THE
BLICKLING
CONCORDANCE

THE
BLICKLING
CONCORDANCE
A LEXICON TO
THE BLICKLING HOMILIES

continuum

Published by Continuum

The Tower Building	80 Maiden Lane
11 York Road	Suite 704
London	New York
SE1 7NX	NY 10038

www.continuumbooks.com

First published 2009

British Library Cataloguing-in-Publication Data

A catalogue record for this book is available from the British Library.
ISBN 9780826497734

Typeset at Continuum
Printed and bound by Ashford Colour Press, Hampshire, UK

CONTENTS

Preface   7

Introduction   9

Editorial Procedures   21

Abbreviations and Symbols   25

Concordance   31

Vitae Andreas from Camb. CCC MS 198   137

Appendix   141

Bibliography   158

5

PREFACE

Those unfamiliar with textual scholarship might assume that the earlier the copy of a text, the closer it will be to the original. But given the vagaries of transmission in the written page, and the problems of ensuring copies free from scribal errors or scribal interventions, this need not be the case. Age alone does not guarantee authenticity or purity of text and the oldest surviving copies may not always be the most accurate. So the compiling of this Concordance to *The Blickling Homilies* aims to enhance further the linguistic, historical and social contexts in which these texts were composed and copied.

This work is the product of over five years of painstaking work, where every word has been checked and rechecked in Anglo-Saxon dictionaries and grammars. I wish to thank my colleague and friend, Ciarán L. Quinn, for his insightful and constructive comments; Michelle P. Brown of the University of London for her continual support and encouragement; Mika Kinose of Rutgers University, New Jersey, for her invaluable comments on the content of the Introduction; and Robin Baird-Smith, Publishing Director of Continuum, for his unfaltering interest in this project. I would also like to extend my appreciation to Jim & Anne Fox, Tadgh & Catherine Foley, Toshi Furomoto, Mimbu Kawamura, Mary C. Keane, Joan & Andrew Kelly, Kimiko Koi, Jerry O'Riordain, Alan Titley, Takao Saijo, Kenichi Sakamoto and Shiro Shiba.

Thanks is finally offered to those who through the forces of fate inspired my interest in lexicography and textual transmission; I mention especially Éamonn O'Carragáin, emeritus of the National University of

Ireland at Cork, and Eric G. Stanley, emeritus of the University of Oxford. This work is dedicated to Daniel Kelly, who sadly passed away from a short illness borne with dignity before its completion; he was an ordinary man who always inspired and encouraged the extraordinary.

Richard J. Kelly
Kobe, Japan
March 2009

CONCORDANCE INTRODUCTION

This Concordance is a companion to the recent edition and translation of *The Blickling Homilies* by Richard J. Kelly.[1] It was undertaken to correct shortcomings in the text of the manuscript, which was first edited by Richard Morris.[2] Respecting Morris's approach, minimal editorial input to the manuscript text is made so as to present as faithful a manuscript rendering as possible. The Concordance deals with scribal inconsistency (and occasional inaccuracy) in word citation and grammatical forms. While Morris's glossary is a milestone of an achievement by any yardstick, it now needs updating. With the aid of the most recent linguistic scholarship in Old English (hereafter abbreviated as OE), the aim is to present a lexicon of *The Blickling Homilies* that is a reliable resource for those who wish to further unlock the linguistic, religious and social treasures that these texts abound with. The editorial procedures are outlined in detail at the end of the Introduction, and one of the significant features of the present work is that each word is cited in its dictionary form, which is particularly important for OE verbs because they are classified by type (strong or weak) and class.

This Introduction begins with an outline of the purpose and structure of the Concordance; it is followed by an excursus on some of the specific linguistic and stylistic features of the Blickling homiletic texts, such as the traces of Anglian and Mercian words in the vocabulary. The lexicographical sources for the compilation of the Concordance are then discussed; these include dictionaries, grammars and other relevant reference works. Such works form the basis for dealing with the issues of

9

word formation and dialectal forms. The preliminaries conclude with a detailing of the editorial procedures used throughout the Concordance.

Purpose and Structure

There are several fields of information to be considered when formulating a lexicon, but the issue of word-definition is to the fore in this work. *The Oxford English Dictionary* (hereafter abbreviated as OED) catalogues and defines English vocabulary with an accuracy and scope that have merited it a well-deserved reputation as the finest historical dictionary of any language. It might seem appropriate to model the entries of the Concordance on those of the OED, but the range and scope of the languages dealt with by the two works are very different, making it unfeasible to apply such an all-encompassing methodology.

There are various strategies for defining, and in the OED the definitions of Modern English (hereafter abbreviated as MnE) are often analytical, offering definitions with explanatory exempla. Such definitions make the relationship between the meanings of a word – its semantic structure – clear. But they are not always particularly helpful to one seeking a straightforward translation in that they frequently require more knowledge of the meaning of a word than OE may be able to supply, thereby leading to an ambiguous definition.

Another strategy for defining is contextual glossing. Definitions describe in some detail the extended context in which a word is used. Such definitions are generally conventional since they remain close to the evidence of the citations and are descriptive rather than interpretive, but they may possibly suggest a degree of semantic possibility beyond what OE linguistic evidence would permit.

A third strategy for defining is by direct translation. Translation equivalents represent the most straightforward form of word definition and it can usefully serve to refine and signify which suggested meanings might be applicable within a given contextual use. However, a limited number of exact word equivalents exist between OE and MnE.

This Concordance is primarily a translation and grammatical lexicon, although all three strategies discussed are considered, when necessary, for defining. The goal is to provide a reliable translation, to outline the range of meaning and grammatical application of the word, to indicate typical collocations and uses, and to present a contextual overview. While the entries in the Concordance are cited with their MnE equivalent, it also cites variations in spellings and identifies dialectal words that are non-West-Saxon.

In general, the Concordance aims for accuracy. A plain translation equivalent, where possible, is used (e.g. *folc* 'folk', 'people'). Each word definition begins with the assumption that the senses of the word under consideration are essentially the same, except when the linguistic evidence within the manuscript determines otherwise and indicates other related meanings. This leads to a certain number of definitions being defined more contextually than in general dictionaries and grammars. A case in point is the subtle but important distinction between pronouns and pronominals as outlined in the Appendix, pp. 145–8.

The senses of a word are collated according to a systematic pattern. Although it is not often the case that OE vocabulary can be defined according to a chronological development of sense, whenever it is possible to point to a sequential change in meaning, this is reflected in the ordering of the entry. A noun like *eorl* reflects the semantic development evident in the narrowing of the earlier sense 'man, nobleman, warrior' to 'chief, ruler of a shire, earl' from the later Norse influence of *jarl*. When applicable to the linguistic context, the most common sense is given first, with other related meanings following in a sequential order.

One of the main principles in defining is not to claim more knowledge than one has. What seems the likeliest definition is cited first, with other possibilities cited that depend on the MS context. For words of uncertain meaning, the collator of the Concordance relies on the knowledge attained from translating the Blickling homiletic texts, which can prove useful in shedding some light on interpreting the context of the meaning; yet readers should also judge for themselves. The word *fers*,

11

which is of Latin origin, is a good example of a word of ambiguous meaning because it could be interpreted as 'sentence' or 'verse'. However, words are defined primarily according to their etymological meaning(s), such as (a) *feorm* 'harbouring of (criminals)' and (b) *feorm* 'cleaning' – this is one of the important goals of the Concordance.

The other important goal of the Concordance is to carefully document the grammatical form(s) for each entry. The structure of this is discussed and outlined in detail in the second part of this Introduction, pp. 21–3. Occasionally, where it is helpful, etymological information is given like the dialectal origin of a particular word (e.g. *eorclanstān* 'jewel' and *geornnes* 'longing', which are of Anglian origin). The various spellings of a word as they appear in the MS are listed. Spelling variants that are due to scribal error are corrected in square brackets with the symbol ➤ to indicate the correction (e.g. [bone ➤ þone]). In addition, a few words in the Blickling texts that are not extant in standard OE dictionaries and grammars are cited and referenced.

The words in the Concordance are cited according to the line number and page number of the homiletic text in Kelly (2003). Words that are frequently used, such as conjunctions, prepositions and adverbs are cited in the Appendix, pp.149–51. A note where appropriate informs of any restrictions in use or occurrence of a word by the date of the manuscript; the Blickling texts were compiled at a West-Saxon scriptorium towards the late tenth century which is very early for a homiliary in OE vernacular.

Blickling Homilies – Linguistic and Stylistic Features
When the Blickling texts were collated sometime in the late tenth century, the West-Saxon dialect had emerged with precedence over the other dialects. This was due in part to the policy of King Ælfred (849–899) to create a sense of cultural hegemony through learning and translation. However, the texts of *The Blickling Homilies* do occasionally display variation in spelling and syntax. This indicates that OE was not a uniform written language even by the late tenth century, and one can best identify

12

the language of the Blickling texts as late West-Saxon which contains certain Anglian and Mercian word forms. One of the important aims of this Concordance is to record and document the vocabulary of the Blickling manuscript because it presents an important word-list of OE as much closer uniformity was evolving. As an example, the later uncorrupted version of the Life of St Andrew, which complements the fragmented Blickling version, shows variation in spelling and syntax; this indicates that this continued into the period of Ælfric and Wulfstan and until the end of the OE period in the twelfth century.

The great masters of OE prose (Ælfred, Ælfric and Wulfstan) all wrote in West-Saxon, so the OE inevitably became associated with that dialect. This has resulted in scholars of historical linguistics not always adequately recognizing the existence of certain Anglian and Mercian influences in manuscripts that emanated from West-Saxon scriptoria. Besides Werferth's *Dialogues of Gregory* and an unknown Mercian translation of Bede's *Ecclesiastical History*, there exists the *Martyrology* and the *Life of St Guthlac* as well as several shorter pieces of this ilk such as the colophons in the *Lindisfarne Gospels*. OE texts were composed in the Anglian kingdoms before the time of Ælfred and continued to be produced in parts of Mercia even after the first major wave of Danish Wars (*c.* 865–79), which resulted in the Danes controlling almost half of the country to the north and east.

There is still some debate about the original dialect of the Blickling homiletic texts, which were transcribed and collated in a late West-Saxon scriptorium, with several traces of Anglian spellings and some instances of early West-Saxon and Mercian word forms. The history of scholarship on the phonology and morphology of the texts has been varied and conflicting. Nineteenth-century German philologists such as Wyld and Bülbring concluded in their linguistic studies of *The Blickling Homilies* that the collection was originally Anglian and that it had been transcribed into West-Saxon.[3] Wyld listed the texts under the heading of 'Saxon Patois', following Bülbring (1902), pp. 11–12. Hardy (1899) reached similar conclusions to that of Wyld and Bülbring.[4] Rauh (1936) concluded that the homilies were not purely Anglian, but did not fully identify the non-West-Saxon words.[5] Her study only focused on comparable words or synonyms in the late Saxon Gospel of Matthew. Rauh's work, however, embarked on an important line of inquiry, which led Menner (1949) to state that the Blickling texts are not purely Anglian in origin but were dialectally more complex.[6] This does explain why several of the texts vary considerably in both style and structure, indicating that they were authored by more than one individual and perhaps from more than one location.

This Concordance cites the non-West-Saxon words of the Blickling homiletic texts by identifying them as described in p.19 below. The historical research shows that Anglian words are the most numerous and are found with reasonable frequency throughout the Blickling collection. The Anglian vocabulary of the Blickling texts contain some words that are Mercian and not Northumbrian (e.g. *eno* 'moreover', *hālettan* 'to greet' and *semninga* 'suddenly'); this indicates that at least some of the homiletic texts possibly originated from earlier versions from the Mercian region.

The Blickling texts, due of their Christian content, have a higher than normal proportion of classical vocabulary, such as *cantica* 'canticle', *ċiriċe* 'church', *discipul* 'disciple' and *pāpa* 'pope'. Non-Germanic vernacular words are fewer in number; words of Celtic origin in the manuscript are *cnoll* 'hill', *drȳ* 'druid' and *dūn* 'mountain'.

Some linguistic scholars of the Blickling texts concluded that they were Anglian in origin, even though a number of them were composed by various authors. What does this imply? It signifies that most of the texts seem to have an Anglian source; the exceptions are Blickling IV and Blickling XVIII which have very few Anglian words, but they also contain the Anglian *ac* and *ned* for *þearf*.

The Anglian vocabulary of *The Blickling Homilies* contains some words that are Mercian and these are labeled (M) 'Mercian' in the Concordance. Many of these Mercian words may have coexisted in Anglian and Mercian; for example, those in poetic texts such as

Cynewulf's 'Elene' like *instæpes* (l. 127) and *semninga* (l. 1109). Therefore, those Blickling texts that contain such vocabulary may have come into Anglian from Mercian.

Whether one can assign any of the Blickling texts to a particular part of the Mercian district is a more problematic issue to deal with. Miller placed them under the heading of East Anglia, but without substantiating the reason.[7] Jordan commented that Miller's hypothesis is not incorrect due to the linguistic evidence.[8] However, Hardy concluded that the Anglian phonological and morphological traces were too unclear to signify a precise location, but stated that they are linguistically closer to the *Rushworth Gospels* than to the early 9th century Mercian *Vespasian Psalter*.[9] The Blickling collection accords with the vocabulary of the *Rushworth Gospels* which contains an independent translation of the Gospel of St Matthew and a gloss on SS Mark, Luke and John, derived from the Lindisfarne glosses. From a note in the manuscript we learn that two men, Færman and Owun, wrote the version.[10] Færman translated the St Matthew and wrote the gloss of St Mark i.–ii. 15 and St John xviii. 1–3. The remaining part is by a scribe called Owun. The similarity of the text of St Matthew to Blickling partly depends on the focus on New Testament themes, and would for that reason naturally resemble the Gospels rather than the Psalter. The fact that the Rushworth and Blickling manuscripts contain *hālettan* and *witedōm*, not in the *Vespasian Psalter*, is not of important significance because the Latin Psalter contains neither *salutare* nor *prophetia*. It is important to note that for some Latin words appearing in the Gospels and the Psalter, Rushworth is in agreement with Blickling where, for example, both write *tān* ('sors') where Vespasian has *hlet*; also, *hehnǣgan* ('humiliare') for *ġehēnan*; and *ġesǣlan* ('alligare') for *āwrīdan* and *ġebindan*. The number of such words is too few to make a definitive conclusion, yet there seems to be some affinity between the Blickling and Rushworth vocabulary.

This raises the question of the date, since the *Vespasian Psalter* is early ninth century and the *Rushworth Gospels* is late tenth, so the resemblance may be due to the similar dating rather than the dialect. The famous reference in Blickling XI to 971 has naturally lead scholars to date the collection to the late tenth century, but this does not mean that older words from earlier dialects were excluded in the transcription of the texts into the Blickling manuscript. Scholars like Scherer, in spite of the presence of late West-Saxon words like *cynehelm* and *scrȳdan*, dated the homilies to before 868.[11] This is now considered to be untenable and the best that can be said in support of Scherer is that some of the earliest versions of the homilies may date from that time, but there is little doubt that they were copied in their present form during the late tenth century. The dating issue of the Blickling manuscript is also referred to in Kelly (2003).[12] However, the linguistic scholarship on the subject is documented in more detail here as it is the more appropriate context in which to do so.

The Blickling homiletic texts, with a few possible exceptions, were originally composed in Anglian; the linguistic evidence supports this hypothesis. Though copied in a West-Saxon scriptorium, the texts were not subject to strict conversion into West-Saxon dialectal forms as was the case with late versions of Bede's *Historia* and Werferth's *Dialogues*.[13] But similar to these works, they appear to be a product of Mercian learning and Mercian spirituality that was later established in Anglia.

Sources

A number of sources were used to complete this Concordance because no single dictionary, lexicon or grammar of Anglo-Saxon have proven to be adequate, so by consulting a variety of them one can employ the best that each has to offer.[14] Clark Hall's *Concise Anglo-Saxon Dictionary with a Supplement by Herbert D. Meritt* (1984) is a work of great importance and an invaluable source for Anglo-Saxon lexicography; but it is at times uncritical and contains a certain number of words that are given dubious meaning(s). Another useful work is the Anglo-Saxon dictionary in German by Grein (1912; repr. 1974). *The Dictionary of Old English*

(1882–98; repr. 1972) compiled by Bosworth and Toller consists of two sections. The first part (A ➤ FIR) was compiled by Bosworth and is not entirely reliable. Toller completed the second part (FIS ➤ W) and is a significant improvement in both completeness and accuracy. The most up-to-date edition plus supplements has been consulted for this Concordance. Every dictionary is necessarily a compromise. If it is to be done well and on an adequate scale, it requires a long time span. This is the case with *The Toronto Dictionary of Old English* which was begun in 1986; it is rather problematic to consult as parts are still in the process of being compiled – a process that is likely to take several more years to complete. The principal other dictionaries consulted are the *Middle English Dictionary* (*MED*), the *Dictionary of the Older Scottish Tongue* (*DOST*), the *English Dialect Dictionary* (*EDD*), the *Dictionary of Old Irish* (*DOI*) and the *Oxford English Dictionary* (*OED*).

Ettmüller's *Lexicon Anglo-saxonicum* (1851) is still an important and scholarly work, but its awkward arrangement of the words under hypothetical stems makes it difficult and time-consuming to consult. Mitchell (1985) is the most comprehensive study of OE syntax, and the work by Visser (1963–73) is useful for presenting the syntax within the history of the language. The standard OE reference grammars are Wrenn & Quike (1977), Campbell (1959; repr. 1977), Wright & Wright (1925; repr. 1972), and More & Knott (1925) which is more general reference work.

The spellings for the Latin and Greek equivalents follow the established practice for OE words: verbs are in the infinitive; nouns in the nominative singular; adjectives (strong and weak) in the nominative masculine singular. The standard Latin dictionaries used are the *Dictionary of Medieval Latin from British Sources* (*DMLBS*), the Lewis and Short, *A Latin Dictionary* (*LD*) and Latham's *Revised Medieval Latin Word - List from British and Irish Sources* (*WLBIS*). The *Oxford Latin Dictionary* (*OLD*), Niermeyer's *Mediae Latinitatis Lexicon Minus* (*MLLM*), Blaise's *Dictionnaire Latin - Français des Auteurs Chrétiens* (*DLFAC*), DuCange's *Glossarium Mediae et Infimae Latinitatis* (*GMIL*) and the *Thesaurus Linguae Latinae* (*TLL*) have also been consulted. The large classical vocabulary in the Blickling texts originates from the Christian nature of their content and makes them a field of special interest to Anglo-Classicists.

Few English personal or place names are extant in the Blickling homiletic texts, and where they occur the following works are important: Smith's *English Place-Name Elements* (*PNE*), Ekwall's *The Oxford Dictionary of English Place-Names* (*DEPN*) and *The Vocabulary of English Place-Names* (*VEPN*). Biblical and Christian personal and place names are quite common especially in the Blickling hagiographical pieces and these names are source referenced to the leading and authoritative works on biblical and Christian scholarship; these inlcude the *Jerome Biblical Commentary* (*JBC*) and *Encyclopedia of Early Christianity* (*EEC*).[15]

Word Formation

A restriction in Anglo-Saxon lexicographical studies is that the source material comes from a rather limited number of manuscripts, of which the Blickling manuscript is one of the most important due to its early dating to the late tenth century. As the Blickling texts rely on classical sources they contain a certain number of words which are directly imported from Greek and Latin, e.g. *dēofol* 'devil' from Greek *diabolos*; *ċyriċe* ' church' from Greek *kuriakon* 'God's house'; *bisceop* 'bishop' from Greek *episkopos* via popular Latin *ebisco*; *engel* 'angel' from Latin *angelus*. Some such borrowed words appear as constructed hybrids in OE and have a certain awkwardness; examples are *bisceophad* 'office of the bishop' and *mæsseprēost* 'mass-priest'. Personal names and place names from classical sources frequently show inconsistency in spelling. The Blickling texts also contain a few words of Celtic origin (e.g. *drȳ* 'druid' from Gaelic *druí*), being the other principal vernacular language in the British Isles. Words in the Blickling texts are also formed by making compounds of two words already existing in the language, which include words from Slavic and other Germanic languages. There is a particularly high concentration of these throughout the texts with words like *eorþware* 'people on earth', *fyrdweorod* 'army' and *olyhtword* 'flattering words'. The most common trait in OE is to add affixes to modify or change the meaning of existing words, like adding the prefix *ġe* before a verb to indicate a stronger meaning (e.g. *ġefaran* 'to die' and *ġemunan* 'to remember').

The language of the Blickling homiletic texts comprises of both core words from OE and those garnered from a variety of other linguistic sources ranging in scope from the classics to various vernacular tongues. But the greatest range of words and their meanings were formulated by adding affixes and by devising hybrids by compounding OE words, foreign words and a combination of OE and foreign words.

Dialects
The greater number of OE words were preserved in West-Saxon, which is the dialect that the Blickling texts were copied in. Trace words from early West-Saxon and other dialects also exist, and these are indicated in the Concordance with the abbreviations (EWS) early West-Saxon, (A) Anglian and (M) Mercian, cited after the relevant word citation. All other words are West-Saxon. The parts of speech are generally clearer in OE than in ME and MnE. The noun *drinc* 'drink' has a corresponding verb *drincan* 'to drink'; whereas 'drink' can be used both as a noun and a verb in MnE.

The Blickling texts have a number of common variants in spellings and alternations, and these are recorded in the Concordance as they occur in the manuscript. Instances are the common patterns by which *geonġ* and *iung* 'young' or *þeġn* and *þen* 'servant' can be recognized as the same word; the alternation of *a* and *o* in the non-past third person singular forms of some Class III strong verbs, e.g. *band* and *bond* of *bindan* 'to bind' and *ġelamp* and *ġelomp* of *ġelimpan* 'to happen'; and the alternation of *a* and *e* in instances of adjective comparison, e.g. *lang* 'long' *lengra / longest* and *strang* 'strong' *strenga / strengest*. Most of these variants are called morphophonemic alternations. Most recent formulations purport to give an account of the 'phonological component' of the grammar of OE conceived in the transformational-generative mode. The efforts to account in terms of a system of rules for so-called surface structure and corresponding phonetic representation constitute an enterprise that is beyond the scope of this Introduction, but I intend to make it the basis of a separate study of the lexicographical significance of words in this Concordance.

EDITORIAL PROCEDURES

The vocabulary of *The Blickling Homilies* is cited alphabetically with the dictionary form in bold type. The letter 'æ' follows 'a', ' þ'/'ð' follows 't'. The prefix *ġe-* is generally ignored in alphabetizing words in dictionaries and glossaries; but it is alphabetized under 'g' in this Concordance because it allows for easier cross-referencing to the texts, so *ġeleornian* ('to learn') appears under 'g' with *ġe–* in a slightly lower pitch to distinguish it as a prefix that is added to the word. Regular OE 'g' words are cited in normal pitch, e.g. *ġēar* ('year'). Long vowels are indicated by a superscript stroke (e.g. 'ā' & 'ū') as are diphthongs with a long vowel (e.g. 'ēa' & 'īe'). The palatalization of 'c' and 'g' by a front vowel or diphthong is indicated by a dot over the letter in the initial citation of the word (e.g. *ċiriċe* & 'ġeorne'). The script in the Blicking manuscript does not adhere to such precise lexicographical rules, as stressing is both sporadic and inconsistent; the Concordance standardizes this.

The vocabulary of the Blickling texts is identified by page and line number according to Kelly (2003). The variations of spelling forms are generally maintained, except when the scribe is clearly in error; it is then corrected within square brackets with the original manuscript form proceeded by the symbol ➤ to indicated the correct form (e.g. [swē ➤ swā]). Such editorial changes are generally kept to a minimum and indicate emendations of manuscript readings or contextual clarifications. The Andreas text, which is a fragment at the end of the Blickling manuscript, is edited in pp. 137–40 from the complete later version in Camb. CCC MS 198, fols 386r–94v; it is cross-referenced to the

Concordance by simple line number. It is the intention of the editor to present a Concordance that is a reliable reference work for further scholarship and research. All abbreviations employed in the Concordance are expanded in Abbreviations and Symbols, pp. 25–9. Nouns are expanded according to gender (*m.*, *f.* or *nt.*) case (*nom.*, *acc.*, *gen.*, *dat.* or *inst.*) and number (*sg.* or *pl.*). Adjectives are similarly cited and expanded, beginning with indefinite ('strong') adjectives in their normal, comparative and superlative forms and then by definitive (weak) adjectives in their normal, comparative and superlative forms. Ordinal numbers (*first, second, third,* etc.) are abbreviated as *num. adj.*, function as adjectives, and all of them are declined weak; whereas cardinal numbers (*one, two, three,* etc.) are abbreviated as *num.* and function as adjectives or as nouns followed by the genitive (see Appendix, p.144).

Adverbs and their variant forms are followed by the abbreviation *adv.* ('adverb'), and those that are commonly identifiable and occur frequently are cited in the Appendix, p.151, along with their variant forms. As these frequently occurring adverbs are easily identifiable throughout *The Blickling Homilies*, it is unnecessary to identify each occurrence according to homiletic text and line number; however, when the word form is worthy of attention, it is cited in the Concordance or referenced to the homiletic text by citing the line and page number in the Appendix. A similar policy is adhered to for conjunctions, which are abbreviated as *conj.* ('conjunction') and for prepositions, which are abbreviated as *prep.* ('preposition'). After common adverbs, conjunctions and prepositions, the Concordance cites the cross-reference to the Appendix. Pronouns, like adjectives, are declined by gender, case and number. As pronouns are generally uniform, they are cited in tables in the Appendix, pp. 145–8; but any pronoun with a special form is cited in the Concordance or specifically referenced to the homiletic text in the Appendix. The symbol > is used after certain words that are common in the Blickling texts when the form has been sufficiently cited.

The verbs are cited in the infinitive form. Strong verbs are classed in Roman numerals and weak verbs are classed in Arabic numbers imme-

22

diately after the infinitive form of each verb in a smaller pitch (e.g. I, II, III, IV, V, VI, VII and 1, 2, 3). The verbs are expanded as follows: infinitive, indicative present and past, subjunctive present and past, imperative, inflective infinitive and participle present and past (with gender, case and number cited when appropriate). The citing of the first, second and third person plural in the indicative and subjunctive present and past forms is omitted because the endings are uniform. The person and number are cited for the plural imperative mode. Terms like 'indicative' or 'subjunctive' mood as well as 'present' or 'preterite' are cited only once if there are more than one form of the verb in the particular mood and/or time.

The Concordance has a different but complementary function to the edition *The Blickling Homilies* (2003) whose aim is to present as faithful a manuscript rendering of the texts as possible, inclusive of dialectal and word variation. Adhering to standard lexicographical principles, it complements the edition by providing standard dictionary forms and definitions of the Blickling vocabulary.

1 R. J. Kelly, ed. & trans. *The Blickling Homilies: Edition and Translation* (Continuum Academii: London and New York, 2003).
2 R. Morris, ed. & trans. *The Blickling Homilies*, EETS os 58, 63, 73 (Oxford, 1874, 1876, 1880); repr. as 1 vol. (Oxford, 1967).
3 H. C. Wyld. *Short History of English* (1921). K. D. Bülbring. *Altenglisches Elementarbuch* (1902).
4 A. K. Hardy, *Die Sprache der Blickling Homilien* (Leipzig, 1899).
5 H. Rauh, *Der Wortschatz der altenglischen Uebersetzungen des Matthaeus-Evangeliums* (Berlin, 1936).
6 R. J. Menner, 'The Anglian Vocabulary of *The Blickling Homilies*'. In T. Kirby & H. B. Woolf, eds. *Philologica: The Malone Anniversary Studies* (1949), pp. 63-4.
7 T. Miller, ed. *The Old English Version of Bede's Ecclesiastical History*, EETS 95 (Oxford, 1890), pp. xxix–xxxii.
8 R. Jordan. *Eigentümlichkeiten des Anglischen Wortschatzes* (Heidelberg, 1906), p. 11.
9 A. K. Hardy (1899), p. 125. *The Rushworth Gospels*, also known as the Irish 'MacRegol Gospels', is preserved in Bodl. MS Auct. D. 2 19. The Vespasian

Psalter is preserved in BL Cotton MS Vespasian A I

10 Færman was a priest at Harewood (Harwood) in the West Riding of
Yorkshire, and he completed the greater part of the work. Owun was a scribe
under the guidance of Færman.

11 G. Scherer. *Zur Geographie und Chronologie des angelsächsischen
Wortschatzes im Anschluss an Bischof Wæferth's Übersetzung des 'Dialoge'
Gregors* (Leipzig, 1928), p. 44.

12. Kelly, op.cit., pp. xv–li.

13 There are four surviving copies of Bede's *Historia ecclesiastica gentis
Anglorum*, the best known of which is BL Cotton MS Tiberius C. II, an 8th
century illuminated manuscript. A standard edition in 2 vols is C. Plummer.
(1896; repr. 1969); this work has been translated from the Latin several
times, and most recently by J. McClure, and R. Collins (1994). Werferth's
Dialogues of St Gregory has been edited by H. Hecht. *Bishof Wæferths von
Worcester Übersetzung der Dialoge Gregors des Grossen* (Hamburg, 1907),
and more recently by D. Yerkes. *The Two Versions of Wæferth's Translation
of Gregory's Dialogues* (Toronto, 1979). This work is preserved in fragment
form in three manuscripts, one of which is Cant. MS Add. 25. We know
from Asser, King Ælfred's biographer, that Wærferth, bishop of Worcester,
was a Mercian who was involved in the literary activities promoted by the
king.

14 All of the linguistic reference works referred to are cited in the Bibliography, pp. 158–61.

15 All of these reference works are cited in the Bibliography, pp. 158–61.

ABBREVIATIONS AND SYMBOLS

Grammatical Terms

acc.	accusative
adj.	adjective
adjvl.	adjectival
adv.	adverb
anom.	anomalous
com. adj.	composite adjective
comp.	comparative
comp. adv.	comparative adverb
conj.	conjunction
cons.	consonant
dat.	dative
def. art.	definite article
dem. adj.	demonstrative adjective
dem. pron.	demonstrative pronoun
f.	feminine
fut.	future
gen.	genitive
ger.	gerund
imp.	imperative
ind.	indicative
indecl.	indeclinable
infl.	inflected
infl. inf.	inflected infinitive
inst.	instrumental
interj.	interjection
inter. pron	interrogative pronoun
intr.	intransitive
m.	masculine
neg.	negative
nom.	nominative

nt.	neuter
num.	numeral
num. adj.	numeral adjective
part.	participle
pass.	passive
pers.	person
pers. n.	personal name
pers. pron.	personal pronoun
pl.	plural
poss.	possessive
poss. adj.	possessive adjective
post prep.	post preposition
pp.	past participle
prep.	preposition
pres.	present
pres. p.	present participle
pret.	preterite
pret. pres.	preterite-present
pron.	pronoun
pronom.	pronominal
prop. n.	proper noun
refl.	reflexive
rel. pron.	relative pronoun
sg.	singular
sv.	strong verb
subj.	subjunctive
superl.	superlative
tr.	transitive
voc.	vocative
wv.	weak verb

LANGUAGES AND DIALECTS

A	Anglian
EWS	Early West-Saxon
Gr.	Greek
Gmc.	Germanic
IE	Indo-European
Lt.	Latin
M	Mercian
ME	Middle English
MnE	Modern English
nWS	non-West-Saxon
OE	Old English
OHG	Old High German
OI	Old Irish
ON	Old Norse
S	Saxon
WS	West-Saxon

GENERAL ABBREVIATIONS

AB	*Analecta Bollandiana*
Add.	Additional
ASE	*Anglo-Saxon England*
ASSAH	*Anglo-Saxon Studies in Archaeology and History*
BN	Paris, Bibliothèque Nationale
BL	British Library
Camb.	Cambridge
Cant.	Canterbury

CCC	Corpus Christi College
ch/chs	chapter/chapters
Bodl.	Bodleian
DEPN	*The Oxford Dictionary of English Place-Names*
DLFAC	*Dictionnaire Latin - Français des Auteurs Chrétiens*
DOI	*Dictionary of Old Irish*
DOST	*Dictionary of the Older Scottish Tongue*
ed./eds	editor/editors
edn	edition
EDD	*English Dialect Dictionary*
EEC	*Encyclopedia of Early Christianity*
EEMF	Early English Manuscripts in Facsimile
EETS	Early English Texts Society
—, os	—, ordinary series
—, ss	—, supplementary series
EHR	*English Historical Review*
ELN	*English Language Notes*
EPNS	English Place-Name Society
ES	*English Studies*
frag.	fragment
GMIL	*Glossarium Mediae et Infimae Latinitatis*
JBC	*Jerome Biblical Commentary*
JBS	*Journal of British Studies*
JEGP	*Journal of English and German Philology*
JEH	*Journal of Ecclesiastical History*
JMH	*Journal of Medieval History*
JTS	*Journal of Theological Studies*
JWCI	*Journal of the Warburg and Courtauld Institutes*
LD	*A Latin Dictionary*
MÆ	*Medium Ævum*
MED	*The Middle English Dictionary*
MGH	Monumenta Germaniae Historica
—, AA	—, Auctores Antiquissimi
—, Epist.	—, Epistolae (in quarto)
—, ES	—, Epistolae Selectae

—, PLAC	—, Poetae Latini Aevi Carolini
—, SS	—, Scriptores (in folio)
MLLM	*Mediae Latinitatis Lexicon Minus*
MLN	*Modern Language Notes*
MP	*Modern Philology*
MS	Manuscript
MMLBS	*Dictionary of Medieval Latin from British Sources*
OED	*The Oxford English Dictionary*
OEG	*Old English Grammar*, A. Campbell, ed.
OES	*Old English Syntax*, B. Mitchell, ed.
OLD	*Oxford Latin Dictionary*
OEN	*Old English Newsletter*
p./pp.	page/pages
PBA	*Proceedings of the British Academy*
PL	Patrologia Latina
PMLA	*Publications of the Modern Language Association of America*
PNE	*English Place-Name Elements*
RB	*Revue Bénédictine*
repr.	reprinted
RES	*Review of English Studies*
rev	revised
Settimane	*Settimane di studio del Centro italiano di studi sull'alto medioevo*
SM	*Studi medievali*
SN	*Studia Neophilologica*
SP	*Studies in Philology*
T	Title (of Homily in MS)
TLL	*Thesaurus Linguae Latinae*
TRHS	*Transactions of the Royal Historical Society*
VEPN	*The Vocabulary of English Place-Names*
WLBIS	*Revised Medieval Latin Word-List from British and Irish Sources*
ZCP	*Zeitschrift für celtische Philologie*

A

ā *adv.* always (see Appendix, p. 151)

ābær (see āberan)

ābbiddan [ābbiddan → ābiddan] (V) to pray for 130:239; *ind. pres. pl.* ābiddaþ 44:151

ābidan (I) to await; *ind. pret. 3 sg.* ābād 150:98

ābeodan (II) to announce; *infl. inf.* to ābeodenne 40:64

āberan (IV) to bear, endure 94:59; *ind. pret 3 sg.* ābær 22:107

abisgian (2) to be occupied; *pp.* abisgod 146:17; *pl.* abisgode 12:67

ābitan (I) to bite; *subj. pres. 3 pl.* ābitan 126:148; *pret. 3 pl.* ābiton 66:187, 132:317

ablendan (1) to blind; *ind. pret. 3 sg.* ablende 106:216; *pp.* ablinde 106:192

ablinnan (III) to cease 16:146; *ind. pres. 2 sg.* ablinnest 130:255; *ind. pres. 3 sg.* ablinneþ 14:97, 14:112; *ind. pret 3 sg.* ablon 154:228; *imp. 1 pl.* ablinnan 30:114

ābycgan (1) to redeem; *ind. pret. 3 sg.* ābohte 62:122

abolgen (see abylgþ)

Abraham *pers. n* Abraham; *nom. sg.* 62:105; *dat. sg.* Abrahame 112:330

ābrecan (IV) to break, break down, destroy 152:151; *ind. pret. 3 sg.* ābræc 2:35, 14:117, 54:194; *pp.* ābrocen 52:175

abregdan (1) to be alarmed; *pp.* abregde 58:30

ābrocen (see ābrecan)

ābuton *adv.* about, around (see Appendix, p. 151)

ābyligan (1) to make angry, offend; *ind. pres. 3 sg.* ābylgþ 22:105; *pp.* ābolgen 4:79

āc *conj.* but (see Appendix, p. 149)

ācennan (1) to be born; *pp.* ācenned 12:73, 20:74, 20:76, 30:102, 40:83, 64:149, 118:94, 118:103; ācynned 114:42; *pl.* ācennede 40:73, 40:74, 64:167; *def. m. gen. sg.* ācendan 116:61

āceorfan (III) to cut off; *subj. pres. 3 sg.* āceorfe 132:279

Achaia *prop. n.* Achaia; *dat. sg.* Achaia 158:26

ācwellan (1) to kill 48:54, 106:185, 158:24, 158:29, 21, 65, 139; *ind. pres. 3 sg.* ācwelþ 44:149; *pret. 3 sg.* ācwælde 50; ācweālde 119; *pl.* ācwealdon 140:105, 86; *subj. pres. pl.* ācwellan 91; *imp. 2 sg.* ācwel 89; *2 pl.* ācwellað 52, 54, 83; *pp.* ācweald 140:105

ādælan (1) to separate; *pp.* ādæled 118:119

Adam *pers. n.* Adam; *nom. sg.* 18:40, 18:41, 60:74a, 60:74b; *gen. sg.* Adames 4:78; *dat. sg.* Adame 60:82

ādīlegian (2) to destroy 94:57; *imp. 2 sg.* ādīlega 60:76; *pp.* ādīlegod 2:19; *pl.* ādīlegode 74:27

adl *f.* illness, disease; *nom. sg.* 16:167; *acc. sg.* adle 88:166; *acc. pl.* adla 60:85, 76:18

ādōn (anom.) to remove 62:112; ādōn [ādoon → ādōn] 66:197; *ind. pret. 3 sg.* ādyde 128:1; *pp.* ādōn 52:181

ādreogan (VII) to suffer, endure 10:26; *ind. pret. 1 sg.* ādreah 122:61; *3 sg.* ādreag 58:23

Adriaticus *prop. n.* Adriaticus; *nom. sg.* 136:15

ādrīfan (I) to drive away, drive out; *ind. pret. pl.* ādrīfon 152:152; *subj. pres. 3 sg.* ādrīfe 28:66

ādrincan (III) to be drowned; *ind. pret. 3 pl.* ādruncan 66:187

ādrygan (1) to dry up 128:185; *ind. pres. 3 sg.* ādrugaþ 62:134; *3 pl.* ādrugiaþ 40:57

ādūne *adv.* down 120:27, 132:285

ādwǣscan (1) to extinguish (fire), destroy (enemies); *3 sg. ind. pret.* ādwǣscte 22:110; *pp.* ādwǣsced 64:158

ādwellan (1) to mislead; *ind. pres. 3 pl.* ādwellaþ 42:105

ādyde (see ādōn)

āfeallan (VII) to fall; *ind. pres. 3 sg.* āfealleþ 20:55

āfēdan (1) to nurture; *pp.* āfēded 40:83, 146:5; *m. dat. pl.* āfēddum 4:69

āflōwan (VII) to flow; *pres. ind. 3 sg.* āflōweþ 70:56

āflȳman [āflīeman] (1) to put to flight; *ind. pres. 3 sg.* āflīemede 80 (A)

āfrefran (1) to comfort 92:17; *subj. pres. 3. sg.* āfrefrige 24:167; *pp.* āfrefrede 10:29, 16:160, 112:334

āfūlian (2) to become foul; *pres. ind. 3 sg.* āfūlaþ 50:109; āfūlað 70:56

āfyllan (1) to throw down 106:201; *ind. pres. 3 sg.* āfylleþ 38:11

āfyrhtan (1) to be afraid; *pp.* āfyrhted 128:223

āfyrran (1) to remove, take away 66:197; *ind. pret. 3 sg.* afyrde 74:20; *pp.* afyrred 46:32

āfyrsan (1) to make haste; *ind. pres. 3 sg.* afȳrseþ 129

āfȳsan (1) to trouble; *pp.* āfȳsed 92:16

āgǣlan (1) to hinder; *ind. pret. 3 sg.* āgǣlde 14:127

āgān (anom.) to possess; *ind. pres. 3 sg.* āh 48:63; *3 pl.* āgān 32:151; *pret. 3 sg.* āhte 78:84, 136:23; *subj. pres. sg.* āge 14:90; *infl. inf.* to āgenne 78:71

āgangan [āgongan] (VII) to pass by; *pp.* āgangen 82:31, 82:36, 82:38; āgan 128:225

āgietan (V) to give up, render; *ind. pret 3 sg.* āgēat 50:97, 68:4; *pp.* āgōten 62:118

āgen *adj.* own; *m. nom. sg.* 10:20; *m. acc. sg.* āgenne 54:212; *m. dat. sg.* āgenum 138:54; *f. dat. sg.* āgenre 62:110; *f. acc. pl.* āgene 76:28; *f. gen. pl.* āgenra 12:54; *m. dat. sg.* āgnum [āgenum] 32:170; *nt. dat. pl.* āgenum 28:78

āgifan [āgiefan] (V) to give up, yield 14:108, 38:3; āgēofan 34:210, 72:102; *ind. pret. 1 sg.* āgēaf 124:98; *3 sg.* āgēaf 118:95, 150:121; *subj. pret. pl.* āgeafon 26:5; *imp. 3 sg.* āgife 32:158, 34:223; *2 pl.* āgifaþ 26:38

āgildan [āgieldan] (III) to yield, render 38:3; āgyldan 34:184, 44:140, 78:81; *subj. pret pl.*

āguldon 128:211; *pres.p. sg.* āgyldende 38:37 (A)

āgimeleasian (2) to neglect; *ind. pres. pl.* agimeleasiaþ 34:194; āgimeleasiað 38:40

Agrippa *pers. n.* Agrippa; *nom. sg.* 132:278; *gen. sg.* Agrippan 120:35; *dat. sg.* Agrippan 120:21, 132:276

Agrippina *pers. n.* Agrippina; *nom. sg.* 120:35

Agustinus *pers. n.* Augustine; *nom. sg.* 68:33

āgyltan (1) to sin; *ind. pres. 1 sg.* āgylte 156:235; *3 pl.* āgyltaþ 22:125; āgyltað 22:127; *pret. 3 sg.* āgylte 118:115

āh (see āgān)

ah *conj.* but (see Appendix, p. 149)

āheardian (2) to be hard; *pp.* āheard 154:230

āhebban (VI) to lift, raise, exalt 90:214; *ind. pres. 3 sg.* āhefþ 24:163; *pl.* āhebbað 100:46; *pret. 3 sg.* āhōf 86:105, 102:112, 106:221, 110:296, 110:297, 130:253; *subj. pret. sg.* āhōfe 84:76; *pp.* āhafen, 86:114, 94:54, 110:294, 128:198, 148:70; āhefen [→ āhafen] 82:4; *m. acc. sg.* āhafenne 86:90; *f. nom. pl.* āhafana [→ āhafene] 60:68; āhafene 160:74

āhangian (2) to hang; *ind. pret. pl.* āhengon 4:54, 16:141, 52:183, 54:190; āhengan 50:96, 124:99; *pp.* āhangen 132:296; 142:176; *m. acc. sg.* ahangenne 22:92; 60:50

āhof (see āhebban)

āhopian (2) to ask; *ind. pres. 3 sg.* āhopað 12:44

ahreddan (1) to save; *subj. pres. sg.* ahredde 28:67

ahsode (see ascian)

āhweorfan (III) to turn away 30:97; *imp. 2 sg.* āhwyrf 62:91

ālǣdan (1) to lead away; *ind. pret. 3 sg.* ālǣdde 46:19, 46:21, 58:29; *imp. 2 sg.* ālǣd 60:80; ālǣde 158:27, 162:102

aldor *m.* elder, prince, chief, ruler; *nom. sg* 58:37, 60:47 ; *acc. sg.* aldor 58:15, 60:71; *nom. pl.* aldoras 22:120

aldorleas *adj.* without a leader; *m. acc. sg.* aldorlease 92:10

aldorliċ *adj.* princely; *f. nom. sg.* 52:171

aldorman *m.* ruler, chief; *nom. sg.* 106:194, 146:8; *nom. pl.* aldormen 28:84; *dat. pl.* aldormannum 148

ālefan (1) to allow, permit; *pp.* ālefed 96:95

ālecgan (1) to lay down; *ind. pret. 3 sg.* ālegde 88:156, 98:14, 98:16; *pl.* ālegdon 130:265; *pp.* ālegd 94:86

ālesan [ālȳsan] (1) to liberate 42:117, 58:36, 70:65; *ind. pret. 2 sg.* ālesdest 62:108; *3 sg.* ālesde 50:97, 62:120, 68:3, 72:92, 72:95, 80:108; *subj. pres. pl.* ālesan 34:191; *pret. 3 sg.* ālesde 72:94; *imp. 2 sg.* āles 60:63; *1 pl.* ālesan 70:61; *pp.* ālesde 56:233, 94:56 (A)

ālesnes *f.* deliverance; *gen. sg.* ālesnesse 52:163

Alleluia *interj.* Alleluia 104:175, 104:176

ālūcan (VII) to pluck, separate; *pp.* ālōcen 38:5

ālȳfan (1) to allow; *pp.* ālȳfed 30:108; *def. f. acc. sg.* ālȳfdon 66:195

ālȳsan (1) to set free, absolve 20:73, 28:59; *subj. pret. 3 sg.* ālȳsde 32:149; *infl. inf.* to ālȳsenne 48:84; *pp.* ālȳsde 74:13

Ālȳsend *m.* Redeemer; *nom. sg.* 46:2, 60:60

Ambinensus *prop. n.* Ambinens; *nom. sg.* 146:40

amen *interj.* amen 16:172, 24:178, 36:241>

āmetan (V) to measure; *pp. f. nom. pl.* āmetene 136:16

ān *adj.* one, alone; *m. nom. sg.* 28:75, 54:229, 106:194, 130:229, 152:164, 99, 168]; *f. nom. sg.* ān 122:68; *nt. nom. sg.* ān 58:35, 70:57, 90:186; *m. acc. sg.* ānne 32:167, 112:327, 126:165, 128:218, 146:32; ænne 160:79, 19, 148; *f. acc. sg.* āne 34:186, 46:28, 90:186, 95; *nt. acc. sg.* ān 46:33, 82:40,

128:226, 132:322; *m. gen. sg.* ānes 74:5; *m. dat. sg.* ānum 18:5, 18:15, 20:69, 22:111, 60:77, 82:28, 82:42, 86:122, 86:130, 118:93, 118:131, 124:111; *f. dat. sg.* ānre 20:56, 62:125, 78:81, 90:188, 92:35, 132:277; *nt. dat. sg.* ānum 82:33, 88:183, 118:115, 122:45, 152:148; *m. inst. sg.* āne 62:136; *f. inst. sg.* ānre 54:218; *m. nom. pl.* āne 52:149, 128:201, 101; *m gen. pl.* ānra 6:116, 40:51, 44:139, 70:78, 76:1, 76:3, 84:72, 100:86, 162:100; *m. dat. pl.* ānum 6:135, 8:137, 54:189, 76:36, 96:92, 126:153, 128:212; *def. m. nom. sg.* āna 46:33, 100:50; *nt. nom. sg.* āne 20:44

ān *prep.* on, at (see Appendix, p. 150)

ānbidian (2) to await; *pres. p. m. dat. sg.* ānbidende 44

and *conj.* and (see Appendix, p. 149)

andefn *f.* proportion; *dat. sg.* andefne 30:99

andetnes *f.* confession; *dat. sg.* andetnesse 44:151, 120:7, 120:10, 120:17, 120:26

andetta *m.* confessor; *nom. sg.* 44:148

andettan (1) to confess 78:52; *ind. pres. pl.* andettaþ 52:164; *subj. pres. sg.* andette 16:158

andfeng *adj.* acceptable; *f. nom. pl.* andfenge 80:103

andġit *nt.* understanding; *nom. sg.* 94:81; *dat. sg.* andġite 74:22, 76:7

andleofa *m.* sustenance, food; *acc. sg.* andleofan 146:32; *gen. sg.* andleofan 118:126

Andreas *pers. n.* Andreas; *nom. sg.* 158:29, 158:34, 158:40, 160:46, 160:49, 160:52, 160:59, 160:64, 160:71, 160:79, 160:80, 162:90, 162:95a, 162:95b, 162:98 >; *voc. sg.* Andrea 62; *acc. sg.* Andreas 158:17, 160:81 >; *dat. sg.* Andrea 158:25, 32

andrysn *adj.* adverse; *nt. dat. pl.* andrysnum 24:141

andswar *f.* answer; *dat. sg.* andsware 142:149

33

andswerian (2) to answer 22:107; *ind.*
pret. 3 sg. andswarode 104:135, 110:277,
22; andswarede 124:124, 128:189, 158:29;
andswerede 160:46 [ondswerede → andswerede],
160:49; *pl.* andswarodon 86; andswaredon
160:65; andsweredan 108:265
andweard *adj.* present; *m. nom. sg.* 58:4,
82:35; *m. nom. pl.* andwearde 90:210; *def.
m. acc. sg.* andweardan 88:139, 88:177,
92:29, 130:266; *m. dat. sg.* andweardan
120:1
andweardnes *f.* presence, present time;
dat. sg. andweardnesse 82:2-3, 82:10,
120:33; anweardnesse 146:3
andwleota *m.* face; *dat. sg.* andwleotan
88:157, 154:192
āne (see ān)
ānes (see ān)
ānfeald *adj.* single; *m. acc. sg.* ānfealdne
148:47, 148:52
ānforlætan (VII) to quit, forsake 38:31,
70:49; *ind. pres. 3 sg.* ānforlæteþ 38:29,
76:22; *pl.* ānforlætaþ 38:26; *pret. 3 sg.*
ānforlēt 150:131; *subj. pres. pl.* ānforlætan
130:262
ānforlætnes *f.* forsaking; *dat. sg.*
ānforlætnesse 60:48
ānlīcnes *f.* likeness, image; *nom. sg.*114;
acc. sg. anlīcnesse 113; *dat. sg.*
anlīcnesse 94:55, 100:46, 131
anmēdla *m.* proud, arrogance; *nom. pl.*
anmēdlan 78:77
ānmōdlīċe *adv.* unanimously 98:27,
102:103, 150:133
anna *adj.* only 116:76
ānne (see ān)
ānnes *f.* oneness, unity; *dat. sg.* ānnesse
98:33, 98:36
ānra (see ān)
ānrædliċ *adj.* undoubted; *f. nom. sg.*
ānrædlicu 8:141
ānre (see ān)
ānrōd *adj.* steadfast; *m. nom. pl.* ānrōde
94:87

ānsīn *f.* sight, vision; *dat. sg.* ānsīne 155
Antecrīst *m.* Antichrist; *nom. sg.* 64:176,
82:33
āniman (IV) to take; *pp.* anumen 38:6
anwald *nt.* power; *acc. sg.* anwald 94:75;
dat. sg. anwalde 20:73, 32:182, 46:20, 62:120
anwig *m.* single combat; *gen. sg.*
anwigges 138:70
anwilnes *f.* obstinacy; *dat. sg.*
anwilnesse 130:250
apostol *m.* apostle; *nom. sg.* 50:102,
50:134, 116:76, 120:4, 124:124, 41; *acc. sg.*
apostol 126:150; *gen. sg.* apostoles 120:3;
dat. sg. apostole 158:26; *nom. pl.*
apostolas 46:42, 92:34, 98:6, 100:41, 100:51,
100:62, 100:70, 100:76, 100:77, 100:87, 102:124,
104:146 [apostolas → apostolas], 104:163, 104:173,
104:177, 106:196, 106:224, 108:252, 108:265,
110:277, 110:304, 110:306; apostoli 1; *acc.
pl.* apostolas 92:26, 92:41, 94:49, 102:92,
102:132, 106:185, 106:189, 108:264, 112:331;
gen. pl. apostola 98:40, 100:86, 104:170,
106:182, 114:7, 120:2, 132:313, 132:319; *dat.
pl.* apostolum 16:170, 30:91, 52:175, 92:4,
96:91, 96:92, 100:53, 102:96, 102:100, 102:116,
106:195, 108:259, 110:276, 110:283, 110:298,
120:40
apostoliċne *adj.* apostolic; *m. acc. sg.*
150:108; *def. m. gen. sg.* apostolican
32:146, 130:266; *nt. dat. sg.* apostolican
118:105
Appia *prop. n.* Appia; *nom. sg.* 132:321
ār *m.* copper; *dat. sg.* āre 88:161
ār *f.* honour, mercy; *nom. sg.* 136:1; *acc.
sg.* āre 34:187, 50:121, 76:10; *gen. sg.* āre
126:163; *dat. sg.* āre 26:36, 148:44
āra (see arisan)
āræcan (1) to stretch out; *imp. 2 sg.* āræce
106:251
ārædan (1) to discover, read 126:147; *pp.*
āræded 124:107
āræfnan (1) to suffer, endure 162:110;
āræfnan 52:144; *ind. pres 1 sg.* aræfnie 75;
pl. āræfnaþ 8:138; *pret 1 sg.* āræfnede
162:109; *3 sg.* āræfnde 120:31; *pl.*

ārefnedon 16:144; *imp. 2 sg.* āræfna 11;
āræfne 162:107; *infl. inf.* to āræfnenne
40:62
ārǣran (1) to raise; *ind. pret. 3 sg.* ārǣrde
150:120; *pl.* ārǣrdon 140:122; *pp.* ārǣred
62:131
āras (see ārisan)
ārdǣd *adj.* merciful; *m. nom. pl.* ārdǣde
90:217
areċċan (1) to tell; *pp.* areaht 2:28
ārfæst *adj.* merciful; *m. nom. sg.* 60:84; *f.
dat. sg.* ārfæstre 24:165; *f. gen. pl.*
ārfæstra 146:37; *f. dat. pl.* ārfæstum
146:25; *def. m. nom. sg.* ārfæsta 62:93
ārfæstnes *f.* piety; *nom. sg.*; *acc. sg.*
ārfæstnesse 154:194
ārian (2) (with *dat.*) to have mercy upon,
spare 34:188, 124:119, 148:46; *imp. 2 sg.* āra
62:100, 131; 62:101 [āre → āra]; *3 sg.* ārige
64:148
ārīman (1) to count 40:81, 42:116
ārīsan (I) to arise 12:74, 66:189, 106:185,
130:268, 130:270, 145; *ind. pres. 1 sg.* ārīse
126:176, 126:177; *3 sg.* ārīseþ 10:8, 26:32,
76:15, 130:268; *pl.* ārīsaþ 120:15; *pret. 1 sg.*
ārās 126:174, 128:186; *3 sg.* arās 58:12,
90:200, 110:291, 124:101, 130:261, 158:41,
160:75, 63, 110; *pl.* ārīson 104:173, 106:187;
subj. pret. sg. ārīse 106:214; *imp. 2 sg.*
ārīs 98:4, 98:38, 108:229, 110:286, 110:290,
162:101, 62; *2 pl.* ārīsað 160:87; *infl. inf.* to
ārīsenne 150:119; *pres. p.* ārīsende 102:118,
154:207
ārlēas *adj.* impious; *def. m. nom. sg.*
ārlēasa 106:199; *f. nom. sg.* ārlēase 60:55;
m. nom. pl. ārlēasan 34:205
ārn (see yrnaþ)
Aron *pers. n.* Aron; *gen. sg.* Arones
114:22
Arrea *prop. n.* Sabarea; *dat. sg.* 146:5
ārweorþian (see ārwyrþian)
ārwyrðe *adj.* honourable, venerable;
f. nom. sg. 144:185; *def. m. nom. sg.*
ārwyrða 140:127; *f. nom. sg.* ārwyrþe 2:20;

nt. nom. sg. ārwyrðe 142:154; *f. dat. sg.*
ārwyrðan 146:2
ārwyrþian (2) to honour 48:81; *imp. 1 pl.*
ārweorþian 6:108
ārwyrþnes *f.* honour, respect; *acc. sg.*
ārwyrþnesse 128:204; *gen. sg.*
ārwyrðnesse 142:147; *dat. sg.*
ārwyrþnesse 46:1, 82:2
āscinan (I) to shine; *ind. pret. 3 sg.* āscān
153; āscean 102:108; *pl.* āscinon 114:15
āsceacan [āscascan] (VI) to drive; *pp.*
asceofene 10:38
āscian (2) to ask; *ind. pret. 3 sg.* āhsode
10:12, 126:158, 130:270, 132:194, 150:112; *pl.*
āhsodon 82:14; āhsodan 82:20; *imp. 2 sg.*
āxa 160:62
āscinon (see āscian)
āscyran [āsciran] (1) to made clear; *pp.*
āscyred 78:48
āsecgan (3) to speak out, tell 102:110;
āseccgan [→āsecggan] 72:99; āsecggan
146:39, 150:125; *subj. pres. sg.* āsecgge
28:62
āsettan (1) to lay down; *ind. pret. 3 sg.*
āsette 6:98, 18:7, 58:15, 110:317, 152:137,
160:79; *2 sg.* āsettest 60:65; *pl.* āsetton
104:164, 110:305, 132:310, 40; *subj. pres. pl.*
āsetton 160:82; *pret. pl.* āsetton 108:262;
imp. 2 pl. āsettað 160:82; āsette 104:154;
pp. āseted 106:215; *m. acc. sg.* āsetedne
[āsetene → āsetedne] 6:108; *m. nom. pl.* āsette
134:325 (?)
āsmēagan (1) to imagine, consider; *ind.
pres. pl.* āsmēagaþ 20:88; *pp.* āsmēade
58:6
āspringan (III) to fail; *ind. pres. 3 sg.*
āspringeþ 62:131
āstīfian (2) to become stiff; *pp. sg* āstīfod
132:318
āstīgan (I) to ascend 82:13, 160:62, 160:65;
ind. pres. 3 sg. āstīgeþ 2:26, 64:138; *pret. 2
sg.* āstīge 60:64; *3 sg.* āstāg 6:125, 22:119,
46:3, 46:18, 58:23, 62:115, 68:3, 74:6, 74:23,
84:70, 84:79, 86:113, 86:116, 88:150, 94:45,
100:60, 116:78, 122:61, 130:245, 132:285,

138:88, 158:38, 160:59, 160:83; āstāh 14:131, 98:9, 104:162, 1, 12, 122, 158, 161; āstāhg 12:49; *pl.* āstīgon 142:178; *subj. pret. sg.* āstīge 8:146, 88:138, 92:7, 94:53, 112:327; *pl.* āstīgan 128:205; *imp. 2 sg.* āstīg 60:70, 158:36; *2 pl.* āstīgað 160:51, 160:58; *pres. p. m. acc. sg.* āstīgendne 86:115
āstreċċan (1) to stretch out; *ind. pret. 3 sg.* āstreahte 150:96, 150:117 (EWS)
āswāpan (VII) to deprive; *pp.* āstȳpte 74:26
āstyrian (1) to stir; *ind. pret. 3 sg.* āstyrede 150:99
āswǣman (1) to pine 28:45
āsweltan (III) to die; *pp.* āswolten 150:113
ātēon (II) to apply; *ind. pret 3 sg.* ātēah 148:48; *pp.* ātogen 18:34
āttor *nt.* poison, venom; *acc. sg.* āttor 2:14, 7, 10, 158:2,
āwǣgan (1) to be disappointed; *ind. pret. 3 pl.* āwǣgdon 62:126
āweahte (see āweccan)
āwellan (VII) to swarm; *ind. pres. 3 sg.* āwealleþ 70:56
āweorpan (III) to cast down; *ind. pret. 3 sg.* āwearp 48:77, 60:69; *pp.* āworpen 2:35, 86:94; *pl.* āworpene 110:319
āweċċan (1) to awake 110:281, 124:92; āweċċean 52:159; *ind. pres. pl.* āwecceaþ 66:186; *pret 3 sg.* āwehte 46:9, 46:24, 48:52, 48:55, 48:87, 50:123, 52:159, 122:48, 124:133, 160:86; āweahte 118:91; *subj. pres. sg.* āwecce 144; *pp.* āweht 62:110, 120:40; *pl.* āwehte 22:102
āweg *adv.* away
āweht (see āweċċan)
āwehte (see āweċċan)
āwenian (2) to wean; *ind. pres. pl.* aweniaþ 42:105
āwierġan (1) to curse; *ind. pret. 3 sg.* āwergde 50:90; *pp. m. nom. pl.* āwyrgde 28:71; *m. acc. pl.* āwergde 62:132; *m. dat. pl.* āwergdum 64:175; *def. m. nom. sg.* āwyrigda 82:33; āwergda 20:49; *m. acc. sg.*

āwerigdan 18:39; āwergdan 156:242; *m. acc. pl.* āwergdan 64:180; *m. dat. pl.* āwergdum 58:17, 144:193
āweaxan (VII) to grow up; *pp.* āwexene 144:200
awiht *pron.* aught 78:49
aworpen (see awearp)
āwrītan (I) to write; *pp.* āwrīten 14:111, 18:9, 18:15, 32:168; āwrītene *pl.* 10:6
āwundian (2) to wound; *pp.* āwunden 118:116
āwunian (2) to abide; *pres. p. m. nom. sg.* āwunigende 76:20
āxa (see ahsode)
āxe *f.* ashes; *nom. sg.* 62:95; āxan *dat. sg.* 62:133
āþenian (2) to stretch out; *ind. pret 3 sg.* āþenede 109, 113; *pp. m. dat. pl.* āþenedum 126:150, 130:245
āþēodan (1) to separate; *subj. pres. sg.* āþēode 40:43
āþwēan (II) to wash; *pp.* āþwǣgen 104:145
āðȳwan (1) to impress; *pp.* āðȳde 140:112

Æ

ǣ *f.* law; *acc. sg.* 114:28, 116:46, 116:49, 128:227, 148:77; *pl.* 116:89
ǣbyligð *m.* offence; *acc. pl.* ǣbyligða 4:83
ǣfæst *adj.* pious; *m. nom. pl.* ǣfæste 122:49
ǣfen *m.* evening; *nom. sg.* 71; *acc. sg.* ǣfen 30:120, 64:140, 64:144; *dat. sg.* ǣfenne 107
ǣfengereord *nt.* evening-feast; *acc. pl.* ǣfengereordu 46:25; ǣfengerordu [→ ǣfengereordu] 68:42; *dat. pl.* ǣfengereordum 50:95, 100:73
ǣfest *m.* envy; *acc. sg.* ǣfest 4:53, 124:95
ǣfest *f.* envy *acc. sg.* ǣfeste 66:197, 122:84; *dat. sg.* ǣfeste 16:148
ǣfestian (2) to be envious; *ind. pres. 3 sg.* ǣfestgaþ 18:42

36

æfestig *adj.* envious; *m. nom. sg.* 44:148, 132:280; *m. nom. pl.* æfestige 132:276; *def. m. nom. pl.* æfstigan 44:153, 44:154

ǽfre *adv.* ever (see Appendix, p. 151)

æfter *adv.* after, afterwards 70:69, 70:72

æfter *prep.* (with acc. / dat.) after (see Appendix, p. 150)

æftera *adj.* following, second; *comp. m. dat. sg.* æfteran 48:89, 64:141; *f. dat. sg.* æfteran 134:327; *nt. nom. sg.* æfterre 54:228

æfterfylġan (1) to follow after; *pres. p. nt. nom. sg.* æfterfylgende 54:220; *nt. gen. sg.* æfterfylgendan 92:31

æfterre (see æftera)

æfterðon *adv.* 150:105

ǽghwǽr *adv.* everywhere 12:77, 42:134; ǽghwār 14:129

ǽghwǽt *pron.* anything; *m. nom. sg.* 94:84

ǽghwēþer (ge ... ge) both ... and 86:131, 148:55; ǽghwēðer (ge) 150:128; ǽghwēþer (ge) 154:216; ǽgwēðer (ge) 154:222

ǽghwilcre (see ǽghwylc)

ǽghwonon *adv.* on all sides 80:123a, 80:123b, 80:124a, 80:124b

ǽghwylc *adj.* each, every; *m. nom. sg.* 2:37, 24:146, 30:99, 32:176, 84:72, 90:213, 114:38, 124:89, 5; *m. acc. sg.* ǽghwylcne 32:160; *f. acc. sg.* ǽghwylce 46:31, 90:184, 90:188; *nt. acc. sg.* ǽghwylc 88:152, 92:18a, 92:18b; *m. gen. sg.* ǽghwylces 58:6, 116:56; *m. dat. sg.* ǽghwylcum 32:157, 78:59, 82:42, 86:95, 86:121, 86:130, 90:189, 154:187; ǽgwylcum 114:29; *f. dat. sg.* ǽghwylcre 55; *nt. dat. sg.* ǽghwylcum 88:183, 150:129; *m. inst. sg.* ǽghwylce 62:136

ǽgweðer (see ǽghweþer)

Ǽgypt *prop. n.* Egypt; *dat. pl.* Ǽgyptum 104:175

ǽgþēr (ge ... ge) both ... and 32:162, 116:46, 130:242; ǽgþær (ge ... ge) 26:10; ǽgþēr (ge) 2:9

ǽht *f.* possessions, property; *acc. sg.* ǽht 74:5; *nom. pl.* ǽhta 34:195, 34:200; *acc. pl.* ǽhta 26:2, 34:217, 34:221, 36:236, 42:103; *gen. pl.* ǽhta 32:155, 34:209; *dat. pl.* ǽhtum 36:238

ǽhtspedig *adj.* wealthy; *m. nom. sg.* 136:21

ǽlc *adj., pron.* every, each one; *m. nom. sg.* 20:80, 40:47a, 52:181, 68:17, 98:36, 104:181, 106:185, 128:203; *f. nom. sg.* ǽlc 40:47b; *m. acc. sg.* ǽlcne 62:112, 122:69; *f. acc. sg.* ǽlce 12:77, 24:146, 86:134, 90:184, 114:28; *f. gen. sg.* ǽlcere 92:26; *nt. gen. sg.* ǽlces 18:30, 124:115; *m. dat. sg.* ǽlcum 146:22; *f. dat. sg.* ǽlcere 60:56; *nt. inst. sg.* ǽlce 152:151

ælmesdǽd *f.* almsdeed; *nom. pl.* ælmesdǽda 24:170; *dat. pl.* ælmesdǽdum 24:163

ælmesgeorn *adj.* charitable; *m. nom. pl.* ælmesgeorne 66:196, 76:30, 90:217

ælmesse *f.* alms; *acc. sg.* ælmessan 26:35, 26:42; *dat. sg.* ælmessan 24:159, 28:43, 28:44; *acc. pl.* ælmessan 34:224; *dat. pl.* ælmessum 24:149, 26:33

ælmessyle *m.* almsdeed; *nom. pl.* ælmessylena 50:113

ælmesweorc *nt.* almswork; *dat. pl.* ælmesweorcum 16:156/7

ælmihtig *adj.* almighty; *m. nom. sg.* 100:45, 130:229, 150:122; *m. acc. sg.* ælmihtigne 76:5, 84:89, 86:128, 98:26, 108:248, 128:218, 130:260, 152:154; *m. dat. sg.* ælmihtigum 78:81, 80:103, 150:101; *def. m. nom. sg.* ælmihtiga 18:27, 20:74, 74:20, 78:45, 86:99; æmihtiga [→ ælmihtiga] 50:102 *m. gen. sg.* ælmihtigan 84:51; *m. dat. sg.* ælmihtigan 20:74, 140:108; ælmihtegan 80:120

37

ælþeodig *adj.* foreign, strange; *m. acc. sg.* ælþeodigne 52; *m. dat. sg.* ælþeodigum 125; *m. nom. pl.* ælþeodige 14:116; *def. m. acc. sg.* ælþeodigan 135; *m. gen. sg.* ælþeodigan 129

ælþeodignes *f.* exile, pilgrimage; *acc. sg.* ælþeodignesse 6:130; *gen. sg.* ælþeodignesse 14:115a; *dat. sg.* ælþeodignesse 14:115b

ælþeodisc *adj.* strange; *m. nom. sg.* 6

æmetig *adj.* empty, void; *m. nom. sg.* 24:151; *f. nom. sg.* æmetugu 2:18

ænig *adj.* any, some; *m. nom. sg.* 24:164, 44:148, 78:87, 118:116, 124:106, 146:39; *f. nom. sg.* ænigu 54:188; ænig 26:10, 62:114; *nt. nom. sg.* ænig 16:167, 46:41, 66:199, 66:200; *m. acc. sg.* ænigne 116:60, 58; *f. acc. sg.* ænige 54:184, 66:188, 148:53; *nt. acc. sg.* ænig 58:8, 146:35; *m. gen. sg.* æniges 42:115; ænges 82:22; *f. gen. sg.* ænigre 88:158; *m. dat. sg.* ænigum 30:117, 76:33; *nt. dat. pl.* ænigum 30:104, 32:157

ænne (see ān)

ær *conj.* before (see Appendix, p. 149)

ær *adj.* early; *m. acc sg.* ærne 30:119; *comp. nt. nom. sg.* ærre 54:227; *f. dat. sg.* ærran 60:44; *superl. nt. nom. sg.* ærest 44:145, 150:105; *def. m. nom. sg.* æresta 12:49, 14:116, 120:4, 146:14; *f. nom. sg.* æreste 2:33; *nt. nom. sg.* æreste 88:161; *m. acc. sg.* ærestan 2:15; *m. gen. sg.* ærestan 60:47; *nt. gen. sg.* ærestan 2:18; *m. dat. sg.* ærestan 86:101; *m. inst. sg.* ærestan 62:136; *m. nom. pl.* ærestan 10:38, 16:142; *m. acc. pl.* ærestan 4:75

æren *adj.* brazen; *f. acc. sg.* ærne 43; *f. acc. pl.* ærene 120:42, 122:43; *def. m. acc. pl.* ærenan 58:28

ærende *nt.* errand, message; *acc. sg.* ærende 4:84, 140:130, 160:49

ærendgewrit *nt.* epistle, letter; *acc. sg.* ærendgewrit 122:80

ærendwreca *m.* messenger; *nom. sg.* 2:11, 4:58, 4:84, 6:93; *dat. pl.* ærendwrecum 140:93

ærest (see 'ær' *adj.*)

æresta (see 'ær' *adj.*)

æreste (see 'ær' *adj.*)

ærist *m.* resurrection; *nom. sg.* 92:25; *gen. sg.* æristes 78:56; *dat. sg.* æriste 56:234, 58:19, 82:8, 82:16, 92:34, 100:76

ærist *f.* resurrection; *acc. sg.* æriste 10:29, 54:217, 62:114, 62:119, 84:65; *gen. sg.* æriste 58:7

ærn *nt.* place, dwelling; *dat. sg.* ærne 152:147

ærðæm þe *conj.* (with *subj.*) before 118:134; ærðon 138:65; ærþon þe 92:7, 116:72, 116:73, 116:74, 116:75, 116:82, 116:86, 116:87/8, 116:88/9

æsprenge *f.* fountain; *dat. sg.* æsprenge 18:34

æswica [æ swica → æswica] *m.* traitor; *nom. sg.* 122:58

æt (see etan)

æt *prep.* (with *acc.*) onto (see Appendix, p. 150)

æt *prep.* (with *dat.*) at, on (see Appendix, p. 150)

ætēowan (1) to show, reveal, manifest 46:5; *ind. pres. 3 sg.* ætēoweð 58:1; ætēoweþ 64:158; *3 pl.* ætēowaþ 40:71; *pret. 3 sg.* ætēawde 128:183, 136:5; ætēowde 18:12, 162:94; ætīwde 154; *3 pl.* ætēawdon 86:110; ætēawdan 132:307; ætēowdon 126:152; *subj. pres. 1 sg.* ætēowe 142:147, 162:93, 162:109; *pp* ætēowed 136:13, 142:142, 142:154, 142:157, 144:185, 144:190; ætīwed 138:51, 138:79; *pl.* ætēowde 76:12; *infl. inf.* to ætēowenne 162:100

ætfēolan (III) to diligently occupy; *ind. pret. 3 pl.* ætfūlgon [æt fūlgon → ætfūlgon] 138:67

ætgædere *adv.* together 92:37, 92:42

38

æthrīnan (I) (with gen. or dat.) to touch; *subj. pres. 3 sg.* æthrīne 116:72; *imp. 2 sg.* æthrīn 108:234

ætīewed (see ætēowan)

ætīwde (see ætēowan)

ætnehstan *adv.* at last 146:8, 152:180

ǣton (see etan)

ætsomne *adv.* together 2

ætstandan (VI) to stand by; *ind. pret. pl.* ætstōd 106:183; *imp. 2 pl.* ætstondað [MS ætsondað] 142:144; *pres. p. m. dat. sg.* ætstondendum 126:136

ǣw *f.* law; *acc. sg.*; ǣwe 28:52, 28:81, 28:83, 30:94

ǣweweard *m.* priest; *nom. sg.* 114:20

æþele *adj.* noble; *m. gen. pl.* æþelra 146:6; *def. m. nom. sg.* æþela 26:1, 26:24, 28:52, 28:73, 30:96, 32:142, 32:163, 34:190, 38:1, 42:101, 142:139; *m. dat. sg.* æþelan 74:1, 74:7; *m. nom. pl.* æþelan 114:24; *superl. def. f. nom. sg.* æþeleste 156:231

æþelnes *f.* nobleness; *nom. sg.* 80:117

B

bān *nt.* bone; *nom. sg.* 62:100; *nom. pl.* bān 80:95; *acc. pl.* bān 80:97; *dat. pl.* bānum 62:100

baptist *m.* baptist; *gen. sg.* baptistan 140:125

barn (see byrnan)

basu *adj.* purple, crimson; *nt. inst. sg.* baswe 142:155

bǣr *f.* bier; *nom. sg.* 106:195; *acc. sg.* bǣre 104:165, 104:168, 104:171, 104:172, 104:173, 104:177, 106:217, 106:220; *dat. sg.* bǣre 104:146

bǣrnan (1) to burn 152:138, 152:140; bǣran [→ bǣrnan] 152:148; *subj. pres. pl.* bǣrnan 102:101

bæþ *nt.* bath; *dat. sg.* bæþe 18:19

be *prep.* (with acc. / dat.) by, about, (see Appendix, p. 150)

bēag *m.* crown; *acc. sg.* bēag 16:140, 120:5

beahsian (2) to ask *ind. pret. 3 pl.* beahsodan 138:47, 140:129

beald *adj.* bold; *m. nom. sg* 76:41 (we)

bealo *nt.* wickedness; *gen. sg.* bealwes 76:41

bēam *m.* tree, timber; *dat. pl.* bēamum 126:165, 130:234

bearn *nt.* child; *nom. sg.* 116:77; *gen. sg.* bearnes 114:32a, 114:32b, 116:48; *nom. pl.* bearn 30:110, 30:114, 92:14, 156:233, 160:87, 54, 83, 86, 141; *gen. pl.* bearna 116:67; *acc. pl.* bearn 2:3, 2:7, 76:31, 119; *dat. pl.* bearnum 108:270, 128:209

bearu *m.* wood, copse; *nom. pl.* bearwas 144:200; *dat. pl.* bearwum 144:202

bebēodan (II) to command 30:122, 30:134, 32:140, 124:92; *ind. pres. 1 sg.* bebēode 20:44, 104:155, 124:119, 126:166, 130:262; *2 sg.* bebēodest 154:207; *pl.* bebēodaþ 28:81; *pret. 3 sg.* bebēad 26:4, 26:8, 26:19, 28:52, 48:67, 54:210, 76:30, 102:125, 104:172, 108:238, 108:246, 108:254, 108:256, 108:257, 122:47, 146:33, 160:76, 37, 166; *subj. pres. sg.* bebēode 30:122; *pret. sg.* bebude 30:92; *pp.* beboden 22:130, 30:118, 32:137, 32:157, 42:124, 76:35, 76:38, 126:180, 148:58, 160:83

bebeorgan (III) (with dat.) to guard; *ind. pres. 3 pl.* bebeorgaþ 42:135; *infl. inf.* to bebeorhgenne 44:142

bebōd *nt.* commandment; *nom. sg.* 32:147; *acc. sg.* bebōd 32:145, 62:125, 160:53; *dat. sg.* bebōde 30:126; *gen. pl.* bebōda 16:164, 18:32, 24:150, 64:181, 72:97, 72:103, 94:63, 100:72, 104:137, 104:158, 114:27; *acc. pl.* bebōdu 2:35, 6:130, 8:150, 14:117, 16:150, 22:103, 22:123, 30:125, 32:164, 36:240, 58:8, 68:18, 128:194, 147; bebōda 24:175; *dat. pl.* bebōdum 114:24; bebōdum (bebōdudum → bebōdum) 120:19

bebycgan to sell; *ind. pret. 3 sg.* bebohte 42:120 (A)

bebude (see bebēodan)

bebyrgean (1) to bury 14:124; *ind. pret. 3 pl.* bebyrigdon 108:254; *pp.* bebyrged 124:99; *infl. inf.* bebyrgenne 98:6 (A)

39

bebyrgednes *f.* burial; *gen. sg.*
bebyrgednesse 48:48
bēc (see bōc)
beceorfan (III) to cut off 126:175; *pp.*
becorfen 120:28, 126:179
becuman (IV) to come 52:168, 60:51; *ind.*
pres. 3 sg. becymeþ 34:190; *pret. 1 sg.*
becom 124:105; *pret. 3 sg.* becom 6:101,
70:85, 74:11, 116:72, 116:87, 122:53, 132:313;
subj. pret. 3 sg. become 116:88
bēd *nt.* prayer; *dat. pl.* bēdum 122:46
bedīeglian (2) to conceal; *pp.* bedīgled
78:49, 138:50, 138:53; *pl.* bedīglede 10:10
bedrīfan (I) to drive; *ind. pres. pl.*
bedrīfaþ 64:180; *pp.* bedrīfen 64:178
bedȳpan (1) to dip; *pp.* bedȳped 128:198
bedydrian (2) to hide, conceal; *pp.*
bedyrned 118:108
beēodan (anom.) to practice; *ind. pret. 3*
sg. beēode 78:80; *pl.* beēodan 140:118;
subj. pret. pl. beēodan 128:218
befæstan (1) to apply, use 122:73; *ind.*
pres. 1 sg. befæste 132:303; *pret. 2 sg.*
befæsttest 132:302
befealdan (I) to fold; *pp.* befealden 60:83,
62:133
befēng (see befōn)
befēran (1) to encompass; *ind. pret. 3 sg.*
befērde 54:200
beflēogan (II) to escape; *subj. pret 3 pl.*
beflugon 118:123
beforan *adv.* before 48:68, 48:70, 54:215,
64:176, 114:11, 116:47, 148:48, 148:73, 154:195
beforan *prep.* (with acc. / dat.) before (see
Appendix, p. 150)
beforan *post prep.* (with dat.) before 10:12,
58:4, 70:52, 74:17, 78:62, 84:76
befriġnan (III) to question; *ind. pret. 2 sg.*
befrūne 128:200; *subj. pret. 3 pl.* befrīnon
140:129
begān (anom.) to practice, perform,
surround, take care of 28:51, 76:22; *ind.*
pres. 3 sg. begǣþ 126:142; *pl.* begāngaþ
38:26, 42:97, 42:104, 42:127; *pret. pl.*
biggēngan 142:174

begang *m.* business, undertaking; *dat. pl.*
begangum 80:105
bēgan (1) to bow; *ind. pres. 1 sg.* bēge
130:238; *pret. 3 sg.* bēgde 130:240; *imp. 1*
pl. bēgan 38:42
bēgen *pron.* both; *m. nom. pl.* 120:5,
140:136; bēgan 120:5; *adj.* both; *m. acc. pl.*
bēgen 106:202
beġytan (V) to obtain 18:26, 34:223, 36:239,
88:165; begēotan 68:17; *ind. pres. 3 sg.*
begyteþ 34:215, 66:203, 68:18; *pret. 2 sg.*
begeate 60:47; *3 sg.* begeat 146:31; *3 pl.*
begēaton 36:236 (A)
behabban (3) to contain 142:153
behēafdian (2) to behead 126:180; *pp.*
behēafdod 132:283; *m. acc. sg.*
behēafdodne 124:134
behealdan (VII) to keep, behold 24:176;
ind. pres. 2 sg. behealdest 62:96; *pret. 1*
sg. behēold 162:92; *3 sg.* behēold 130:241;
pl. behēoldan 6:112; *imp. 2 sg.* behēald
158:6, 158:12, 76, 100, 105; *2 pl.* behēaldað
68:38, 59
behindan *adv.* behind 72
behindan *prep.*(with dat.) behind 44:146
beholan (1) to hide; *pp. def. f. nom. sg.*
beholene 52:152 (A)
behȳdan (1) to hide; *pp.* behȳded 64:173
behydig *adj.* heedful; *f. nom. sg.* 46:30
belēac (see beluceþ)
belean (VI) to lie; *ind. pret. 3 sg.* beleah
130:272
belimpan (III) to pertain; *ind. pres. 3 sg.*
belimpeþ 10:24, 26:36
belūcan (II) to lock up; *ind. pres. 3 sg.*
belūceþ 2:28; *pret. 3 sg.* belēac 4:79; *pp.*
belocen 4:75, 42:93; *pl.* belocene 40:66
bēme *f.* trumpet; *nom. sg.* 116:43, 116:53;
acc. pl. bēman 66:185
bemīðan (VI) to hid, conceal; *pp.*
bemīðen 138:49
bēn *f.* prayer, petition; *nom. sg.* 60:66,
116:63; *nom. pl.* bēna 80:103, 138:80; *acc.*
pl. bēna 76:9, 90:209

bend *m.* bond; *acc. sg.* bend 6:96; *nom. pl.* bendas 60:82, 62:103; *dat. pl.* bendum 58:13, 58:36, 60:43, 60:74, 60:81, 60:87, 62:102
Beneuentius *prop. n.* Beneuentius; *nom. sg.* 138:70
bēo (see bēon)
bēodan (II) to bid, command 30:126; *ind. pret. 3 sg.* bēad 108:261, 110:283, 130:234; *pl.* budon 10:15
bēodlaf *m.* table-leavings; *acc. pl.* bēodlafa 34:225
bēon (anom.) to be; *ind. pres. 1 sg.* eom; *1 sg.* nelle (am not); *3 sg.* nis (is not) (see Appendix, p. 152-3)
beorht *adj.* bright, splendid, glorious *m. nom. sg.* 58:31, 154:223, 158:11; *comp. f. acc. sg.* beohtran 104:141
beorhte *adv.* brightly 90:184,
beorhtnes *f.* brightness; *acc. sg.* beorhtnesse 12:52, ; *dat. sg.* beorhtnesse 58:40; *acc. pl.* beorhtnessa 10:39
beorþor *m.* offspring; *acc. sg.* beorþor 2:33; *dat. sg.* beorþre 108:274, 108:275
bēotan (VII) to beat; *ind. pres. 3 sg.* bēotaþ 64:177; *3 pl.* bēotiaþ 22:106; *ind. pret. 3 pl.* bēotan 16:140
beran (IV) to bear, carry 44:139, 46:42; *ind. pres. 3 pl.* beraþ 100:76, 126:167, 130:259; *pret 3 sg.* bær 2:5, 8:144; *3 pl.* bæron 46:10, 48:58, 104:173, 104:177, 108:252; *subj. pres. 3 pl.* bēran 54:207, 104:168, 104:171, 130:262; *infl. inf.* to berenne 62:123; *pres. p. f. acc. sg.* berendan 2:14; *pp.* geboren 16:163, 114:18, 118:94
berēofan (II) to spoil, plunder; *ind. pret. 3 sg.* berēafode 46:19; *pp.* berēafod 52:175, 60:71
beren *nt.* barn; *acc. sg.* beren 26:13, 26:14, 26:26
beren *adj.* made of barley; *m. acc. sg.* berenne 126:145; berene 124:130
bergean [beorgan] (1) to bury 14:125
bescēawian (2) to consider; *ind. pres. 3 pl.* bescēawiaþ 40:72, 42:91, 42:94

bescyerian (2) to deprive; *ind. pret. 2 sg.* bescyredest 32:164 (A)
besencean (1) to plunge 22:99; *ind. pret. 3 pl.* besencton 28:71; *subj. pres. 3 pl.* besencean 44:157; *pp.* besencte 32:141 (A)
besīncan (1) to sink 88:174
besmītan (VI) to defile 60:52; *ind. pret. 3 sg.* besmāt 118:118; *pp.* besmīten 50:104; *pl.* besmitene 16:148 (A)
besorgian (2) to be anxious about 120:12
bestæppan (II) to proceed, trod; *pp.* bestapene 88:173
beswāc (see beswican)
beswingan (III) to beat, flog; *ind. pres. 1 sg.* beswang 124:98
beswēopan to envelop, wrap; *ind. pret. 3 sg.* beswēop 148:51
beswīcan (I) to deceive, beguile, weaken, frustrate 38:13, 38:15, 38:17, 138:76; *ind. pres. 3 sg.* beswīceþ 128:195; *3 pl.* beswīcaþ 42:105; *pret. 3 sg.* beswāc 2:15; *infl. inf.* to beswīcenne 130:260; *pp.* beswīcen 124:110
bet *adv.* better 50:136
bētan (I) make good, make amends 30:99, 86:128; *ind. pres. pl.* bētaþ 134:330; *subj. pres. sg.* bēte 16:158; *pl.* bēton 16:156
Betfage *prop. n.* Bethphage; *nom. sg.* 52:163; *dat. sg.* 48:59, 52:161,
Bethania *prop. n.* Bethany; *dat. sg.* 46:23, 48:82
Betleem *prop. n.* Bethlehem; *acc. sg.* 64:149
betre *adj.* better; *comp. m. nom. sg.* 90:220; *nt. nom. sg.* betere 16:163; *nt. gen. sg.* betran 148:53; *m. nom. pl.* beteran 78:64; betran 98:40; *superl. m. nom. sg.* betsta 126:170; *m. acc. sg.* betstan 46:32; *f. acc. sg.* betstan 132:281; *m. dat. sg.* betstan 74:7; *m. nom. pl.* betstan 50:108
betuh *prep.* (with *acc.*) between 2:31, 100:82
betuh *prep.* (with *dat.*) between 42:123, 94:50, 114:18, 144:205
betux *prep.* (with *dat.*) between 118:101

41

betwēonum *postprep.* (with dat.) between, among 64:153, 154:198, 2, 158:23; betwynum 108; betwēonon 76:31, 122:84, 20; betwēonan 90:218, 128:203, 152:146, 49; be ... twēonum 98:31; be ... twēonum 100:77

betȳnan (1) to shut 150:117; *ind. pres. 3 sg.* betȳnde 158:22; *3 pl.* betȳndon 60, 78, 108; *pp.* betȳned 4:56, 126; *pl.* betȳnede 108:233, 50; betȳnde 40:65

bewerian (2) to ward off; *ind. pret. 3 sg.* bewerede 92:18

bewitan (1) to guard; *ind. pret. 3 sg.* bewiste 128:182

bewrēon (I) to cover; *ind. pres. 3 sg.* bewrihþ 42:98; *pret. 3 sg.* bewreāh 2:42; *imp. 2 pl.* bewreoþ 64:171; *pp. sg* beþeāht 136:26; bewrigen 66:187, 142:155; *pl.* bewrigene 10:10

bī *prep.* (with dat.) by 132:309, 152:140

biddan (V) to pray 12:68, 12:86, 86:127, 112:335, 128:196, 138:71, 142:137, 144:195, 144:209; biddon 68:5; *ind. pres. 1 sg.* bidde 40:51, 98:20, 98:27, 100:84, 102:100, 104:136, 106:211, 132:302, 158:7, 162:93, 115; bide 106:208; *3 sg.* bideþ 12:53, 72:100; *pl.* biddaþ 34:187, 44:156, 52:165, 54:226, 64:166, 76:10, 102:113, 102:114; *pret 1 sg.* bæd 24; *3 sg.* bæd 12:89a, 12:89b, 14:123, 26:9, 146:14, 146:42, 152:155; *pl.* bædon 60:59, 132:293, 156:232, 150, 156; bædan 156:237; *subj. pres. sg.* bidde 12:83; *pl.* biddan 12:87; *imp. 1 pl.* biddon 14:94; biddan 16:165; *2 pl.* bidde 156:233; *pres. p. def. m. dat. sg.* biddendan 12:84

bīdan (I) to await; *ind. pres. 3 sg.* bīdeþ 4:71, 78:45

bifian (2) to tremble; *pres. p. f. inst. sg.* bifigendre 4:89; *def. m. acc. sg.* bifigendan 34:207; bifgendan 40:89; *m. dat. sg.* bifigendan 38:41; *m. nom. pl.* bifigendan 76:8

big *adv.* by 152:153

big *prep.* (with dat.) by 46:25

big *post prep.* (with dat.) by 32:179, 38:31, 76:23, 136:17, 146:32

biġġengan (see bēgan)

bigswic *m.* deceit; *dat. sg.* bigswice 122:49

bigswica *m.* deceiver; *nom. sg.* 120:41; *nom. pl.* bigswicon 130:248

bindan (III) to bind; *ind. pres. pl.* bindað 10:7; *pret. pl.* bundon 16:139

binne *m.* manger; *nom. sg.* 6:108

bisceop *m.* bishop; *nom. sg.* 32:143, 138:73, 140:127, 142:139, 142:168, 148:75, 150:123; biscep 138:46; biscop 28:75, 28:77, 28:87, 30:90, 30:96, 30:100, 30:126; biscep [→ biscop] 28:82; *acc. sg.* biscop 30:90; *dat. sg.* bisceope 138:61, 138:79, 142:142, 148:75, 148; biscepe 138:51; biscope 28:80; *nom. pl.* biscopas 30:133, 76:37; *dat. pl.* biscopum 28:79

bisceophād *m.* office of bishop; *acc. sg.* bisceophād 150:129; *dat. sg.* bisceophāde 150:124

bisceopscīr *f.* bishopric; *dat. sg.* bisceopscīre 154:198

bismere (see bysmor)

bīst (see bēon)

biswica *m.* deceiver *acc. sg.* biswican 106:187

bite *m.* sting; *nom. sg.* 46:18a; *acc. sg.* bite 46:18b

biter *adj.* bitter; *m. nom. pl.* bitere 40:63; *def. f. dat. sg.* biteran 16:148; *superl. m. acc. sg.* biterestan 158:9

bitere *adv.* bitterly 34:211

biternes *f.* bitterness; *dat. sg.* biternesse 80:125

biwist *f.* living, food; *dat. sg.* biwiste 128:207

blǣd *m.* blast; *nom. sg.* 136:40

blāwan (VII) to blow 66:185; *ind. pres. pl.* blǣstan 84

blēo *f.* colour, appearance; *gen. pl.* blēona 122:56

bletsian (2) to bless 30:109, 118:98; *ind. pres. 1 sg.* bletsige 98:19, 102:90, 102:91,

102:92, 102:134; *3 sg.* bletsaþ 60:83; *pl.*
bletsiaþ 102:113, 102:114 [blessiaþ → bletsiaþ];
pret. 3 sg. bletsode 98:18, 102:132 [beltsode
→ bletsode], 106:219, 106:221, 123; *imp. 2 pl.*
bletsiað 100:54, 100:57
bletsung *f.* blessing; *acc. sg.* bletsunge
110:294; bletsunga 50:122, 98:21; *gen. sg.*
bletsunga 32:164; *dat. sg.* bletsunga 4:57,
142:166; bletsunge 102:91; *acc. pl.*
bletsunga 2:40, 32:174, 98:21
blīnd *adj.* blind; *m. nom. sg.* 10:11, 12:52,
14:90, 58; *f. gen. sg.* blīndre 74:18; *m. nom.*
pl. blīnde 48:79; *m. acc. pl.* blīnde 124:90;
def. m. nom. sg. blīnda 10:18, 10:36, 12:50,
12:57, 12:64, 12:81, 12:89, 14:120, 14:122; *m.*
acc. sg. blīndan 12:69, 12:71, 14:92; *m. dat.*
sg. blīndan 12:47
blindnes *f.* blindness; *acc. sg.* blindnesse
14:115; *gen. sg.* blindnesse 12:78; *dat. sg.*
blindnesse 10:37, 108:231 [bindness →
blindness], 108:241
blis *f.* joy, bliss; *nom. sg.* 16:166, 16:169,
24:154, 60:49, 86:106; bliss 68:37; *acc. sg.*
blisse 16:160, 24:142, 60:72, 84:87, 150:134,
154:191; *gen. sg.* blisse 8:153; *dat. sg.*
blisse 2:4, 38:29, 56:239, 86:96, 136:18,
140:107, 142:166; *nom. pl.* blissa 70:43; *acc.*
pl. blissa 68:41
blissian (2) to rejoice 144:210; *ind. pres. 3*
sg. blisseþ 40:50; *pres. 3 pl.* blissiaþ
32:151; *imp. 2 sg.* blissa 2:24; *3 pl.* blissian
[→ blessian] 62:117; *pres. p.* blissigende 2:21,
98:17/8; blissiende 110:282
blīþe *adj.* joyful; *f. inst. sg.* blīþre 62:107;
nt. inst. sg. blīþe 4:46, 24:175; *m. nom. pl.*
blīþe 26:41, 60:45; *comp. f. nom. sg.* blīþre
26:42
blīðe *adv.* joyfully 6:101; bliþe 24:167,
32:172
blīþlīce *adv.* joyfully 70:72
blōd *nt.* blood; *nom. sg.* 6:103, 62:118,
128:183, 162:104, 71; *acc. sg.* blōd 50:96,
50:97, 68:4, 128:184, 5; *dat. sg.* blōde 62:122

blōdig *adj.* bloody; *m. nom. sg.* 64:140,
64:144; *nt. nom. sg.* blōdig 64:138
blōstm *m.* blossom, flower; *dat. pl.*
blōstmum 4:70
blōwan (VII) to bloom, blow 78:52; *ind.*
pres. 3 sg. blōweþ 40:59; *pres. p.*
blōwende 80:115, 80:121; *acc. pl.*
blōwende 40:56, 46:10, 48:57; *dat. pl.*
blōwendum 46:12; *def. m. nom. sg.*
blōwenda 40:54; *nom. pl.* blōwendan
40:54
bōc *f.* book; *nom. sg.* 62:133, 136:19; *acc.*
sg. bōc 118:133; *nom. pl.* bēc 50:112; *acc.*
pl. bēc 20:49, 78:62; *gen. pl.* bōca 42:118,
106:222; *dat. pl.* bōcum 14:111, 26:21, 28:79,
32:169, 64:168, 92:6, 92:32, 98:1, 114:1
bōcere *m.* scribe; *dat. pl.* bōcerum 58:24
bodian (2) to proclaim, announce 84:68,
110:306; *ind. pres. 1 sg.* bodige 130:230; *3*
sg. bodaþ 38:40, 122:63; *pret. 3 sg.* bodode
4:86; *pl.* bodedon 6:112; *subj. pres. sg.*
bodige 100:87; *pp.* bodad 38:22, 48:49
bodung *f.* preaching; *acc. sg.* bodunga
120:38; *dat. sg.* bodunga 128:220
boga *m.* bow; *acc. sg.* bogan 136:38
borh *m.* pledge, security; *nom. sg.* 26:28
bōsm *m.* bosom; *acc. sg.* bōsm 4:43,
116:77, 116:79, 116:81; *dat. sg.* bōsme 74:7,
116:67, 116:81
bōt *f.* amends; *acc. sg.* bōte 24:143, 54:187,
68:23, 70:60, 138:71; *dat. sg.* bōte 70:65,
90:204, 90:216
brād *adj.* broad; *f. dat. sg.* brādre 16:139
bræc (see brecan)
breġdan (III) to bend, weave; *ind. pret. 3*
sg. bræd 122:56
brecan (V) to break 152:143; *ind. pret. 3*
sg. bræc 152:144, 152:167, 152:176, 152 :178;
imp. 2 sg. brec 24:160
breġd *m.* craft; *gen. pl.* bregda 76:41
brēman (1) to celebrate; *ind. pret. pl.*
brēmdon 92:1
brēost *nt.* breast; *acc. sg.* breost 88:161;
dat. pl. brēostum 74:8

43

breþer (see broþor)
brid *m.* bird; *nom. pl.* briddas 14:134
brīdlian (2) to bridle, control; *ind. pret 3 sg.* brīdlodan 114:13
brim *nt.* sea, flood; *nom. sg.* 100:72
bringan (1) to bring 24:158, 50:111, 124:130; *ind. pres. pl.* bringe 50:133; *pl.* bringaþ 50:115; *pret. 1 sg.* brōhte 98:5; *3 sg.* brōhte 2:6, 2:14, 2:34, 2:39, 4:84, 104:165, 126:154, 126:179, 154:184; *imp. 2 pl.* bringaþ 24:169, 26:13; *pp.* broht 2:17
broc *nt.* disease, misery; *acc. sg.* broc 122:61; *acc. pl.* brocu 40:81
brōga *m.* fear, terror; *nom. sg.* 30:116, 108:241; *dat. sg.* brōgan 138:87
brōht (see bringan)
brōhte (see bringan)
brōþor *m.* brother; *nom. sg.* 20, 22; brōþer 120:14; brōðor 98:38, 160:47, 27; *acc. sg.* brōþor 158:15, 26; *dat. sg.* brēþer 162:102; *nom. pl.* brōþor 28:49, 32:150, 34:208, 92:28, 100:57, 100:69, 102:100, 102:104, 108:257, 108:265, 160:43, 160:61; brōðor 96:90, 150:91, 156:239; brōþer 100:83; brōþra 150:102; *acc. pl.* brōþor 158:15; *dat. pl.* brōðrum 154:196
brūcan (II) (with gen.) to enjoy 26:12, 34:227, 70:70
brūn *adj.* brown; *nt. gen. sg.* brūnes 50:108
brȳd *f.* bride; *gen. sg.* brȳde 6:107, 6:127
brȳdbūr *m.* bridal-chamber; *nom. sg.* 4:70; *dat. sg.* brȳdbūre 4:81, 6:94, 6:99
brȳdguma *m.* bridegroom; *nom. sg.* 6:99; *gen. sg.* brȳdguman 6:107
brȳdloca *m.* bridal-chamber; *dat. sg.* brȳdlocan 4:82
brȳdþing *nt.* nuptials; *gen. pl.* brȳdþinga 2:11
bryn *m.* burning; *dat. sg.* bryne 94:46, 140:91
budon (see bēodan)
bufan *adv.* above 28:71
bufan *prep.* (with dat.) above 88:179

bundon (see bindan)
burggeat *nt.* city-gate; *dat. sg.* burggeate 146:42
burgwar *m.* citizen; *nom. pl.* burgware 138:43, 138:60, 138:69
burh [→ þurh] *prep.* through 128:202
burh *f.* city; *nom. sg.* 48:73, 52:175, 136:14; *acc. sg.* burh 52:169, 52:172, 54:191, 54:192, 54:193, 90:187, 128:202, 140:96; burg 146:40; *gen. sg.* burge 52:176, 54:209, 90:189, 136:16; *dat. sg.* byrig 54:193, 108:240, 132:322, 138:46, 146:5, 148:75, 150:124; burh 136:21
burhġerefa *m.* provost; *dat. sg.* burhgerefan 130:275
burhleod *m.* citizen; *dat. pl.* burhleodum 68
burhwaru *f.* citizens; *nom. pl.* burhware 52:173; *gen. pl.* burhwara 136:11; *dat. pl.* burhwarum 140:136
burnon (see byrnan)
burþra *m.* birth; *acc. sg.* burþran 74:12
būtan *conj.* except, unless 14:102, 156:234 >
būton *prep.* (with acc. / dat.) without (see Appendix, p. 150)
būton *adv.* outside 136:34
būton *conj.* except, unless, but 6:118, 12:73, 14:105, 22:107, 24:158, 26:14, 26:16, 28:62, 36:235, 40:77, 50:100, 54:188, 54:205, 54:212, 54:215, 68:16, 70:57, 70:59, 72:96, 72:101, 78:75, 78:76, 82:28, 82:42, 84:57, 104:140, 118:133, 122:64, 126:141, 126:155, 126:162, 128:201, 146:31, 148:47, 152:147, 154:194 > (see Appendix, p. 149)
būtū *pron.* both; *m. nom. sg.* 114:23
bydenfæt *nt.* bushel; *nom. sg.* 88:161
byldu *f.* boldness; *dat. sg.* byldo 124:122
bylewit *adj.* mild, gentle; *def. m. acc. sg.* bylewitan 118:128
byrġen *f.* tomb, sepulchre, *acc. sg.* byrgenne 80:93, 104:154a; *gen. sg.* byrgenne 50:127, 108:255, 110:284; *dat. sg.* byrgenne 46:9, 50:124, 62:110, 68:30, 68:33, 102:92, 102:97, 104:154b, 108:254, 110:290, 110:291

byrnan (III) to burn 42:121; *ind. pres. pl.*
byrnaþ 90:184; *pret. 3 sg.* barn 124:101; *pl.*
burnon 70:52, 92:42; *pres. p.* byrnende
88:181
byrnsweord *nt.* fiery sword; *acc. sg.*
byrnsweord 78:46
byrþen *f.* burden; *nom. sg.* 50:126, 50:128
acc. sg. byrþenne 94:59; *gen. sg.*
byrþenne 94:58
bysen *f.* example; *nom. sg.* 52:141; *acc.
sg.* bysene 4:51, 14:126, 18:30, 22:101, 28:86,
42:145, 54:213, 58:2, 68:34, 72:90, 80:110; *dat.
sg.* bysene 10:24, 12:66, 22:116, 50:110,
52:142, 58:13, 70:58, 130:274, 148:86; *inst. sg.*
bysene 132:278; *acc. pl.* bysena 84:63; *dat.
pl.* bysenum 16:151
bysmerlīċe *adv.* shamefully 138:77
bysmor *nt.* mockery, scorn; *acc. sg.*
bysmor 16:138; *dat. sg.* bismere 138:71; *f.
dat. sg.* bismre 81; *acc. pl.* bysmra 10:26
bysmerian (2) to mock ; *pres. 3 sg.*
bysmraþ 128:192; *pl.* bysmriaþ 58:42; *pret.
3 pl.* bismrōdan 148:52; *subj. pres. pl.*
bysmrian 10:7; *pres. p. m. acc. sg.*
bismriende 81

C

cafortūn *m.* hall; *dat. sg.* cafortūne
150:120
camp *m.* fight, battle; *dat. sg.* campe
18:41, 152:158, 154:219, 154:220
Campania *prop. n.* Campania; *gen. sg.*
Campania 136:13
campian (2) to fight; *infl. inf.* to
campienne 116:87 (A)
campung *f.* fighting, warfare; *dat. sg.*
campunga 154:221
campweorod *nt.* host; *dat. sg.*
campweorode 6:122
can (see con)
cantic *m.* song; *dat. sg.* cantice 2:21, 4:46
Cantica Canticorum *prop. n.* Song of
Songs; *acc. sg.* Cantica Canticorum 6:114

carcern *nt.* prison; *acc. sg.* carcern 58:40,
158:2, 158:11, 158:21, 18, 24, 47, 50, 72, 80;
gen. sg. carcernes 60:81, 15, 17, 45, 134; *dat.
sg.* carcerne 12:75, 158:18, 158:20, 158:28, 27,
38, 42, 78, 108, 109, 112, 126, 127, 133 (EWS)
cāsere *m.* emperor; *nom. sg.* 54:191,
54:194, 54:200, 122:60, 124:109,124:116,
124:123, 126:141, 126:159, 126:171; *acc. sg.*
cāsere 132:290, 132:292; *gen. sg.* cāseres
146:10; *dat. sg.* cāsere 120:21, 120:33,
122:53, 122:81, 126:148
Catacumb *prop. n.* Catacomb; *dat. sg.*
Catacumbe 132:321
cēap *m.* bargain, gain; *acc. sg.* cēap
26:23; *gen. sg.* cēapes 26:38, 32:153, 136:27;
dat. sg. cēape 26:6, 26:9, 136:29; *dat. pl.*
cēapum 124:100, 136:24
cearian (2) to be sorrowful; *imp. 2 sg.*
ceara 100:71
ċeaster *f.* city; *nom. sg.* 52:171, 122:68;
acc. sg. ceastre 18:7, 20:86, 48:73, 100:59, 9,
158:27, 160:46, 160:47, 162:101, 14, 42, 121,
123, 158, 162; *gen. sg.* ceastre 162:104, 32,
60, 67, 70, 97; *dat. sg.* ceastre 108:231, 158:8,
160:48, 160:82, 160:85, 162:102, 3, 5, 11, 116,
119, 159, 164, 167
ċeasterwar *nt.* citizen; *nom. pl.*
ceastreware 48:73
ċeasterwīċ *f.* village; *acc. sg.* ceasterwīc
48:61
cennan (1) to bring forth; *ind. pres. 2 sg.*
cennest 4:60, 4:73; *ind. pret. 3 sg.* cende
2:4a, 2:4b, 2:7, 2:8; *pl.* cendon 64:169; *subj.
pret. sg.* cende 2:3
cennend *nt.* parent; *nom. pl.* cennende
114:25; *gen. pl.* cennendra 116:48; *dat. pl.*
cennendum 114:38
ċeorl *m.* man, husband; *gen. pl.* ċeorla
42:97
cerran [cyrran] (1) to turn 148:44; *ind. pret.
3 sg.* cerde 126:158
cete *f.* hut, cell; *acc. sg.* cetan 150:94,
150:115
cherubin *m.* cherubim; *acc. pl.*
cherubine 100:45 (cherubin, Lt. 100:44)

ċīegan (1) to cry out, call 128; *ind. pres. 2 sg.* cēgst 116:64; *3 sg.* cēgþ 130:244; *pl.* cēgeaþ 100:50; *ind. pret. 3 sg.* cīgde 93; cēgde 12:65, 60:75, 102:95; *ind. pret. pl.* cīgdon 124; cēgdon 48:71, 48:73, 62:107, 160:75; *pres. p.* cēgende 98:24; *pres. p. m. acc. sg.* cīgendne 130:243 (A)
cild *nt.* child; *acc. sg.* cild 157; *gen. sg.* cildes 162:94, 155; *gen. pl.* cilda 48:76
cining *m.* king; *nom. sg.* 48:65, 52:141; *acc. sg.* cining 132:312; *gen. sg.* cininges 146:8, 146:9, 146:18; *dat. sg.* cininge 80:130, 122:76, 126:181, 154:186; cinige 48:58; cinge 48:88; *nom. pl.* ciningas 46:11
ċiriċe *f.* church; *nom. sg.* 52:149, 88:146, 90:187, 136:12, 136:13; circe 142:153; *acc. sg.* ciricean 88:145, 140:116, 140:120, 140:122, 140:130, 140:132, 142:143, 142:150, 146:14, 152:137; circean 114:7; *gen. sg.* ciricean 136:17, 140:110, 142:169; circean 148:73; *dat. sg.* ciricean 88:160, 136:3, 136:20, 138:64, 140:109, 140:118, 142:171; cirican 88:181; *nom. pl.* ciricean 114:7; *dat. pl.* ciricum 128:217
cīrm [cierm] *m.* outcry, clamour; *nom. sg.* 157
clamm *m.* fetter; *dat. pl.* clammum 58:14
Claudio *pers. n.* Claudius; *acc. sg.* Claudium 122:83; *dat. sg.* Claudio 122:81
clāþ *m.* cloth, garment; *acc. pl.* clāþas 6:110
clǣne *adj.* clean, pure; *m. nom. sg.* 148:79; *nt. nom. sg.* clǣne 24:168; *f. acc. sg.* clǣne 50:101, 122:88; *m. dat. sg.* clǣnum 128:201; *f. dat. sg.* clǣnre 54:221; *def. m. nom. sg.* clǣna 4:64; *m. gen. sg.* clǣnan 6:96; *f. gen. sg.* clǣnan 2:30, 6:100, 6:118, 14:131, 22:95; *f. dat. sg.* clǣnan 6:91; *nt. acc. sg.* clǣne 2:8; *f. nom. pl.* clǣnan 8:151; *m. acc. pl.* clǣnan 8:146; *f. acc. pl.* clǣnan 50:103; superl. *def. f. nom. sg.* clǣnoste 104:168; clǣneste 108:274, 110:278

clǣnnes *f.* cleanness, purity; *nom. sg.* 114:41; *acc. sg.* clǣnnesse 142:162; *gen. sg.* clǣnnesse 2:31, 8:147, 52:142; *dat. sg.* clǣnnesse 28:50, 128:226; *gen. pl.* clǣnnessa 4:74
clǣnsian (2) to cleanse, purify 24:149, 24:154, 94:54, 124:91; *ind. pres. pl.* clǣnsiaþ 24:174; *subj. pres. pl.* clǣnsian 24:138
clǣnsung *f.* cleansing; *dat. sg.* clǣnsunga 90:216
cleopian (2) to call, cry 12:70, 54:221; *ind. pres. 1 sg.* cleopie 62:93; *pl.* cleopiað 76:10; *ind. pret. 3 sg.* cleopode 10:14, 62:103, 104:156, 106:199, 106:205, 126:147, 150:101; *pl.* cleopodan 54:218, 60:70, 64:149; *imp. 1 pl.* cleopian 12:57; *pres. p.* cleopigende 98:24
cleopung *f.* crying; *nom. sg.* 150:112
clif *nt.* Cliff; *dat. sg.* clife 142:158, 144:201, 144:204
cnēorisn *f.* kindred, kin; *acc. sg.* cnēorisne 158:5; *nom. pl.* cnēorisna 4:48
cnēow *nt.* knee; *acc. pl.* cnēowa 28:72, 130:238, 130:240; *dat. pl.* cnēowum 60:83
cniht *m.* boy, lad, servant; *nom. sg.* 122:55, 122:78; *gen. sg.* cnihtes 51; *dat. sg.* cnihtum 112:325
cnihtġebēorþor *m.* childbirth, childbearing; *dat. sg.* cnihtgebēorþre 2:10
cnihthād *m.* youth; *dat. sg.* cnihthāde 146:38
cnoll *m.* hill, summit; *nom. sg.* 138:88, 142:162; *dat. sg.* cnolle 136:12, 136:17, 136:36
cōlian (2) to become cool; *ind. pres. 1 sg.* cōlaþ 76:20
Constantīne *pers. n.* Constantine; *gen. sg.* Constantīnes 146:10
costian [costnian] (2) to try, tempt 8:137, 22:97, 22:112; *ind. pret. 3 sg.* costode 20:45; *subj. pret. sg.* costode 20:53, 22:114; *imp. 2 sg.* costa 18:10, 20:52; *infl. inf.* to costianne 160:73; costiænne 162:90; *pp.*

costad 18:23; costod 18:2, 18:37, 22:93; *pl.*
costode 18:24
costigend *m.* tempter; *nom. sg.* 18:3,
18:16; *acc. sg.* costigend 22:99
costnung *f.* temptation; *dat. pl.*
costnungum 8:139
costung *f.* temptation; *nom. sg.* 20:43;
acc. sg. costunge 22:94b; *dat. sg.*
costunge 22:94a, 22:98; *acc. pl.*costunga
22:107; *gen. pl.* costunga 12:68; *dat. pl.*
costungum 68:26, 128:196
cræft *m.* craft; *acc. pl.* cræftas 12:68
cræftig *adj.* skilful, cunning; *m. nom. sg.*
32:157
Crīst *pers. n.* Christ; *nom. sg.* 2:25, 6:108,
6:119, 6:126, 26:4, 30:92, 38:26, 52:150 >; *acc.*
sg. Crīst 42:120, 52:149, 52:155, 52:182, 60:50,
78:53 >; *gen. sg.* Crīstes 4:70, 8:149, 10:9,
10:35, 18:20, 20:82, 52:154, 60:49 > ; *dat. sg.*
Crīste 20:50, 40:50, 42:97, 50:101, 52:177,
108:260 >
Crīsten *adj.* Christian; *nt. acc. sg.*
Crīsten 30:102, 30:109; *m. dat. sg.*
Crīstenan 156:234; *m. nom. pl.* Crīstene
30:106; *nt. gen. pl.* Crīstenra 30:97; *m. dat.*
pl. Crīstenum 30:118; *f. dat. pl.*
Crīstenum 140:98, 140:102; *def. nt. acc. sg.*
Crīstenan 30:93; *m. nom. pl.* Crīstenan
140:95, 140:103
culufre [culfre] *f.* dove; *nom. sg.* 110:287;
gen. sg. culfran 14:134, 94:53
cuma *m.* stranger; *nom. sg.* 82:33
cuman (IV) come 2:37, 10:2, 74:4, 84:80,
86:117, 116:52, 116:54, 126:137, 142:171; *ind.*
pres. 3 sg cymeþ 4:63, 6:104, 14:108, 18:21,
48:65, 58:10, 64:177, 64:179, 84:46, 86:114,
86:115, 92:20; cymþ 128:191; cumeþ 4:73,
70:77; *pl.* cumaþ 12:61, 18:33, 70:55, 78:79;
cumað 154:207; *pret. 2 sg.* come 54:219,
54:228, 60:60, 80:95; *3 sg.* cōm 4:51, 6:126,
12:81, 18:39, 22:93, 46:38, 48:50, 48:55, 48:82,
48:83, 70:45, 84:75, 102:102; cwōm 22:96,
52:161, 140:98; cwōn [→ cwōm] 6:100, 46:23;
pl. cōmon 15, 134; cōman 82:13, 88:137,
88:148, 100:84, 106:225, 118:120, 142:150, 125;

subj. pres. sg. cume 68:11, 68:15, 70:62,
78:70, 90:219, 102:102; *pl.* cuman 104:171,
124:119; *pret. sg.* cōme 18:38, 124:90,
130:234; *pl.* cōman 108:254; *imp. 2 sg.* cum
34, 74; *3 pl.* cuman 126:148; *pres.p. sg.*
cumende 92:36, 144:187; *m. acc. sg.*
cumendne 116:85; *pp.* cumen 136:9, 146:5;
m. acc. pl. cumene 76:14
cunnan (pret. pres.) to know; *ind. pres. 1 sg.*
con 158:33; *3 sg.* can 12:52, 124:126; *pret.*
pl. cūðan 74:19; cūþon 150:132; *subj. pres.*
pl. cunnon 28:60; *pp.* cūþ 14:100, 18:18,
20:48, 20:89, 84:69, 88:149, 118:101, 126:169,
130:258; cūð 142:163, 148:63; *f. dat. sg.*
cūðre 148:61
cunnian (2) to try, prove 48:43
cuþlīċe *adv.* certainly 42:110, 44:157,
54:210, 88:178
cuðre (see con)
cwacian (2) to quake; *pres. p. def. f. nom.*
pl. cwacigendan 76:8
cwalu *f.* slaughter, death; *dat. sg.* cwale
132:313
cwealm *m.* slaughter, destruction, death;
dat. sg. cwealme 16:166
cwellan (1) to kill; *subj. pres. sg.* cwelle
126:164; *pp.* cwelmed 28:44, 38:33
cwellere *m.* killer, murderer; *nom. pl.*
cwelleras 158:22
cwēman (1) (with *dat.*) to please; *subj. pres.*
pl. cwēmon 30:115
cwēn *f.* queen; *nom. sg.* 74:9
cweþan (V) to say, speak 50:121, 104:181,
106:185, 128 >; *ind. pres. 1 sg.* cweþe
120:4; *2 sg.* cwist 52:145, 126:142, 126:162,
128:222, 128:224, 130:274; *3 sg.* cwiþ 42:136,
126:169; cwið 94:52, 118:129; cwyþ 82:11;
cweþ 64:147; *pl.* cweþaþ 16:145, 64:166,
64:168, 64:170, 106:183; *pret. 2 sg.* cwǣde
162:98, 76, 96, 98; *3 sg.* cwæð 98:34, 98:36,
100:56, 142:142, 154:213, 154:214, 162:98 >;
cwǣþ 2:21, 2:22, 2:31, 4:46, 4:59, 4:61, 4:62,
4:64, 4:70, 52:145, 106:225 >; *pl.* cwǣdon
10:13, 48:71, 48:74, 54:218, 54:223, 54:224,

47

54:225 >; cwǣdan 52:177, 152:164 >;
cwǣþon 60:70; *subj. pres. sg.* cweþe
110:312; *pl.* cweþan 14:99, 104:169; *pret. sg.*
cwǣde 26:21, 32:169, 54:228, 92:6; *imp. 2 sg.*
cweþ 18:4, 106:218, 106:226 >; cwæþ 46:28,
108:232 >; *1 pl.* cweþan 12:58, 16:158; *pres.*
p. cweþende 20:48, 38:25, 98:4, 98:18, 98:21,
98:25, 100:43, 100:68, 100:81, 102:89, 102:98 >;
cweðende 100:53; *m. acc. sg.* cweðendne
148:61; *pp.* cweden 2:18, 160:69
cwic *adj.* alive, living; *m. nom. sg.*
150:118; *m acc. sg.* cwicenne 132:292; *m.*
dat. sg. cwicum 26:9; *m. dat. pl.* cwicum
6:105
cwicsūsl *f.* hell-torment; *dat. sg.*
cwicsūsle 60:68; *inst. sg.* cwicsūsle 40:85
cwide *m.* saying, word, speech; *nom. sg.*
86:100, 98:33; *acc. sg.* cwide 34:208, 42:136,
118:128, 148:66; *gen. sg.* cwides 148:64
cwielmian (2) to kill; *ind. pret. 3 sg.*
cwylmde 140:94; *pp.* cwylmed 42:120 (A)
cyfes [ciefes] *f.* concubine; *acc. pl.* cyfesa
68:39
cyle [cield] *m.* cold; *acc. sg.* cyle 42:114;
dat. sg. cyle 40:83, 132:318, 146:42
cym *m.* coming, advent; *acc. sg* cyme
82:17; *dat. sg.* cyme 54:220, 56:232, 60:43
cynedōm *m.* kingdom; *gen. sg.*
cynedōmes 60:56
cynehelm *m.* royal crown; *dat. sg.*
cynehelme 16:141 [EWS]
cyneliċ *adj.* royal, kingly; *def. f. acc. sg.*
cynelican 52:169
cynerīċe *nt.* kingdom; *acc. pl.* cynerīce
[cynerīcu → cynerīce] 74:5
cynestōl *m.* royal seat; *dat. sg.* cynestōle
74:4
cyning *m.* king; *nom. sg.* 2:29, 4:81, 6:119,
6:123, 6:124, 22:90, 46:14, 104:157, 122:79,
122:87, 130:231; *acc. sg.* cyning 4:74, 8:144,
54:190, 84:88; *gen. sg.* cyninges 76:29,
114:20, 120:37, 146:7; *dat. sg.* cyninge
116:87, 140:99; *nom. pl.* cyningas 76:37;

gen. pl. cyninga 94:88, 140:99; *dat. pl.*
cyningum 114:12;
cyninge *f.* queen; *gen. sg.* cyningan 6:132
cynn *nt.* kin, race; *nom. sg.* 2:33, 2:40, 58:5,
64:163, 70:87, 110:312, 118:121, 122:72; cyn
10:37; *acc. sg.* cynn 2:31, 52:162, 64:164
[mannacynn → manna cynn]; cyn 72:100, 56; *gen.*
sg. cynnes 2:34, 4:81, 14:117, 14:135, 46:2,
106:216; *dat. sg.* cynne 2:36, 4:50, 4:51,
12:48, 50:129, 96:93, 100:42, 108:269, 110:314;
gen. pl. cynna 44:145, 50:107
cypeman *m.* dealer, merchant; *gen. pl.*
cypemanna 48:78
ċyrran [ċierran] (1) to turn; *ind. pret. 1 sg.*
cyrde 132:296; *3 sg.* cyrde 12:47, 12:48;
subj. pres. sg. cyrre 60:65; *pret. pl.*
cyrdon 122:49
ċyriċe *f.* church; *nom. sg.* 6:107, 26:40,
28:48, 88:141; *acc. sg.* cyrican 26:39b, 28:46,
30:128, 146; cyricean 28:53, 50:100, 52:163,
78:55; *gen. sg.* cyricean 120:3; *dat. sg.*
cyrican 26:39a, 34:230; *gen. pl.* cyricena
22:120, 28:54; *acc. pl.* cyricean 30:135
cyrre (see cyrde)
cyssan (1) to kiss 88:164; *ind. pret. 3 sg.*
cyste 110:296; *imp. 2 sg.* cys 106:217; *pres.*
p. cyssende 110:299, 20
cȳþan (1) to make known 78:63, 84:58,
84:64; *ind. pres. 1 sg.* cȳþe 126:152; *3 sg.* c
ȳþ 14:123; *pl.* cȳþeþ 4:88; *pret. 3 sg.* cȳ
ðde 8:141; cyþde 4:59, 6:97, 8:142, 46:22,
48:87, 74:17, 82:23, 126:155, 128:226; *pl.* cȳ
þdon 18:21, 74:3, 114:11, 122:52; *subj. pret.*
sg. cȳðde 142:138; *pl.* cȳþdon 102:126
cȳþnes *f.* witness, testimony; *acc. sg.* cȳ
þnesse 20:67; *dat. sg.* cȳþnesse 20:70,
48:47, 130:266
cȳþþo *f.* acquaintance; *acc. sg.* cȳþþe
80:92; *dat. sg.* cȳþþe 78:89, 100:46

D

daru *f.* damage; *nom. sg.* 14:91

48

Dauid *pers. n.* David; *nom. sg.* 20:67, 38:8, 38:24, 58:15, 76:7, 94:46; *gen. sg.* Dauides 10:14, 10:16, 12:58, 14:135, 48:71, 54:218, 98:34

dǽd *f.* deed, action; *dat. sg.* dǽde 148:63, 148:66, 148:71, 150:106; *nom. pl.* dǽda 38:9, 58:6; *acc. pl.* dǽda 20:70, 42:123, 44:139, 50:122, 66:206, 76:28, 122:70; *gen. pl.* dǽda 20:89, 90:216, 146:37, 146:38; *dat. pl.* dǽdum 10:42, 18:25, 20:64, 38:38, 44:141, 50:134, 66:191, 70:75; *inst. pl.* dǽdum 2:41

dǽdbōt *f.* amends, penance; *acc. sg.* dǽdbōte 54:185; *dat. sg.* dǽdbōte 44:150 (EWS)

dǽġ *m.* day; *nom. sg.* 18:21, 68:11, 68:15, 70:82, 92:26, 92:30, 92:33, 114:4 >; *acc. sg.* dæg 14:108, 30:120, 40:88, 40:89, 46:15, 62:136, 64:159, 70:77, 96:91 >; *gen. sg.* dæges 20:56, 22:121, 30:115, 62:128, 64:147, 82:2, 86:129, 88:180, 92:32, 96:90, 98:3 >; *dat. sg.* dæge 6:104, 6:113, 6:124, 46:9, 62:132, 62:133, 62:134, 62:135, 62:136, 64:161, 66:184, 82:3, 130:268 >; *inst. sg.* dæge 10:8, 50:91, 50:93, 50:94, 50:96, 50:124, 64:152, 64:156, 64:162, 64:174; *nom. pl.* dagas 24:139, 24:140, 158:24, 158:28, 21 >; *acc. pl.* dagas 22:134, 24:141, 24:153, 48:86, 102:111, 110:302, 130:270, 138:48 >; *gen. pl.* daga 18:3, 22:118, 22:122, 22:131, 22:132, 22:135, 40:75, 138:66, 138:73 >; *dat. pl.* dagum 68:30, 98:5, 114:20, 132:293, 146:10, 158:30, 162:99 >; *inst. pl.* dagum 46:23, 48:82, 62:135

dæġhwāmliċ *adj.* daily; *def. m. acc. sg.* dæghwāmlican 146:32; *f. acc. pl.* dæghwāmlican 16:155; *f. dat. pl.* dæghwāmlicum [dæg hwamlicum → dæghwamlicum] 24:148

dæġhwāmlīċe *adv.* daily 30:101, 70:47, 88:168, 142:169

dæġred *nt.* daybreak; *acc. sg.* dægred 142:171

dǽl *m.* deal, part, portion, share; *nom. sg.* 78:75, 82:38, 88:152, 146:14; *acc. sg.* dǽl 22:130, 22:131, 22:136, 24:137, 26:5, 26:9, 26:38, 32:153, 32:158, 46:32, 54:194; *gen. sg.*

dǽles 32:168, 104:153; *dat. sg.* dǽle 72:98, 76:33, 84:72; *acc. pl.* dǽlas 32:166, 32:167, 106:202, 130:264, 32; *dat. pl.* dǽlon 34:225

dǽlan (1) to share, divide, distribute 32:154, 32:172, 34:217, 68; dǽlon 34:230; *ind. pres. 3 sg.* dǽleþ 26:42; *pl.* dǽlaþ 32:161; *subj. pres. sg.* dǽle 26:7, 32:177; *imp. 3 sg.* dǽle 34:224; *1 pl.* dǽlon 34:227; *2 pl.* dǽlaþ 28:50

dǽlnimend *m.* partaker; *nom. pl.* dǽlnimende 132:302; *acc. pl.* dǽlnimende 6:103

dēad *adj.* dead; *m. nom. sg.* 126:173, 130:269, 136:42, 68; *m. acc. sg.* dēadne 124:133, 150:104, 150:121; *m. acc. pl.* dēade 14:125, 124:91, 46; *m. gen. pl.* dēadra 28:58; *m. dat. pl.* dēadum 6:105, 122:48, 126:174; *def. m. nom. sg.* dēada 40:66, 150:99, 150:118; *m. gen. sg.* dēadan 80:94, 150:96, 150:116; *m. dat. sg.* dēadan 34:194, 50:126; *m. nom. pl.* dēadan 14:125, 78:47; *m. acc. pl.* dēadan 122:47

dēadliċ *adj.* mortal; *def. m. nom. sg.* dēadlica 40:53

dēagol [dīegle] *nt.* secret, mystery; *acc. pl.* dēagol 124:126

dēað *m.* death; *nom. sg.* 40:63; dēaþ 46:17a, 46:17b, 58:32, 58:33, 70:62, 70:91 >; *acc. sg.* dēað 68:22; dēaþ 22:95, 40:79, 46:16, 52:183, 58:25, 58:36, 72:92 >; *gen. sg.* dēaþes 34:220, 40:77, 40:80, 44:154, 50:127, 58:14, 58:27, 60:71, 60:81, 62:102, 62:108, 78:88 >; *dat. sg.* dēaþe 10:8, 22:94, 32:155, 42:91, 46:16, 46:24, 48:52, 48:55, 48:87 >; *inst. sg.* dēaþe 34:191; *acc. pl.* dēaþas 76:14

dēaþberend *adj.* deadly, fatal; *def. f. nom. sg.* dēaþberende 44:156

dēaþliċ *adj.* mortal; *m. nom. sg.* 14:109; *m. nom. pl.* dēaþlice 136:11

dēaþliċnes *f.* mortality; *acc. sg.* dēaþlicnesse 12:45

dēgol *adj.* secret; *f. nom. sg.* dēgol 82:26; *nt. dat. sg.* dēglum 126:143; *m. gen. pl.* dēgolra 114:12

dēgol *nt.* secret; *acc. sg.* dēgol 126:147

dēgollīċe [dēogllīċe] *adv.* secretly 124:130

dehter (see dohtor)

dēma *m.* judge; *nom. sg.* 42:110, 66:202, 116:52; *acc. sg.* dēman 66:206; *gen. sg.* dēman 34:221; *nom. pl.* dēman 42:127, 42:132, 42:134; *gen. pl.* dēmena 42:122; *dat. pl.* dēmum 42:108, 42:128

dēman (1) (usually with *dat.*) to judge; *ind. pres. 2 sg.* dēm[est] 132:281; *3 sg.* dēmeþ 66:203; *pl.* dēmaþ 42:107, 42:130, 42:132; *pret. 1 sg.* dēmde 108:271; *3 sg.* dēmde 70:50; *pl.* dēmdon 28:55; *subj. pres. sg.* dēme 28:57; *imp. 2 pl.* dēme 42:109; *infl. inf.* to dēmenne 6:104, 56:236

dēofol *nt.* devil; *nom. sg.* 18:11, 22:111, 22:113, 32:146, 86:93, 106:184, 56, 59, 79, 86 >; *acc. sg.* dēofol 18:41, 20:55, 20:70, 22:117, 28:66, 30:116 >; *gen. sg.* dēofles 4:55, 8:139, 12:61, 12:68, 16:151, 20:73, 22:90, 22:92, 22:107, 86:124; *dat. pl.* dēofle 18:2, 18:24, 18:37, 20:86, 46:16, 126:171, 55; *nom. pl.* dēoflu [dēoflum → dēoflu] 110:319; dēofla 84; *acc. pl.* dēoflu 30:124; dēoflo 79; *gen. pl.* dēofla 58:15, 58:29, 72:95, 120:22; *dat. pl.* dēoflum 30:111, 38:42, 42:95, 42:112, 42:120, 52:156, 86:125

dēofolgild *nt.* idol; *acc. sg.* dēofolgild 152:139, 152:155, 152:176; dēofolgyld 150:136; dēofolgeld 152:137, 152:160; *dat. sg.* dēofolgelde 152:148; *nom. pl.* dēofolgyld 64:157; *dat. pl.* dēofolgeldum 138:78

dēofolliċ *adj.* devilish; *nt. nom. pl.* dēofollicu 122:79; *def. m. gen. sg.* dēofollican 96:94

dēofolsēoc *adj.* possessed of the devil; *m. dat. pl.* dēofolsēocum 122:47

dēogollīċe *adv.* secretly 132:309

dēop *adj.* deep; *def. m. acc. sg.* dēopan 72:96

dēopnes *f.* deepness, depth; *acc. sg.* dēopnesse 100:45

dēor *nt.* animal, beast; *nom. sg.* 66:200

dēore [dīere] *adj.* dear, beloved; *def. m. nom. sg.* dēora 46:22

dēorwyrþ *adj.* precious; *f. gen. sg.* dēorwyrþre 46:34, 50:105; *m. gen. pl.* dēorwyrþra 70:46; *nt. gen. pl.* dēorwyrþra 68:39; *nt. dat. pl.* dēorwyrþum 20:57; *def. f. acc. sg.* dēorwyrþan 50:94; *nt. acc. sg.* dēorwyrðe 68:4; *f. gen. sg.* dēorwyrðan 46:35

diernan (1) to hide; *subj. pres. sg.* dyrne 28:63

dihtan (1) to compose; *ind. pret 3 sg.* dihtode 92:22

discipul [Lt. discipulus] *m.* disciple; *nom. sg.* 160:68; *nom. pl.* discipuli 160:53, 160:65; discipulos 156:232, 160:86; *acc. pl.* discipuli 158:26, 160:81; discipulos 154:203; *gen. pl.* discipula 160:79; *dat. pl.* discipulum 154:199, 154:202, 158:35, 158:36, 158:38, 158:41, 160:59, 160:69, 160:71, 162:95, 14, 18, 40, 149, 159, 167

dohtor *f.* daughter; *dat. sg.* dehter 62:99; *dat. pl.* dohtrum 48:65, 114:22

dolh [dolg] *nt.* wound; *acc. pl.* dolh 62:113

dōm *m.* judgement; *nom. sg.* 2:2, 62:127, 66:204; *acc. sg.* dōm 40:63, 42:111, 66:202; *gen. sg.* dōmes 6:104, 14:108, 16:143, 18:21, 22:121, 30:124, 38:41, 40:89, 42:135, 70:77; dōmos [dōmes → dōmos] 78:56; *dat. sg.* dōme 66:189, 124:98, 134:330; *nom. pl.* dōmas 60:88; *acc. pl.* dōmas 28:57, 30:134, 42:107, 42:130, 54:211, 70:50; *dat. pl.* dōma 114:12; *dat. pl.* dōmum 32:170, 110:283

dōmsetl *nt.* judgement-seat; *dat. sg.* dōmsetle 58:4, 62:124 [dōm setle → dōmsetle]

dōn (anom.) to do, make, cause 24:171a, 24:171b, 34:193, 48:47, 50:135, 54:185, 58:39, 62:126, 68:23, 88:165; *ind. pres. 1 sg.* dō 110:277 [doo → dō]; dō 104:135, 124:127, 126:143, 132:301, 91a, 91b, 111; *2 sg.* dest 32:166; *3 sg.* deþ 14:104, 34:197, 70:71, 70:72, 126:137, 126:140, 128:192, 130:253; dōþ

126:172; *pl.* dōþ 18:31, 34:185, 48:79, 90:193, 158:7; dōð 148:66, 75, 77; *pret. 2 sg.* dydest 108:266, 110:313, 65; *3 sg.* dyde 4:45, 10:26, 10:30, 12:57, 12:64, 14:120, 46:18, 64:176, 70:79, 110:315; *pl.* dydon 36:234, 48:67, 54:227, 118:130, 118:132, 138:72, 160:83, 73, 135, 140; dyde 138:53; *subj. pres. sg.* dō 126:164, 128:213, 156:234; *pret. pl.* dydon 138:73; *imp. 2 sg.* dō 60:80, 162:107, 76, 114, 135; *3 sg.* dō 118:125; *1 pl.* dōn 24:143, 26:3, 70:60; *2 pl.* dōð 20:44; *infl. inf.* to dōnne 92:21, 138:47, 162:100; *pres. p.* dōnde 32:175, 154:188, 126; *m. dat. pl.* dōndum [rihtdōndum → riht dōndum] 42:93; dōndum 42:125

dorste (see durran)

drāf *f.* herd, drove; *acc. sg.* drāfe 136:30

dragen (see hwem dragen)

drēam *m.* song, music; *acc. pl.* drēamas 28:47; *dat. pl.* drēamum 26:40

drēfan (1) to trouble; *ind. pret. 3 sg.* drēfde 114:27

drēgde (see drȳgan)

drenc *m.* drink; *acc. sg.* drenc 7; *dat. sg.* drence 38:32

drīfan (I) to drive 124:91

Drihten *m.* Lord; *nom. sg.* 2:12, 2:17, 4:51, 6:94, 6:98, 6:101, 6:119, 8:138, 10:2, 10:40, 12:83, 14:108, 18:18 >; *acc. sg.* Drihten 4:47, 6:128, 6:134, 6:135, 8:150, 12:81, 14:93, 14:94, 16:137, 16:165, 18:11, 18:15, 84:70 >; *gen. sg.* Drihtnes 2:16, 4:71, 6:90, 8:140, 10:35, 12:61, 16:150, 22:114, 44:158, 84:84 >; Drihtenes 82:7, 131; *dat. sg.* Drihten 10:21, 16:144, 16:171, 20:71, 24:158, 24:170, 26:3, 44:151, 44:166, 50:111 >; Drihtene 130; *voc.* Drihten 10:19

drihtenliċ *adj.* belonging to the Lord; *def. m. dat. sg.* drihtenlican 48:88; *f. dat. sg.* drihtenlican 82:10; *m. inst. sg.* drihtenlican 84:65

drincan (III) to drink 7; drincan [drinccan → drincan] 10; *ind. pres. 3 sg.* drincþ 116:66; *pret. pl.* druncon 4, 5, 8; *subj. pres. sg.* drince 38:29

drȳ *m.* magician, sorcerer; *nom. sg.* 120:31, 120:39, 122:48, 122:50, 122:51, 122:66, 122:72, 122:77, 126:176, 130:250; *acc. sg.* drȳ 120:33, 122:54, 126:160; *gen. sg.* drȳs [drȳg → drȳs] 130:239; *dat. sg.* drȳ 120:26, 120:32, 122:52, 128:190

drȳcræft *m.* magic art, sorcery; *acc. sg.* drēocræft 120:42; drȳcræft 122:76; *dat. sg.* drēocræfte 128:192/3; *dat. pl.* drȳcræftum 126:175

drȳg *adj.* dry; *nt. acc. pl.* drȳge 80:97; *m. inst. pl.* drȳgum 124:92

drȳgan (1) to dry; *ind. pret. 3 sg.* drēgde 50:106; drȳgde 46:35, 50:131

dugoþ *f.* nobility; *nom. sg.* 130:235

dugoþ *adj.* good, honourable; *def. m. nom. sg.* dugoþa 122:60; 122:79

dūn *f.* mountain, hill; *acc. sg.* dūne 18:12, 22:91, 90:186; *dat. sg.* dūne 48:60, 88:141; *dat. pl.* dūnum 64:171

durran (pret. pres.) to dare; *ind. pret. 3 sg.* dorste 22:111; 142:171; *pl.* dorston 140:130, 85; dorstan 138:44, 140:120; *subj. pres. sg.* durre 124:128

duru *f.* door; *nom. sg.* 4:75, 42:92, 88:163; *acc. sg.* duru 100:64, 150:95, 150:117, 45; *dat. sg.* dura 28:46, 108:255, 136:31, 136:36, 142:150; duru 110:285, 17, 134; dyru 15; *nom. pl.* dura 17; *acc. pl.* dura 138:63

duruweard *m.* doorkeeper; *nom. sg.* 106:209

dūst *nt.* dust; *nom. sg.* 62:95; *acc. sg.* dūst 40:49, 80:97; *dat. sg.* dūste 70:55, 156:235

dūstscēawung *f.* contemplation of dust; *dat. sg.* dūstscēawunga 80:104

dwēlian (2) to err; *ind. pres. pl.* dwēlgaþ 130:257, 130:258; *pres. p.* dwēlgende 138:69

dwolian (2) to go astray; *pres. p.* dwolgende 132:318

dyrne (see diernan)

dyru (see duru)

dysiġ *adj.* foolish; *m. nom. sg.* 34:211; *m. nom. pl.* dysige 40:72; *def. m. nom. sg.* dysega 26:19, 32:163

dysliċ *adj.* foolish; *f. acc. pl.* dyslice 68:40

E

eā *f.* water; *acc. sg.* eā 28:72; *dat. sg.* eā 28:67, 28:70

ēac *prep.* also (see Appendix, p. 150)

ēac *adv.* also (see Appendix, p. 151)

ēadiġian (2) to bless; *infl. inf.* to ēadgienne 6:111

ēadiġ *adj.* blessed, happy; *m. nom. sg.* 154:189; *f. acc. sg.* ēadige 4:48, 6:112; *m. nom. pl.* ēadige 8:151, 16:159, 64:168, 112:332, 112:333a, 102:333b; ēadge 114:24; *def. m. nom. sg.* ēadiga 100:53, 100:63, 100:79, 102:99, 102:115, 102:121, 104:167, 124:124, 138:78; ēadega [ēadega → ēndega] 98:29; ēadga 108:238; *f. nom. sg.* ēadige 4:76, 4:88, 6:113, 102:105; *m. acc. sg.* ēadigan 148:76, 150:122, 19, 39; *m. gen. sg.* ēadigan 146:2, 80; ēadygan 150:132; *f. gen. sg.* ēadigan 102:132, 104:148, 104:152, 104:156, 104:159, 108:258, 108:262, 110:285; *m. dat. sg.* ēadigan 114:38, 148:68, 154:222; *f. dat. sg.* ēadigan 102:124, 102:127; ēadgan 136:2; *superl. m. nom. sg.* ēadegust 112:331; *def. f. nom. sg.* ēadgeste 8:143; ēadgoste 110:312

ēadiġliċ *adj.* happy; *f. acc. sg.* ēadiglice 140:127

ēadiġnes *f.* blessedness; *nom. sg.* 68:19, 70:83, 136:1; *acc. sg.* ēadignesse 35 3, 66:208, 68:9; *dat. sg.* ēadignesse 24:145

ēadmōdliċ *adj.* humble; *def. f. acc. pl.* ēadmodlican 20:88

ēadmōdlīċe *adv.* meekly, humbly 28:60

ēadmōdnes *f.* meekness, humility; *dat. sg.* ēadmōdnesse 18:31; ēadmōdnessum 72:98/9

ēage *nt.* eye; *nom. pl.* ēagan 40:65, 108:233, 130:253, 158:23; *acc. pl.* ēagan 108:234,

150:99, 6, 9, 158:22, 30; *gen. pl.* ēagena 14:90, 158:7; *dat. pl.* ēagum 10:36, 14:101, 68:38, 70:54, 88:140, 156:236; *inst. pl.* ēagon 84:66

ēagþӯrel *nt.* window; *nom. pl.* ēagþӯrelu 88:182 *acc. pl.* ēagþӯrelo 90:185

eahta *num.* eight 38; ehta [→ eahta] 88:182

eal *adv.* all, quite 40:77

eal *adj.* (see eall)

ēalā *interj.* oh (see Appendix, p. 151)

eald *adj.* old; *m. nom. sg.* 122:55; *m. acc. sg.* ealdne 28:70; *m. dat. sg.* ealdum 86:131, 92:23; *nt. acc. pl.* ealde 76:2; *def. m. nom. sg.* ealda 28:74; *m. acc. sg.* ealdan 60:68; *nt. acc. sg.* ealde 34:225; *f. gen. sg.* ealdan 116:46

ealdian (2) to grow old; *ind. pres. 3 sg.* ealdaþ 40:48

ealdor [aldor] *m.* ancestor, parent; *nom. sg.* 14:116; *acc. sg.* ealdor 58:27

ealdorman *m.* ruler, chief; *nom. sg.* 108:237, 108:244; ealderman 102:130, 106:211, 106:219; *gen. sg.* ealdormannes 120:2; ealdermannes 106:197; *nom. pl.* ealdormen 48:54, 52:157, 106:184, 124:95; *dat. pl.* ealdormannum 114:12, 47

eall *adj.* all, every; *m. nom. sg* 58:37, 64:174, 73; eal 32:179, 34:188, 40:61; *f. nom. sg.* eall 4:76, 64:146, 118:107; eal 48:73, 54:230, 60:49; *nt. nom. sg.* eall 2:33, 2:40, 46:35, 62:117, 64:147, 64:163; eal 10:22, 10:37, 48:68, 48:80, 50:106; *m. acc. sg.* ealne 22:136, 30:118, 42:102, 48:49, 58:27, 64:139, 64:140, 64:159; *f. acc. sg.* ealle 32:176, 64:159; *nt. acc. sg.* eall 2:31, 4:82, 8:138, 8:143, 34:184, 38:18, 58:20; eal 14:103, 16:141, 18:12, 22:96, 30:102; *m. gen. sg.* ealles 20:56, 26:38, 38:37, 48:44, 62:98, 74:10, 94:66, 124:111; *f. gen. sg.* ealre 2:30, 8:147, 52:142, 70:89, 80:105, 80:114; eallre 44:164; *nt. gen. sg.* ealles 44:140, 54:199, 74:9, 78:81, 84:67, 88:167, 90:196; *m. dat. sg.* eallum 86:121; *f. dat. sg.* ealre 6:135, 20:71, 86:108, 86:118, 98:15; *nt. dat. sg.* eallum 2:36, 4:50, 6:128,

18:6, 50:128, 96:93, 110:314; *nt. inst. sg.*
ealle 4:44, 58:7, 76:25, 108:242; *m. nom. pl.*
ealle 16:171; *f. nom. sg.* ealle 4:48, 6:105;
nt. nom. sg. ealle 6:124, 8:152, 10:5, 18:33;
m. acc. pl. ealle 4:86, 6:124, 14:128, 14:129;
nt. acc. pl. ealle 6:28, 12:83; *m. gen. pl.*
ealra 20:89, 30:106 [earla → ealra], 30:108,
30:110, 30:113; *f. gen. pl.* eallra 4:74, 20:77;
m. gen. pl. eallra 54:195; *f. gen. pl.* eallra
16:172; *m. dat. pl.* eallum 2:39, 10:41,
22:116; *f. dat. pl.* eallum 4:67, 16:152, 20:70,
20:74; *nt. dat. pl.* eallum 6:133; *m. inst. pl.*
eallum, 114:42, 118:106; *nt. inst. pl.* eallum
108:245
eallinga *adv.* altogether 114:37, 116:65;
eallunga 86:97, 116:63, 120:39
ealo *nt.* ale; *acc. sg.* ealu 116:66
earc *f.* chest, box; *acc. sg.* earcan [earan →
earcan] 156:231
eard *m.* native country; *dat. sg.* earde
78:89
eardian (2) to dwell, live 24:152; *ind. pres.*
1 sg. eardige 50:101; *3 sg.* eardað 6:124;
eardaþ 32:146; *pl.* eardiaþ 26:40; *pret. 3 sg.*
eardode 6:123, 74:8; *subj. pres. sg.* eardige
98:35; *infl. inf.* to eardienne 50:103
eardung *f.* dwelling; *nom. sg.* 8:149,
110:287, 144:201; *acc. pl.* eardunga 52:156,
106:198 [eadrunga → eardunga]
ēare *nt.* ear; *acc. pl.* ēaron 74:24; *inst. pl.*
ēarum 38:20; earon 84:67
earfoþe *f.* difficulty, trouble; *nom. sg.*
94:79; *nom. pl.* earfoþa 60:51; *dat. pl.*
earfoþum 34:187, 50:136
earfoþnes *f.* difficulty, trouble; *acc. sg.*
earfoðnesse 88, 129; *acc. pl.* earfoðnessa
162:106; *dat. pl.* earfoþnessum 76:24;
earfoðnessum 139
earm *m.* arm; *acc. pl.* ear[m]an 110:315;
inst. pl. earmum 130:245
earm *adj.* poor; *f. nom. sg.* earm 62:93; *m.*
acc. sg. earmne 42:124; *m. dat. sg.*
earmum 66:204, 148:65; *m. acc. pl.* earme
42:129, 90:217, 146:30; *m. gen. pl.* earmra
26:37, 34:218; *m. dat. pl.* earmum 26:38,

32:150, 32:161, 32:172, 34:225, 36:237, 76:30,
118:129; *def. m. acc. sg.* earman 24:170; *m.*
gen. sg. earman 24:167, 24:173, 50:136; *m.*
dat. sg. earman 26:30, 36:232; *m. nom. pl.*
earman 26:41; *superl. m. dat. pl.*
earmestum 34:230; earmestan 26:39
earmlic *adj.* miserable; *m. acc. sg.*
earmlicne 150:114; *m. inst. sg.* earmlice
150:113; *f. inst. sg.* earmlicre 60:75
ēastan *m.* east part; *nom. sg.* 140:122
ēastdæl *m.* east quarter; *dat. sg.* ēastdæle
64:143, 64:162, 40
ēastend *m.* east end; *dat. sg.* ēastende
64:152
Ēaster *m.* Easter; *dat. sg.* Ēastrum 46:23,
48:82
Ēasterdæg *m.* Easter Day; *acc. pl.*
Ēasterdagas 24:142
ēastorlic *adj.* belonging to Easter; *def. nt.*
nom. sg. ēastorlice 58:1; *m. nom. pl.*
ēasterlican 24:140
ēastrīce *nt.* east kingdom; *acc. sg.*
ēastrīce 132:320
ēaþe *adv.* easily 14:98, 46:39, 136:8
ēaþelīce *adv.* easily 142:160
ēaþmōd *adj.* meek, humble; *m. nom. sg.*
8:145, 58:6, 90:195; ēaðmōd 146:22; *f. nom.*
sg. ēaðmōd 8:143; *f. dat. sg.* ēaþmōdre
30:132; *m. nom. pl.* ēaþmōde 66:196,
90:217; *m. acc. pl.* ēaþmōde 110:320; *def.*
m. acc. sg. ēaþmōdan 8:144; *f. acc. pl.*
ēaþmōdan 68:27; ēaðmōdan 76:7; *comp. f.*
nom. sg. ēaþmōddre 6:133
ēaþmōdian (2) to humble; *imp. 2 pl.*
ēaþmōdgiaþ 68:25
ēaþmōdlic *adj.* humble; *f. dat. sg.*
ēaþmōdlicre 120:7
ēaþmōdlīce *adv.* meekly, humbly 92:29,
94:70; ēaðmōdlīce 4:89, 138:52, 138:63,
140:99, 140:109, 142:139
Ebrēas *prop. n* Jews; *gen. pl.* Ebrēa
124:90
Ebrēisc *adj.* Hebrew; *nt. acc. sg.* Ebrēisc
103; *f. inst. sg.* Ebrēiscre 106:220
ēca (see ēce *adj.*)

53

ecan (1) to increase, add to 54:212 (A)
ece *m.* pain; *nom. sg.* 16:167, 72:113; *dat.*
pl. ecum 40:60
ēċe *adj.* eternal; *m. nom. sg.* 4:88, 12:77,
34:216, 72:111; *nt. nom. sg.* ēce 44:159; *m.*
acc. sg. ēcne 64:178; *f. nom. sg.* ēce 16:166,
20:75, 68:19; *f. acc. sg.* ēce 2:40, 16:160,
56:238; *nt. acc. sg.* ēce 12:84, 18:26, 24:138,
24:144, 24:176, 38:42, 40:89, 66:193, 68:24,
86:125; *nt. gen. sg.* ēces 4:51, 10:25, 70:73,
72:109, 90:199, 94:89; *f. dat. sg.* ēcere
24:157; ēcre 88:174, 92:42; *nt. dat. sg.* ēcean
70:89, 72:115; *nt. inst. sg.* ēce 136:7; *m. acc.*
pl. ēce 64:177; *m. dat. pl.* ēcum 42:113,
58:9, 68:8, 70:65, 130:269; *f. dat. pl.* ecum
70:69, *def. m. nom. sg.* ēcea 78:75; eca
20:75, 22:91; *m. acc. sg.* ēcean 144:192;
ēcan 36:238, 44:137, 46:16; *m. gen. sg.*
ēcean 58:27, 136:11; ēcan 34:220; *nt. gen.*
sg. ēcean 58:1; ēcan 10:42, 12:52, 12:53,
12:55, 32:159, 40:44, 60:45, 92:31, 134:331; *m.*
dat. sg. ēcan 20:75, 42:91b; *f. nom. sg.* ēce
44:162; *f. acc. sg.* ēcean 24:140, 66:207, 68:9,
70:76, 82:6, 84:78, 86:90; ēcan 88:176; *nt.*
acc. sg. ēce 58:14, 58:25, 78:57; *f. dat. sg.*
ēcean 60:86; ēcan 24:145, 42:112; *nt. dat.*
sg. ēcean 12:44, 52:168, 94:56, 96:95; ēcan
18:29, 42:91a, 68:17; *nt. dat. pl.* ēcum
42:120; ēcan 24:147
ēceliċe *adv.* eternally 78:67
ēcndōm *m.* eternal kingdom; *acc. sg.*
ēcndōm 84:82
ēcnes *f.* eternity; *dat. sg.* ēcnesse 8:154,
16:162, 24:178, 26:17, 36:241, 40:50, 44:158,
44:166, 50:102, 56:240, 66:209, 80:131
ēcre (see ēce)
edhwyrft *m.* return; *nom. sg.* 96:95
edlean *nt.* reward; *acc. sg.* edlean 70:79,
72:101; *dat. sg.* edleane 26:29
edwit *nt.* disgrace; *acc. sg.* edwit 70:59,
70:75; *acc. pl.* edwita 68:7
efenhāliġ *adj.* equally holy; *m. nom. sg.*
30:90
efenþrōwian (2) to sympathize; *ind. pres.*
pl. efenþrōwiaþ 132:301; *pres. p.*

efenþrōwiende 12:80; efenþrōwgende
50:136
efne *adv.* even 50:126, 54:223, 82:38, 90:198,
90:205, 146:24, 148:65, 148:89, 150:129,
152:144, 152:145, 152:157, 156:234 >
efnēce *adj.* co-eternal; *m. nom. sg.*78:54
efngemyndig *adj.* equally mindful; *m.*
nom. pl. efngemyndige 70:54
efnhlete *adj.* equal in lot; *m. nom. sg.*
30:91
efstan (1) to strive, hasten 76:25; *ind. pres.*
3 sg. efsteþ 40:47, 40:76; *imp. 2 pl.* efstað
54; *pres. p.* efstende 167
eft *adv.* afterwards, hereafter 4:64, 4:70,
4:80, 6:93, 10:24, 14:108, 14:118, 16:137,
16:159, 16:161a, 16:161b, 38:17, 38:29, 38:40>
eġe *m.* awe, fear, dread, terror; *nom. sg.*
16:168, 58:33, 132:316; *acc. sg.* ege 34:207,
64:172, 90:218, 94:87, 128:212, 160:70; *dat. sg.*
ege 6:117, 6:121, 28:56, 42:130
eġeleasnes *f.* boldness; *dat. sg.*
egeleasnesse 60:48
eġesan (see eġsa)
eġesfull *adj.* awful, dreadful; *m. nom. sg.*
58:31; *f. nom. sg.* egesfull 62:128; *def. m.*
acc. sg. egesfullan 70:77
eġesliċ *adj.* awful, dreadful; *def. m. nom.*
sg. egeslica 18:21; *m. gen. sg.* egeslican
22:121; *m. dat. sg.* egeslican 118:129
eġle *adj.* troubled; *nt. dat. sg.* eglum
12:57
eġsa [eġesa] *m.* awe, fear, dread; *nom. sg.*
62:127; *acc. sg.* egsan 86:130, 94:89; *gen.*
sg. egsan 128:209; *dat. sg.* egesan [egsan →
egesan] 86:121; egsan 84:50, 86:117
ehtatēne [eahtatīene] *num.* eighteen 50:107;
ehtatȳne 54:198
ēhtere *m.* persecutor; *nom. sg.* 128:227
ēhtan (1) (with *gen.*) to persecute; *ind. pres.*
2 sg. ēhtest 122:69
ēhtnes *f.* persecution; *dat. pl.*
ēhtnesssum [→ ēhtnessum] 120:11
eldo *f.* age; *acc. sg.* eldo 82:35; *dat. sg.*
eldo 82:36

54

ele *m.* oil; *nom. sg.* 50:108; *gen. sg.* eles 90:185; *dat. sg.* ele 28:66, 50:111, 88:183
ellen *m.* strength; *dat. sg.* elne 18:32
Elian *pers. n.* Elias; *gen. sg.* Elian 116:68
Elizabeþ *pers. n.* Elizabeth; *nom. sg.* 114:21, 114:31; Elizabet 116:64; *gen. sg.* Elizabethe 116:80; *dat. sg.* Elizabet 114:33
elles *adv.* else 6:118, 26:14, 26:16, 40:76 [ealles → elles], 70:57, 78:75, 78:76, 140:132 [ealles → elles], 148:47, 154:193 [ealles → elles], 156:231, 156:234 >
embe *prep.*(with acc.) about, around 68:10, 68:28; emb 28:69, 52:176a, 52:176b, 62:114, 70:81, 102:122, 102:132, 148:61 >
embgān (anom.) to compass, go around; *subj. pres. sg.* embgānge 121 (A)
embsellan (1) to surround; *ind. pres. 3 sg.* embseleþ 4:63; *pret. pl.* embsealdon 100:62
embsettan (1) to surround; *ind. pret. 3 sg.* embsæt [embæst → embsæt] 54:191 (A)
embþringan (III) to thronged round; *ind. pret. pl.* embþrungon 70:53
end (see ond)
ende *m.* end, quarter; *nom. sg.* 8:153, 34:189, 40:71, 58:10; *acc. sg.* ende 14:113, 92:27; *dat. sg.* ende 8:154, 16:153, 24:178, 28:43, 36:241, 40:47, 40:76, 42:113; *dat. pl.* endum 64:146, 64:174, 66:185
endebyrdnes *f.* order, arrangement, manner; *dat. sg.* endebyrdnesse 64:148, 142:170, 146:27, 148:73; *acc. pl.* endebyrdnessa 144:195/6
endedæġ *m.* day of death; *dat. sg.* endedæge 34:192
endestæf *m.* end, conclusion; *dat. sg.* endestæfe 58:38
endian (2) to come 82:35, 82:36
endleofan *num.* eleven 54:196
endlyfta *num. adj.* eleventh; *acc. sg. f.* endlyftan 64:147
engel [Lt. angelus] *m.* angel; *nom. sg.* 2:16, 2:22, 2:31, 4:70, 4:71, 6:91, 8:141, 28:74, 98:4, 98:7, 98:13; *acc. sg.* engel 118:110, 158:31, 120; *gen. sg.* engles 2:32, 4:57, 98:11, 98:15,

104:166, 114:36, 116:61; *dat. sg.* engle 28:74, 98:7; *nom. pl.* englas 6:112, 6:123, 18:9, 20:51, 22:112, 22:115, 22:116, 28:71, 84:84, 84:86; *acc. pl.* englas 14:127, 124:121, 126:136, 126:154, 126:155, 126:166; *gen. pl.* engla 6:111, 6:122, 58:5 [eagla →engla], 64:148, 64:163, 64:165, 70:82, 72:115, 82:5, 84:81, 84:85, 102:130; *dat. pl.* englum 14:96, 16:170, 32:141, 64:172, 68:33, 86:96, 86:105, 102:131, 110:303, 116:43
engelliċ *adj.* angelic; *inst. sg.* engelice 118:113; *def. f. dat. sg.* engellican 56:239; *nt. dat. pl.* englicum [englicum → engelicum] 92:8
eno *conj.* moreover 6:117, 162:103 (A) (M)
eorclanstān *m.* jewel; *nom. sg.* 104:161 (A)
ēorendel *m.* dawn; *nom. sg.* 116:51
eornes *f.* anger, wrath; *acc. sg.* eornesse 86:101
eorþe *f.* earth; *nom. sg.* 4:43, 26:7, 32:178, 50:127, 62:129, 62:133, 64:142, 64:146, 64:152; eorðe 104; *acc. sg.* eorþan 14:128, 26:11, 32:181, 64:145, 64:153, 64:154, 80:116, 80:117, 88:172, 94:51; eorðan 130:230, 156:240, 162:105; *gen. sg.* eorþan 32:174, 32:180, 34:188, 64:145, 64:174, 84:56; eorðan 90:213; *dat. sg.* eorþan 2:28, 8:146, 32:148, 32:149, 34:184, 36:236, 46:3, 50:123, 52:161; eorðan 70:55, 82:22, 86:103, 138:53, 138:57, 156:232, 101
eorþcyning *m.* earthly king; *acc. pl.* eorþcyningas 84:53
eorþhrērnes *f.* earthquake; *nom. sg.* 64:154
eorþliċ *adj.* earthly; *f. acc. sg.* eorþlice 32:162; *f. dat. sg.* eorþlicre 94:69; *nt. acc. pl.* eorþlicu 20:59; *f. gen. pl.* eorþlicra 14:94, 30:106, 30:113; eorðlicra 94:88; *f. dat. pl.* eorþlicum 30:108; *def. nt. nom. sg.* eorþlice 20:61; *m. acc. sg.* eorðlican 94:89; *m. dat. sg.* eorþlican 102:106; *m. nom. pl.* eorþlican 34:204; *f. acc. pl.* eorþlican 94:77; *nt. acc. pl.* eorþlican 34:202; *nt. dat. pl.* eorþlicum 32:159

55

eorþscraf [eorþscræf] *nt.* grave; *dat. sg.*
eorþscrafe 78:44
eorþstyr[ung] *f.* earthquake; *nom. sg.*
132:320
eorþwaru *f.* mankind; *nom. pl.* eorþware
6:105; *gen. pl.* eorþwara 60:61; *dat. pl.*
eorþwarum 124:89
eorþwela *m.* earthly wealth; *gen. pl.*
eorþwelena 34:198
eosel *m.* ass; *nom. sg.* 54:205; *acc. sg.*
eosol 48:67
eosele *f.* she ass; *acc. sg.* eoselan 48:62,
54:204; *gen. sg.* eoselan 48:66
ēow (see ġē)
ēowde *nt.* flock; *acc. sg.* eowde 132:303,
132:304
ēower *pron.* of you (see Appendix, p. 145)
ēower *poss. adj.* your; *m. nom. sg.* 12:85;
f. nom. sg. ēower 94:74; *nt. nom. sg.*
ēower 82:24; *m. acc. sg.* ēowerne 26:13,
26:25, 160:51, 91; *nt. acc. sg.* eower 24:169,
26:26; *m. gen. sg.* ēoweres 118:126;
ēowres 120:14; *m. dat. sg.* ēowrum 160:57;
nt. dat. sg. ēowrum 99; *m. acc. pl.*
ēowere 28:49; ēowre 32:150, *f. dat. pl.*
ēowre 106:216; *m. gen. pl.* ēowerra
32:152; *m. dat. pl.* ēowrum, 110:283; *f. dat.
pl.* ēowrum 26:32, 34:191, 36:238
ēowian (2) to show; *ind. pret. 3 sg.*
ēowode 126:151
ermð *m.* misery; *acc. pl.* ermða 10:39
erre *m.* wrath; *acc. sg* erre 30:127,
118:123; *dat. sg.* erre 62:92, 118:122
erre *adj.* angry; *m. nom. sg.* 126:146; *nt.
inst. sg.* erre 130:273; *m. nom. pl.* erre
104:180, 152:168
Esaias *pers. n.* Isaiah; *nom. sg.* 24:160,
118:109
etan (v) to eat 158:2; *ind. pret. 3 sg.* ǣt 118,
124; *3 pl.* ǣton 4a, 4b; *subj. pres. 1 sg.* ete
38:28; *imp. 2 pl.* etað 33
Eua *pers. n.* Eve; *nom. sg.* 2:4, 2:5, 2:7,
60:74, 60:87; *gen. sg.* Euan 2:2, 4:56; *dat.
sg.* Euan 62:102

ēþel *m.* native land; *nom. sg.* 86:91; *acc.
sg.* ēþel 14:118; ēðel 144:192; *gen. sg.*
ēþles 56:232, 92:5
ēþelīċe *adv.* easily 40:78; *comp.* ēþelīcor
44:142, 94:62; *superl.* ēþelīcost 38:15

F

fācen *m.* guile, deceit; *nom. sg.* 154:189;
acc. sg. 66:196: fācen; *dat. sg.* fācne 2:15
fācenfull *adj.* guileful; *def. nom. pl.*
fācenfullan 38:13
faran (vı) to go 12:74, 14:124, 2, 160:49; *ind.
pres. 2 sg.* færest 160:68; *pl.* faraþ 10:4;
pret. pl. fōran 48:50, 140:107; *subj. pres. pl.*
faran 160:54; *imp. 2 pl.* farað 36; *pres. p.*
farende 154
fæc *nt.* period of time, interval; *acc. sg.*
fæc 150; *dat. sg.* fæce 6:97, 16:138, 80:100
fæder *m.* father; *nom. sg.* 12:85, 82:25,
92:13, 92:15, 92:20, 94:65, 106:209; *acc. sg.*
fæder 14:124, 98:26, 118:96, 120:14; *gen. sg.*
fæder 4:43, 20:47, 70:85, 108:272, 110:301,
116:47; *dat. sg.* fæder 20:74, 64:167, 72:116,
94:74, 118:94, 106:210, 108:267, 110:295; *nom.
pl.* fæderas 18:19, 28:55, 122:86; *acc. pl.*
fæderas 128:208; *dat. pl.* fæderum 112:329
fæderliċ *adj.* fatherly; *def. m. gen. sg.*
fæderlican 46:3; *m. dat. sg.* fæderlican
2:26; *nt. dat. sg.* fæderlican 82:5, 84:89
fæġer *adj.* fair, beautiful; *m. nom. sg.*
80:118, 80:120; *f. nom. sg.* fæger 6:90; *nt.
nom. sg.* fæger 52:177, 76:17; *m. acc. sg.*
fægerne 80:94; *nt. gen. sg.* fægeres 14:91,
162:94, 155; *nt. acc. pl.* fægre 80:98; *def. m.
dat. sg.* fægran 102:88; *superl. m. nom. sg.*
fægerost 40:59; fægrost 88:143; *def. m.
nom. sg.* fægresta 4:64
fægere *adv.* beautifully 88:145; fægre
[fægere → fægere] 88:142
fægernes *f.* fairness, beauty; *nom. sg.*
40:47, 40:48, 40:49, 40:53; *acc. sg.*
fægernesse 52:176, 80:119; *gen. sg.*
fægernesse 26:12, 40:72, 80:114; *dat. sg.*

56

fægernesse 110:322; *acc. pl.* fægernessa 52:178; *dat. pl.* fægernessum 4:68

fǣmne *f.* virgin; *nom. sg.* 2:20, 2:24, 2:39, 4:45, 4:71, 4:88, 6:121, 104:168, 108:274a, 108:274b, 108:275, 110:279, 110:312; *acc. sg.* fǣmnan 112:335, 122:88; *gen. sg.* fǣmnan 2:30, 4:56, 6:94, 6:100, 8:147, 14:131, 22:95, 116:81; *dat. sg.* fǣmnan 6:91, 74:12, 98:2, 118:103; *nom. pl.* fǣmnan 102:125, 104:163; *gen. pl.* fǣmnena 74:9

fǣmnliċ *adj.* maidenly; *def. m. acc. sg.* fǣmnlican 116:79

fǣr *m.* sudden marvel; *dat. sg.* fǣre 138:43

fǣringa *adv.* suddenly 90:192, 122:44, 122:54, 126:149, 150:118, 152:173, 152:177, 154:203

fǣrliċ *adj.* sudden; *m. nom. sg.* 78:86

fǣrlīċe *adv.* suddenly 86:133, 148:89

fæstan (1) to fast 24:166; *ind. pres. 3 sg.* fæstte 18:19, 18:23; fæste 18:2, 152:154; *subj. pres. pl.* fæston 18:23; *pret. pl.* fæston 138:48

fæste *adv.* fast 28:53, 78:51, 154:221

fæsten *nt.* fast, fasting; *nom. sg.* 24:157, 24:162, 24:168, 50:113; fasten 22:118; *acc. sg.* fæsten 22:120, 24:169, 138:73, 140:136, 142:140; *gen. sg.* fæstenes 18:20; fæstennes 22:133; *dat. sg.* fæstenne 18:25, 24:149, 28:43, 28:44, 138:50; *dat. pl.* fæstenum 16:156, 24:174, 42:101

fæstendæġ *m.* fastday; *gen. pl.* fæstendaga 22:134

fæstlīċe *adv.* firmly 30:122, 90:218, 94:78, 120:19, 120:26, 120:35, 134:329; *comp.* fæstlīcor 94:62

fæstnung *f.* bond; *nom. sg.* 116:46; *dat. sg.* fæstnunga 118:95

fæt *nt.* vessel; *nom. sg.* 110:288, 142:175; *acc. sg.* fæt 110:278; *dat. sg.* fæte 142:178

fæþmliċ *adj.* embracing, enclosing; *def. nt. nom. sg.* fæþmlice 4:67

feala *indecl. pron.* (with *gen. pl.*) much, many 14:91, 26:29, 34:218, 74:17, 80:90, 120:40, 122:56, 150:104; feale 88:169

fealasprecolnes *f.* talkativeness; *gen. sg.* fealaspreolnesse [→ fealasprecolnesse] 118:118

feallendliċ *adj.* likely to fall; *f. nom. sg.* 80:112

feallan (VII) to fall down; *ind. pres. 2 sg.* feallest 18:13, 20:55; *3 sg.* fealleþ 40:76; *pret. 3 sg.* feol 132:316, 152:172; *pl.* feollan 106:192; *imp. 2 pl.* feallaþ 64:171; *pres. p. m. acc. sg.* feallendne 80:125

fear [fearr] *m.* bull; *nom. sg.* 136:30

fearhrȳþer *nt.* bull; *nom. sg.* 136:27

fēaw *adj.* few; *m. nom. pl.* fēawa 34:194; *m. dat. pl.* fēawum 68:30, 132:292; *def. m. acc. pl.* fēawan 24:153

fēdan (1) to feed 26:40; *pp.* fēded 38:31, 38:33

feforādl *f.* fever; *dat. sg.* feforādle 142:180, 148:87, 154:227

feld *m.* field; *acc. sg.* feld 136:25; *dat. sg.* felda 142:164

fēogan [fēoan → fēogan] (1) to fight; *ind. pret. 3 pl.* fēodan 122:85

feoh *nt.* wealth, cattle; *acc. sg.* feoh 124:101, 124:103, 124:105, 160:55; *gen. sg.* feos; *dat. sg.* feo 28:56, 42:110, 48:44, 54:199; *inst. sg.* feo 136:25

feohtan (III) to fight 144:194

fēond *m.* enemy; *nom. sg.* fȳnd 106:216; *acc. sg.* fēond 20:79, 60:68, 72:114; *dat. sg.* fȳnd 124:119; *nom. pl.* fȳnd 102:109, 114:203, 144:203; *gen. pl.* fēonda 74:14, 138:76; *dat. pl.* fēondum 32:176, 46:11, 70:64, 70:81, 138:82

feor *adv.* far 28:68, 48:53, 82:29, 82:34, 118:118, 148:70, 162:91

feorh *nt.* life, soul; *acc. sg.* feorh 128:194, 146:41; *gen. sg.* feores 34:187; *dat. sg.* feore 30:95, 44:165, 72:107

feorhner *nt.* preservation of life; *dat. sg.* feorhnere 74:23

fēorþa *num. adj.* fourth; *m. acc. sg.*
fēorþan 90:199; *m. inst. sg.* **fēorþan** 30:120,
46:9, 50:93, 50:124, 64:156
feoung *f.* hatred, enmity; *dat. sg.*
feounge 120:16; **feounga** 132:313
fēower *num.* four, 22:123, 22:124, 22:125,
22:126, 28:71, 64:146, 64:174, 66:185a,
66:185b, 94:50
fēowerfealdlīċe *adv.* fourfold 6:108/9
fēowerteoþ *num. adj.* fortieth; *nt. dat. sg.*
fēowertigoþan [fēowerteoþan → fēowertigoþan]
22:129
fēowertig *num.* forty 18:2 18:3, 22:122,
54:184, 38; **fēowertiges** 22:118, 24:139;
fēowertigum 22:128
fēran (I) to go, come 10:12, 14:98, 130:251,
152:158, 154:202, 156:241, 160:43; *ind. pres.*
3 sg. **fēreþ** 48:74; *pret. 3 sg.* **fērde** 12:69,
48:56, 48:68, 48:70, 54:215, 136:32, 136:33,
136:37, 146:39, 150:109, 154:198, 154:200,
154:201, 166; *pl.* **fērdon** 70:44, 70:53, 86:136,
138:84, 37; **fērdan** 148:43
fersceat *m.* passage money; *acc. sg.*
fersceat 160:51, 160:52
fēþa *m.* warfare; *acc. sg.* **fēþan** 116:88;
dat. sg. **fēþan** 154:221
fīctrēow *nt.* figtree; *acc. sg.* **fīctrēow**
50:90, 33
fīf *num.* five 20:68, 22:132, 82:31, 142:153
fīfe *num.* five 82:35
fīfta *num. adj.* fifth; *m. inst. sg.* **fīftan**
30:120, 50:94, 64:162
fīftene *num.* fifteen 146:17
fīftig *num.* fifty 92:34
fihtan (I) to fight; *ind. pres. 2 sg.* **fihtest**
55 (A)
findan (III) to find; *ind. pres. 3 sg.* **findeð**
72:114; *pret. 3 sg.* **fand** 138:48, 138:73;
funde 154:191; *pl.* **fundon** 140:122; *subj.*
pres. sg. **finde** 56:237; *pp.* **funden** 114:37,
136:20
firen *f.* sin, crime; *nom. sg.* 114:26; *gen.*
pl. **firena** 116:45; **fyrenra** [→ fyrena] 94:55
firenlust *m.* sinful lust; *acc. sg.* **firenlust**
2:4; *dat. sg.* **firenluste** 16:149; *nom. pl.*

fyrenlustas 78:80; *acc. pl.* **fyrenlustas**
68:40
fisc *m.* fish; *nom. pl.* **fixas** 66:188
fiscere *m.* fisher; *acc. sg.* **fiscere** 124:117
flǣsc *nt.* flesh; *nom. sg.* 62:99, 70:56, 78:75;
dat. sg. **flǣsce** 62:99
flǣschoma *m.* covering of flesh, the
body; *nom. sg.* 78:48
flǣsclic *adj.* carnal; *m. nom. sg.* 158:32; *f.*
dat. sg. **flǣsclicre** 80:98; *nt. gen. sg.*
flǣsclices 10:30; *def. m. acc. pl.*
flǣsclican 12:60
flēam *m.* flight; *dat. sg.* **flēame** 138:85
flēogan (II) to fly, flee 130:246; **flēon** 119;
ind. pres. 3 sg. **flȳhþ** 30:116, 80:124; *pl.*
flēoþ 64:165, 160:48; *pret. 3 sg.* **flēah**
114:40, 146:13; *pl.* **flūgon** 138:89, 140:94, 85,
92; *infl. inf.* to **flēonne** 118:121; *pres. p. m.*
acc. sg. **flēogendne** 130:254; *pres. p. m.*
dat. sg. **flēondum** 80:125
flēon (II) to put to flight; *ind. pres. 3 sg.*
flēmeþ 62:132
flōwan (VII) to flow; *ind. pres. 3 sg.* **flēwþ**
162:105; *pret. 3 sg.* **flēow** 71 (A)
flītan (VI) to strive, dispute; *ind. pres. 3*
sg. **flīteþ** 122:62
flyge *m.* flight, flying; *dat. sg.* **flyge**
136:40
flytere *m.* quarreller; *nom. pl.* **flyteras**
42:103
fola *m.* foal; *acc. sg.* **folan** 48:62, 48:66,
54:204
folc *nt.* folk, people; *nom. sg.* 10:22, 30:91,
30:104, 30:123, 30:130, 48:53, 48:68, 48:74;
acc. sg. **floc** 30:93, 30:102, 30:109, 42:129,
54:206, 54:215, 100:65; *gen. sg.* **folces** 18:19,
52:179, 54:197, 54:199, 74:10, 120:34, 122:67,
130:235; *dat. sg.* **folce** 22:130, 28:86, 30:101,
30:122, 46:7, 100:77, 108:239; *gen. pl.* **folca**
30:97, 82:15; *dat. pl.* **folcum** 76:35, 108:272,
120:24
folgað *m.* service, employment; *dat. sg.*
folgaðe 146:31

folgian [foligan → folgian] (2) (with *dat.*) to follow 118:127; *ind. pret. pl.* folgodan 122:51; folgedan 132:308

for *prep.* (with *acc. / dat.*) for (see Appendix, p. 150)

fōr *m.* journey; *dat. sg.* fore 148:88

fōran (see fāran)

fōran *adv.* before (see Appendix, p. 151)

forbærnan (1) to burn 106:202, 132:292; forbærnon 106:186; *ind. pret. 3 sg.* forbærnde 108:242; *infl. inf.* to forbærnenne 64:145; *pp.* forbærned 62:133

forbelgan (III) to be enraged; *ind. pret. 3 sg.* forbealh 136:32

forbēodan (II) to forbid; *pp.* forboden 36:236

forbrecan (V) to break in pieces 106:202

forburstan (III) to burst asunder, broke; *ind. pret. pl.* forburston 144:206

forbyrnan (III) to be burnt 152:141

fordēman (1) to condemn; *ind. pres. pl.* fordēmaþ 42:124; *pret. 3 sg.* fordēmde 154:190; *pp. m. acc. pl.* fordēmde 60:54 (EWS)

fordīlegian (2) to destroy, abolish; *pp.* fordīlegod 86:100

fordōn (anom.) to ravage; *ind. pret. 3 sg.* fordyde 54:201

fore *post prep.* for (see Appendix, p. 150)

forebēanc [foretænc] *m.* foretoken; *nom. pl.* forebēacno 82:30 (A)

forebringan [fore bringan → forebringan] (1) to bring for 30:109

forefēran (1) to go before; *pres. p. def. m. nom. pl.* forefērendan 10:15

forehīeran (1) (with *dat.*) to hear of; *ind. pret. pl.* forehȳrdon 150:132

forelæran (1) to teach; *pres. p.* forelærende 104:170

foremǣre *adj.* great, illustrious; *m. nom. sg.* 148:75; *m. gen. sg.* foremǣres 118:127; *m. nom. pl.* foremǣre 114:9; *def. f. nom. sg.* foremǣre 114:3

foresecgan (3) to foretell; *ind. pret. 1 sg.* foresǣgde 92:21; *3 sg.* foresǣgde 140:91; *pl.* foresǣgdon 54:216

foresetenes *f.* purpose; *acc. sg.* foresetenesse 150:130/1

foreþingian (2) to intercede 30:103

forġeorne *adv.* very earnestly 78:68

forġifan [forġiefan] (V) to give 58:25; *ind. pres. 2 sg.* forgifest 100:48; *3 sg.* forgifeþ 4:82, 68:24, 72:107; *pres. 2 sg.* forgeafe 110:293; *3 sg.* forgeaf 12:83, 20:77, 28:76, 72:105, 86:99, 94:89; *subj. pres. sg.* forgife 158:7; *sg.* forgeafe 12:84; *imp. 2 sg.* forgif 162:96; *pres. p.* forgifende 12:80; *pp.* forgifen 90:216, 120:12

forġifnes *f.* forgiveness; *nom. sg.* 32:155, 96:93, 116:45; *acc. sg.* forgifnesse 30:131, 44:152, 68:24; forgifenesse 44:151, 44:155; *gen. sg.* forgifnesse 152:174; *dat. sg.* forgifnesse 24:156; *acc. pl.* forgifnessa 12:79, 32:152, 60:63

forgietan (V) to forget; *ind. pres. pl.* forgytaþ 38:19; *pp.* forgiten 12:55; *def. gen. m. sg.* forgytenan 38:27

forglendrian (2) to devour; *pp.* forglendred 68:31

forgyldan (III) to repay 26:30, 38:18, 62:125; *ind. pres. 1 sg.* forgylde 130:274; *3 sg.* forgyldeþ 34:185; *pl.* forgyldað 65; *pp.* forgolden 28:78, 34:211

forhæfdnes *f.* abstinence; *nom. sg.* 24:155, 24:170; *dat. sg.* forhæfdnesse 22:122, 22:127, 22:131, 24:138, 24:141, 24:153, 54:213

forhealdan (I) to defile; *ind. pres. 3 sg.* forhealdeþ 128:215; *pret. 3 sg.* forheold 28:76

forhogian (2) to despise, disregard; *ind. pres. 3 sg.* forhogaþ 58:8, 76:9; *pret. 3 sg.* forhogode 136:30; *pl.* forhogodan 4:53, 94:87; *pp.* forhogde 52:173

forhogdlīċe *adv.* contemptuously 52:172

forhogodliċ *adj.* contemptuous; *m. inst. sg.* forhogodlice 52:170

forht *adj.* fearful; *m. nom. pl.* forhte 58:30, 138:43

forhtian (2) to be afraid; *ind. pres. pl.* forhtigað 114; *ind. pres. pl.* forhtiaþ 6:105; *pret. 3 sg.* forhtode 4:89, 154:223; *pres. p. def. m. nom. pl.* forhtgendan 76:7/8

forhwon *adv.* why 12:64, 80:95, 128:188, 154:206

forhwierfan (1) to change; *pp. def. m. nom. sg.* forhwyrfda 20:58

forhwyrfedliċ *adj.* perverse; *nt. acc. pl.* forhwyrfedlice 20:58

forhycggan [forhicgan] (3) to distain, despise 30:130; forhycggaþ 28:46, 42:122 (A)

forieldan (1) to put off; *subj. pret. sg.* forylde 146:35; *pl.* foryldon 66:195

forlǣtan (VII) to forsake, dismiss 40:78, 154:209, 127; forlǣton 78:67; *ind. pres. 1 sg.* forlǣte 92:10, 104:160a, 104:160b, 110:300, 158:14; *2 sg.* forlǣtest 154:206; *3 sg.* forlǣteþ 2:22, 48:64, 72:114, 160:78; forlǣteð 78:70; *pl.* forlǣtaþ 22:133, 28:46; forlǣtað 72:97; *pret. 2 sg.* forlēte 96, 107, 156, 163; *3 sg.* forlēt 12:49, 18:16, 22:91, 40:70, 48:84, 52:142, 88:173, 148:74, 152; *pl.* forlēton 10:39, 112:324, 150:104, 158:5, 73; forlētan 130:263; *subj. pres. pl.* forlǣtan 78:67; *imp. 2 sg.* forlǣt 60:64, 60:79, 158:8, 120; *2 pl.* forlǣtað 156:240; forlētað 156:239; *pp.* forlǣten 24:172, 52:181; *def. f. nom. sg.* forlǣtene 28:48

forlǣtnes *f.* remission, intermission; *acc. sg.* forlǣtnesse 24:144, 90:208; *dat. sg.* forlǣtnesse 102:126; *acc. pl.* forlǣtnessa 78:56

forleornung *f.* deception; *nom. sg.* 128:191

forlēosan (II) to lose; *ind. pres. 2 sg.* forlēosest 128:194; *pl.* forlēosaþ 26:35; *subj. pres. pl.* forlēosan 70:63

forma *nt.* first; *dat. sg.* forman 88:172

fornēah *adv.* almost 150:132

forniman (IV) to take off, take away; *ind. pret. 3 sg.* fornam 150:90; *pp.* fornumene 62:95

fornumene (see forniman)

forsēarian (2) to dry up; *pp. nt. dat. sg.* forsēaredum 106:201

forsēon (V) to overlook; *ind. pres. 3 sg.* forsyhþ 68:26, 76:9; *pret. 3 sg.* forseah 16:137, 70:88; *pl.* forsawon 94:89; *subj. pres. pl.* forsēon 106:207, 106:212; *imp. 2 sg.* forseoh 24:162

forspillan (1) to destroy; *subj. pres. sg.* forspille 132:277

forstelan (IV) to steal; *ind. pret. pl.* forstælan 124:103

forstandan (II) to defend; *ind. pres. 3 sg.* forstandeþ 154:207

forswelgan (III) to swallow up, devour 64:153; *ind. pret. 3 sg.* forswealh 137; *subj. pres. 3 sg.* forswelge 64:166; *infl. inf.* to forswylgenne 64:145

forwiernan (1) to refuse, deny; *ind. pres. 3 sg.* forwyrneþ 32:168; *pret. 3 sg.* forwyrnde 100:64; *pl.* forwyrndon 34:222; *subj. pres. sg.* forwyrne 36:232

forswīgian (2) to conceal 124:104

forwlencan (1) to be proud; *pp. def. nt. acc. sg.* forwlencte 136:35

forwordenliċ *adj.* perishing; *f. nom. sg.* forwordenlic 80:111

forwyrcan (1) to forfeit; *ind. pret. pl.* forworhtan 16:143

forwregan (1) to accuse; *subj. pret. sg.* forwregde 126:181

forwȳrd *f.* perdition, destruction; *nom. sg.* 128:191; *acc. sg.* forwȳrd 16:154, 28:87; forwȳrde 70:64, 112:325, 122:64; *dat. sg.* forwȳrde 60:86

forwyrnednes *f.* abstinence, self-denial; *nom. sg.* forwyrnednesse 150:128

forwyrdan (1) to perish; *inf. pres. 3 sg.* forwyrð 99; *pret. 3 sg.* forwearþ 18:40, 60:78; *subj. pres. 3 pl.* forweorþon 128

fōrþ *adv.* forth 6:100, 12:69, 34:224, 40:57, 58:2, 62:123, 64:159, 84:75; fōrð 138:81, 148:43, 150:120, 152:171

forþberan (IV) to bring forward, produce 16:144; forþbearn [→forþberan]70:78

forþbringan (1) to bring forth, produce 110:293; *ind. pres. 3 sg.* forþbringeþ 26:7; *pret. 3 sg.* forðbrohte 140:128

forþcuman (IV) to come forth; *ind. pres. 3 sg.* forþcymeþ 64:143

forðgan (anom.) to go forth; *ind. pret. 3 sg.* forðeode 6:97

forðfēran (1) to go forth, die 150:93, 154:204; *ind. pret. 3 sg.* forðfērde 150:90; *pp.* forþfēred 46:23; *m. acc. sg.* forðfēredne 148:89

forþfōr *f.* departure, death; *gen. sg.* forþfōre 40:88; forðfōre 154:195; *dat. sg.* forðfōre 146:2

forþgān (anom.) to go forth 66:189

forðġelǣdan (1) to bring forward; *subj. pres. sg.* forðgelædde 142:139

forþlǣtan (VII) to send forth; *ind. pres. 3 sg.* forþlǣteþ 94:46

forlaðian (2) to invite; *ind. pret. 3 sg.* forþlaþode 70:84

forðlōcian (2) to look forth; *ind. pret. 3 sg.* forðlōcade 150:100, 150:118

forþon / forðon *conj.* therefore (see Appendix, p. 149)

fōt *m.* foot; *nom. sg.* 18:10, 20:50; *nom. pl.* fēt 88:159, 120:27, 132:287, 132:298; *acc. pl.* fēt 46:34, 50:95, 50:106, 50:130, 50:134, 88:173, 110:291, 132:289; *dat. pl.* fōtum 46:25, 50:116, 124:92, 134

fōtlāst *m.* footprint; *nom. pl.* fōtlāstas 140:111

fōtsceamul *m.* footstool; *nom. sg.* 20:61

fræġn (see friġnan)

frætwan (1) to adorn; *ind. pret. 3 sg.* frætwode 78:79

frætwodnes *f.* adorning, decoration; *nom. sg.* 70:46; frætwednes 34:201; *acc. sg.*

---

frætwodnesse 142:162; *dat. sg.* frætwednesse 88:158

fram *prep.* (with dat.) from (see Appendix, p. 150)

framfundung *f.* departure; *gen. sg.* framfundunga 92:5; *dat. sg.* framfundunga 94:66

frea beorht *adv.* very bright 158:11

frēċennes *f.* danger, ruin; *acc. sg.* frēcennesse 140:97; frēcenesse 20:53; *dat. sg.* frēcennesse 158:15; *nom. pl.* frēcenessa 76:12; *dat. pl.* frǣcenessum 76:24

frēfran (1) to comfort, console 146:30; *ind. pret. 3 sg.* frēfrede 94:72

Frēfrend *m.* Comforter; *nom. sg.* 92:12; *acc. sg.* Frēfrend 74:10, 94:81

fremde *adj.* strange, alien; *m. nom. pl.* fremde 160:66

fremman (1) to perform, accomplish, commit; *ind. pres. 3 sg.* fremeþ 128:214; *3 pl.* fremmað 146:21; *pret. pl.* fremedon 86:125; *imp. 2 sg.* freme 130:255; *infl. inf.* to fremmenne 40:61

fremsumnes *f.* benefit; *gen. pl.* fremsumnessa 80:130

frēo *adj.* free; *m. acc. sg.* frēone 60:53; *m. acc. pl.* frēo 58:21

freodōm *m.* freedom, deliverance; *nom. sg.* 96:93

freolsian (2) to deliver, liberate; *ind. pret. 3 sg.* freolsode 58:15

freond *m.* friend; *nom. sg.* 70:69, 80:98; *acc. sg.* freond 72:114; *gen. sg.* freondes 42:116; *nom. pl.* frynd 132:312; *gen. pl.* freonda 70:51, 86:96

freondscipe *m.* friendship; *nom. sg.* 34:213; *acc. sg.* freondscipe 34:215

fretan (V) to devour; *ind. pret. 3 pl.* frǣton 132:317; *pp.* freten 68:31

froren (VII) to freeze; *ind. pres. 3 sg.* freoseþ 64:160

freoþian (2) (with acc or dat.) to intercede, to keep peace between; *ind. pres. 1 sg.* freoþige 94:74

fricca *m.* crier; *nom. sg.* 116:44; friccea 116:52 (EWS)

fringan (III) to ask, inquire; *ind. pret. 3 sg.* frægn 104:142, 106:209; *pl.* frugnon 118:122; frunan 82:13, 82:21 (EWS)

frōfer *f.* comfort, consolation; *acc. sg.* frōfre 92:11b, 140:99, 140:102; *gen. sg.* frōfre 92:11a, 92:20, 94:80, 138:75; *dat. sg.* frōfre 84:60, 92:4

from *prep.* (with *dat.*) from (see Appendix, p. 150)

from *adj.* firm, stout, bold; *m. nom. pl.* frome 94:83, 94:87

fruma *m.* beginning; *nom. sg.* 92:30, 114:30; *acc. sg.* fruman 4:61; *dat. sg.* fruman 46:20, 62:106, 62:108, 80:114, 114:19, 136:19

fruman *adv.* at first 42:90, 60:47, 108:241

frumliehtan (1) to dawn; *ind. pret. 3 sg.* frumlyhte 142:171

frymþ *f.* beginning; *acc. sg.* frymþe 92:26; *dat. sg.* frymþe 138:86

frymþliċ *adj.* primeval, primitive; *def. m. dat. sg.* frymþlican 74:27

fugel *m.* bird; *nom. pl.* fuglas 66:187

ful *adv.* full, very 38:2, 56:237, 92:13, 94:78, 126:169 >

ful *adj.* foul, rotten; *m. nom. sg.* 50:124; *superl. m. acc. sg.* fulostan 40:64

fulfremed *adj.* perfect; *m. nom. sg.* 50:104, 148:82 (EWS)

fulfremedliċ *adj.* perfect; *nt. dat. pl.* fulfremedlicum 52:167

fulfremedlīċe *adv.* perfectly 22:135, 124:94, 148:77

fulfremednes *f.* perfection; *gen. sg.* fulfremednesse 14:98

full *adj.* full; *m. nom sg.* 50:126, 76:41, 80:115, 100:41; *f. nom. sg.* full 2:12; ful 2:17, 2:18, 2:23, 100:82

fullian (2) to complete 24:160; *ind. pret. 3 sg.* fullade 146:29

fullīċe *adv.* fully 38:11, 134:329, 146:27, 152:138

fulostan (see ful *adj.*)

fultmian (2) (with *dat.*) to help, aid 146:29; *subj. pres. sg.* fultumie 46:29; *pres.p.* fultumiende 104:176

fultum *m.* help, assistance; *nom. sg.* 158:6; *acc. sg.* fultum 36:236, 90:220, 138:78, 140:98, 140:102; *gen. sg.* fultomes 84:75, 94:83, 138:75; *dat. sg.* fultume 20:51, 138:83, 144:193, 144:196

fulwiht *nt.* baptism; *acc. sg.* fulwiht 52:153; *gen sg.* fulwihtes 18:18; *dat. sg.* fulwihte 18:23, 18:24, 20:47, 22:119, 140:101, 146:15, 146:19, 148:62

fulwiht *f.* baptism; *gen. sg.* fulwihte 146:28

fulwihtere *m.* baptist; *nom. sg.* 118:102

fulwiht fæder *m.* baptismal father, baptizer; *nom. sg.* 140:125/6

fulwiht had *m.* baptismal vows; *acc. pl.* fulwiht hadas 76:39

fulwihtwer *m.* baptist; *gen. sg.* fulwihtweres 114:3/4

fundian (2) to endeavour; *ind. pres. pl.* fundiaþ 64:145, 64:175

furþon *adv.* even 124:110; furþum 82:27

feallan (VII) to cast down; *ind. pret. 3 sg.* fylde 152:176; *3 pl.* fyldon 152:181

fylġean (1) (with *dat.*) to follow 14:125, 150:133; fylgeon 68:5; *ind. pres. 1 sg.* fylge 20:66; *3 sg.* fylgeþ 72:109; *pl.* fylgað 16:150; fylgaþ 16:151; flygeað 16:151; fylgeaþ 30:105, 56:234, 80:125; fylge 50:132; *pret. 3 sg.* fylgde 153; fylgde 48:71; *subj. pres. pl.* fylgeon 54:214, 78:49; *infl. inf.* to fylgenne 142:138; *pres. p.* fylgende 10:21, 14:122, 108:269, 158:5, 99; fyliende 157; *def. f. dat. sg.* fylgendan 148:56 (A)

fyllan (1) to fill; *ind. pres. 3 sg.* fylleþ 88:180

fylnes *f.* fulness; *nom. sg.* 124:111

fynd (see feond)

fӯr *nt.* fire; *nom. sg.* 94:54; *acc. sg.* fӯr 86:126, 108:242; *gen. sg.* fӯres 140:94; *dat. sg.* fӯre 22:124, 40:85, 106:186, 122

fyrd *f.* army; *acc. sg.* fyrde 64:138

fyrdweorod *nt.* host, army; *gen. sg.*
fyrdweorodes 64:141

fȳren *adj.* fiery; *m. nom. sg.* 64:144; *nt.
nom. sg.* fȳren 122; *m. nom. pl.* fȳrene
138:89; *m. gen. pl.* fȳrenra 94:55; *f. dat. pl.*
fȳrenum 28:72; *def. f. acc. sg.* fȳrenan
28:72; *f. dat sg.* fȳrenan 28:67, 28:80; *m.
dat. pl.* fȳrenum 140:105

fyrhtu *f.* fear; *acc. sg.* fyrhto 86:129

fyrst *m.* interval, space of time; *dat. sg.*
fyrste 78:70

fyrstmearc *m.* respite; *dat. sg.*
fyrstmearce 106:221

fyrwetgeornnes *f.* curiosity; *dat. sg.*
fywetgeornnesse [→fyrwetgeornnesse] 48:51

fȳst *f.* fist; *dat. pl.* fȳstum 16:140

G

Gabriel *pers. n.* Gabriel; *nom. sg.* 2:11,
116:62; *dat. sg.* Gabriele 110:284

gǣlan (1) to hinder; *ind. pres. 3 sg.* gǣleþ
124:115; *imp. 2 pl.* gǣle 132:298

gǣst (see gān)

gǣstum (see gāst)

gǣþ (see gān)

gafol *nt.* tribute, tax; *nom. sg.* 26:37; *acc.
sg.* gafol 58:32, 128:211; *gen. sg.* gafoles
28:89, 74:14

galdorcræft *m.* magic trick; *acc. pl.*
galdorcræftas 42:104

galga *m.* gallows; *acc. sg.* galgan 68:3;
dat. sg. galgan 18:22

Galilea *prop. n.* Galilee; *dat. sg.*
Galileam 86:112; *dat. pl.* Galileum 48:75

Galileisc *adj.* Galilean; *def. m. nom. pl.*
Galileiscan 86:111

gān (anom.) to go 106:188, 124:92; *ind. pres.
2 sg.* gǣst 156; *3 sg.* gǣþ 72:109, 94:51,
116:68, 118:104; *pl.* gāþ 18:6; *imp. 2 sg.* gā
18:14, 20:64, 44:137; *2 sg.* gāþ 52:169

gang *m.* way; *acc. sg.* gang 76:32

gangan [gongon] (VII) to go 86:102, 118:134,
130:243, 132:294, 150:95, 150:116, 40, 42, 127;
ind. pres. 1 sg. gange 98:27; *3 sg.* gangeþ
34:199; *pret. 3 sg.* geong [geondweardode →
geong weardode] 110:285; *subj. pres. sg.* gange
149; *imp. 2 sg.* gang 108:230, 124:129,
158:27, 158:35, 162:101, 159; *3 sg.* gange
116:54, 142:146; *pl.* gangaþ 48:61, 110:298;
gangað 32; *pres. p.* gangende 98:26,
102:118, 102:120, 104:153, 104:175, 104:177,
110:299

Garganus *prop. n.* Garganus; *nom. sg.*
136:21, 138:86; *dat. sg.* Garganus 136:15

gāst [halga] *m.* ghost, spirit; *nom. sg.* 4:47,
4:62 [halga], 4:72 [halga], 20:58, 74:7 [halga],
78:74, 92:18 [halga], 92:20 [halig], 92:22 [halga],
110:310; *acc. sg.* gāst 34:203, 58:26 [halges],
84:47 [halgan gaste → halgan gast], 132:306, 98,
144; *gen. sg.* gāstes 10:30, 80:107[haliges] ,
84:46 [halges], 92:25[halga] , 92:36 [halgan], 92:37
[halgan], 102:104 [halgan], 114:10 [haliges],
114:36 [halgan], 114:37 [halgan], 116:71[halgan];
dat. sg. gāste 6:114 [halgan], 92:38 [halgan],
102:89, 116:66 [halgum], 116:68 [halgum],
116:73[halgum], 156:241; *inst. sg.* 100:51
[halige]; *nom. pl.* gastas 112:332; *acc. pl.*
gāstas 62:132, 140:93; *gen. pl.* gāsta 64:179,
74:10; *dat. pl.* gāstum 16:169, 58:17, 64:175,
144:194; gǣstum 144:191

gāstliċ *adj.* spiritual; *m. nom. sg.* 148:84
[gāstic → gāstlic]; *m. acc. sg.* gāstlicne 38:6,
38:21; *nt. gen. sg.* gāstlices 18:32; *m. inst.
sg.* gāstlice 38:33; *nt. acc. pl.* gāstlico
102:101; *nt. gen. pl.* gāstlicra 24:151; *nt.
dat. pl.* gāstlicum 38:36, 50:114; *def. f. acc.
sg.* gāstlican 38:30; *nt. acc. sg.* gāstlice
14:99, 80:106; *m. dat. pl.* gāstlicum 14:97;
nt. dat. pl. gāstlicum 38:34; *nt. inst. pl.*
gāstlicum 94:72

gāstliþnes *f.* hospitality; *nom. sg.* 114:35

gātu (see geat)

ġe *conj.* and / both ... and (see Appendix, p.
149)

ġē *pron.* you (see Appendix, p. 145)

ġeācsige (see geāxiað)

ġeǽttrian (2) to poison; *pp. m. dat. sg.*
geǽttredum 136:38

ġeāgnian (2) to own, possess 74:5

ġeāhsode (see ġeāxiað)

ġeald (see ġyldan)

ġean [īsigean] *prep.* over against, opposite
144:202

ġeandettan (1) to confess 28:60; *ind. pres.*
3 pl. geandettiaþ 134:329

ġēar *nt.* year; *acc. sg.* gēar 132:322; *dat.*
sg. gēare 22:132; *inst. sg.* gēare 82:38,
146:41; *nom. pl.* gēar 62:94, 128:225; *acc.*
pl. gēar 148:73; *gen. pl.* gēara 150:104; *dat.*
pl. gēarum 68:30

ġēar *m.* year; *acc. sg.* gēar 22:136

ġēara *adv.* long ago 4:74, 4:79, 22:130,
60:61, 64:167, 72:93 (A)

ġēare *adv.* readily, surely, certainly 8:148,
22:132, 56:237, 90:207, 122:74, 144:188; *comp.*
gēaror 8:147, 90:192

ġēarelīċe *adv.* readily 76:11

ġeārn (see ġeiernan)

ġearo *adj.* ready, prepared; *m. nom. sg.*
26:15, 149; *m. nom. pl.* gearwe 70:89,
86:135; *m. acc. pl.* gearwe 56:237

ġearian (2) honoured, endowed; *pp.*
gearode 74:15

ġearwian (2) to prepare; *ind. pres. 3 sg.*
ġearwaþ 4:81, 20:59; *pres. pl.* gearwiaþ
50:100, 52:156; *pret. 3 sg.* gearwode 46:24,
133

ġearwe (see gearo)

ġeat *nt.* gate; *acc. pl.* geatu 58:28; gātu 60

ġeatwa *f.* provisions; *dat. pl.* geatwum
152:157

ġeaxian (2) to learn; *ind. pres. pl.* geaxiað
76:13, 76:18; geaxiaþ 76:19; *pret. 3 sg.*
geahsode 136:31; *subj. pres. 3 sg.* geacsige
28:62

ġebǽran (1) to behave; *ind. pret. pl.*
gebǽrdon 154:205

ġebǽru *nt.* proceeding; *acc. pl.* gebǽro
138:82

ġeband (see ġebindan)

ġebēagian (2) to crown; *pp.* gebēagod
130:246; *pl.* gebēgde 140:107

ġebed *nt.* prayer; *nom. sg.* 102:120; *acc.*
sg. gebed 150:117; *gen. sg.* gebedes 12:88;
dat. sg. gebede 12:63, 98:40, 102:119,
104:170, 150:97, 150:118, 29; *acc. pl.* gebedo
134:328; gebedu 152:147; *gen. pl.* gebeda
142:149; *dat. pl.* gebedum 16:156, 24:174,
30:113, 42:101, 54:222, 92:30

ġebedhūs *nt.* house of prayer; *nom. sg.*
48:78

ġebedrǽden *nt.* prayer; *acc. sg.* gebed-
rǽdene 38:27; *dat. sg.* gebedrǽdenne
30:106

ġebedstōw *m.* place of prayer; *dat. sg.*
gebedstōwe 92:38

ġebēgde (see gebēagian)

ġebelgan (III) to be angry; *pp.* gebolgen
46:37, 52:138

ġebendan (1) to bend; *ind. pret. 3 sg.*
gebende 136:38

ġebēorscip *m.* feast; *dat. sg.* gebēorscipe
38:28

ġebeorþor *nt.* birth, childbearing; *acc. sg.*
gebeorþor 74:13

ġebēotian (2) to threaten; *pp.* gebēotod
58:17

ġeberan (IV) to bear; *ind. pres 3 sg.*
gebereþ 116:64; *pret. 3 sg.* gebær 106:187;
pp. geboren 16:163, 114:18, 118:94

ġebētan (1) make amends for, atone for
44:142, 62:125, 78:44; gebēton 42:100; *pres.*
pl. gebētaþ 40:47; *subj. pres. sg.* gebēte
12:55

ġebīdan (I) (with *gen.*) to await, expect
146:36; *ind. pret. 3 sg.* gebād (with *acc.*)
120:29

ġebiddan (V) (with *refl. pron. in acc.*) to pray
12:85, 98:36; *ind. pres. 1 sg.* gebæd 132:294;
3 sg. gebæd 102:119, 130:240, 150:96, 162:95,
16, 111, 136, 143; *pl.* gebǽdon 138:62, 29;
subj. pret. pl. gebǽdon 100:59; *imp. 2 sg.*
gebide 98:38; *pres. p.* gebiddende 98:3,
158:4, 103; *pp.* gebǽded 58:22

ġebindan (III) to bind 132:281; *ind. pret. 3 sg.* geband 58:27, 118:96; *pl.* gebunden 72; *subj. pret. sg.* gebunde 32:148; *pp. m. nom. sg.* gebunden 32:148; *m. acc. sg.* gebundenne 60:69, 60:72; *f. acc. sg.* gebundene 54:204; *f. nom. pl.* gebundne 144:203; *def. m. acc. pl.* gebundenan 53

ġeblandan (VII) to blend; *pp.* geblanden 7

ġebletsian (2) to bless; *pp.* gebletsod 2:31, 54:219, 82:20, 100:82; gebletsad 2:32, 48:72, 54:228, 62:104; *pl.* gebletsode 32:175

ġeblinnan (III) to ceases; *ind. pres. 3 sg.* geblinneþ 12:54

ġeblissian (2) to rejoice; *ind. pres. 3 sg.* geblissaþ 24:171; *subj. pres. pl.* geblissian 60:73; *pp.* geblissad 160:70

ġeblōwan (VII) full-blown; *pp.* geblōwen 106

ġebod *nt.* commandment; *nom. sg.* 160:57; *dat. sg.* gebode 75

ġebolgen (see ġebelgan)

ġeboren (see ġeberan)

ġebrecan (V) to break 152:156; *ind. pret 3 sg.* gebræc 150:136; *pl.* gebrǣcan 152:161; *subj. pret. 3 sg.* gebræce 152:155

ġebreġdan (III) to draw; *ind. pret. 3 sg.* gebrægd 152:169; *pp. def. m. acc. pl.* gebregdnan 70:50

ġebringan (1) may bring; *subj. pres. sg.* gebringe 142:139; *pret. pl.* gebrōhton 36:235

ġebrosnian (2) to decay; *pp. m. nom. pl.* gebrosnode 80:101

ġebrosnodliċ *adj.* corruptible; *m. nom. sg.* 80:112

ġebrosnung *f.* decay, defilement; *dat. sg.* gebrosnunga 2:9/10

ġebrōðor *m.* brethren; *nom. pl.* gebrōðor 100:54; gebrōþor 160:52; *gen. pl.* gebrōðra 98:36

ġebūan (1) to inhabit; *pp.* gebuen 86:92; *f. nom. sg.* gebūennes 114:36

ġebūgan (II) to submit, obey; *subj. pres. pl.* gebūgon 26:11

ġebunde, ġebunden (see ġebindan)

ġebundne (see ġebindan)

ġebyċgan (1) to buy; *subj. pret. pl.* gebohtan 30:95

ġebyrd *f.* birth, nativity, birthday, lineage; *nom. sg.* 114:3, 116:50, 118:107; *acc. sg.* gebyrd 114:6, 116:65, 118:99; *gen. sg.* gebyrde 116:86, 118:90, 118:97; *dat. sg.* gebyrde 114:19, 116:89; *inst. sg.* gebyrde 116:49; *gen. pl.* gebyrda 146:6; *dat. pl.* gebyrdum 114:18, 118:101

ġebyrd *nt.* birth; *dat. sg.* gebyrde 118:93

ġebyrdo *f.* manner; *dat. pl.* gebyrdum 124:118

ġebyrian (1) to be fitting; *ind. pres. 3 sg.* gebyreð 78:59

ġeċeas (see ġeċeosan)

ġeċēosan (II) to choose 14:132; *ind. pret. 1 sg.* gecēas 138:58; *2 sg.* gecure 110:278; *3 sg.* gecēas 6:118, 46:32, 160:53; *pp.* gecoren 8:142, 130:239, 146:4; *m. acc. pl.* gecorene 60:44; *f. dat. pl.* gecorenum 66:193; *def. nt. dat. sg.* gecorenan 74:8; *m. nom. pl.* gecorenan 60:73; *nt. nom. pl.* gecorenan 72:93; *m. acc. pl.* gecorenum 58:29, 86:123; *m. dat. pl.* gecorenum 108:263; *comp. m. nom. sg.* gecorenra 118:107

ġeċiegan (1) to call; *ind. pres. 1 sg.* gecege 126:166; *pret. 3 sg.* gecegde 128:227; *pp.* geceged 48:79, 102:106; *pl.* gecegede 30:110

ġeċignes *f.* calling, entreaty; *dat. sg.* geċignesse 102:91

ġecirdon (see gecyrran)

ġeclǣnsian (2) purify 12:88, 22:128; *ind. pres. 3 sg.* geclǣnsaþ 24:156; *subj. pres. pl.* geclǣnsian 24:175; *pp.* geclǣnsod 114:34

ġecnāwan (VII) to recognise, perceive 80:126; *pp.* gecnāwen 48:89

ġecompian (2) to fight 18:39

ġecrīstnian (2) to christen; *subj. pret. sg.* gecrīstnode 146:14; *pp.* gecrīstnod 146:28, 148:62, 148:85

ġecunnian (2) to try 20:53

ġecure (see geċēosan)

ġecwēme *adj.* pleasing; *nt. nom. sg.*
24:163; *nt. acc. sg.* gecwēme 24:158; *comp.*
f. nom. pl. gecwēmran 28:64

ġecwēmnes *f.* satisfaction; *dat. sg.*
gecwēmnesse 46:27

ġecweþan (V) to say, speak 28:73; *ind.*
pret. 1 sg. gecwæþ 124:134; *3 sg.* gecwæþ
114:17, 132:306; gecwæð 148:64; *pp.*
gecwēden 4:85, 6:115, 20:50, 48:52, 48:65,
66:203, 92:39, 94:44

ġecynd *nt.* nature, kind; *nom. sg.* 6:110,
12:71, 86:97, 90:185; *acc. sg.* gecynde
14:132; gecynd 22:113, 24:162, 86:103, 88:138,
88:175, 90:202; *gen. sg.* gecynde 18:28,
116:50; gecynd 20:80; *dat. sg.* gecynde
12:48, 12:76, 40:58, 80:98, 86:93; gecynd
84:89; *gen. pl.* gecynda 22:111

ġecyndeliċ *adj.* natural; *def. f. nom. sg.*
gecyndelice 4:66

ġecyrran [ġecierran] (1) to turn 10:34, 54:184,
68:23, 70:65, 76:7; gecyrron 30:93, 30:98; *ind.*
pres. 1 sg. gecyrre 70:84; *3 sg.* gecyrreþ
40:60; *pl.* gecyrraþ 44:151, 90:204, 90:206;
pret. 3 sg. gecyrde 70:85, 152:180; *pl.*
gecyrdon 120:36, 120:38; gecirdon 152:163;
subj. pres. sg. gecyrre 68:22, 76:4; *pl.*
ġecyrran 76:7; *pret. sg.* gecyrde 30:95; *imp.*
2 sg. gecyr 62:92, 80:102; *1 pl.* gecyrron
70:83; *2 pl.* gecyrraþ 70:84; *pp.* gecyrred
40:49, 40:65, 58:42, 94:43, 132:287, 136:41,
146:15; *pl.* gecyrrede 54:221

ġecȳþan (1) to make known, manifest
18:42, 22:99, 110:279, 116:82, 130:236; gecȳ
þon 26:11; *ind. pres. 1 sg.* gecȳþe 126:140,
138:58, 162:103; *pret. 3 sg.* gecȳþde 52:143,
52:147, 58:17, 80:130, 86:120, 136:5, 136:19;
gecȳðde 72:91, 74:25; *subj. pres. sg.* gecȳ
þe 126:162, 142:147; *pret. 3 sg.* gecȳþde
138:49; *imp. 2 sg.* gecȳþ 60:72; gecȳð 62;
gecȳþe 100:56, 160:56; *pp.* gecȳþed 22:110,
22:116, 88:178, 140:98, 154:196; gecȳðed
138:60, 144:185, 148:76; *def. f. dat. sg.*
gecȳþdan 92:34

ġecȳþnes *f.* testimony; *nom. sg.* 130:242;
dat. sg. gecȳþnesse 122:52

ġedælan (1) to separate divide, deal,
distribute 34:198; gedælon 68:11; *ind. pres.*
3 sg. gedæleþ 14:105, 86:134; *subj. pres. pl.*
gedælan 26:8; *pret. 3 sg.* gedælde 52:139;
pp. gedæled 46:40; *pl.* gedælde 78:74

ġedafen *adj.* fit, becoming; *m. nom. sg.*
80:122

ġedafenian (1) to be fitting; *ind. pres. 3*
sg. gedafenaþ 8:146, 38:2, 104:168, 104:170;
gedafenað 156:234; *pret 3 sg.* gedafenode
46:13, 52:161, 54:227

ġedafenliċ *adj.* fitting, meet; *nt. dat. pl.*
gedafenlicum 26:25

ġedāl *nt.* separation; *nom. sg.* 44:161,
94:79

ġedēf *adj.* quiet, fit worthy; *m. nom. pl.*
gedēfe 114:8, 114:23; *m. gen. pl.* gedēfra
150

ġedēfelīċe *adv.* quietly, mildly, 150:129

ġedēgan [ġedīegan] (1) to escape 28:57

ġedēman (1) to judge; *pp.* gedēmed 42:109

ġedōn (anom.) to do, make 38:41, 82:41,
126:168, 126:178, 146:35, 148:44, 156:233,
158:22 [dōn → gedōn], 22; *ind. pres. 3 sg.*
gedēþ 24:165, 70:69; *pret. 1 sg.* gedyde
60:78; *3 sg.* gedyde 6:103, 58:21, 106:209,
126:146, 146:38, 40; *pl.* gedydon 48:68,
54:186, 62:126, 130:273, 132:309, 140:124;
subj. pres. sg. gedō 98:37; *pl.* gedōn
24:137; *pret. sg.* gedyde 68:17; *imp. 2 sg.*
gedō 110:309, 110:312; *2 pl.* gedōþ 26:15; *pp.*
gedōn 22:136, 44:150, 46:39, 48:49, 50:110,
70:71, 122:80, 124:132, 138:50, 138:55; *m. acc.*
pl. gedōne 20:71

ġedrēfan (1) to trouble; *ind. pret. 3 sg.*
gedrēfde 58:28; *pp.* gedrēfed 12:63, 94:73,
100:71; gedrēfede 10:28

ġedrēosan (II) to perish; *pp.* gedrorene
80:101

ġedrofenliċ *adj.* troublesome; *f. nom. sg.*
80:112

ġedrync *m.* drinking; *dat. sg.* gedrynce 68:41

ġedwīnan (VI) to wasted away; *ind. pret. 3 sg.* gedwān 38:22

ġedwola *m.* deceiver; *acc. sg.* gedwolan 4:55; *acc. pl.* gedwolan 42:104; *dat. pl.* gedwolum 70:88

ġedwolcræft *m.* deceitful arts, deceptions; *acc. pl.* gedwolcræftas 42:126; *dat. pl.* gedwolcræftum 42:106

ġedwolian (2) to err; *ind. pret. 1 sg.* gedwolede 60:78

ġeēacnian (2) become pregnant; *pp.* geēacnod 2:9, 2:10, 2:13, 6:113, 40:82

ġeēacnung *f.* conception; *acc. sg.* geēacnunge 100:87

ġeearnian (2) to earn, merit 10:42, 14:119 [geernian → geearnian], 16:161, 24:138, 44:152, 50:114, 56:238, 70:68, 78:50; *ind. pres. 3 sg.* geearnaþ 66:203; *pl.* geearniað 144:193; *pret. 2 sg.* geearnodest 44:138/9; *3 sg.* ġeearnode 80:106; *subj. pres. sg.* geearnige 70:75, 70:76; *pl.* geearnian 36:238; *imp. 2 sg.* geearna 80:103; *1 pl.* geearnian 70:82; *infl. inf.* to geearnienne 116:69

ġeearnung *f.* merit; *nom. sg.* 132:315; *dat. pl.* geearnungum 14:110

ġeēaþmēdan (1) humble; *ind. pres. 3 sg.* ġeēaþmēdeþ 2:26; *pret. 3 sg.* geēaþmēdde 6:129, 14:130, 46:2; geeaðmēdde 136:9, 148:67, 160:89; *subj. pret. pl.* geēaþmēdon 30:130

ġeēcian [geēacian] (2) to increase; *ind. pres. 3 sg.* geēceþ 68:2; *subj. pres. sg.* geēce 24:158; *pp.* geēced 86:91 (A)

ġeednēowian (2) to renew; *pp.* geednēowod 6:110; *pl.* geednēowode 106:227/8

ġeendian (2) to end; *ind. pres. 3 sg.* geendað 14:95; geendaþ 24:147, 40:86; *pret. 3 sg.* geendode 58:16; *infl. inf.* to geendenne 56:236; *pp.* geendod 58:33, 78:86, 130:275

ġeendebyrdan (1) to arrange; *pp.* geendebyrd 20:72; geendebyrded 58:34

ġeendung *f.* ending, finish; *acc. sg.* ġeendunga 110:302; *dat. sg.* geendunge 44:160

ġefæstan (1) to fast; *pp.* gefæst 142:141

ġefæstnian (2) to fasten 58:24; *pp.* ġefæstnod 106:203, 120:27, 132:288

ġefagian (2) embroidered; *pp.* gefagod 80:97

ġefaran (VI) to journey, travel, die 158:30, 162:99; *ind. pres. 3 sg.* gefærþ 92:13

ġefēa *m.* joy; *nom. sg.* 16:168, 44:160, 70:82, [gelea→ gefēa] 72:111, 86:91, 86:106, 116:65; *acc. sg.* gefēan 4:82, 16:166, 34:223, 36:238, 44:137, 84:85, 84:86, 110:305, 128:208, 144:209, 154:192; *dat. sg.* gefēan 40:50, 58:42, 60:70, 70:81, 86:96, 140:117, 142:166, 168; *inst. sg.* gefēan 98:12, 164; *nom. pl.* gefēan 34:204

ġefeallan (VII) to fall 38:42; *ind. pret. 3 sg.* gefealleþ 126:161; *pl.* gefeallaþ 64:157; *pret. 3 sg.* gefeol 130:263; *pp.* gefeallen 64:146

ġefēċċean [gefētian] (2) to fetch 130:236 (A)

ġefēlan (1) to feel; *ind. pret. 3 sg.* gefēlde 150:99

ġefeoht *nt.* fight; *gen. sg.* gefeohtes 138:86; *dat. sg.* gefeohte 140:114; *nom. pl.* gefeoht 76:15

ġefeohtan (III) to fight 20:68, 152:146

ġefeol (see gefeallan)

ġefēon (V) to rejoice 8:153, 56:239, 118:98, 118:99; *ind. pres. pl.* gefēoþ 116:65; *imp. 2 pl.* gefēoþ 132:299, 132:310; *pres. p.* gefēonde 2:21, 52:137, 98:17, 100:41, 138:60, 138:83, 142:148, 150:101, 154:230, 158:42, 164 (EWS)

ġefeormian (2) to cleanse 128:184

ġefēr *m.* companion; *dat. pl.* gefērum 146:25

ġefēran (1) to travel, journey 158:31, 158:32; *pp.* gefēred 140:109

ġefērrǣden *f.* fellowship, company; *dat. sg.* gefērrǣdenne 146:9; gefērrǣdenne 146:18 (EWS) ġefērscipe *m.* companionship, company; *acc. sg.* gefērscipe 58:28, 136:27; *gen. sg.* gefērscipes 136:11/2

ġeflēogan (II) to put to flight; *pp.* geflēmed 58:40

ġeflit *nt.* strife, contention; *nom. sg.* 16:168; *nom. pl.* geflitu 128:228

ġeflitan (VI) to strive; *ind. pret. pl.* gefliton 120:26

ġeflȳman (1) to put to flight 152:159

ġefōg *m.* joint; *dat. pl.* gefōgum 70:57

ġefrætwan (1) to adorn, ornament; *ind. pres. pl.* gefrætwiað 68:29; *pret. pl.* gefrætwodan 66:190; *pp.* gefrætwod 4:68, 4:70, 34:202, 88:162; *pl.* gefrætwode 66:191

ġefremman (1) perform, commit, accomplish 94:84; *ind. pret 2 sg.* gefremedeste 130:271; *3 sg.* gefremede 76:4, 78:82; *pp.* gefremed 56:231

ġefrēolsian (2) to liberate, set free 18:41/2, 46:4; gefrēolsian [gefrēclsian → gefrēolsian] 20:54; *ind. pres. 1 sg.* gefrēolsige 158:15; *3 sg.* gefrēolseð 82; *pret. 3 sg.* gefrēolsode 58:16; *subj pres. sg.* gefrēolsige 90; *pp.* gefrēolsode 20:82; gefrēoþode 74:14

ġefullian (2) to fulfil, baptize 132:300; *ind. pret. 3 sg.* gefullode 148:72, 149

ġefultmian [gefultumian] (2) to help, aid 152:159; *subj. pres. sg.* gefultmige 70:60; *imp. 3 sg.* gefultumige 112:336

ġefulwian (2) to baptize; *ind. pret. 3 sg.* gefulwade 150:104; *pp.* gefulwad 146:27

ġefyllan (1) to fulfil, accomplish 14:121, 24:150, 108:267, 110:294; *ind. pres. 3 sg.* gefylleþ 2:22, 14:129, 26:26; gefylþ 12:77; *pret 2 sg.* gefyldest 60:86, 62:98; *3 sg.* gefylde 6:109, 10:29, 58:20, 92:40a, 92:40b; *subj. pres. sg.* gefylle 24:167, 160:63; *pl.* gefyllon 26:16, 160:50; gefyllan 68:29; *pp.* gefylled 2:19, 6:114, 8:151, 16:169, 46:35, 48:52, 92:40; *pl.* gefyllede 108:243, 130:253, 142:165; gefylde 10:5, 68:37, 86:93, 90:184, 94:49

ġefyllan (1) to cast down 152:151, 152:160; *ind. pret 3 sg.* gefylde 60:68, 150:136, 152:137; *pl.* gefyldan 152:161; *subj. pret. sg.* gefylde 152:155

ġefylnes *f.* fulfilment, completion; *acc. sg.* gefylnesse 94:73; *dat. sg.* gefylnesse 18:32; gefyllnesse 56:231

ġefyrenian (2) to sin; *ind. pret. 1 sg.* gefyrenode 162:97; *2 sg.* gefyrenodest 162:98; *pp.* gefyrenode 144:208

ġefyrhtan (1) to terrify; *pp.* gefyrhte 152:162

ġefyrhto *f.* doubt; *dat. pl.* gefyrhtum [gewyrhtum → gefyrhtum]116:48

ġegaderung *f.* gathering; *dat. sg.* gegaderunge [gegaderung → gegaderunge] 116:86

ġegān (anom.) to obtain; *ind. pret. 3 sg.* geēode 84:73

ġegangan [ġegongan] (VII) to go, happen 70:69; *subj. pres. sg.* gegange 28:80; *pp.* gegangen 142:177

ġeġearnian (2) to earn; *subj. pres. pl.* gegearnian 24:144

ġeġearwian [geġearcian] (2) to prepare 54:214; *ind. pres. pl.* gegearwiaþ 128:202; *pret. 2 sg.* gegearwodest 160:67; *3 sg.* gegearwode 112:324; *pp.* gegearwod 102:107, 118:113, 132:311; *pl.* gegearwode 134:327 (A)

ġegerelan (see ġegyrela)

ġegrīpan (VI) to seize, grasp 106:201; *ind. pret. 3 sg.* gegrāp [gegrāþ → gegrāp] 116:87; *pl.* gegrīpan 100:62; gegrīpon 106:211

ġegyrean (1) to clothe; *ind. pret. 3 sg.* gegyrede 62:111, 70:86, 98:17, 152:153; *2 sg.* gegyredest 148:63; *pl.* gegyredon 140:171; *imp. 2 sg.* gegyre 24:161; *pp.* gegyred 98:16; *m. acc. sg.* gegyredne 148:57; *pl.* ġegyrede 152:157

ġegyrela *m.* garment, clothing; *acc. sg.* gegyrelan 102:96, 148:47, 148:52; *dat. sg.* gegyrelan 148:67; gegerelan 118:115; *nom. pl.* gegyrelan 78:79

ġegyrwan [ġegierwan] (1) furnished; *pp.*
gegyrwed 118:115 (A)
ġehadian (2) to ordain; *pp.* gehadode 28:53
ġehæftnan (2) to hold captive; *pp.*
gehæftnede 60:58, 62:106
ġehæftworld *f.* captive world; *nom. sg.*
4:77
ġehǣlan (1) to heal; *ind. pret. 2 sg.*
gehǣldest 60:85; *3 sg.* ġehǣlde 48:80; *pp.*
gehǣled 2:33, 14:93, 106:217; *m. acc. sg.*
gehǣldedne 10:20; *pl.* gehǣlde 56:234,
74:13, 88:166, 142:182, 144:184, 144:189
ġehālgian (2) to consecrate; *ind. pret. 1 sg.*
gehālgode 108:273, 142:143; *pl.* gehālgodan
140:124; *subj. pret. pl.* gehālgodan
140:123; *pp.* gehālgod 136:4; *pl.* gehālgode
42:98, 114:9, 114:10; *def. f. acc. sg.*
gehālgodan 78:55
ġehāt *nt.* promise; *nom. sg.* 94:76; *acc. sg.*
gehāt 100:78, 102:91; *dat. pl.* gehātum
122:86
ġehātan (VII) to promise; *ind. pret. 1 sg.*
gehēht 128:186; gehēt 102:134, 108:269; *2 sg.*
gehēte 58:39, 102:91; *3 sg.* gehēht 120:10,
138:80, 138:82; gehēt 10:29, 82:17, 84:60, 92:9,
126:154; *pp.* gehāten 78:58, 92:4
ġehealdan (VII) to hold, keep 30:127; *ind.*
pret. 3 sg. geheold 146:20, 148:45, 150:130;
subj. pres. sg. gehealde 78:59, 94:74; *pl.*
gehealdan 76:39; *pret. pl.* geheoldan 30:94;
pp. gehealden 34:226, 104:150; *pl.*
gehealdene 32:143, 128:207, 132:322
ġehēapian (2) heaped; *pp.* gehēapod 122:65
ġehelpan (III) (with *acc.* or *dat.*) to help; *ind.*
pres. 2 sg. gehelpest 4:80
ġehēowian [ġehīwian] (2) to form, colour,
shape; *ind. pret. 3 sg.* gehēowede 20:67; *pl.*
gehēowodan 60:79
ġehēowung *f.* fashioning; *acc. sg.*
gehēowunga 62:95
ġehēran [ġehīeran] (1) to hear 78:83; *ind.*
pret. pl. gehēradon; gehērdan 100:61, 92;
imp. 2 pl. gehērað 10:1; gehēraþ 26:1; *infl.*
inf. to gehērenne 28:47

ġeherean [ġeherġean] (1) to praise; *pp.*
gehered 48:76, 48:89, 64:148, 102:107;
gehiered 116:58
ġehlēatan [ġehlēotan] (VII) to allot; *ind. pret.*
3 sg. gehlēat 3
ġehnīgan (I) to humble; *ind. pret. 3 sg.*
gehnǣde 56 (A) (M)
ġehrīnan (1) to touch 142:160
ġehweþer ge … ge (both … and) 136:4
ġehwylċ [hwilċ / hwelċ] *inter. pron., adj. &*
pronom. which, each, every; *m., f. & nt.*
(see Appendix, p. 148)
ġehwyrfan [ġehwierfan] (1) to turn; *ind. pres.*
2 sg. gehwyrfest 163; *3 sg.* gehwyrfþ
116:67; *subj. pres. sg.* ġehwyrfe 104:136;
pp. gehwyrfed 108:268; *pl.* gehwyrfede
34:206; gehwyrfde 160:45; gehwerfede 130
ġehȳdan (1) hide; *subj. pres. sg.* gehȳde
64:166; *imp. 2 pl.* gehȳdað 64:171
ġehygd *f.* heed, care; *dat. pl.* gehygdum
128:211
ġehyhtan (1) to trust 78:55; *ind. pret. 3 pl.*
gehyhtton 72:93; gehyhton 112:323; *subj.*
pres. pl. gehyhton 60:73
ġehȳnan (1) to humble; *ind. pret. 3 sg.*
gehȳnde 58:27; *pp. m. acc. pl.* gehȳnde
60:54
ġehȳran (1) to hear 4:44, 38:27, 46:26, 58:2;
gehīeran 152; *ind. pres. 1 sg.* gehīere 57; *2*
sg. gehȳrstu 58:37, 126:169, 126:170; *3 sg.*
gehȳreþ 12:78; gehȳreð 76:9; *pl.* gehȳraþ
16:160, 38:19, 38:39; gehȳrað 16:137; *pret. 2*
sg. gehȳrdest 4:72, 23; *3 sg.* gehȳrde 10:12,
12:69, 98:9, 56; gehīerde 69; *pl.* gehyrdon
2:29, 10:23, 10:25, 18:36; gehȳrdan 52:165;
subj. pres. gehȳre 38:4; *pl.* gehȳron
38:2, 78:62; gehȳran 30:129; *imp. 2 sg.*
gehȳr 62:93, 122:60; *pl.* gehȳre 158:34; gehīere
11; *1 pl.* gehȳron 2:20, 14:111; gehȳran
12:64, 12:89; *2 pl.* gehȳraþ 98:1, 98:25,
100:58; *infl. inf.* to gehȳrenne 20:87, 38:15;

pp. gehȳred 2:32, 20:47, 60:46, 60:55, 60:67; *pl.* gehȳrede 138:80

ġehȳran (1) to oppress; *ind. pret. 3 sg.* geh ȳrde 80:91

ġehȳrnes *f.* hearing; *nom. sg.* 38:23

ġehȳrsum *adj.* obedient; *m. nom. pl.* geh ȳrsume 114:28

ġeiernan (III) to run; *ind. pret. 3 sg.* ġeārn 152:167

ġelācnian (2) to heal 124:91

ġelǣdan (1) to lead, bring 86:123, 162:105; gelǣdon 10:17, 68:9; *ind. pres. 3 sg.* gelǣdeþ 16:154, 24:156, 24:176, 54:208; *subj. pres. sg.* gelǣde 16:166, 144:209; *pret. sg.* gelǣdde 90:202; *imp. 2 pl.* gelǣdaþ 48:62, 160:47; *pp.* gelǣded 28:87, 68:12, 120:30; *pl.* gelǣdde 70:63, 94:56, 132:282

ġelǣran (1) to learn; *ind. pret. 3 sg.* gelǣrde 148:77; *pp.* gelǣred 120:40; *pl.* gelǣrede 12:66

ġelǣstan (1) to perform 36:240; *ind. pres. 3 sg.* gelǣsteþ 38:11; *subj. pres. sg.* gelǣste 78:59; *pp.* gelǣsted 74:6

ġelamp (see ġelimpan)

ġelaþian (2) to invite 18:41; *ind. pret. 3 sg.* gelaþode 70:89

ġelēafa *m.* belief, faith; *nom. sg.* 2:28, 10:20, 14:98, 54:229; *acc. sg.* gelēafan 10:32, 14:121, 38:12, 52:153, 159; *dat. sg.* gelēafan 44:138, 52:166, 74:24

ġelēaffull *adj.* believing, faithful; *nt. nom. sg.* 62:117; *m. nom. pl.* gelēaffulle 8:152, 2:121, 50:100, 54:221; *m. dat. pl.* gelēaffullum 2:39, 6:109, 20:60, 20:87, 22:116, 50:135, 52:151, 76:35; *def. nt. acc. sg.* gelēaffulle 54:205/6

ġelēaffulnes *f.* belief; *acc. sg.* gelēaffulnesse 78:53

ġelēafsum *adj.* believing; *def. nom. pl.* gelēafsuman 82:12/3

ġelēanian (2) reward; *ind. pres. 3 sg.* gelēanað 70:73

ġelēfan (1) to believe 78:57; *ind. pres. pl.* gelēfaþ 30:133

ġelēofan [ġelīefan] (1) to believe 12; *ind. pres. pl.* gelēofað 128; *subj. pres. pl.* gelēofon 142; gelēofan 159; gelīefon 145

ġelīċ *adj.* like; *m. nom. sg.* 12:44, 14:110, 32:141, 62:90, 116:43

ġelīċe *adv.* like, similarly 10:29, 28:80, 40:58, 42:128, 82:39, 118:112, 140:94; *superl.* gelicost 140:111, 152:145

ġelīchomian (2) to incarnate; *pp.* gelīchomod 22:95

ġelīcnes *f.* likeness; *acc. sg.* gelīcnesse 46:14

ġelīcian (2) to please; *ind. pret. 3 sg.* gelīcode 20:48

ġelīefon (see ġelēofan)

ġelīffæstan (1) to quicken, bring to life; *pp.* gelīffæsted 114:40

ġelimpan (III) to happen 44; *ind. pres. 3 sg.* gelimpeþ 38:29, 62:127, 62:135, 62:136, 86:133, 90:190, 92:13; gelimpeð 68:29; *pl.* gelimpaþ [gelimpeð → gelimpaþ] 138:59; *pret. 3 sg.* gelamp 20:65, 52:182, 78:85, 122:49, 122:83, 136:27, 146:39, 148:83, 148:85, 148:87, 150:109; gelomp 58:33; *subj. pres. sg.* gelimpe 26:31; *pret. sg.* gelumpe 54:188

ġelimpliċ *adj.* meet, fitting; *nt. nom. sg.* gelimplic 92:11, 92:42; *f. dat. sg.* gelimplicre 142:169

ġelimplīċe *adv.* fittingly 12:84

ġelōme *adv.* frequently 30:109, 76:16, 144:184

ġelōmliċ *adj.* frequent; *nt. nom. sg.* gelōmlic 152:178; *def. f. dat. sg.* gelōmlican 94:72

ġelōmlīċe *adv.* frequently 68:28, 142:158

ġelōmlician (2) to become frequent 76:19

ġelȳfan [ġelīefan] (1) to believe 14:119, 38:7, 42:118, 56:235, 78:56, 124:106; *ind. pres. 1 sg.* gelȳfe 142:161; *2 sg.* gelȳfest 106:213, 106:214; *3 sg.* gelȳfeþ 12:53, 14:102, 108:232, 108:235, 108:247; gelȳfþ 108:250; *pl.* gelȳfaþ 26:31, 40:89, 102:115. 128:193; gelȳfað 158:6,

158:16; *pret. 3 sg.* gelȳfde 108:229, 118:96; gelȳfde [gelȳfd → gelȳfde] 128:187; *pl.* gelȳfdon 48:55, 56:232, 118:131, 120:41, 122:71; *subj. pres. sg.* gelȳfe 106:218, 106:226, 108:233; *pl.* gelȳfon 16:145; *imp. 3 sg.* gelȳfe 24:157; *pl.* gelȳfan 8:150; *pl.* gelȳfaþ 98:25; gelȳfað 142:144; *infl. inf.* to gelȳfenne 18:37, 20:56, 144:187/8 (A)

ġelȳfd *adj.* believing; *m. nom. pl.* gelȳfde 108:251

ġelȳsan (1) to defeat; *pp.* gelȳsed 73

ġemǣcc *m.* mates; *nom. pl.* gemǣccan 14:135

ġemǣn *adj.* common; *nt. acc. sg.* gemǣne 14:95, 14:96

ġemǣre *nt.* limits, bounds; *acc. pl.* gemǣro 58:35, 94:52, 136:14; *dat. pl.* gemǣrum 84:57

ġeman (1) to heed, remember 14:126, 46:28; *ind. pret. pl.* gemdon 70:48

ġemāna *m.* fellowship; *nom. sg.* gemānan 6:106a, 6:106b

ġemanian (2) to admonish; *pp.* gemanode 90:191, 90:203

ġemdon (see ġeman)

ġemedemian (2) to be humbled; *ind. pret. 3 sg.* gemedemode 26:6; *pp.* gemedemod 104:138; *pl.* gemedemode 98:33

ġemeleaslīce *adv.* heedlessly, negligently [gemeleaslīce → gemeleaslīce] 42:133

ġemengan (1) to mingle; *pp.* gemengeð 71; *pl.* gemengde 101

ġemet *nt.* measure, capacity; *nom. sg.* 20:52, 42:115, 82:22, 84:43, 116:56, 130:238, 140:132; *acc. sg.* gemet 8:138; *dat. sg.* gemete 2:20, 4:44, 50:113, 86:114; *inst. sg.* gemete 100:57, 100:84; *inst. pl.* gemetum 142:183

ġemētan (1) to find; *ind. pres. 2 sg.* gemētest 4:59, 81; *2 sg.* gemētst 158:36; *pl.* gemētaþ 54:204, 104:154; gemētað 33; gemēte 48:61; *pret. 3 sg.* gemētte 100:65, 102:103, 102:132, 136:35; *pl.* gemētton

104:148, 15, 45, 47, 48; gemittan 140:110; *subj. pres. pl.* gemēton 66:206; *pp.* gemēt 21; gemēted 6:91, 16:167, 24:151, 126:180, 136:20, 142:152

ġemetfæst *adj.* modest, moderate; *m. nom. sg.* 146:22, 148:80

ġemiltsian (2) to have mercy; *imp. 2 sg.* gemiltsa 135

ġemittan (see ġemetest)

ġemolsnian (2) to rot; *ind. pres. 3 sg.* gemolsnaþ 78:44; *pp.* gemolsnode 80:102

ġemonigfealdian (2) to multiply; *pp.* gemonigfealdode 76:13

ġemunan (pret. pres.) to remember 38:7, 40:88, 70:77, 70:80, 86:127, 86:130; *ind. pres. pl.* gemunaþ 90:193; *pret. 3 sg.* gemunde 92:15, 146:32; *subj. pres. pl.* gemunan 78:61, 90:202; *imp. 1 pl.* gemūnon 16:154, 50:112; *2 pl.* gemūne 11

ġemyclian (2) to magnify; *imp. 2 sg.* gemycla 110:309; *3 sg.* gemycclige 6:134

ġemynd *nt.* memory; *nom. sg.* 46:41, 120:24; *acc. pl.* gemynd 48:49, 58:8; *dat. sg.* gemynde 42:106, 130:266; gemynde (*f.*) 18:26, 88:174, 136:2; *dat. pl.* gemyndum 80:109

ġemyndig *adj.* mindful; *m. nom. sg.* 32:183, 58:6, 62:91, 104:157, 104:158, 106:209, 112:326, 136:9, 148:63; *f. nom. sg.* gemyndig 46:30; *m. nom. pl.* gemyndige 16:164, 26:4, 70:67, 72:104, 114:27

ġemyndgian (2) to remember; *imp. 2 sg.* gemyne 20:64, 80:99, 80:100, 154:209

ġenǣson (see ġenesan)

ġenean (1) to be sufficient; *ind. pret. 3 sg.* geneah 116:61

ġenēalǣcan (1) (with acc. or dat.) to draw near, approach 106:194, 138:45, 85; genēalǣcean 52:160; *ind. pret. 3 sg.* genēalǣhte 10:11, 10:18, 12:46, 46:5, 48:59

ġenēdan (1) to compell; *pp.* genēded 18:38

ġenēh *adv.* enough, abundantly 70:80; genēhge 142:145

71

ġenemnam (1) to name; *ind. pret. 3 sg.*
genemede 6:92; *pp.* genemned 4:64, 122:87
ġenēosian (1) to visit 122
ġenērian (1) to save, preserve 68:8; *ind.*
pres. 3 sg. genȳreþ 68:25; *pret. 2 sg.*
genēredest 62:105; *3 sg.* genērede 46:19,
80:107; *subj. pres. sg.* genērige 16:165; *imp.*
2 sg. genēre 62:101
ġenesan (V) to be saved, preserved; *ind.*
pres. 3 sg. geneseþ 120:18; *pret. 2 sg.*
genæson 140:97
ġenēþēowian (2) to be subdued; *ind. pret.*
3 sg. geneþērode 4:55
ġenihtsum *adj.* plentiful, abundant; *m.*
nom. pl. genihtsume 68:37
ġenihtsumian (2) to abound; *ind. pres. 3*
sg. genihtsumað 68:14; *pl.* genihtsumiað
94; *pret. pl.* genihtsumedan 14:134; *subj.*
pres. sg. genihtsumige 24:157
ġenihtsumnes *f.* plenty, abundance; *nom.*
sg. 80:117; *acc. sg.* genihtsumnesse 26:18;
dat. sg. genihtsumnesse 26:27
ġeniman (IV) to take, seize 106:186;
genimon 64:175; *ind. pres. 3 sg.* genimþ
32:166; genimeþ 34:217; *pret. 3 sg.* genam
10:4, 18:6, 18:11, 46:33, 82:4, 100:64, 136:38,
148:49, 150:119, 79, 110; *pl.* genamon 6, 9,
64; genaman 4:53, 54:197, 124:95, 130:264,
132:319; *subj. pres. sg.* genime 32:168; *pl.*
genimon 35; *pret. sg.* genāme 50:105; *pl.*
genamon 61; *imp. 2 pl.* genimaþ 160:81; *pp.*
genumen 62:109, 98:5; *pl.* genumene
32:156; *m. acc. pl.* gemumene 60:49
ġenōg *adv.*enough 122:74, 148:56
ġenyreþ (see ġenerian)
ġenyþerian (2) to humble, subdue; *pp.*
genyþerod 130:269; genyþerad 20:84; *pl.*
genyþerade 20:83
ġenyþerung *f.* humiliation,
condemnation; *acc. sg.* genyþerunge 46:6;
dat. sg. genyþerunga 42:112
ġeō *adv.* long ago 32:141, 52:179
ġeofu *f.* gift, grace; *nom. sg.* 2:17, 86:106,
94:86, 96:92; *gen. pl.* geofa 14:94; geofena

2:12, 2:17, 2:23, 72:105, 80:129, 132:302; *dat.*
pl. geofum 92:24, 114:10
ġeogoþ *m.* youth; *nom. sg.* 44:159, 72:112;
dat. sg. geogoðe 146:11
ġeogoþhād *m.* youth; *nom. sg.* 40:58; *dat.*
sg. geogoðhāde 146:9
ġeogoðlust *m.* youthful lusts; *acc. pl.*
geogoðlustas 40:61
ġēomor *adj.* sad; *m. nom. sg.* 80:103
ġēomrung *f.* grief, lamentation; *dat. sg.*
gēomrunga 62:94, 78:88
ġeond *prep* (with acc.) over, all over,
throughout 48:49, 76:14, 84:58, 84:68, 88:168,
94:51, 128:225, 130:251, 136:25, 136:28, 136:32,
136:33, 136:34, 150:135, 162:104 >
ġeondettan (1) to confess; *ind. pres. 3 pl.*
geondettaþ 40:46 (A)
ġeondweardian (2) to present, manifest;
ind. pret. 3 sg. geondweardode 110:285,
[geondweardodne → geondweardode] 124:134]; *pp.*
geondweard 14:101
ġeong *adj.* young; *m. nom. sg.* 122:55; *m.*
dat. sg. geongum 86:131; *m. acc. pl.*
geonge 76:2; *comp. m. dat. pl.* geongrum
76:24
ġeopenian (2) to open, manifest, reveal;
subj. pres. pl. geopenian 130:237; *pp.*
geopenod 4:80; *pl.* geopenode 158:23
ġeorn *adj.* eager, desirous, greedy; *m.*
nom. sg. 28:57, 76:40; *comp. m. nom. pl.*
geornran 22:103
ġeorne *adv.* eagerly 6:112, 16:158, 16:165,
24:148, 30:128, 30:134, 38:10, 68:38, 76:28,
78:64, 80:128a, 80:128b, 86:128, 142:137 >;
comp. geornor 10:24, 12:65, 122:64; *superl.*
geornost 78:62
ġeornful *adj.* desirous, eager, anxious;
nom. sg. 148:80; *f. nom. sg.* geornful
46:26; *m. nom. pl.* geornfulle 76:26
ġeornfullīċe *adv.* diligently 92:28
ġeornlīċe *adv.* earnestly, diligently 12:67,
24:145, 26:3, 38:3, 80:113, 86:127, 138:66,
140:101, 140:113, 144:209 >; *comp.*
geornlīcor 148:58

72

ġeornnes *f.* earnestness, diligence, longing; *nom. sg.* 38:23; *acc. sg.* geornnesse 60:86 (A)

ġēotan (II) to pour; *ind. pret. 3 sg.* gēat 50:93

ġerǣċan (1) to stretch forth, extend; *ind. pret. 3 sg.* gerǣc 128:183

ġerǣċean (1) to reach 142:160; *pp.* gerēahte 132:288 (A)

ġerās (see ġeriseþ)

ġerēafian (2) to steal; *ind. pret. 3 pl.* gerēafodan 124:102

ġerēahte (see ġerǣcean)

ġerēccean [gerēcenan] (1) to tell, declare, explain 126:144; *imp. 2 sg.* gerēce 126:143; *pp.* gerēht 4:85, 54:209 (A)

ġerēccan (1) to rule, direct; *ind. pres. 3 sg.* gerēceþ 54:208

ġerēfa *m.* ruler, governor; *nom. sg.* 106:199; *nom. pl.* gerēfan 42:106

ġerēgnian [gerēnian] (2) to arrange; *pp.* gerēgnod 88:179

ġerēht (see ġerēccean)

ġereord *m.* speeches; *nom. pl.* gereordo 106:225

ġerestan (1) to rest, abide; *infl. inf.* to gerestenne 114:37

Gerichō *prop. n.* Jericho; *acc. sg.* Gerichō 10:11, 12:46

ġerihtnes *f.* setting right; *nom. sg.* 116:45

ġerihtwīsian (2) to justify; *ind. pres. 2 sg.* gerihtwīsige 128:222

ġerīm *m.* number; *dat. sg.* gerīme 22:129

ġerīsan (VI) to befit; *ind. pres. 3 sg.* gerīseþ 48:59; *pret. 3 sg.* gerās 8:143

ġerīsnliċ *adj.* fitting; *def. nt. nom. sg.* gerīsnlican 6:95

ġerisn *adj.* fitting; *superl. nt. nom. sg.* gerisnost 140:132

Ġerusalem *prop. n.* Jerusalem; *nom. sg.* 54:209, *acc. sg.* Gerusalem 10:5, 48:59, 52:160, 52:172, 54:191

ġerӯman (1) to manifest; *ind. pres. 3 sg.* gerӯmeþ 124:124; *subj. pret. pl.* gerӯmdon 138:65

ġerӯne *nt.* mystery, sacrament; *nom. sg.* 10:37, 52:164; *acc. sg.* geryne 146:28; *gen. sg.* gerӯnes 10:32, 10:33

ġerӯnelliċ *adj.* mysterious; *def. f. nom. sg.* gerӯnelican 116:86

ġeryno *nt.* festival; *nom. sg.* 58:1 [genrio → geryno]

ġesǣgen *f.* saying, record, narration; *gen. sg.* gesǣgene 38:19

ġesǣlan (1) to be tied; *pp. f. acc. sg.* gesǣlede 48:62 (A)

ġesǣlan (1) to happen; *ind. pres. 3 sg.* gesǣleþ 34:195

ġesǣlig *adj.* happy, blessed; *m. nom. sg.* 70:58

ġesǣliglīċe *adv.* happily 120:6

ġesamnian (2) to gather together, collect, assemble 26:3; *ind. pret. 3 sg.* gesamnode 136:33; *pl.* gesamnodan 70:48, 120:31; *pp.* gesamnode 46:20, 100:61, 142:172

ġesamnung *f.* gathering together; *nom. sg.* 44:162; *acc. pl.* gesamnunga 74:14

ġesceaft *f.* creature; *nom. pl.* gesceafta 6:105, 32:182, 64:182, 152:145; *acc. pl.* gesceafta 4:86, 14:128, 22:115, 84:77; *gen. pl.* gesceafta 50:122, 64:137, 84:89, 128:216, 130:230; *dat. pl.* gesceaftum 22:124, 62:127, 62:128, 84:81

ġescēawian (2) to regard, consider 118:90

ġesceldan [gescieldan] (1) shield; *ind. pres. 3 sg.* gesceldeþ 32:175; *pp.* gesceldode 152:157 (A)

ġescendan (1) to be shamed; *ind. pret. 3 sg.* gescende 83

ġesceppan (VI) to create; *ind. pret. 2 sg.* gesceōpe 50:122; *3 sg.* gesceōp 14:128, 14:132, 34:203, 72:102; *pp.* gesceapen 14:107, 22:124, 40:82, 80:114; *pl.* gesceapene 40:88, 42:90

73

ġescierpla *m.* garment; *nom. pl.*
gescyrplan 78:78 (A)
ġescyldan (1) to shield; *ind. pres. pl.*
gescyldaþ 42:131; *subj. pres. sg.* gescylde
12:68, 86:129; *pp.* gescylded 88:152
Ġescyppend *m.* Creator; *gen. sg.*
Gescyppendes 6:126
ġesēċean [ġesēċan] (1) to seek, visit 72:96,
84:61, 86:121; *ind. pres. 3 sg.* gesēceþ
72:114; *pret. 3 sg.* gesōhte 6:119, 6:129,
86:118, 90:194, 152:183; *pl.* gesōhtan 138:46;
pp. gesōht 6:133 (A)
ġesecgan (3) to delcare, proclaim 116:57,
116:82; gesecgean 116:85; *infl. inf.* to
gesecgenne 116:61; *pp.* gesægde 58:20
ġesegen *f.* record; *gen. sg.* gesegene 38:5
ġeseġnian (2) blessed; *ind. pret. 3 sg.*
gesegnode 126:151; *pp.* gesegnod 126:145
ġesellan (1) to give, to sell; *ind. pret. 3 sg.*
gesealde 48:44, 146:42, 148:49; *subj. pret.*
sg. gesealde 52:139; *pp.* geseald 10:6, 26:32,
46:39, 50:92, 68:19
ġesēman (1) to reconcile 126:139; *pp.*
gesēmde 126:173
ġesendan (1) to send; *pp.* gesended 6:96
ġeseneliċ *adj.* visible; *def. m. nom. sg.*
gesenelica 14:103
ġesēon (V) to see 10:19, 14:91, 14:100, 14:101,
14:103, 14:122, 20:56, 48:51, 64:160, 68:13,
68:34, 76:11; *ind. pres. 1 sg.* gesēo 130:242,
160:61; gesie 27; *2 sg.* gesihst 58; *3 sg.*
gesyhþ 20:43, 108:236; *pl.* gesēoð 8:152,
90:206; gesēoþ 40:55, 52:178, 64:164, 64:181,
90:190, 90:203; gesēo 86:133; *pret. 2 sg.*
gesawe 80:96, 80:97; *3 sg.* gesēah 10:22,
28:81, 54:186, 70:87, 122:56, 124:90; gesēh
10:21; *pl.* gesēgon 84:88; gesawon 48:57,
74:20, 84:63, 84:83, 86:114; *subj. pres. sg.*
gesēo 24:161, 158:8; *pl.* gesēon 102:105;
pret. sg. gesawe 22:114, 28:68, 116:83,
116:89, 154:217; *imp. 2 sg.* gesēoh 130:252,
158:6, 74, 76, 100, 105; *2 pl.* gesēoþ 26:40;
gesēoð 59; *pres. p.* gesēonde 106:195,

144:197; *pp.* gesēwen 34:209; *pl.* gesawene
122:44
ġesettan (1) to set, place, establish 82:14,
82:21, 82:28, 84:44; gesetton 84:82; *ind. pres.*
1 sg. gesette 104:135; *pret. 2 sg.* gesettest
102:92; *3 sg.* gesette 12:87, 54:212, 82:25,
100:42, 136:22, 140:115, 142:168, 148; *pl.*
gesetton 18:19, 22:120, 54:201, 102:88,
132:314; *subj. pret. pl.* gesetton 128:206; *pp.*
geseted 86:92, 100:86, 136:12, 136:15,
156:237; *pl.* gesette 42:108, 52:171
ġeset *m.* liar; *dat. pl.* gesetum 136:29
ġesewenlīċe *adv.* visibly 110:279
ġesibb *m.* kindred; *gen. sg.* gesibbes
14:126
ġesibbian (2) to reconcile; *pp. m. acc. sg.*
gesibbodne 154:201
ġesibsum *adj.* peaceable; *def. m. nom. sg.*
gesibsuma 6:119, 6:124
ġesiġefæstan (1) to be victorious; *imp. 1*
pl. gesigefæstan 104:172; *pp.* gesigefæsted
46:15/16, 106:195
ġesihþ *f.* sight, vision; *acc. sg.* gesihþe
108:251, 148:69; *dat. sg.* gesihþe 84:79,
108:247, 110:297, 138:56, 138:79, 142:142, 63,
80, 136; gesihðe 8:152
ġesingan (III) to sing 30:102; *subj. pres. 3*
sg. gesinge 142:146; *pp.* gesungen 6:114
ġesittan (V) to sit down 48:68, 58:4; *ind.*
pres. 3 sg. gesitteþ 62:124; *pret. 3 sg.*
gesæt 46:25, 62:115, 112:327, 160:59, 44; *infl.*
inf. to gesittenne 96:95/6
ġesmeran [ġesmieran] (1) to anoint; *pp.*
gesmered 50:109
ġesomnian (2) to gather, assemble 98:37
ġesomnung *f.* collection, assemblage;
nom. sg. 70:46
ġesperian (2) to arm with spears; *pp.*
gesperode 152:157
ġesprecan (V) to speak; *pp.* gesprecen
100:79, 132:300, 138:60
ġestandan (VI) to stand 120:33; *ind pret. 3*
sg. gestōd 10:17, 12:70, 46:27, 150:112,
152:142; *pl.* gestōdon 80; gestōdan 114:39;
subj. pres. pl. gestōndan 120:11; *pret. 3 sg.*

gestōde 140:111; *pp.* gestānden 114:29, 154:227

ġestaðelian (2) to establish, restore; *ind. pret. 1 sg.* gestaðelode 158:34; *3 sg.* gestaþelade 10:41; *pl.* gestaþelodon 94:78; *pp.* gestaþelod 62:117

ġestīgan (I) to ascend; *ind. pres. 1 sg.* gestīge 126:166

ġestillan (1) be still, quiet; *ind. pres. 3 sg.* gestilleþ 4:67; *subj. pret. sg.* gestilde 160:76; *pp.* gestilled 114:39

ġestincan (III) to smell; *ind. pres. pl.* gestincað 40:56

ġestrangian (2) to strengthen; *ind. pret. 2 sg.* gestrangodest 98; *subj. pres. sg.* gestrangie 159; *imp. 2 sg.* gestranga 102; *pp.* gestrangod 100:77, 158:14

ġestrēon *nt.* acquisition, treasure; *nom. sg.* 68:14, 70:47; *acc. pl.* gestrēon 34:202, 78:69, 78:84; *dat. pl.* gestreōnum 16:147, 32:159, 32:170, 36:234

ġestrēonian [gestrēowian] (2) to gain; *pret. 3 sg.* gestrēonde 84:74

ġestrēonfull *adj.* treasured, precious; *def. nt. acc. pl.* gestrēonfullan 92:15

ġesund *adj.* sound, whole; *m. nom. sg.* 110; *m. acc. sg.* gesundne 124:100, 150:121; *m. nom. pl.* gesunde 76:6

ġeswencan (1) to trouble, afflict, distress; *ind. pres. pl.* geswencaþ 120:16; *subj. pres. 3 sg.* geswence 24:168; *pp.* geswenced 40:60, 154:229; *pl.* geswencede 160:61

ġeswīcan (1) (with *gen.*) to cease from 30:98, 42:127, 144:208; *ind. pres. pl.* geswīcaþ 134:329; *subj. pres. pl.* geswīcon 30:125

ġeswinc *m.* toil; *dat. sg.* geswince 40:75

ġesyhþ (see ġesēon)

ġesyhþ *f.* sight, vision; *nom. sg.* ġesyhþ 54:209; *acc. sg.* ġesyhþe 54:208; *dat. sg.* gesyhþe 62:115, 76:29, 106:206, 108:235, 132:282

ġesyne *adj.* manifest, evident; *nt. nom. sg.* gesyne 64:172, 142:151; *m. nom. pl.* gesyne 140:112

ġesyngian (2) sinned; *ind. pret. 1 sg.* gesyngade 60:77

ġēt *adv.* yet, still 26:23, 88:139, 118:92

ġetācnian (2) to betoken, signify; *ind. pres. 3 sg.* getācnaþ 50:90, 50:124, 52:163; *pl.* getācniaþ 50:98, 84:85; *pret. 3 sg.* getācnode 114:16; *pp.* getācnod 48:83

ġetēah (see ġetyhþ)

ġeteld *nt.* tent, tabernacle; *nom. sg.* 4:65

ġetellan (1) to reckon; *ind. pret. 3 pl.* getealdon 140:104; *pp.* geteald 28:67

ġeteohhian (2) to determine, appoint; *pp.* geteohhod 16:163; geteohhad 128:191

ġetēon (II) to draw, drag; *pp.* getēod 12:84, 18:29, 20:72, 24:147, 66:204; *pl.* getēode 52:150

ġetēorian (2) to fail, wear away; *ind. pret. 3 sg.* getēorode 80:91; *pp.* getēorod 95

ġetimbrian (1) to build 126:165, 146; *ind. pret. 3 sg.* getimbrede 148:84, 152:138; *pl.* getimbredon 134:323; *pp.* getimbred 88:142, 88:154, 90:187 (A)

ġetimbre *nt.* building; *nom. pl.* getimbro 52:180; *gen. pl.* getimbra 52:179

ġetremman [getrymman] (1) to strengthen, support; *ind. pret. 3 sg.* getremede 6:102; *pp.* getremede 10:31, 84:48

ġetrēow *adj.* faithful; *m. nom. pl.* getrēowe 34:194; *def. m. nom. sg.* getrēowa 70:69; *superl. dat. sg. m.* getrēowestan 138:75

ġetrēowfull *adj.* faithful; *def. m. nom. sg.* getrēowfulla 44:137

ġetrēowliċ *adj.* faithful; *nt. gen. sg.* getrēowlices 34:193

ġetrēowlīċe *adv.* faithfully 128:213, 128:216

ġetrymman (1) to strengthen, fortify 94:57, 148:66; *ind. pret. 1 sg.* getrymede 158:35; *3 sg.* getrymede 10:32; *pp.* getrymed 154:251; *m. nom. pl.* getrymede 82:18, 84:171

ġetrymnes *f.* setting in order; *gen. sg.* getrymnesse 64:142

ġetrȳwan [ġetrūwian] (1) to trust 110:317; *ind.
pret 3 sg.* getrȳwde 150:93 (A)

ġetȳdran (1) to bring forth; *ind. pret. 3 sg.*
getȳde 148:77

ġetyhtan (1) to persuade, instruct; *ind.
pres. 3 sg.* getyhþ 16:152, 24:155, 78:46;
pret. 3 sg. geteah 148:49; *pp.* getogen 28:70,
97, 101

ġeþafian (2) (*with acc. or dat.*) to permit,
allow; *ind. pres. 3 sg.* geþafaþ 30:91; *subj.
pres. pl.* geþafian 28:85

ġeþafung *f.* permission, consent; *gen. sg.
pl.* geþafunga 4:72, 4:77

ġeþang *m.* thought; *acc. sg.* geþang
124:127

ġeðeah (see ġeþicgan)

ġeþeaht *m.* decision; *nom. sg.* 132:316;
acc. sg. geðeaht (→)

ġeþeld (see ġeþyld)

ġeþenċean (1) to think, consider 52:158,
58:21, 62:123, 62:126, 66:194, 70:80;
geþencan 32:178, 34:186, 34:189, 38:8, 40:80;
ind. pres. 3 sg. geþencþ 38:10; *pret. 2 sg.*
geþohtest 32:165; *subj. pres. pl.* geþencean
[geþencan → geþencean] 68:2; *imp. 2 sg.*
geþenc 26:19; *1 pl.* geþencan 16:159;
geþencean 14:127, 18:28, 24:145; *2 pl.*
geþenceaþ 68:28; *3 pl.* geþencean 14:102;
infl. inf. to geþencenne 18:22, 18:26/7, 20:70,
22:104, 22:122, 24:173; *pp.* geþōht 124:132,
126:140

ġeþicgan (V) to prosper, gain; *ind. pret. 3
sg.* geðeah 146:8

ġeþingian (2) to intercede for; *pp.*
geþingod 4:78

ġeþoftscip *m.* fellowship; *dat. sg.*
geþoftscipe 30:110

ġeþoht (see geþencean)

ġeþoht *m.* thought, mind; *acc. sg.* geþoht
6:130, 22:125; *dat. sg.* geþohte 76:40; *acc.
pl.* geþohtas 126:141; *gen. pl.* geþohta
12:67; *dat. pl.* geþohtum 12:88, 24:154

ġeþrēan (1) afflicted; *pp.* geþrēad 152:174

ġeþrēatian (2) to restrain, bound; *pp.*
geþrēatod 152:146; *m. acc. sg.*
geþrēatodne 28:72

ġeþrōwian (2) to suffer; *ind. pret. 3 sg.*
geþrōwode 16:145, 58:25, 62:122, 72:92,
90:197; geþrōwade 16:138; *pl.* geþrōwodan
120:23

ġeþungen [ġeþingan] (1) to be pious; *pp.*
geþungen 148:78

ġeþungennes *f.* piety; *gen. sg.*
geþungennesse 2:30

ġeþwærnes *f.* agreement; *acc. sg.*
geþwærnesse 76:31

ġeþȳen [ġeþīen] (1) to urge; *subj. pres. pl.*
geþȳdon 92:29

ġeþyld *f.* patience; *acc. sg.* geþyld 54:184

ġeþyld *m.* patience; *nom. sg.* 22:104;
geþeld 54:203; *acc. sg.* geþyld 86:119; *dat.
sg.* geþylde 22:101; *inst.* geþylde 52:144

ġeþyldelīċe *adj.* patient; *f. acc. sg.* 52:145

ġeþyldelīċe *adv.* patiently 22:107

ġeþyldiġ *adj.* patient; *m. nom. sg.* 146:22

ġeūnlustian (2) to loathe; *ind. pres. 3 sg.*
geūnlustaþ 40:61

ġeūnrōtan (1) to be sad; *pp.* geūnrōted
[geūnrēted → geūnrōted] 98:23

ġeūnrōtsian (2) to be sad; *pp.* geūnrōtsod
104:172

ġewaldum (see ġeweald)

ġewanian (2) to diminish; *ind. pret. 3 sg.*
gewanode 62:119

ġeweald *nt.* power; *nom. sg.* 169; *acc. sg.*
geweald 34:196, 152:173; *dat. sg.* gewealde
70:62, 118:105, 82; *dat. pl.* gewealdum
42:117; gewaldum 30:112

ġeweaxan (VII) to grow, grew; *ind. pret. 3
sg.* geweox 136:24

ġewelegian [ġeweligan] (2) to enrich; *ind.
pret. 2 sg.* gewelegodest 62:108; *pp. m.
acc. sg.* gewelegode [→ gewelegodne] 124:118;
m. nom. pl. gewelgade 74:15 (A)

ġewemmednes *f.* impurity; *gen. sg.*
gewemmednesse 50:125

ġewemman (1) to violate; *ind. pres. 2 sg.*
gewemmest 4:74; *pp.* gewemmed 20:75; *pl.*
gewemmede 116

ġewendan (1) to turn; *ind. pres. pl.*
gewendað 134:330; *pp.* gewended 120:27

ġewenn *m.* battle, storm; *nom. sg.* 44:161

ġeweorc *nt.* work; *nom. sg.* 52:177; *acc.*
sg. geweorc 136:4

ġeweorþan (III) to become, happen 4:61,
58:3, 76:25, 82:31, 82:34, 86:106; geweorðan
90:208; *ind. pres. 3 sg.* geweorþeþ 6:104,
16:154; *pl.* (ge)weorþaþ 90:206; *pret. 3 sg.*
gewearþ 84:69, 86:107, 132:320; gewearð
148:84; *subj. pres. pl.* geweorþan 18:4;
pret. sg. gewurde 66:200, 112:331; *imp. 3
sg.* geweorþe 6:90; *pp.* geworden 10:11,
14:114, 48:64, 48:80, 56:235, 60:50; *pl.*
gewordene 64:159, 106; gewordne 70:55

ġeweorþian (2) to honour; *ind. pret. 2 sg.*
geweorþodest 62:97; *pp.* geweorþod 48:76,
88:140, 92:24, 116:58, 136:8; *pl.* geweorþode
74:15, 120:23

ġewīcian (2) to dwell; *ind. pret. 3 sg.*
gewīcode 54:192

ġewindan (III) to blow; *pp.* gewindwod
4:66

ġewinn *m.* labour, toil, strife, battle; *nom.
sg.* 72:112; gewin 154:225; *gen. sg.*
gewinnes 98:28, 156; *dat. sg.* gewinne 40:84,
42:117, 154:215; *gen. pl.* gewinna 132:300
(A)

ġewinnan (III) to win 154:226; *ind. pret. 3
pl.* gewunnon 120:26 (A)

ġewita *m.* witness; *nom. sg.* 84:67, 124:89;
nom. pl. gewitan 84:55, 84:57, 114:11

ġewītan (I) to depart, pass away, die 98:22,
104; *ind. pres. 2 sg.* gewītest 154:206; *3 sg.*
gewīteþ 38:35, 40:48, 40:59, 62:129, 62:130;
pl. gewītaþ 14:94, 40:57, 40:70, 160:66; *pret.
3 sg.* gewāt 38:22, 52:152, 78:89, 80:104, 82:6,
84:79, 86:90, 132:293; *pl.* gewīton 66:188,
70:43, 70:44; gewītan 126:152, 144:206; *subj.
pres. sg.* gewīte 102:113; *pl.* gewītan
90:215; *pres. p.* gewītende 44:158; *pp.*

gewīten 68:38, 88:176, 106:183; *pl.* gewītene
70:54, 70:56, 70:88, 80:101

ġewītendliċ *adj.* transitory; *def. nt. acc.
sg.* gewītendlice 50:99

ġewītgian (2) to witness; *pp.* gewītgod
64:168; *pl.* gewītgode 58:18

ġewitnes *f.* witness; *nom. sg.* 114:26; *dat.
sg.* gewitnesse 106:222

ġeworden (see ġeweorþan)

ġewrecan (V) to avenge 22:106; *ind. pret.
3 sg.* gewrecþ 128:214; *subj. pres. pl.*
gewrecan 22:104

ġewreot *nt.* writing, scripture; *nom. pl.*
gewreotu 10:5, 12:43, 28:81; *acc. pl.*
gewreotu 106:222; gewreoto 128:226; *gen.
pl.* gewreota 38:2, 54:222

ġewrīdan (VI) to flourish; *ind. pret. 3 sg.*
gewrīdode 136:25

ġewrit *nt.* writing, scripture; *nom. sg.*
86:100, 118:99, 124:107, 124:108; *acc. sg.*
gewrit 122:82; *gen. sg.* gewrites 22:100; *dat.
sg.* gewrite 114:2

ġewrixl *nt.* change, turning; *acc. sg.*
gewrixle 62:131

ġewuldrian (2) to glorify; *pp.* gewuldrod
98:32, 104:145; gewuldrad 98:12, 136:6; *def.
m. nom. sg.* gewuldroda 104:157

ġewuna *m.* custom, manner; *nom. sg.*
142:176; *dat. sg.* gewunan 142:156;
gewunon 138:61; *dat. pl.* gewunon 50:125

ġewundian (2) to wound; *ind. pret. 3 sg.*
gewundode 114:26

ġewuneliċ *adj.* customary, usual; *nt. nom.
sg.* ġewunelic 60:46

ġewunian (2) to dwell, abide
78:89; *ind. pret. 3 sg.* gewunode 136:28,
136:30

ġewunnon (see ġewinnan)

ġewurde (see ġeweorþan)

ġewyrcean (1) to work, make 130:233;
gewyricean 78:46; gewercean 88:171; *ind.
pret. 1 sg.* geworhte 142:143, 158:34; *3 sg.*
geworhte 32:182, 130:230, 140:122, 150:106;
pl. geworhtan 44:141, 60:79, 140:116; *pp.*

geworht 16:155, 46:11, 50:107, 88:160, 88:162, 88:182a, 88:182b; *pl.* geworhte 88:145; *def. m. acc. pl.* geworhtan 16:158, 86:128

ġewyrht *nt.* deed; *acc. pl.* gewyrhto 118:90; *dat. pl.* gewyrhtum 28:78, 60:88, 70:80 [gewyrthum → gewyrhtum], 86:125, 148:81

ġīet (see ġīt)

ġif *conj.* if (see Appendix, p.149)

ġifernes *f.* greed, avarice; *acc. sg.* gifernesse 16:143

ġifre *adj.* greedy; *def. m. nom. sg.* gifra 42:94

ġifu *f.* gift, grace, favour; *nom. sg.* 92:25; *acc. sg.* gife 4:59, 80:106, 84:73 88:151, 90:192, 92:37; *gen. sg.* gife 100:41; *dat. sg.* gife 2:18, 102:104; *gen. pl.* gifa 20:77; gifena 32:183, 92:24; *dat. pl.* gifum 116:74, 118:135

ġīgant *m.* giant; *nom. sg.* 6:101; *acc. sg.* gīgant 20:69

ġild *nt.* idol; *nom. sg.* 152:150; *acc. sg.* gild 152:160, 152:167; gyld 152:151; *dat. sg.* gilde 152:140; *nom. pl.* gild 152:165; *acc. pl.* gild 152:178; gyld 152:181

ġilþ [ġielþ] *m.* boasting; *nom. sg.* 82; *dat. sg.* gilþe 20:65

ġimelēas *adj.* careless; *def. m. gen. sg.* gimelēasan 38:27

ġimm *m.* gem; *gen. pl.* gimma 34:201, 70:46

ġingra *m.* disciple; *nom. sg.* 30:90; *nom. pl.* gingran 94:65; *dat. pl.* gingrum 62:111, 92:6, 92:19, 94:64

ġīsl [ġīsel] *m.* hostage; *dat. sg.* gīsle 4:77

ġīsternes *f.* liberality; *nom. sg.* 114:35

ġit *dual pron.* you two (see Appendix, p. 145)

ġīt *adv.* yet, still (see Appendix, p. 151)

ġītsere *m.* coveter, covetous man; *nom. sg.* 46:41, 48:43; *nom. pl.* gītseras 42:103

ġītsian (2) to covet; *pres. p. def. m. nom. sg.* gītsigenda 32:165

ġītsung *f.* coveting, covetousness; *gen. sg.* gītsunga 48:43; *dat. sg.* gītsunga 16:147, 20:65; gītsunge 52:146; *dat. pl.* gītsungum 40:43

glæs *nt.* glass; *nom. sg.* 78:48; *dat. sg.* glæse 88:182

glæsen *adj.* made of glass; glæsen *nt. nom. sg.* 142:175; *nt. dat. sg.* glæsenum 142:178

glaunes *f.* skill; *nom sg.* 70:49

gleng *m.* ornament, splendour; *nom. pl.* glengas 70:43; glengeas 78:78; *acc. pl.* glengas 68:39, 80:110

gnornian (2) to mourn; *pres. p.* gnorngende 80:104

gnornung *f.* mourning, lamentation; *nom. sg.* 60:56, 62:136

God *m.* God; *nom. sg.* 4:77, 12:49, 18:27, 24:172, 30:108, 30:112, > *acc. sg.* God 8:152, 16:145, 18:11, 18:15, 26:25, > *gen. sg.* Godes 2:34, 4:63, 4:85, 6:106, 14:111, 14:112, 14:117, 18:8, 18:21, 18:27, 18:32, 18:33, 18:34, > *dat. sg.* Gode 4:60, 20:43, 22:135, 26:22, 138:54, 138:80, > *acc. pl.* godas 138:77

gōd *adj.* good; *m. nom. sg.* 90:215; *nt. nom. sg.* gōod [→ gōd] 98:35; *m. acc. sg.* gōdne 38:28; *f. acc. sg.* gōde 28:86; *nt. acc. sg.* gōd 48:45, 50:131, 52:146, 78:60; *m. gen. sg.* gōdes 54:213; *m. dat. sg.* gōdum 12:44, 24:166, 54:206, 68:16; *m. nom. pl.* gōde 90:204, 90:212; *m. acc. pl.* gōde 142:168; *f. gen pl.* gōdra 146:38; *nt. gen. pl.* gōdra 50:91, 50:112, 50:115, 76:26; *f. dat. pl.* gōdum 10:42, 14:121, 66:191, 70:75, 146:29; *def. m. nom. sg.* gōda 28:86, 42:136, 124:109, 124:116, 126:159, 132:301; *m. gen. sg.* gōda 38:9; *nt. acc. sg.* gōdan 76:21; *f. acc. pl.* gōdan 90:214

gōd *nt.* good, benefit; *nom. sg.* 70:68, 148:76; *acc. sg.* gōd 14:112, 14:113, 28:75; gōd [good → gōd] 148:70; *gen. sg.* gōdes 18:30, 78:58; *dat. sg.* gōde 18:31, 52:137, 60:86, 148:65; *inst. sg.* gōde 28:89; *nom. pl.* gōd 18:33, 70:73; *acc. pl.* gōd 50:112, 70:73; *gen. pl.* gōda 146:35; *dat. pl.* gōdum 2:22, 24:164, 26:16, 160:67

gōdcund *adj.* divine; *f. acc. sg.*
gōdcunde 58:12, 84:77; *nt. acc. sg.*
gōdcund 54:224, 116:47, 116:61; *f. dat. sg.*
gōdcundre 22:103, 34:190; *nt. dat. sg.*
gōdcundum 152:162, 152:174; *m. acc. pl.*
gōdcunde 30:109 [gōdcundre → gōdcunde],
126:155; *nt. gen. pl.* gōdcundra 24:150,
136:6; *m. dat. pl.* gōdcundum 26:39; *f. dat.
pl.* gōdcundum 92:24; *nt. dat. pl.*
gōdcundum 88:139, 114:14; *def. f. nom. sg.*
gōdcunde 12:72a, 12:72b; *f. acc. sg.*
gōdcundan 30:129, 38:39, 152:155; *m. gen.
sg.* gōdcundan 70:86; *nt. gen. sg.*
gōdcundan 22:100; *m. dat. sg.* gōdcundan
82:17; *f. dat. sg.* gōdcundan 12:76, 114:28,
148:66; *m. gen. pl.* gōdcundra 114:31;
f. dat. pl. gōdcundum 116:74
godcundlīċ *adj.* divine; *nt. nom. sg.*
150:97
godcundnes *f.* divinity, deity; *nom. sg.*
12:47; *acc. sg.* godcundnesse 22:115,
62:116, 82:6, 86:90, 88:176, 100:87, 124:124;
gen. sg. godcundnesse 92:7, 124:125; *dat.
sg.* godcundnesse 6:95, 12:50, 82:4, 90:198
godspel *nt.* gospel; *nom. sg.* 114:6; *acc.
sg.* godspel 10:23, 30:131, 160:54; godspell
78:63, 114:19; *gen. sg.* godspelles 38:4,
94:49; *dat. sg.* godspelle 26:4, 26:37, 46:22,
94:52, 116:58, 146:33
godspellere *m.* evangelist; *nom. sg.* 4:88,
10:1, 12:46, 12:69, 14:123, 18:1, 18:36, 20:85;
gen. sg. godspelleres 118:93; *gen. pl.*
godspellera 22:123
godweb *nt.* purple; *acc. sg.* godweb
80:96; *inst. sg.* godwebbe 142:155
godwebben *adj.* purple; *nt. dat. pl.*
godwebbenum 66:190
godwrāc *adj.* godless; *def. m. acc. sg.*
godwrācan 52:142 (A) (M)
gold *nt.* gold; *gen. sg.* goldes 12:89, 34:197,
70:47, 94:47, 136:5; *dat. sg.* golde 20:57,
66:190, 80:96, 88:155, 88:162
goldblōma *m.* golden blossom; *nom. sg.*
74:11

goldhord *nt.* treasure, treasury; *nom. sg.*
6:96, 6:125, 28:63, 28:65; *acc. sg.* goldhord
104:159; *dat. sg.* goldhorde 34:226; *dat. pl.*
goldhordum 94:47
goldwlenc *m.* gold ornaments; *gen. pl.*
goldwlenca 34:201
Goliaþ *pers. n.* Goliath; *acc. sg.* Goliaþ
20:68
gong *m.* path, way; *acc. sg.* gong 10:41
gongan (VII) go, walk; *ind. pres. pl.*
gongað 132:299; *subj. pres. pl.* gongan
68:33; *pret. pl.* gongan 138:65; *imp. 2 sg.*
gong 106:217; *pres. p.* gongende 100:58,
100:67, 100:70, 100:85, 106:202; gangende
102:120
gōod (see gōd)
grǣdiġ *adj.* greedy; *m. nom. sg.* 144:204
grammōd *adj.* angry; *m. acc. sg.*
grammōdne 154:191
grāpian (2) to touch, handle; *ind. pret. pl.*
grāpodan 106:193
Grēce *prop. n.* Greek; *nom. pl.* Grēcas
132:319
grēne *adj.* green; *nt. dat. sg.* grēnum
88:161, 142:164
grētan (1) to greet; *ind. pres. 3 sg.* grēteþ
122:83; *pret. 3 sg.* grētte 116:81, 152 (A)
grēweþ (see grōwan)
grim *adj.* fierce, savage; *m. nom. sg.*
16:153, 146:41; *def. m. gen. sg.* grimman
42:117; *superl. m. acc. sg.* grimmestan
42:114
grimlīċe *adv.* grimly, severely 42:127
grimnes *f.* grimness, cruelty, severity;
dat. sg. grimnesse 38:18, 42:125
gripan (VI) to seize; *pres. p.* gripende
144:203
gristbitung *f.* gnashing; *nom. sg.* 128:199
grōwan (I) to grow 78:52; *ind. pres. 3 sg.*
greweþ 118:111; *pres. p.* grōwende 40:55,
136:18
grund *m.* ground, pit, abyss; *acc. sg.*
grund 22:99, 44:157, 60:64, 60:69, 64:180,
72:96, 110:320, 152:161; *dat. sg.* grunde
46:21, 58:26; *gen. pl.* grunda 100:45

ġrymetian (2) to rage; *ind. pres. pl.*
grymetiaþ 64:153
ġyfylnes *f.* completion, end; *acc. sg.*
gyfylnesse 102:111/12
ġyldan [ġieldan] (III) to render 86:122; *ind.*
pret. 3 sg. geald 58:32, 154:190 (A)
ġylp [gielp] *m.* boasting / glory; *nom. sg.*
36:231, 40:69; *dat. sg.* gylpe 34:228; *nom.*
pl. gylpas 34:205
ġylpan (1) to boast 122:76
ġylt *m.* guilt, sin; *nom. sg.* 4:78; *gen. sg.*
gyltes 30:99; *dat. sg.* gylte 14:117; *gen. pl.*
gylta 134:331; *dat. pl.* gyltum 76:4
ġymeleas *adj.* careless; *def. m. dat. pl.*
gymeleasum 38:24
ġyman [ġīeman] (1) (with gen.) take heed,
care; *ind. pres. 3 sg.* gymeþ 66:198; *pres.*
pl. gymaþ 112:333
ġyrnan [ġiernan] (1) to yearn, desire 136:11;
ind. pret. pl. gyrndon 36:235 (A)
ġyte *m.* shedding (of tears / blood); *dat. pl.*
gytum 42:102 [see ġit]

H

habban (3) to have 14:96, 24:142, 32:167,
38:4, 38:6, 58:12, 76:6, 76:21 >; *ind. pres. 2*
sg. hafast 54:224, 60:71; *3 sg.* hæfþ 10:20,
24:172, 42:114, 58:41, 58:42, 92:26; hafaþ 4:77,
30:108, 32:182, 58:40, 58:41, 60:49, 60:53,
72:109, 90:216, 126:170; hafað 84:77; *pl.*
habbaþ 14:95, 14:114, 16:155, 22:117, 30:111,
42:122, 48:46, 52:143, 52:149, 52:151 >;
habbað 38:12, 52:148, 132:311, 160:50,
160:52; hæbbað 126; hæbbe 22:135; *pret. 1*
sg. hæfde 80:100; *2 sg.* hæfdest 58:41,
122:74; *3 sg.* hæfde 2:35, 4:86, 6:116, 6:133,
12:72, 12:84, 52:140, 58:17, 62:110 >; *pl.*
hæfdon 14:133, 28:72, 46:11, 64:173, 68:38,
68:39, 68:41, 84:87a, 84:87b, 94:73, 100:79 >;
hæfdan 122:85, 140:118, 148:54 >; *subj. pres.*
sg. hæbbe 44:146, 44:150, 58:8, 68:12, 86:95,
104:143, 118:124, 118:125 >; *pl.* habban 18:9,
22:131, 26:6, 26:38, 34:228, 36:237, 62:123,
70:62, 76:31a, 76:31b, 132:304 >; *infl. inf.* to

hæbbenne 34:200, 36:235, 40:66/7, 154:215 >;
to hæbbene 78:71; *pp.* hæfde 60:74 >
hād *m.* person, order, office; *gen. sg.*
hādes 6:110, 30:133, 32:147, 92:8; *dat. sg.*
hāde 22:111, 146:23; *inst. sg.* hāde 138:64;
acc. pl. hādas 28:50, 76:39; *dat. pl.* hādum
76:36
hæftned *m.* captivity; *acc. sg.* hæftned
54:198; *dat. sg.* hæftnede 58:41, 60:63,
62:122
hǣlan (1) to heal, cure 74:17; *imp. 2 sg.*
hǣl 48:72, 54:219, 54:223, 54:224, 54:225,
54:230; *infl. inf.* to hǣlenne 152:181/2
hǣle *adj.* whole; *m. nom. pl.* hǣle 120:22
hǣl *f.* salvation; *dat. sg.* hǣle 46:4, 50:97,
74:23, 76:22, 90:197, 154:226
Hǣlend *m.* Saviour; *nom. sg.* 6:119, 10:11,
10:13, 10:17, 10:19, 10:25, 12:46, 12:65, 12:69;
acc. sg. Hǣlend 48:55, 74:10, 108:232,
116:85; Hǣlende [Hǣlende →Hǣlendne]
128:220; Hǣlendne 106:219, 112:336,
130:261; *gen. sg.* Hǣlendes 10:35, 46:25,
46:34, 46:37, 50:106, 50:115, 50:129, 50:130;
dat. sg. Hǣlende 4:47, 14:122, 46:24, 46:27,
46:33, 60:58, 76:21; Hǣlendum 108:260,
130:229, 160:75, 142
hǣlo *f.* salvation; *acc. sg.* hǣlo 2:40; *gen.*
sg. hǣlo 54:226; *dat. sg.* hǣlo 16:142,
24:157, 52:183, 110:310
hǣmedþing *m.* sexual commerce; *gen.*
sg. hǣmedþinges 40:67
hǣren *adj.* hairy; *nt. dat. sg.* hǣrenum
152:153
hǣr *m.* hair; *dat. pl.* hǣrum 118:116
hǣs *f.* command; *dat. sg.* hǣse 60:67,
108:272
hǣto *f.* heat; *nom. sg.* 32:181; hǣtu 4:66;
dat. pl. hǣton 40:57
hǣþen *adj.* heathen; *m. nom. pl.* hǣþene
150:136; hǣþne 90:205; hǣðne 146:7; *m.*
gen. pl. hǣþenra 32:145, 116:45, 138:85,
152:168, 152:176; *m. dat. pl.* hǣþnum 10:6,

120:14; hǣðnum 138:68; *def. m. nom. sg.*
hǣþena 152:172; *m. acc. sg.* hǣþenan
152:161; *m. dat. sg.* hǣþnum 120:21; *m.*
nom. pl. hǣþenan 152:150, 152:152; *nt.*
nom. pl. 152:165; hǣðnan 138:77, 140:94,
140:100, 152:179; *m. acc. pl.* hǣþnan
140:96; hǣðnan 138:89; *m. dat. pl.*
hēðnum 138:84
hāl *adj.* whole; *m. nom. sg.* 14:114, 120:18,
154:185; *m. acc. sg.* hālne 124:100, 150:121;
m. nom. pl. hāle 76:6
hālettan (1) to greet; *ind. pret. 3 sg.*
hālette 100:80, 108:264; *pl.* hāletton 98:32
(A) (M)
hālettung *f.* greeting; *nom. sg.* 4:58; *dat.*
sg. hālettunga 4:57; hālettunge 2:13 (A)
hālgian (2) to make holy 140:130, 140:132;
subj. pres. pl. hālgian 142:143; *pret. pl.*
hālgedon 140:120; *imp. 2 pl.* hālgiaþ
24:169; *infl. inf.* to hāligienne 18:29
hāliġ *adj.* holy; *m. nom. sg.* 4:49, 4:63,
82:26, 92:20, 110:313, 138:46; *nt. nom. sg.*
hālig 24:168; *m. gen. sg.* hāliges 80:107,
92:39, 114:37; hālges 84:46; *m. dat. sg.*
hālgum 116:66, 116:68, 116:73; *m. inst. sg.*
hālige 100:51; *m. nom. pl.* hālige 6:127,
12:43, 18:19, 20:46, 20:62, 20:82, 50:113,
72:111; hālge 114:8; *nt. nom. pl.* hāligu
28:81; *m. acc. pl.* hālige 24:176, 138:74;
hālie 100:83; *m. gen. pl.* hāligra 30:108,
30:110, 30:113, 38:2, 42:130, 44:162, 54:186; *m.*
dat. pl. hālgum 20:50, 20:51, 24:149, 66:191,
74:29, 86:92; *nt. dat. pl.* hālgum 92:30; *def.*
m. nom. sg. hāliga 14, 16, 20, 30, 32, 36, 39,
40, 41, 54, 57, 63, 74; hālga 4:62, 4:72, 6:118,
30:114, 54:215, 74:7, 16, 20, 22, 29; *f. nom. sg.*
hālige 2:20, 2:39, 4:45, 6:107, 6:121, 52:149,
102:95, 104:135, 136:12; *nt. nom. sg.* hālige
6:103, 38:21; *m. acc. sg.* hālgan 4:79, 60:84,
78:54, 84:47, 61; *f. acc. sg.* hālgan 18:7,
20:86, 24:173, 52:163, 52:172, 54:229, 140:136;
nt. acc. sg. hālige 10:23, 48:77, 52:153, 68:5,
114:5; *m. gen. sg.* hālgan 4:67, 82:2b, 82:16,
92:3, 92:25, 92:36, 92:37, 94:47; *f. gen. sg.*

hālgan 6:132, 8:146, 18:34, 38:5, 38:19, 82:2a;
nt. gen. sg. hālgan 38:4; *m. dat. sg.*
hāligan 62; hālgan 6:113, 72:116, 84:51,
92:38, 116:71; *f. dat. sg.* hālgan 46:1, 82:9,
88:174, 90:189, 169; *nt. dat. sg.* hālgan
146:2; *m. nom. pl.* hālgan, 36:234, 56:232,
82:17; *f. nom. pl.* 60:69 [hagan →halgan]; *nt.*
nom. pl. hālgum 10:5; *f. acc. pl.* hālgan
46:19, 86:93; *m. dat. pl.* halgan 96:91;
hālgum 82:15, 58; *f. dat. pl.* hālgum
62:106; *nt. dat. pl.* hālgum 84:43; hālgan
74:8; *superl. f. nom. sg.* hālgost 58:11
hāliġdōm *m.* holiness; *nom. sg.* 118:100
hāliġnes *f.* holiness; *gen. sg.* hālignesse
114:34; *dat. sg.* hālignesse 20:83, 108:273
hālsian (2) beseech, entreat; *ind. pres. 1*
sg. hālsige 40:51, 62:96, 68:33, 106:207,
130:259
hālsung *f.* embrace; *acc. sg.* halsunga
68:41; *dat. pl.* hālsunga 60:59
hālwend *adj.* wholesome; *m. acc. sg*
hālwendne 6:130; *f. nom. sg.* hālwende
80:116, 142:180; *def. m. nom. pl.*
hālwendan 82:12
hālwendliċ *adj.* wholesome; *f. acc. sg.*
hālwendlice 140:127
hām *adv.* elsewhere 6:93, 46:12, 148:88
hām *m.* home; *nom. sg.* 16:169; *acc. sg.*
hām 4:79; *dat. sg.* hām 48:50, 140:107
hand *f.* hand; *acc. sg.* hand 50:92, 108:235,
140:100, 30, 31; *dat. sg.* handa 98:11, 98:15,
104:166, 106:204, 120:3, 142:160, 150:119;
nom. pl. handa 60:79, 106:227; *acc. pl.*
handa 24:163, 84:77, 100:43, 100:46, 106:226;
gen. pl. handa 68:25; *dat. pl.* handum
104:174, 106:193, 136:10, 144:202, 152:181;
inst. pl. handum 126:150
handlean *nt.* recompense; *acc. sg.*
handlean 62:123
hangian (2) to hang; *ind. pres. 3 sg.*
hangaþ 88:179; *pret. 3 sg.* hangode
106:204; *pret. pl.* hangodan 144:202,
144:206
hār *adj.* hoary; *m. acc. sg.* hārne 144:199

81

hāt *adj.* hot; *f. nom. sg.* hāt 154:222; *def. m. gen. sg.* hātan 72:96

hātan (VII) to bid, command, order; *ind. pres.* 2 *sg.* hātest 132:278; *3 sg.* hāteþ 14:108, 66:184; *pret.* 3 *sg.* hēht 120:33, 122:53, 122:65, 122:81, 126:136, 130:235, 130:267, 130:269, 150:95, 150:116, 154:203; hēt 10:17, 126:178, 130:233, 145, 146; *3 pl.* hēton 158:2; *subj. pres. sg.* hāte 98:21; *pret. 3 sg.* hēte 28:45; *imp.* 2 *sg.* hāt 122:80, 124:129, 126:165, 126:175, 128:184, 132:280

hātan (VII) to name, call; *ind. pret. 3 sg.* hātte 46:38, 122:68, 132:310, 136:22, 146:40; hāte 132:321; *pret. pl.* hātton 138:70; *pp.* hāten 46:37, 130:264, 136:16, 138:46, 150:110, 152:150

hātheort *nt.* wrath; *nom. sg.* 106:197

hātheort *f.* anger; *dat. sg.* hātheortan 163

hātheort *adj.* wrathful; *comp. m. nom. sg.* hātheortra 152:169

hātheortlīċe *adv.* heartily 40:62, 40:68, 132:291

hatian (2) to hate; *ind. pres. pl.* hatigaþ 64:161; *subj. pres. sg.* hatige 44:146, 44:147

hatung *f.* hatred; *dat. sg.* hatunga 132:313

hē, hēo, hit *pron.* he, she, it; *m. f. & nt.* (see Appendix, p. 145)

hēaf *m.* mourning, lamentation; *nom. sg.* 60:46, 80:123; *acc. sg.* hēaf 34:206, 150:111

hēafda *m.* head of a couch, bed; *dat. sg.* hēafdan 102:121

hēafliċ *adj.* sorrowful; *def. nt. nom. sg.* hēaflice 86:100

hēafod *nt.* head, chief; *nom. sg.* 20:89, 88:163, 120:27, 126:180, 132:287; *acc. sg.* hēafod 16:140, 50:94, 128:183, 130:252, 130:253 132:279, 132:284, 132:289, 160:79, 154; *gen. sg.* hēafdes 30:117, 100, 105; *dat. sg.* hēafde 120:28, 126:175, 126:179, 128:185, 142:160, 99; *acc. pl.* hēafdu 106:192

hēafodliċ *adj.* chief, principal; *def. m. acc. pl.* hēafodlican 24:146

hēah *adj.* high, exalted; *m. nom. sg.* 88:161; *m. acc. sg.* hēahne 126:165; *f. nom. sg.* hēh 52:171; *f. acc. sg.* hēa 18:12; *def. m.*

nom. sg. hēa 22:90, 138:51; *m. acc. sg.* hēan 20:86; *f. nom. sg.* hēa 74:6; *f. acc. sg.* hēan 22:91; *m. gen. sg.* hēan 136:1, 136:17b; *m. dat. sg.* hēan 20:58, 136:12, 136:17a; *f. dat. sg.* hēan 20:63; *nt. dat. sg.* hēan 90:195; *m. acc. pl.* hēan 46:21; *superl. f. nom. sg.* hēhst 58:11; *def. m. gen. sg.* hēhstan 4:63, 4:73, 76:29; *nt. dat. sg.* hēhstan 54:219, 54:223, 54:230

hēahdiacon *m.* archdeacon; *nom. pl.* hēahdiaconas 76:37

hēahengel *m.* archangel; *nom. sg.* 102:130, 110:285, 116:62, 118:95, 136:8, 138:52, 138:56, 142:161; hēahengl [→ hēahengel] 66:185; *acc. sg.* hēahengel 138:62, 142:137, 144:195; *gen. sg.* hēahengles 136:2; *dat. sg.* hēahengle 104:139, 108:258, 110:284, 110:297, 138:74, 140:108; *nom. pl.* hēahenglas 72:110; *dat. pl.* hēahenglum 16:170

hēahfæder *m.* patriarch; *nom. sg.* 62:106; *gen. sg.* hēahfæder 114:22; *nom. pl.* hēahfæderas 72:110, 74:2; *acc. pl.* hēhfæderas [→ hēahfæderas] 48:85; *gen. pl.* hēahfædera 114:6, 118:105; hēhfædera [→ hēahfædera] 54:216; *dat. pl.* hēahfæderum 16:170

hēahġerēfa *m.* high officer; *nom. sg.* 124:89; *dat. pl.* hēahgerēfum 120:11

hēahġeþungen *adj.* illustrious; *m. acc. pl.* hēahgeþungene 128:204

hēahsetl *nt.* throne; *dat. sg.* hēahsetle 6:102, 6:125, 34:221; hēahsettle 44:139; hēhsetle [→ hēahsetle] 108:271

hēal *adj.* whole; *f. nom. sg.* 80:116

healdan (VII) to hold, keep 6:131, 22:123, 28:89, 36:240, 38:5, 38:6, 68:18, 90:219, 130:269; healdon 130:267; *ind. pres.1 sg.* healde 104:158; *pl.* healdað 6:124; healdaþ 16:150, 38:12; *pret. 3 sg.* hēold 34:221, 146:29; *subj. pres. sg.* healde 58:8; *pl.* healdan 22:103, 24:145, 28:50, 28:81, 30:126, 30:135, 30:136; *pret. sg.* heolde 28:52; *pl.* heoldan 76:30, 128:213; *imp.1 pl.* healdan 8:151; *2 pl.* healdaþ 104:155; *infl. inf.* to healdenne 6:122

healf *adj.* half; *m. acc. sg.* healfne 148:50;
nt. acc. sg. healf 148:48; *m. dat. sg.*
healfum 148:50

healf *f.* half; *acc. sg.* healfe 62:116, 66:192,
104:153

healfcwiċ *adj.* half-alive, half-dead; *m.
nom. pl.* healfcwice 140:96

healiċ *adj.* high, exalted, lofty; *m. nom.
sg.* 118:111; *m. gen. sg.* healices 118:127; *f.
nom. sg.* healico 140:119; *def. nt. acc. pl.*
healican 118:90; *nt. dat. pl.* healicum
146:20

healīċe *adv.* highly 86:96, 88:139; *comp.*
healīcor 22:109

heall *f.* hall; *nom. sg.* 114:36; *dat. sg.*
healle 120:39

healt *adj.* halt; *m. nom. pl.* healte 48:79

hēan *adj.* poor; *m. dat. sg.* hēanum
86:131; *superl. m. nom. sg.* hēanosta
118:131

hēanes *f.* height; *acc. sg* hēanesse. 84:53;
dat. sg. hēanesse 18:9, 142:159; *dat. pl.*
hēanessum 2:25, 36:235, 48:72, 64:150

hēap *m.* troop; *nom. sg.* 54:215; *nom. pl.*
hēapas 118:122

heard *adj.* hard, severe; *m. nom. sg.*
66:204; *nt. nom. sg.* heard 154:225; *m. acc.
sg.* heardne 66:202; *f. gen. sg.* heardre
38:39; *nt. dat. sg.* heardum 152:154; *def. m.
gen. sg.* heardan 72:96; *m. dat. sg.*
heardan (heardam → heardan) 154:219; *f. acc.
pl.* heardan 68:7; *superl. m. gen. sg.*
heardestan 32:139; *f. nom. sg.* heardeste
55

heard *adv.* hard; *superl.* heardost 154:224

hēaþrym *m.* exalted; *nom. sg.* 92:8

hebban (VI) to raise up; *ind. pret. pl.*
hofan 104:173, 110:304

hefiġ *adj.* heavy, grievous; *m. nom. pl*
hefige 48:45; *def. f. nom. sg.* hefige
50:126; *f. acc. sg.* hefian 74:59; *comp. nt.
nom. sg.* hefigre 70:74; *superl. def. f. gen.
sg.* heofogoston 50:125

hēh (see hēah)

hēhfædera (see hēahfæder)

hēhstān (see hēah)

hēht (see hātan)

hēhþ *m.* height; *dat. sg.* hēhþe 46:3

hell *f.* hell; *acc. sg.* helle 32:141, 60:69;
gen. sg. helle 22:99, 40:85, 42:94, 44:157,
46:21, 56:233, 58:14, 58:26, 58:28; *dat. sg.*
helle 22:108, 28:44, 28:80, 42:102, 46:19

hellware *f.* hell's host; *gen. pl.*
helwarena 60:55; *dat. pl.* hellwarum 60:80

help *m.* help; *dat. sg.* helpe 74:23, 124:113

helpan (III) (with gen. or dat.) to help, aid
24:173, 50:135, 152:166

helpend *m.* helper; *acc. sg.* 74:11

helscēað *m.* hell-robbers; *dat. pl.*
helscēaðum 144:196

hēo (see hē, hēo, hit)

heofencund *adj.* heavenly; *def. f. nom.
sg.* heofencunde 116:78

heofogoston (see hefiġ)

heofon *m.* heaven; *nom. sg.* 4:43, 62:129,
62:133, 64:142, 64:145, 64:162, 104; *acc. sg.*
heofon 64:139, 64:144, 84:82, 86:109, 86:113a,
86:113b; heofen 14:128, 86:115, 130:230; *gen.
sg.* heofenes 26:17, 32:173; heofeones
48:44; *nom. pl.* heofonas 74:6; *acc. pl.*
heofenas 62:115, 84:65, 84:70, 84:79, 88:138,
88:175, 90:202, 92:7; heofonas 82:5, 86:105,
86:116, 13, 158, 161; *gen. pl.* heofena 40:50,
96:95, 110:318, 112:332; heofona 2:25, 4:52,
20:61, 26:14, 28:46, 46:21, 62:134, 110:321,
112:334; *dat. pl.* heofnum 64:156, 68:32;
heofenum 12:86, 26:10, 30:105, 50:123,
52:161, 64:137, 64:141; heofonum 2:28,
32:148, 32:149, 76:32, 82:13, 84:47, 116:72 >

heofoncyning *m.* heaven's king; *acc. sg.*
heofoncining [heofon cining → heofoncining]
54:207; *gen. sg.* heofoncyninges 138:56

heofonliċ *adj.* heavenly; *m. acc. sg.*
heofonlicne 132:299; *f. acc. sg.* heofonlice
32:162; heofonlice 154:191; *m. dat. sg.*
heofonlicum 64:179; *f. dat. sg.* heofonlicum
62:97; *nt. acc. pl.* heofonlice 6:130; *m. dat.
pl.* heofonlicum 16:169; *def. m. nom. sg.*

83

heofonlica 2:29, 4:58, 4:81, 6:93, 6:123, 92:15; *nt. nom. sg.* heofonlice 6:130, 12:48; heofenlice 94:76; heofenlice 110:288; *m. acc. sg.* heofonlican 34:223, 94:78; *m. gen. sg.* heofonlican 56:232, 92:5; *f. gen. sg.* heofonlican 4:65; *nt. gen. sg.* heofonlican 6:104, 10:39, 42:92, 74:27; heofenlican 40:89; *m. dat. sg.* heofonlican 20:59a, 80:130; *nt. acc. sg.* heofonlice 78:58, 86:123; heofenlice 94:75; *nt. dat. sg.* heofonlican 6:121, 34:226; heofonlicon 10:32; *m. nom. pl.* heofonlican 6:123; *nt. acc. pl.* heofonlican 20:59b; *nt. gen. pl.* heofonlican 10:31/2, 10:33
heofonrīċe *nt.* heaven's kingdom; *gen. sg.* heofonrīċes 4:74/5
heofonware *f.* dwellers in heaven; *nom. pl.* heofonware 6:105; heofenware 94:67; *gen. pl.* heofonwara 60:60
heonon *adv.* hence 20:62, 132:293
heononweard *adj.* passing away; *f. nom. sg.* 80:126/7
heora (see hē, hēo, hit)
heord *f.* flock; *acc. sg.* heorde 154:207; *dat. sg.* heorde 28:88
heorte *f.* heart; *nom. sg.* 30:131, 48:53, 94:74, 158:3, 160:70; heorta 8; *acc. sg.* heortan 24:154, 80:102, 102; *gen. sg.* heortan 12:63, 44:164, 86:108, 142:162; *dat. sg.* heortan 2:23, 4:45, 6:135, 8:149, 12:57, 12:61, 24:165, 30:132; *nom. pl.* heortan 90:191; *acc. pl.* heortan 76:7; *gen. pl.* heortena 124:126; *dat. pl.* heortum 50:101, 54:207, 62:112, 66:197, 78:51, 80:110, 80:121
hēow *nt.* colour, appearance; *gen. sg.* hēowes 50:109, 136:7; *dat. sg.* hēowe 66:189, 162:94
hēowcūð *adj.* familiar; *m. nom. pl.* hēowcūðe 68:13
hēr *adv.* here 2:37, 14:122, 18:1, 24:143, 26:31, 28:79, 32:137, 32:151 >
hera [hiera] (see hē, hēo, hit)
hēran (1) to hear, obey 64:178
herdebēlig *m.* shepherd's bag; *nom. sg.* 20:68

here *m.* army; *acc. sg.* here 54:190; *gen. sg.* herges 132:313; *dat. sg.* herige 54:189, 54:192
herehȳhþ *f.* spoil; *acc. sg.* herehȳhþ 62:109; herehȳþ 64:176
hererēaf *nt.* spoil, plunder; *acc. sg.* 58:38
heretoga *m.* leader; *nom. sg.* 116:85
herewīc *nt.* dwellings; *nom. pl.* 80:101
herġendliċ *adj.* laudible; *m. nom. sg.* 98:20
herġung *f.* harrowing; *dat. sg.* hergunga 58:19
heriean (1) to praise; *ind. pres. pl.* herigaþ 20:62; hergeaþ 62:108; *pret. 3 sg.* herede 6:134, 6:135, 10:21, 140:91; *pret. pl.* heredon 74:3, 104:180, 120:34; heredan 70:45; *subj. pres. pl.* herian 20:71; *imp 1 pl.* herian 4:44; *infl. inf.* to herianne 6:111; herigenne 42:132; hergenne 154:185; *pp.* hered 46:7
Herod *pers. n.* Herod; *gen. sg.* Herodes 114:20
hersumian [hīersumian] (2) to obey; *ind. pres. pl.* hersumiað 89 (A)
heruwan [hierwan] (1) to despise; *ind. pret. 2 sg.* heruwdest 32:164
hēt (see hātan)
hēte, hēton (see hātan)
hēðnum (see hǣþen)
hī (see hē, hēo, hit)
hider *adv.* hither 4:75, 60:43, 60:53, 70:54, 70:85, 74:4, 80:95, 82:33 >
hidercym *m.* coming hither; *dat. sg.* hidercyme 60:53, 60:62
hīe, hiene (see hē, hēo, hit)
hieora, hiere (see hē, hēo, hit)
Hierusalem *prop. n.* Jerusalem; *acc. sg.* Hierusalem 128; *dat. sg.* Hierusalem 48:57, 132:308
higian (2) to hasten 20:43
hiht *m.* hope; *nom. sg.* 54:229, 82
Hilari *pers. n.* Hillary; *dat. sg.* Hilarie 148:74
him (see hē, hēo, hit)
hindsið *m.* ruin; *nom. sg.* 86:99

hine (see hē, hēo, hit)

hine [hīe] (see hē, hēo, hit)

hingrian (1) to hunger 110:322; *ind. pres. 3 sg.* hingreþ 26:17; *pret. 3 sg.* hingrede 18:3; *pres. p. m. dat. pl.* hingrigendum 146:30; *def. m. acc. pl.* hingrigendan 2:21

hīo, hiora (see hē, hēo, hit)

hira, hire (see hē, hēo, hit))

hīred *m.* household; *acc. sg.* hired 28:84, 154:197, 154:201; *dat. sg.* hīrede 120:39

his (see hē, hēo, hit)

hit (see hē, hēo, hit)

hīw *nt.* colour, hue; *acc. sg.* hīw 18:28; *dat. sg.* hīwe 18:27, 18:29

hīwung *f.* likeness, image; *dat. sg.* hīwunga 42:90

hlǣdder *f.* ladder; *dat. pl.* hlǣddrum 142:177

hlāf *m.* loaf, bread; *acc. sg.* hālf 24:160, 124:130, 126:145, 4, 160:55; *dat. sg.* hlāfe 18:5, 50:96; *dat. pl.* hlafum 18:4

hlāford *m.* lord, master; *nom. sg.* 136:31; *acc. sg.* hlāford 48:44, 116:80, 122:83; *acc. pl.* hlāfordas 128:216; *gen. pl.* hlāforda 120:36; *dat. pl.* hlāfordum 128:217

hleahter *m.* laughter; *nom. pl.* hleahtras 34:205, 40:69

hleonian [hlinian] (2) to lean, recline; *pres. p.* hleonigende 102:121

hlīfian (2) to cross; *pres. p.* hlīfigende 100:72

hliehhan (VI) to laugh; *ind. pres. pl.* hlihaþ 16:161

hlīewan (1) to warm; *ind. pres. 3 sg.* hlȳweþ [hlȳpeþ → hlȳweþ] 32:181

hlot *m.* lot; *acc. sg.* hlot 2

hlūd *adj.* loud; *f. nom. sg.* 104:180; *f. inst. sg.* hlūdre 126:147; hlūddre 10:14

hlūde *adv.* loudly 106:182, 150:101; *comp.* hlūdor 10:16

hlūttor *adj.* pure, clear; *m. nom. sg.* 142:174, 148:79; *nt. inst. sg.* hlūttre 40:46; *nt. dat. pl.* hlūtrum 54:222

hlȳweþ [see hlīewan]

hnescestan *adj.* soft, tender; *superl. f. acc. sg.* 68:27

hofan (see hebban)

hōc *m.* hook; *dat. sg.* hōce 28:68, 28:70

hold *adj.* faithful; *m. gen. pl.* holdra 86:95

hondgeweorc *m.* handiwork; *nom. sg.* 104:158

hond *m.* hand; *dat. pl.* hondum 18:9

hongian [hangian] (2) to hang; *ind. pres. 3 sg.* hongaþ 88:183

hogian (2) to hope; *ind. pret. pl.* hopodan 60:62

hordcofa *m.* closet; *dat. sg.* hordcofan 102:96

hordern *nt.* storehouse; *nom. pl.* hordernu 68:36

hordfæt *m.* treasury; *dat. sg.* hordfæte 74:8

hrædlīče *adv.* quickly, soon 14:94, 38:19, 76:4, 94:76, 160:56; *comp.* hrædlicor 158:31, 158:32

hrægl *nt.* garment, clothing; *acc. sg.* hrægl 34:225, 98:16, 148:59, 152:171, 160:55; *gen. sg.* hrægles 148:43, 154:184; *dat. sg.* hrægle 26:41, 98:17, 118:115, 128:207, 150:128, 152:153; *inst. sg.* hrægle 148:57, 148:62; *nom. pl.* hrægl 84:85; *acc. pl.* hrægl 48:69; *gen. pl.* hrægla 68:39; *dat. pl.* hræglum 20:57, 66:191, 84:84, 86:110

hraþe *adv.* speedily 12:80, 18:18, 106:228, 108:251, 110:283, 8, 25, 110, 117; hraðe 9, 37, 69, 85

hrēam *m.* weeping, lamentation; *nom. sg.* 80:123; *acc. sg.* hrēam 42:115

hrēof *m.* leper; *acc. pl.* hrēofe 124:90

hrēones *f.* roughness; *acc. sg.* hrēonesse 160:73; *dat. sg.* hrēonesse 160:62

hrēow *f.* penitence, repentance; *nom. sg.* 70:60; *acc. sg.* hrēowe 24:143, 54:185, 54:187, 70:60, 90:193; *dat. sg.* hrēowe 16:157, 16:160

hrif *nt.* womb; *nom. sg.* 4:67; *dat. sg.* hrife 22:95

hrīmig *adj.* rimy; *m. nom. pl.* hrīmige [hsomige → hrīmige] 142:163/4, 144:200
hrōf *m.* roof; *nom. sg.* 142:159; *gen. sg.* hrōfes 142:173
hrōp *m.* lamentation; *nom. sg.* 128:199
hrȳman [hrīeman] (1) to cry; *pres. p. m. nom. sg.* hrȳmende 153
hrȳþer *nt.* ox; *nom. sg.* 136:31, 136:32; *acc. sg.* hrȳþer 136:39, 138:45; hrȳþær 136:35; *dat. pl.* hrȳþrum 136:24
hū *adv.* how (see Appendix, pp. 147 & 151)
hugu (see hwa and hwylc)
hund *m.* dog; *nom. pl.* hundas 126:148, 126:149; *acc. pl.* hundas 126:154; *dat. pl.* hundum 126:151
hund *num.* hundred 22:132, 82:38, 140:104, 142:153, 38; hunde 46:40, 52:139
hundliċ *adj.* canine; *m. acc. pl.* hundlice 126:155
hundtēontiġ *num.* hundred 54:196, 54:197, 54:200
hundtēontiġfeald *adj.* hundredfold; *f. dat. sg.* hundtēontigfealdre 26:33
hungor *m.* hunger; *nom. sg.* hungor 44:160, 72:113; *acc. sg.* hungor 42:115; *dat. sg.* hungre 12:67, 40:83, 54:193, 132:318; *inst. sg.* hungre 38:33, 54:192, 54:195; *acc. pl.* hungras 76:18
hunig *m.* honey; *dat. sg.* hunige 118:114
hūru *adv.* yet; 30:101, 30:121, 78:67, 86:97, 154:200, 156:232 >
hūs *nt.* house; *nom. sg.* 46:35, 48:78, 50:106, 88:150, 88:154, 114:34, 142:156, 152:140; *acc. sg.* hūs 6:98, 50:99, 102:120, 102:129, 132:298, 152:141, 152:142; *gen. sg.* hūses 100:64, 150:120; *dat. sg.* hūse 26:15, 50:93, 60:81, 98:14, 100:80, 102:108, 102:119; *gen. pl.* hūsa 70:46; *dat. pl.* hūsum 142:167
hūsl *m.* sacrament; *dat. sg.* hūsle 142:146, 142:177
hwā, hwæt *rel. pron.* who; *m./f. & n. nom. sg.* (see Appendix, p. 146)
hwæm (see hwā, hwæt)

hwǣr *adv.* where 40:67, 40:68, 70:44, 70:45, 70:49, 78:76a, 78:76b, 78:78, 78:79, 78:80, 118:115 >
hwæs (see hwā, hwæt)
hwæt (see hwā, hwæt)
hwǣte *m.* wheat; *nom. sg.* 32:174
hwæþer ... þe *conj.* whether ... or 82:41
hwæþere *conj.* nevertheless 12:85, 14:135, 26:7, 52:141, 52:144, 52:152; hwæþre 10:32, 14:130, 72:99, 118:93; hwēþre 88:151, 110:293, 148:70, 152:162, 154:209, 154:230; hwēðre 124:103, 142:170, 144:186, 146:5, 146:7, 146:20, 146:23, 146:28 >
hwām (see hwā, hwæt)
hwan (see hwā, hwæt)
hwanan *adv.* whence 14:100
hwane (see hwā, hwæt)
hwanne *adv.* when 118:113, 118:118, 154:224
hwearf (see hweorfan)
hwega (see hwā, hwæt and hwilċ)
hwego (see hwā, hwæt)
hwelcum (see hwilċ)
hwēmdragen [hwēm dragen → hwēmdragen] *adj.* oblique; *m. nom. sg.* 142:156
hwēne *adv.* a little 38:19, 88:160
hweorfan (III) to return 68:16; *ind. pres. 2 sg.* hwyrfest 160:64; *pret. 3 sg.* hwearf 136:34; *imp. 2 sg.* hwyrf 158; *2 pl.* hweorfað 160:83; *pres. p.* hweorfende 46:12, 98:14; hwyrfende 136:29, 142:166, 161
hweþer *conj.* whether 20:53, 54:184, 140:120, 140:130, 160:62; hweðer ... þe whether ... or 82:20/1
hwider *adv.* whither 2
hwīle *nt.* time; *acc. sg.* 34:186, 86:131, 88:158, 150:97, 150:98; þa hwīle þe *acc. sg.* whilst 24:142/3, 34:198/9, 66:194, 70:61, 70:61/2, 70:67, 72:103, 80:127, 86:127, 122:54, 154:221; ða hwīle ðe 140:114; þa hwile 106:220; nu hwile 76:23; *dat. pl.* hwilum 34:196a, 34:196b, 42:114, 140:92, 140:93, 154:228
hwiērfan (1) to return; *ind. pret. pl.* hwīrfdon 46 (A)

86

hwīlwendliċ *adj.* temporary, transitory; *m. nom. sg.* 34:213

hwīt *adj.* white; *f. acc. sg.* hwīte 104:143, 104:148, 104:151; *nt. dat. pl.* 86:110; *def. nt. nom. pl.* hwitan 84:84

hwītnes *f.* whiteness; *nom. sg.* 4:69

hwōn (see hwā)

hwonne *adv.* when 68:11, 68:15, 70:48, 78:45, 82:27, 84:44, 86:120

hwonon *adv.* whence 58:31, 106:225

hwugu (see hwā)

hwȳ (see hwā)

hwyder *adv.* whither 68:12, 70:43, 70:44, 106:193, 130:243, 132:294, 160:43

hwylċ *pron., adj.* who, what, which; *m. nom. sg.* 14:105, 40:52, 40:81, 80:93, 104:142, 118:121; *nt. non. sg.* hwylc 34:189; *f. acc. sg.* hwilce 86:131; *nt. acc. sg.* hwylc 26:14, 62:123; *f. dat. sg.* hwylcere 122:75; *nt. dat. sg.* hwylcum 2:20, 26:29, 40:74, 40:75; *nt. inst. sg.* hwylce 100:57, 100:84; hwylcum 162:109; *m. nom. pl.* hwylce 38:8; *m. acc. pl.* hwylce 68:12

hwylċ *pron., adj.* some; *m. nom. sg.* hwylc 20:81, 108:233; *nt. nom. sg.* hwilc 49; *m. acc. sg.* hwylcne 154:184; *m. gen. sg.* hwylces 86:135; *m. dat. sg.* hwylcum 92:13; hwelcum 148:65; *m. dat. pl.* hwylcum 34:229; *f. dat. pl.* hywlcum 34:187

hwylċ [hwilċ] *pronom.* what, which & who; *m., f. & nt. nom. sg.* (see Appendix, p. 148)

hwyrf (see hweorfan)

hwyrfel *m.* circuit; *nom. sg.* 88:142

hȳ [hī] (see hē, hēo, hit)

hycgan (3) to think; *subj. pres. sg.* hycgge 28:48

hȳdan (1) hide; *ind. pres. pl.* hȳdað 64:165; *subj. pres. pl.* hȳdon 34:228

hyht *m.* hope; *nom. sg.* 60:60, 60:61, 94:77, 94:78, 116:65; *acc. sg.* hyht 94:89, 128:206

hyhtan (1) to rejoice; *ind. pret. 3 sg.* hyhte 116:81; *pl.* hyhtan 60:62; *imp. 3 pl.*

hyhton 62:117; *pres. p. def. m. nom. sg.* hyhtenda 6:100

hyll *m.* hill; *dat. pl.* hyllum 64:171

hyp *m.* hip; *dat. sg.* hype 6:117

hyra [hira] (see hē, hēo, hit)

hȳran [hīeran] (1) to hear 32:137, 80:128, 128:193; *ind. pres. 3 pl.* hȳraþ 42:134; *pret 3 sg.* hȳrde 152:164; *pret. pl.* hȳrdon 94:70, 138:69; *subj. pret. pl.* hȳrdon 128:210, 128:217 (A)

hyrde *m.* shepherd, herdsman; *nom. sg.* 120:3, 132:301, 138:59; *gen. sg.* hyrdes 136:30; *nom. pl.* hyrdas 30:97; *acc. pl.* hyrdas 124:99, 15, 46, 50

hȳrsumian (2) to obey; *ind. pret. pl.* hȳrsumedon 94:68

hys [his] (see hē, hēo, hit)

I

iċ, wit, wē *pers. pron.* I, we two, we (see Appendix, p. 145)

īdel *adj.* empty, idle; *m. nom. sg.* 68:16; *nt. acc. sg.* īdel 18:12, 20:45; *f. nom. pl.* īdle 90:215; *nt. nom. pl.* īdelu 152:165; *def. m. nom. sg.* īdla 40:67; *m. dat. sg.* īdlan 20:65; *m. nom. pl.* īdlan 78:78; *f. nom. pl.* īdlan 70:43; *nt. nom. pl.* īdlan 40:69; *nt. acc. pl.* īdlan 146:12, 152:178, 152:181

īdel-hende *adj.* empty-handed; *m. nom. sg.* 32:156

īdelnes *f.* emptiness; *dat. sg.* īdelnesse 2:22, 112:324; *nom. pl.* īdelnessa 40:68

Ierusalem *prop. n.* Jerusalem; *dat. sg.* Ierusalem 54:200

ilca *adj.* same; *def. m. nom. sg.* 20:73, 42:99, 58:38, 68:30, 86:117, 86:120; *f. nom. sg.* ilce 136:19; *nt. nom. sg.* ilce 122:51, 142:156; *m. acc. sg.* ilcan 124:127, 136:22, 136:41; *f. acc. sg.* ilcan 14:131, 86:103, 100:60, 106:190; *nt. acc. sg.* ilce 122:62, 122:63, 73; *m. dat. sg.* ilcan 86:116, 138:51, 142:172; *f. dat. sg.* ilcan 14:107, 62:124,

62:130, 88:172; *nt. inst. sg.* ilcan 148:57; *m. dat. pl.* ilcan 32:142; *nt. inst. pl.* ilcum 108:245

in *prep.* (with *acc. / dat.*) in (see Appendix, p. 150)

in *adv.* in 88:163, 122:65, 140:124

inbelūcan [inbelocan] (II) to shut in; *ind. pret. 3 sg.* inbelēac 150:95

inc (see ġit)

incer *dual pron.* you two; *nt. nom. sg.* incer 122:72; *f. dat. sg.* incre 130:250

incuman (IV) to enter 88:153; *ind. pret. pl.* incoman 120:29

ingān (anom.) to enter; *ind. pret. 3 sg.* inēode 2:29, 48:77, 9, 14 >; inēodan 158:21

infeccan [infetian] (2) to fetch 122:54 (A)

ingang *m.* entrance; *nom. sg.* 4:80

ingangan [ingongan] (VII) to enter; *imp. 2 pl.* ingongað 142:144; *pres. p.* ingangende 102:129, 47, 66, 80; ingongende 100:80, 102:131

inġehygd *m.* intention; *acc. pl.* ingehygd 124:125; ingehyd 94:77

inġelǣdan (1) to lead in; *subj. pres. sg.* ingelǣde 132:297

inġeþanc *m.* mind; *inst. pl.* ingeþancum 38:20

in hlēt [hlīet] *m.* lot; *acc. sg.* in hlēt [inhlēt → in hlēt] 110:306

innan *adv.* within, inwardly; 84:51, 90:191, 90:207, 136:7, 148:78; innon 54:200

inne *post prep.* (after *rel. pron.*) in (see Appendix, p. 150)

inner *m.* inward part, what is within; *nom. pl.* inneran 60:84

inneweard *adj.* inward; *f. dat. sg.* inneweardre 4:45, 12:57, 38:7; *f. inst. pl.* inneweardum 92:41

innon (see innan)

innoð *m.* womb; *nom. sg.* 6:118; *acc. sg.* innoþ 2:25, 2:30, 6:118, 62:97; innoð 4:81, 14:131; *gen. sg.* innoþes 2:32; innoðes 4:65, 6:97; *dat. sg.* innoþe 2:5, 2:24, 74:7, 118:92; innoðe 142:180; *acc. pl.* innoþas 118:91

instæpes *adv.* forthwith, immediately 10:20, 26:28, 44:149, 60:57; instepes 22:99, 22:119; instepe 136:40 (A) (M)

intō *prep.* (with *acc*) into (EWS) (see Appendix, p. 150)

inwit *m.* deceit, guile; *nom. sg.* 76:41; inwid [inwit] 154:189 (A)

inwitfull *adj.* deceitful; *def. nt. acc. pl.* inwitfullan 38:11

iō *adv.* formerly 80:99, 80:100; iū 4:74

Iōhannes *pers. n.* John; *nom. sg.* 46:22, 100:53, 100:57, 100:79, 104:167, 104:169, 114:42, 116:51, 116:53, 116:57, 116:70, 116:77, 118:102, 118:104, 118:112; Iōhannis 116:55; *gen. sg.* Iōhannes 114:3, 114:8, 114:19, 114:25, 118:91, 118:97, 118:100, 140:125; Iōhanne 114:38; *dat. sg.* Iōhanne 48:60, 100:56, 114:8, 114:17, 118:110, 118:133

Iōhel *pers. n.* Joel; *nom. sg.* 24:169

irenum *adj.* iron; *m. dat. pl. sg.* irenum 132:277

is (see eom)

īsige *adj.* ice; *def. m. dat. pl.* īsigean 144:202

īsen *adj.* iron; *def. m. dat. sg.* īsenan 28:68; īs[e]nan 28:70; *m. nom. pl.* īsenan 60:57

Israhēl *prop. n.* Israel; *nom. sg.* 112:325; *gen. pl.* Israhēla 4:51, 82:15, 82:18, 108:271/2, 110:294, 116:67; *dat. pl.* Israhēlum 4:50, 6:116

Ītālia *prop. n.* Italy; *dat. sg.* Ītālia 146:5

iū (see iō)

Iūdah *prop. n* Judah; *dat. sg.* Iūdan 20:76

Iūdas *pers. n.* Judas; *nom. sg.* 42:119, 52:137, 52:140; *dat. sg.* Iūdan 52:145

Iūdēa *prop. n.* Judea; *dat. sg.* Iūdēa 84:56

Iūdēas *prop. n.* Jews; *nom. pl.* 50:96, 104:179, 106:187, 106:191a, 122:84; *acc. pl.* Iūdēas 106:191b, 118:120; *gen. pl.* Iūdēa 46:7, 46:23, 54:206, 68:8, 106:184, 106:194, 108:231, 108:237, 122:67, 122:68, 122:80, 124:93, 124:101, 124:105, 124:106; *dat. pl.* Iūdēum 10:26, 16:138, 58:23, 124:89, 162:108

Iūdisc *adj.* Jewish; *m. nom. sg.* 46:10; *def. nt. nom. sg.* Iūdisce 48:50; *nt. acc. sg.* Iūdisce 54:215

iugoþ *f.* youth; *nom. sg.* 114:29; *gen sg.* iugoþe 62:91

Iulius *pers. n.* Julius; *gen. sg.* Iulius 146:10

K

kyning *m.* king; *gen. sg.* kyninges 116:45; *dat. pl.* kyningum 120:11

L

lā *interj.* lo 40:67, 78:75, 78:76 >
lāc *nt.* offering, gift; *acc. sg.* lāc 24:159, 24:169, 142:137; *acc. pl.* lāc 30:109, 138:63; *dat. pl.* lācum 30:104, 142:150
lād *f.* excuse; *acc. sg.* lāde 38:41
lādian (2) to vindicate; *ind. pret. 3 sg.* lādode 106:210
Lāzarus *pers. n.* Lazarus; *acc. sg.* Lāzarum 48:87
læcedōm *m.* medicine; *acc. sg.* læcedōm 68:20; *dat. sg.* læcedōme 76:5
lǣdon [lǣdan] (1) to lead 22:91, 88:175, 132:319; *ind. pres. pl.* lǣdaþ 88:169; *pret. 2 sg.* lǣddest 60:43, 60:52; *3 sg.* lǣdde 18:7, 18:11, 28:74, 150:120, 167; *pl.* lǣddon 28:71, 48:67, 54:198; *imp. 2 pl.* lǣdað 54:204; *pp.* lǣded 18:1, 20:85
læg (see licgan)
lǣne *adj.* lean, frail; *def. m. gen. sg.* lǣnan 14:93; *nt. gen. sg.* lǣnan 78:86, 92:30
lǣneliċ *adj.* frail; *def. nt. acc. sg.* lǣnelice 50:98
lǣran (1) to teach 28:55, 28:60, 52:167, 70:58, 80:106; lǣron 30:125, 32:142; *ind. pres. 1 sg.* lǣre 32:150, 76:1; *3 sg.* lǣreþ 122:62; *pl* lǣraþ 50:112, 50:132; *pret. 1 sg.* lǣrde 128:202, 128:203, 128:204, 128:206, 128:208a, 128:208b, 128:210, 128:211a, 128:211b, 128:212, 128:216, 128:217; *3 sg.* lǣrde 12:84,

42:99, 68:21, 92:18, 112:331; lǣrede 140:128; *pl.* lǣrdon 132:293; lǣrdan 146:13; *subj. pret. pl.* lǣrdon 128:209; *imp. 3 pl.* lǣran 76:31; *infl. inf* to lǣranne 3; to lǣrenne 160:54; *pres. p.* lǣrende 165
lǣs *adv.* less; þy lǣs (lest); þe lǣs þe / þe lǣs (lest) (see Appendix, p. 151)
lǣssa *adj.* less; *comp. m. dat. sg.* lǣssan 32:158; *nt. nom. sg.* lǣsse 82:39; *nt. acc. sg.* lǣsse 34:228, 126:137; *superl. m. nom. sg.* lǣsta 118:131
lǣstan (1) to perform, accomplish 128:194
lǣst *m.* footprint; *acc. pl.* lǣstas 88:155
lǣt *adj.* slow; *m. nom. sg.* 28:65; *f. nom. sg.* lāta 114:32a, 114:32b
lǣtan (VII) to let, allow 14:125, 86:132; *ind. pres. 2 sg.* lǣtest 126:160; *3 sg.* lǣt 46:28; lǣteþ 8:137, 32:166; *pret. 3 sg.* let 22:91, 58:24; *pl.* lēton 110:322, 150:121; lētan 46:42; *subj. pret. sg.* lēte 22:97; *imp. 2 sg.* lǣt 52:146; *2 pl.* lǣtaþ 48:47
lǣwede *adj.* lay; *m. gen. sg.* lǣwedes 146:25; *m. dat. sg.* lǣwedum 146:23; *m. nom. pl.* lǣwede 28:53; *m. dat. pl.* lǣwedum 32:138; *def. m. nom. pl.* lǣwedan 30:136
lǣwan (1) to betray; *ind. pres. 3 sg.* lǣweþ 120:14, 120:15
lǣþþo *f.* dislike, enmity; *acc. sg.* lǣþþe 44:145
lāf *f.* remainder, leavings; *nom. sg.* 78:76; *acc. sg.* lāfe 80:96; *dat. sg.* lāfe 54:197, 158:24, 158:28, 21, 134
lamb *m.* lamb; *acc. sg.* lamb 14:133
lane *f.* lane; *acc. pl.* lanan 162:104, 67, 70; *dat. pl.* lanum 97
land *nt.* land; *acc. sg.* land 54:201, 138:71; *gen. sg.* landes 136:14; *dat. sg.* lande 32:170, 78:89, 80:90, 86:112, 122:68, 122:80, 158:26, 30; *dat. pl.* landum 68:36
landāgend *m.* land-owning; *acc. pl.* landāgende 128:210

lang *adj.* long; *m. nom. sg.* 158:33; *nt. nom. sg.* lang 82:19; *f. acc. sg.* lange 150:97; *m. nom. pl.* lange 82:39; *def. f. nom. sg.* lange 40:77; *comp. nt. nom. sg.* lengre 82:41

lange *adv.* long, a long time 4:57, 54:192, 58:17, 58:32, 78:49, 82:39, 82:40, 118:130, 132:314; *comp.* leng 48:84, 64:172, 78:88, 94:71, 120:36, 122:63, 124:119, 126:160, 130:262, 154:217, 154:220 >

langian (2) (with *acc.*) to long for 80:92; *ind. pret. 3 sg.* langode 154:224

langung *f.* longing; *nom. sg.* 80:90, 94:70; *acc. sg.* langunga 92:14; *gen. sg.* langunga 94:59; *dat. sg.* langunga 78:88, 92:5

lār *f.* teaching, doctrine; *nom. sg.* 26:20, 94:50, 94:52, 128:219; *acc. sg.* lāre 4:53a, 4:53b, 30:129a, 30:129b, 38:30, 38:39, 46:26, 84:73, 90:199, 94:49, 118:120; *dat. sg.* lāre 22:103, 54:222, 78:64, 94:51, 128:227, 140:101; *acc. pl.* lāra 22:123, 152:179; *dat. pl.* lārum 16:151, 42:96, 50:133, 50:134, 126:161, 150:133

lārēow *m.* teacher; *nom. sg.* 8:147, 26:1, 26:24, 28:52, 28:73, 28:86, 30:96, 30:114; *gen. sg.* lārēowes 38:22, 128:200; *nom. pl.* lārēowas 18:20, 28:54, 28:59, 30:122, 30:124, 30:129, 54:211, 54:212; *acc. pl.* lārēowas 52:166; *dat. pl.* lārēowum 30:93, 48:84

lāst *m.* footprint; *nom. pl.* lāstas 88:171; *acc. pl.* lāstas 88:160; *dat. pl.* lāstum 88:164, 88:165, 88:168, 88:179

lāstweard *m.* successors; *nom. pl.* lāstweardas 34:193

lāta (see lǣt)

late *adv.* late 40:73

latian (2) to delay; *subj. pret. sg.* latode 118:92

lāttēow *m.* guides; *acc. pl.* lāttēowas 68:12

lāþ *adj.* hateful; *f. gen. pl.* lāþra 44:161

laþian (2) to invite; *ind. pres. 3 sg.* laþaþ 130:244, 132:286; *pret. 3 sg.* laþode 4:52; *3 pl.* laþodan 138:78

lāþe *m.* displeasure; *dat. sg.* laþe 28:83

lāþlič *adj.* loathsome; *f. nom. sg.* lāþlico 78:74

lawer *m.* laurel; *dat. sg.* lawere 130:246

Lāzarus *pers. n.* Lazarus; *nom. sg.* 46:23, 46:32, 48:52, 48:54, 50:123; *acc. sg.* Lāzarum 48:87; Lāzarum 46:9, 52:158; *gen. sg.* Lāzares 48:50

leahter [leahtor] *m.* sin, crime; *nom. sg.* 114:27, 114:38; *dat. sg.* leahtre 114:24, 114:29; *nom. pl.* leahtras 110:288; *acc. pl.* leahtras 24:146

lēanigean [lēanian] (2) (with *dat.*) to reward 86:122 (A)

lēan (VI) to blame; *infl. inf.* to lēanne 42:132

lēan *m.* reward; *dat. pl.* lēanum 26:35

lēas *adj.* loose, free; *m. nom. sg.* 94:54

lēas *adj.* false, lying; *m. nom. sg.* 122:57; *f. acc. sg.* lēase 154:186; *f. dat. sg.* lēasre 122:52; *m. nom. pl.* lēase 126:168; *def. m. nom. sg.* lēasa 40:69; *m. acc. pl.* lēasan 138:77; *m. dat. pl.* lēasum 36:233; *superl. m. acc. sg.* lēasostan 124:117

lēascræft *m.* false crafts; *dat. pl.* lēascræftum 16:153

lēasung *f.* lying, deception; *nom. sg.* 128:191; *acc. sg.* lēasunga 66:196; *dat. pl.* lēasungum 124:106; lēasingum 124:110

lēat (see lūtan)

leg *m.* flame, lightning *nom. sg.* 140:94, 152:143, 152:144; *acc. sg.* leg 42:114, 140:94, 152:141, 152:144; *gen. sg.* leges 72:96, 140:90; *dat. sg.* lege 152:143; *inst. sg.* lege 140:104; *gen. pl.* lega 92:39; legea 94:55

leget *nt.* lightning; *nom. pl.* legetu 64:139, 138:89

leng (see lane)

lēode *f.* people; *nom. pl.* 54:190, 138:70, 140:94, 140:100; *acc. pl.* lēode 140:90, 140:96, 140:103; *dat. pl.* lēodum 140:98, 140:102

lēodscipe *m.* nations; *acc. pl.* lēodscipas 54:199

lēof *adj.* beloved; *m. nom. sg.* 14:112, 78:72, 92:13, 146:25; *nt. nom. sg.* lēof 30:105,

36:237, 76:17, 76:41, 80:116; *nt. gen. pl.*
lēofra 44:161; *def. m. nom. sg.* lēofa 20:48,
94:66, 100:56, 158:12; *nt. nom. pl.* lēofan
92:15; *comp. nt. nom. sg.* lēofre 34:188,
86:95, 140:134; *m. nom. pl.* lēofran 34:200;
superl. nt. nom. sg. lēofast 34:209; lēofost
78:71; *f. nom. pl.* lēofoste 38:14; *def. m.
nom. pl.* lēofestan 4:84, 8:150, 10:1, 10:34,
14:92, 14:111, 18:1, 18:18, 26:1, 38:1, 46:1, 58:1,
74:1, 82:1, 92:1, 98:1, 114:1, 120:1, 120:19,
136:1, 146:1; lēofostan 76:1, 78:66;
lēofoston 116:84
leofian (2) to live 38:32; *ind. pres. 3 sg.*
leofað 8:153, 12:52, 28:44, 56:239, 66:208,
72:115, 80:130; leofaþ 24:177, 38:31, 38:36,
40:84,116:76; lyfað 90:221; *pl.* leofiaþ
32:179
lēogan (VII) to lie 124:128; *ind. pres. 1 sg.*
lēoge 124:109; *pret. 3 sg.* lēah 20:49; *subj.
pres. sg.* lēoge 124:106, 124:128; *pres. p.*
lēogende 124:122
lēoht *nt.* light; *nom. sg.* 12:47, 12:48, 14:97,
44:159, 62:131, 64:158; *acc. sg.* lēoht 10:42,
12:64, 12:83, 14:95, 14:96, 14:100, 66:193,
72:109; *gen. sg.* lēohtes 10:39, 12:52, 12:54,
12:55, 14:90, 14:95, 40:44, 42:116, 92:31, 98:39,
102:110; *dat. sg.* lēohte 12:44, 14:97, 58:30,
90:184, 98:13, 158:12
lēoht *adj.* enlightened; *nt. dat. sg.*
leohtum 74:22
lēohtfæt *nt.* lamp; *nom. sg.* 88:179, 88:183;
acc. pl. lēohtfāto 102:102; *gen. pl.*
lēohtfāta 70:52
lēoma *m.* beam, ray; *nom. sg.* 116:51
leom [lim] *nt.* limb; *nom. pl.* leomo 22:90;
acc. pl. leomu 8:146, 80:98, 128:182, 150:96,
150:99; *gen. pl.* leoma 104:140; *dat. pl.*
leomum 22:92, 100:47, 116:88
lēoran (II) to depart; *subj. pres. 3 sg.*
lēore 104:168, 104:170 (A)
leornere *m.* learner; *acc. sg.* leorneras
94:55; *dat. pl.* leornerum 92:10, 92:11, 94:80
leornian (2) to learn 80:105; *ind. pres. pl.*
leorniaþ 82:25, 84:46, 84:70, 86:136, 88:140;

pret. pl. leornedon 94:52; leornodan 92:6;
imp. 2 pl. leorniað 8:145
libban (3) to live 50:132; *ind. pres. 1 sg.*
lybbe 116:76; *pl.* libbaþ 50:133; libbað 142;
ind. pret. pl. lifdon 140:96; *subj. pres. sg.*
libbe 68:22; *pl.* libban 76:33; lybban 30:92
Libia *pers. n.* Livia; *nom. sg.* 120:35
Librassa *prop. n.* Livrassa; *nom. sg.*
152:150
līc *nt.* body, corpse; *acc. sg.* līc 124:102,
130:270, 132:309, 150:91; *nom. pl.* līc
132:322
līcian (2) to please; *ind. pres. 3 sg.* līcað
162:101; *pret. 3 sg.* līcode 69; *pl.* līcodan
54:197; *subj. pres. sg.* līcie 46:31; līcige
140:134, 66; *pl.* līcian 76:35
līce *adj.* pleasing; *m. nom. sg.* 126
līcetung *f.* hypocrisy; *nom. sg.* 70:51
licgan (V) to lie 46; *ind. pres. 3 pl.* licggað
70:55; *pret. 3 sg.* læg 150:116, 156:236; *subj.
pres. 3 sg.* licge 156:235; *pret. 3 sg.* læge
132:318
līchama *m.* body; *nom. sg.* 14:103, 40:53,
78:43; līchoma 14:102, 22:124, 38:31, 38:35,
40:48; *acc. sg.* līchaman 68, 105; līchoman
14:104, 14:105, 24:153, 24:166, 24:167, 24:174,
30:118, 50:95; *gen. sg.* līchoman 24:137,
24:155, 24:170, 38:30, 38:37, 40:58, 40:71; *dat.
sg.* līchoman 14:92, 20:73, 62:111;
līchomon 68:11; *nom. pl.* līchoman 70:55,
134:323, 134:324; *acc. pl.* līchaman 5, 118,
124; līchoman 66:186, 78:47, 132:319,
134:328; *dat. pl.* līchomum 54:225
līchomlič *adj.* bodily; *m. acc. sg.*
līchomlicne 72:91/2; *nt. dat. pl.*
līchomlicum 118:92/3; *m. dat. pl.*
līchomlicum 14:100/1; *def. nt. nom. sg.*
līchomlice 94:79; *nt. dat. pl.* līchomlicum
38:34/5
līchomlīče *adv.* bodily 88:137, 90:196,
90:201, 94:69, 94:71
līcþrōwere *m.* leper; *gen. sg.*
līcþrōweres 50:93
līf *nt.* life; *nom. sg.* 18:5, 40:76, 40:79,
44:160, 62:94, 76:16, 76:17; *acc. sg.* līf 6:131,

12:84, 18:26, 22:96, 24:138, 24:144, 24:147, 76:33, 78:57; *gen. sg.* līfes 10:25, 10:41, 12:43, 14:113, 32:159, 40:44, 40:48; līfæs 78:86 ; *dat. sg.* līfe 6:128, 18:29, 34:193, 36:234, 42:91, 52:150, 52:168 ; *inst. sg.* līfe 118:113

lifdon (see libban)
lifian [libban] (3) to live; 28:43, 40:78; lifgean 22:131, 24:153, 116:75, 146:32; *ind. pres. 3 sg.* lyfað 90:221; *1 pl.* lifiaþ 24:141, 40:75, 42:96, 52:155; *pl* lifgeaþ 22:135; *pl* 28:48; lifgaþ 24:143; *pret. 3 sg.* lifde 22:97, 78:85, 118:113, 146:24, 150:105; *pl.* līfdon 22:136, 140:96, 140:101; *subj. pres. sg.* lifge 76:28, 90:220; *pl.* lifian 24:138; *pl.* lifgean 22:122, 28:85; *pret. sg.* lifde 116:82; *pres. p.* lifgende 62:110; *m. acc. sg.* lifgendne 150:103; *pl.* lifgende 54:226; *def. m. nom. sg.* lifigenda 6:132; *m. acc. sg.* lifgendan 106:207, 138:62; *m. gen. sg.* lifgendan 6:126, 106:223, 108:233, 108:249; lyfgendan 106:214

līxan [līexan] (1) to shine; *ind. pres. 3 sg.* līxeþ 4:68 (A)
līþelīċe *adv.* gently 74:17
loc *m.* lock; *gen. pl.* loca 60:57
loc *m.* lock of hair; *nom. sg.* 99; *nom. pl.* loccas 100; *acc. pl.* loccas 105; *dat. pl.* loccum 46:34, 50:106, 50:131
lōcian (2) look, see 140:90; *ind. pres. pl.* lōciaþ 64:163, 86:113; *pret. 3 sg.* lōcode 130:252, 130:258, 162:90; lōcade 156:237; *pl.* lōcodan 84:83, 86:109, 122:46; *imp. 2 sg.* loca 10:20, 34:208; *infl. inf.* to lōcienne 88:149; *pres. p.* lociende 158:13, 106, 112
lof *nt.* praise; *nom. sg.* 22:109, 36:240, 44:166, 96:96; *acc. sg.* lof 28:50, 80:105, 86:98, 104:169, 104:178, 106:183, 110:302, 154:193, 158:20
loflīċe [loflīċe → loflīċe] *adv.* gloriously 116:70
lofsang *m.* hymn; *dat. sg.* lofsange 134:325; *nom. pl.* lofsangas 142:165; *acc. pl.* lofsangas 138:74; *dat. pl.* lofsangum 142:172

longe *adv.* long 58:38, 154:218
lor *nt.* loss, destruction; *dat. sg.* lore 46:39
losian (2) to perish; *pret. 3 sg.* losode 130:272
Lūcas *pers. n.* Luke; *nom. sg.* 10:1, 82:11, 92:31
lufe *f.* love; *acc. sg.* lufan 52:167, 66:207, 72:91, 72:100, 128:202, 140:118, 146:21; *gen. sg.* lufan 18:33; *dat. sg.* lufan 16:141, [lugan → lufan] 16:144, 16:152, 30:93, 38:42, 42:122, 42:124, 42:131, 48:81, 84:50, 84:61, 120:36; lufon 28:56, 42:111, 42:121, 48:51, 78:60, 120:20; *inst. sg.* lufan 92:42; *dat. pl.* lufon 14:132
lufian (2) to love 14:126, 34:217, 56:235, 80:106, 80:110 >; *ind. pres. 1 sg.* lufige 94:65, 138:57; *3 sg.* lufaþ 34:212a, 34:212b, 44:165, 122:69 >; lufað 78:73; *pl.* lufiaþ 34:229, 40:72, 42:122, 64:161, 80:125 >; *pret. 3 sg.* lufode 4:45, 40:62, 40:68, 78:87, 94:64, 104:149, 118:117 >; lufade 40:54; *pl.* lufodan 56:232; *subj. pres. pl.* lufian 16:146, 20:71, 54:222, 78:66 >; *pret. pl.* lufodan 128:203; lufedan 128:212; *imp. 1 pl.* lufian 4:43, 6:127, 6:136, 8:150, 44:164, >; *2 pl.* lufiað 147; *3 pl.* lufian 2:40
luflīċe *adv.* lovingly, gladly 90:194, 138:52, 140:109
lufu *f.* love; *nom. sg.* 34:200, 40:43, 76:21, 154:222, 154:225; *acc. sg.* lufe 90:218, 148:53 11; *dat. sg.* lufe 28:83, 40:44
Lupicinus *prop. n.* Lupicinus; *nom. sg.* 150:110
lust *m.* desire; *nom. sg.* 40:67
lustfullīċe *adv.* joyfully 24:164
lustfulnes *f.* desire; *acc. sg.* lustfulnesse 10:42
lustlīċe *adv.* joyfully, gladly 30:129, 32:161, 38:19
lūtan (II) to bend; *ind. pret. 3 sg.* lēat 152:171
lybcræft *m.* magic; *dat. sg.* lybcræfte 7
lȳfan [līefan] (1) to allow; *pret. 3 sg.* lȳfde 130:271

lȳefan [līefan] (1) believe; *infl. inf.* to lȳ
fenne 6:112

lyft *f.* air; *acc. sg.* lyfte 130:246; *dat. sg.*
lyfte 22:125, 122:44, 130:259

lystan (1) to list; *ind. pres. 3 sg.* lyst
32:177; *subj. pres. sg.* lyste 70:70

lȳt *adv.* little 28:58

lȳtel *adj.* little; *f. nom. sg.*; lȳtelu 40:77;
nt. acc. sg. lȳtel 32:151; *f. acc. pl.* lȳtle
14:133; *nt. dat. pl.* lȳtlum 26:34

M

mā *adv.* more (see miċle)

magan (pret. pres.) to be able; *ind. pres. 1 sg.*
mæg 14:99a, 14:99b, 14:100, 14:101a; *2 sg.*
miht 58:39, 80:95, 110:279, 110:281, 122:75,
126:171, 130:238; *2 sg.* mihtest 122:73; *3 sg.*
mæg 4:61, 4:72, 14:91, 14:101b, 20:80, 38:6,
38:32, 50:103; *pl.* magon 4:43, 4:45, 10:36,
14:103, 16:160, 22:113; magan 12:86, 64:160,
66:194, 120:25, 126:168; magen 121; *subj.
pres. sg.* mæge 10:19, 37 9, 24:166, 28:59,
38:16, 40:81, 42:116, 42:117, 50:136; *3 sg.*
mihte 12:73, 14:122, 22:99, 30:98, 48:68,
88:155; mehte 46:39; *pl.* mihton 10:31,
32:143, 42:101, 54:193, 74:19, 74:22, 84:54;
mihtan 28:88, 94:84, 114:13, 124:103, 148:55;
mehton 10:9, 30:93; meahton 88:144,
102:110, 65

mǣg *m.* kinsman; *nom. sg.* 80:98; *acc. pl.*
māgas 98:24; *dat. pl.* māgum 128:210

mægden *nt.* maiden; *gen. sg.* mægdenes
[mægenes → mægdenes] 110:311

mæġen *nt.* power; *nom. sg.* 4:63, 4:73,
20:78, 62:134, 64:143, 64:154; *acc. sg.*
mæġen 4:66, 4:86, 50:121, 54:224, 80:106;
gen. sg. mæġenes 18:32, 118:106; *dat. sg.*
mæġene 10:31, 16:156, 18:34, 124:121,
152:162, 152:174; *inst. sg.* mæġene 4:44,
68:23, 72:107, 76:25, 136:8; *gen. pl.* mæġena
24:151, 30:112, 114:31; *dat. pl.* mæġenum
50:114, 114:13, 114:14, 116:71, 160:69

mæġenþrym *m.* majesty; *nom. sg.*
124:112; *acc. sg.* mæġenþrym 52:151,

52:159; *gen. sg.* mæġenþrymmes 4:87, 6:96,
70:86

mǣgsibb *f.* kinship; *acc. sg.* mǣgsibbe
74:25

mǣgwlite *m.* shape; *acc. sg.* mǣgwlite
88:171 (A)

mǣġþ *f.* tribe, group; *dat. sg.* mǣgðe
146:4; *dat. pl.* mǣgþum 108:272

mæġþhād *m.* virginity; *acc. sg.*
mægþhād 4:74

mǣnan (1) to speak of; *ind. pret. 3 sg.*
mǣnde 6:119, 26:14

mǣre *adj.* illustrious, famous; *m. nom.
sg.* 150:135; *f. nom. sg.* mǣre 136:14; *nt.
nom. sg.* mǣre 152:139; *def. m. acc. sg.*
mǣron 92:2; *comp. m. nom. sg.* mǣrra
114:18

mǣrlīċe *adv.* gloriously, grandly 48:74

mǣrsian (2) to celebrate 114:2; *ind. pres.
pl.* mǣrsiaþ 62:119, 114:7; *infl. inf.* to
mǣrsienne 114:4/5

mǣrsung *f.* extolling; *dat. sg.* mǣrsunga
20:71

mæsse *f.* mass; *acc. sg.* mæssan 30:101,
142:146; *dat. sg.* mæssan 136:T, 146:T; *nom.
pl.* mæssan 142:165

mæssedæġ *nt.* mass-day; *inst. pl.*
mæssedagum 30:128

mæsse-prēost *m.* mass-priest; *nom. sg.*
28:55, 28:62, 28:65, 28:87, 30:100, 32:137,
32:139, 32:143; *gen. sg.* mæsse-prēostes
28:69; *nom. pl.* mæsse-prēostas 28:53,
30:133; *acc. pl.* mæsse-prēostas 28:83,
142:168; *dat. pl.* mæsse-prēostum 30:126

Magnificaþ *prop. n.* Magnificat; *nom.
sg.* 110:308

mān *nt.* crime, sin; *acc. sg.* mān 44:150;
gen. sg. mānes 54:185; *gen. pl.* māna
50:126

man *m.* man, person; *nom. sg.* 2:37, 8:148,
12:49, 20:76, 20:81; *acc. sg.* man 28:47,
28:70, 32:160 [nam → man], 38:17; *gen. sg.*
mannes 10:6, 18:5, 26:42, 28:56a, 28:56b,
28:64, 30:131; *dat. sg.* men 12:44, 32:157,

78:59, 82:42, 86:95, 92:13; *nom. pl.* men 4:84, 8:150, 10:38, 14:99, 14:111, 16:142, 16:145, 16:150a, 16:150b, 20:46, 38:12; menn 50:100, 64:164; *acc. pl.* men 4:75, 28:84, 30:134, 32:142, 50:132; menn 126:164; *gen. pl.* manna 4:79, 6:106, 12:61, 18:33, 24:146, 26:2; *dat. pl.* mannum 10:6, 18:42, 20:51, 20:87, 22:92, 22:116, 24:161

mancynn *nt.* mankind; *acc. sg.* mancyn 48:83, 58:15, 72:92; mancynn 86:120; mannacynn 64:164; *gen. sg.* mancynnes 86:99, 90:196; *dat. sg.* mancynne 58:13, 84:58, 84:60, 84:68, 86:99, 90:199 (see also cynn)

māndǣd *f.* wicked deed; *acc. pl.* māndǣda 86:125; *dat. pl.* māndǣdum 52:173, 52:180, 64:181, 70:74

mānfull *adj.* sinful; *def. nt. nom. sg.* mānfulle 20:60

maniġ *adj.* many; *m. nom. sg.* 146:41 ; *nt. nom. sg.* manig 32:146; *f. acc. sg.* manige 84:73; *m. gen. sg.* maniges 30:131, 38:13; *nt. acc. sg.* manig 16:138, 54:206, 76:19, 100:65; 150:122 [manige → manig] >; *m. dat. sg.* manegum 86:133; *m. nom. pl.* manige 30:94, 38:18, 38:25, 38:39, 44:144, 48:55, 52:152 >; *nt. nom. pl.* manegu 128:228; *m. acc. pl.* manige 54:186, 68:39, 154:201; manega 162:103, 11; *f. acc. pl.* manige 58:23, 128:195, 128:203 >; manega 30:111, 162:106; *nt. acc. pl.* manige 108:238; manega 124:93; *m. gen. pl.* manigra 62:115, 148:84; *m. dat. pl.* manegum 90:190; *f. dat. pl.* manegum 52:170, 76:18, 92:24 >; mǣgenum 114:13; *nt. dat. pl.* manegum 50:114, 58:20, 88:139 >

manian (2) remind; *ind. pres 1 sg.* manige 34:190, 76:27, 100:73; *3 sg.* manaþ 28:89, 32:160, 90:207, 114:1, 122:69, 136:1; *pret. 3 sg.* manode 18:24, 118:124, 148:78 (A)

maniġfeald *adj.* manifold; *nt. nom. sg.* manigfeald 144:184; *nt. acc. sg.* manigfeald 62:121, 88:178; *f. dat. sg.* manigfealdre 80:115; *m. nom. pl.* manigfealde 144:188; *nt. acc. pl.*

manigfealde 78:85, 106:222; *m. dat. pl.* manigfealdum 136:24; *def. f. nom. sg.* manigfealde 70:51; *nt. dat. pl.* manigfealdum 72:90

manigfealdliċ *adj.* various; *f. nom. pl.* manigfealdlice 94:68; *f. acc. pl.* manigfealdlice 142:169

maniġo *f.* multitude; *nom. sg.* 153

manliċ *m.* image of man; *acc. pl.* manlican 122:43

mann *m.* man; *dat. sg.* mannan 140

mansleġe *m.* murder; *gen. sg.* mansleges 132:280

mānswara *m.* perjurer; *nom. pl.* mānswaran 42:96; *dat. pl.* mānswarum 42:126

māra *adj.* greater; *comp. m. nom. sg.* 30:116, 86:105, 86:106, 114:42, 118:101; *f. nom. sg.* mǣre 66:201, 68:10, 68:31; *nt. nom. sg.* mǣre 20:78, 70:58, 82:40; *m. acc. sg.* māran 84:86a, 84:86b, 88:170, 116:60, 150:126; *f. acc. sg.* māran 24:142, 54:188, 90:193; *nt. acc. sg.* mǣre 28:75, 34:227, 66:202, 148:48, 148:54; *nt. gen. sg.* māran 82:22; *m. dat. sg.* māran 32:157, 86:117; *f. dat. sg.* māran 24:140; *superl. nt. nom. sg.* mǣst 90:196; *def. m. nom. sg.* mǣsta 30:111, 82:38; *m. acc. sg.* mǣstan 54:194; *f. nom. sg.* mǣste 44:144; *f. acc. sg.* mǣstan 72:91; *nt. acc. sg.* mǣste 2:36; *f. dat. sg.* mǣstan 94:82; *nt. dat. sg.* mǣston 30:126

Maria *pers. n.* Mary; *nom. sg.* 2:12, 2:39, 4:57, 4:76, 4:88, 6:113, 46:26, 46:32, 46:33, 50:98, 50:105, 50:115, 98:4, 98:9, 98:14, 98:21, 98:23, 100:82 >; Mariæ 102:95; Marie 104:143, 104:151, 104:166, 110:312 ; *acc. sg.* Marian 6:111, 100:62, 102:133, 106:218, 106:219 >; *gen. sg.* Marian 46:30, 100:66, 100:80, 102:129, 102:132, 104:144, 104:148, 104:152, 104:156, 104:159, 104:164, 106:186, 106:221, 108:230 >; *dat. sg.* Marian 50:130, 62:97, 74:12, 98:2, 100:66, 110:280, 110:304 >

Marmadonia (see Mermadonia)

marmanstān *m.* marble-stone; *dat. sg.* marmanstāne 140:110, 142:152

Martha *pers. n.* Martha; *nom. sg.* 46:24, 46:26 46:29, 46:30, 50:98, 50:99

Martinus [Lt. Martinus] *pers. n.* Martin; *nom. sg.* 146:9, 146:38, 148:45, 148:62, 148:69, 148:83, 148:88, 150:90, 150:100, 150:114, 150:119, 152:142, 152:151, 152:164, 152:170; *acc. sg.* Martinus 148:77; *gen. sg.* Martines 146:3, 152:147; *dat. sg.* Martine 148:68, 152:159

martyr *m.* martyr; *gen. pl.* martyra 16:171; martira 118:106

mārþon [m[...]on → mārþon] *adv.* moreover 12:74

Matheus [Lt. Matheus] *pers. n.* Matthew; *nom. sg.* 18:1, 52:160, 112:326, 158:10, 158:12, 158:13, 158:14, 158:19, 158:22, 158:25, 3, 9, 19, 22, 29 > ; *acc. sg.* Matheum 158:27, 39; Matheus 19; *dat. sg.* Matheum 162:101

mē (see iċ, wit, wē)

mēaġollīċe *adv.* mightily 138:62

mēagolmōdnes *f.* power; *dat. sg.* mēagolmōdnesse 86:108

mēd *f.* reward; *acc. sg.* mēde 32:162; *dat. sg.* mēde 26:28, 26:33, 30:104, 58:7, 70:73; *dat. pl.* mēdum 70:69

mēdder [mēder] (see mōdor)

medeme *adj.* worthy; *m. nom. sg.* 90:215; *nt. acc. sg.* medeme 24:169; *m. nom. pl.* medeme 90:204, 90:212

medemnes *f.* kindness; *acc. sg.* medemnesse 102:127

medmyccle *adv.* meanly 52:171

medmyċel *adj.* small; *f. nom. sg.* medmycel 88:163; *m. acc. sg.* medmycelne 14:131; *nt. acc. sg.* medmycel 160:49; *m. dat. sg.* medmycclum 78:69; *nt. dat. sg.* medmyclum 128:207; medmycclum 42:110; *m. dat. pl.* medmycclum 76:4; *def. m. acc. sg.* medmycclan 2:29, 2:42; *f. acc. pl.* medmycclan 44:142; *f. dat. pl.* medmyclum 24:152 (A)

medome *adj.* worthy; *m. acc. sg.* medomne 38:3; *nt. acc. sg.* medome 116:69

medstrang *adj.* moderate strength; *def. m. acc. pl.* medstrangan 128:206

megolnes *f.* might; *dat. sg.* megolnesse 44:164

meht [miht] *f.* power; *nom. sg.* 12:72; *acc. sg.* mehte 20:80; meht 84:78

mēngan (1) to mingle, blend; *ind. pret. pl.* mēngdon 68:42

meniġo [meniġu] *f.* multitude; *nom. sg.* 12:59, 48:56, 48:70, 54:215, 60:58, 60:67, 70:51; menego 12:60, 12:65; menigeo 152:168; mengeo 106:182, 132:290, 136:24; *acc. sg.* menigo 10:12; mengeo 102:128, 104:179, 108:257, 148:60; *dat. sg.* mengeo 120:34; menigeo 108:264

mennisc *nt.* people; *nom. sg.* 122:70

mennisc *adj.* belonging to man; *m. nom. sg.* 114:38; *f. nom. sg.* mennisc [mennisc → mennisce] 116:60; mennisce 118:107; *m. acc. sg.* menniscne 74:11, 84:61, 90:195, 116:73; *f. acc. sg.* mennisce 104:141; *nt. acc. sg.* mennisc 116:74, 116:83, 148:70; *m. gen. sg.* mennisces 116:56; *f. gen. sg.* menniscre 116:86; *nt. gen. sg.* mennisces 142:156; *m. dat. sg.* menniscum 86:118; menniscan 118:92, 118:103; *nt. dat. sg.* menniscum 100:42; *m. nom. pl.* mennisce 64:182; *m. dat. pl.* menniscum 146:21; *def. f. nom. sg.* mennisce 12:71, 86:97; *nt. nom. sg.* mennisce 10:37; mennissce 26:21; *m. acc. sg.* menniscan 124:115; *f. acc. sg.* menniscan 12:73, 12:78, 82:4, 86:103, 88:175, 90:202; *nt. acc. sg.* mennisce 52:162, 72:100, 88:138; *f. gen. sg.* menniscan 20:79, 116:50, 118:90; *nt. gen. sg.* menniscan 2:34, 4:80, 14:117, 106:216; *f. dat. sg.* menniscan 12:76, 20:78, 70:87, 84:89, 86:93; *nt. dat. sg.* menniscan 12:48, 50:128, 108:269

meolcian (2) to give milk; *pres. p.* meolcgende 64:170

meolcsūcan (VII) to milk suck; *pres. p. m. gen. pl.* meolcsūcendra 48:76

meregrot *m.* pearl; *nom. sg.* 104:160

mergen *m.* tomorrow; *nom. sg.* 93
mergendæġ *m.* tomorrow; *gen. sg.*
mergendæges 146:36
mergenliċ *adj.* of the morning; *def. m.*
nom. sg. mergenlica 98:10; *m. inst. sg.*
mergenlican 100:85, 104:152
Mermedonia *prop. n.* Mermedonia; *dat.*
sg. Mermedonia 158:27, 160:46, 160:82;
Marmedonia 160:85, 3, 162
mete *m.* food; *nom. sg.* 26:15, 78:76; *acc.*
sg. mete 38:28, 146:30; *gen. sg.* metes
24:166; *dat. sg.* mete 26:41, 38:32, 150:128,
158:22, 158:24, 158:29, 22, 45; *acc. pl.*
mettas 118:125
metan (V) to measure, compare; *pp.*
meten 94:48
mēttas (see mēte)
mētan (1) to find; *ind. pret. 3 sg.* mētte
148:88
mettrumnes *f.* illness; *nom. sg.* 40:77
Michael *pers. n.* Michael; *nom. sg.*
100:63, 110:285, 138:56, 140:113, 142:141;
Michahel 64:179, 66:185, 102:130, 108:259,
138:52, 138:79; *acc. sg.* Michael 138:62,
144:209; Michahel 144:195; *dat. sg.*
Michaele 138:49, 138:75, 140:108;
Michahele 104:139, 108:258, 110:296
mid *prep.* (with *acc.*) when, while (see Appendix,
p. 150)
mid *prep.* (with *dat.*) with (see Appendix, p. 150)
midd *adj.* middle; *m. acc. sg.* midne
30:120, 62:136; *f. acc. sg.* midde 42; *m. dat.*
sg. middum 146:41 [middumwintra → middum
wintra]; *nt. dat. sg.* middum 88:146, 112; *m.*
dat. pl. middum 23
middanġeard *m.* world; *nom. sg.* 32:180,
40:75, 58:32, 58:37, 80:118, 80:124, 82:35; *acc.*
sg. middangeard 40:73, 48:49, 48:83, 48:84,
50:125, 78:47, 82:33; *gen. sg.*
middangeardes 18:12/3, 20:57, 30:102, 40:76,
40:80, 44:157, 48:44; *dat. sg.* middangearde
42:112, 60:72, 62:132, 68:35, 82:26
middel *m.* waist; *acc. sg.* middle 100:63
midfyrhtnes *f.* middle age; *nom. sg.*
114:29

miht *f.* power; *nom. sg.* 20:75, 66:201, 74:6,
144:184; *acc. sg.* mihte 46:5, 82:25, 110:279,
110:315; miht 10:35, 22:98, 92:8, 94:86, 150:94,
152:155; *gen. sg.* mihte 4:87; *dat. sg.*
mihte 20:63, 62:110, 124:118; miht 12:76
mihtiġ *adj.* mighty; *m. nom. sg.* 4:49,
110:313, 152:181, 162:100; *m. acc. sg.*
mihtigne 150:107; *def. m. nom. sg.*
mihtiga 48:74; *m. acc. pl.* mihtigan
110:317
mīl [Lt. milia] *f.* mile; *dat. sg.* mīle 90:188,
134:327; *nom. pl.* mīla 136:16, 144:205; *inst.*
pl. mīlum 132:321
milde *adj.* mild; *m. nom. sg.* 30:132, 48:65,
90:208; *m. acc. sg.* mildne 66:206, 76:5; *f.*
dat. sg. mildre 24:165
mildheort *adj.* merciful; *m. nom. sg.*
8:145, 68:21, 148:80; *m. nom. pl.*
mildheorte 66:196; *nt. dat. pl.*
mildheortum 24:159; *def. m. nom. sg.*
mildheorta 24:163, 46:1; *m. acc. sg.*
mildheortan 2:5, 8:144; *superl. m. nom. sg.*
mildheortost 154:213
mildheortlīċe *adv.* merciful 70:84
mildheortnes *f.* mercy; *nom. sg.* 4:49,
30:107, 32:154, 62:104, 110:314; *acc. sg.*
mildheortnesse 8:148, 62:92, 72:91, 74:18,
86:119, 118:130, 150:98, 154:194, 160:55,
160:87 [mildheortness → mildheortnesse]; *gen. sg.*
mildheortnesse 18:34, 50:111, 66:206,
112:326; *dat. sg.* mildheortnesse 6:129,
18:31, 60:76, 60:80, 66:204; *nom. pl.*
mildheortnessa 134:327; *dat. pl.*
mildheortnessum 72:99
milts *f.* mercy; *acc. sg.* miltse 26:11,
74:24; *acc. pl.* miltsa 72:100; *gen. pl.*
miltsa 72:105, 76:26, 80:129
miltsian (2) (with *dat.*) to have mercy on
30:112, 34:188, 148:45; *ind. pres. 2 sg.*
miltsast 102:115; *subj. pret. sg.* miltsade
12:66; *imp. 2 sg.* miltsa 10:14, 10:15 [miltasa
→ miltsa], 10:16, 10:17, 12:58a, 12:58b, 28:73,
60:75, 60:76, 62:101, 154:209; *3 sg.* miltsige

96

64:148; *pres. p.* miltsiende 12:80, 28:77, 62:102; miltsiend 157; miltsigende 60:82
mīn *per. adj.* my, mine; *m. nom. sg.* 20:48, 62:100, 62:101, 80:98, 94:65, 98:20, 102:90, 104:136; *f. nom. sg.* mīn 4:46, 6:134, 46:28, 60:83, 102:134; *nt. nom. sg.* mīn 48:78, 62:94, 122:62, 142:146; *m. acc. sg.* mīnne 98:8, 108:268, 118:110, 130:242, 132:298; *f. acc. sg.* mīne 60:80, 60:85, 62:93 [min → mine], 62:95, 62:96, 62:105, 108:268, 110:300, 110:301; *nt. acc. sg.* mīn 26:13, 48:49, 60:85, 110:301; *m. gen. sg.* mīnes 8:140, 104:153, 108:272, 110:301, 120:17, 124:121, 128:200, 91; *f. gen. sg.* mīnre 48:47, 52:151, 62:90; *nt. gen. sg.* mīnes 110:287, 100; *m. dat. sg.* mīnum 4:47, 26:32, 92:21, 98:22, 98:26, 108:267; *f. dat. sg.* mīnre 62:99, 98:22, 102:91, 102:92, 110:303, 163; *nt. dat. sg.* mīnum 26:15; *m. nom. pl.* mīne 28:49, 32:150, 60:84, 62:94, 80:100, 80:101, 84:55; *m. acc. pl.* mīne 60:76, 126:166; *f. acc. pl.* mīne 60:85, 122:70; *m. gen. sg.* mīnra 132:300; *m. dat. pl.* mīnum 44:138, 124:119, 149; *f. dat. pl.* mīnum 60:85
misliċ *adj.* various; *f. dat. sg.* mislicre 142:159; *m. nom. pl.* mislice 28:61, 144:188; *f. acc. pl.* mislice 68:41, 76:18; *m. dat. pl.* mislicum 12:62, 40:60; *f. dat. pl.* mislicum 142:181; *nt. dat. pl.* mislicum 138:77,
missenliċ *adj.* various; *m. dat. pl.* missenlicum 4:69
missenlīċe *adv.* variously 26:7
mōd *nt.* mind; *nom. sg.* 66:200, 154:212, 154:230, 8, 158:3; *acc. sg.* mōd 24:174, 38:42, 86:130, 159; *gen. sg.* mōdes 10:30, 10:42, 20:81, 84:53, 148:53, 154:208; *dat. sg.* mōde 104:181, 144:192, 154:191, 154:192; *inst. sg.* mōde 4:46, 24:175, 40:46, 40:52, 46:5, 58:7, 120:8, 130:273, 150:93; mōd 68:23; *dat. pl.* mōdum 54:214
mōddrie *f.* aunt, cousin; *dat. sg.* mōddrian 116:79
mōdeliċ *adj.* proud; *nt. acc. pl.* mōdelico 78:69, 78:84

mōdgeþanc *m.* mind's thought; *nom. sg.* 156:237
mōdig *adj.* proud; *m. nom. sg.* 76:40
mōdor *f.* mother; *nom. sg.* 2:34, 6:92, 146:7; *gen. sg.* mōdor 110:281, 116:47, 116:67, 116:71, 110:77, 116:81, 118:91, 118:134; *dat. sg.* mēder 2:16, 2:27, 64:167, 110:303; mēdder 40:74
molde *f.* earth; *acc. sg.* moldan 88:164, 88:167, 88:168; *gen. sg.* moldan 80:96, 88:169; *dat. sg.* moldan 78:44
molsnian (2) to decay; *ind. pres. 3 sg.* molsnaþ 14:107
mon *m.* man, one; *nom. sg.* 14:90, 14:112, 14:126, 20:80, 24:157, 24:163, 26:19, 26:20, 30:117, 30:131, 32:167, 32:176, 34:196, 38:40, 42:98, 48:63 >; *acc. sg.* mon 24:155, 136:41; *gen sg.* monnes 34:199, 116:56; *gen. pl.* monna 4:50; *dat. pl.* monnum 10:41, 14:94, 22:102, 30:132, 32:161, 42:92, 116:82 >
mōna *m.* moon; *nom. sg.* 12:45, 62:130, 64:158; *acc. sg.* mōnan 12:43
monian [manian] (2) to admonish; *ind. pret. 3 sg.* monade 12:85
mōnaþ *m.* month; *acc. sg.* mōnaþ 26:5, 26:8, 62:98, 74:9, 90:220, 132:322; *inst. sg.* mōnþe 116:76; *gen. pl.* mōnða 6:97
moniġ *adj.* many; *m. dat. sg.* monegum 68:14; *m. nom. pl.* monige 16:145, 44:150, 118:99; *f. nom. pl.* monige 60:51, 88:166
moniġfeald *adj.* manifold; *m. nom. pl.* monigfealde 68:35 *m. dat. pl.* monigfealdum 68:36
monþwǣre *adj.* mild, gentle; *m. nom. sg.* 48:66
monþwǣrnes *f.* meekness; *dat. sg.* monþwǣrnesse 22:108
morgen *m.* morning; *nom. sg.* 160:85; *acc. sg.* morgen 30:119, 48:56, 158:41; *dat. sg.* morgenne 138:81, 138:83, 142:148
morgendæġ *m.* tomorrow; *dat. sg.* morgendæge 146:34
morgenliċ *adj.* of tomorrow; *def. m. inst. sg.* morgenlican 98:26, 100:69/70

97

morþor *m.* murder; *nom. sg.* 44:144; *gen. sg.* morþres 44:153; *nom. pl.* morþras 44:145 (A)

mōtan (pret. pres.) be allowed; *ind. pres. 3 sg.* mōt 32:137, 72:114; *pl.* mōton 70:68, 80:127; mōtan 8:153, 14:96, 16:165, 16:171, 24:177, 56:238, 66:194, 86:127 >; *subj. pres. sg.* mōte 12:62, 40:78, 42:99, 70:68, 78:43, 78:52, 128:196, 154:209 >; *pl.* mōtan 26:12, 30:103, 30:109, 36:239, 72:107, 88:165 >; *pret. sg.* mōste 14:123, 28:73, 146:36, 152:156, 154:224; *pl.* mōston 138:76, 150:133, 156:238; mōstan 156:232

Moyses *pers. n.* Moses; *nom. sg.* 32:144; *gen. sg.* Moyses 106:221; *dat. sg.* Moyse 30:92

mundbora *m.* protector; *gen. sg.* mundboran 118:127; *dat. sg.* mundboran 138:75; *acc. pl.* mundboran [munboran → mundboran] 132:311

mundbyrd *f.* protection; *acc. sg.* mundbyrde 142:144

munuc *m.* monk; *dat. pl.* munecum 76:38

mūnt *m.* mountain; *nom. sg.* 138:86, 142:163; *acc. sg.* mūnt 20:86, 98:9, 112:327, 136:33; *gen. sg.* mūntes 136:13, 136:25, 138:88; *dat. sg.* mūnte 112:328, 136:22, 138:88; *dat. pl.* mūntum 64:165

munuchād *m.* monastic life; *gen. sg.* munuchādes 150:131

munuclīf *nt.* monk's life; *inst. sg.* munuclīfe 146:24

mūþ *m.* mouth; *nom. sg.* 40:65; *acc. sg.* mūþ 40:55, 117, 118; mūð 112:329, 77; *dat. sg.* mūþe 18:6, 38:10, 38:22, 48:76, 48:89, 84:62, 154:193, 132

myclian [miclian] (2) to magnify; *ind. pres. 3 sg.* mycclaþ 4:46 *pret. 3 pl.* myccledon 10:22; *imp.1 pl.* mycclian 6:136 (A)

myċel *adj.* great; *m. nom. sg.* 4:84a, 4:84b, 62:127, 94:77, 98:8, 98:20, 110:313; *m. acc. sg.* mycelne 4:82, 28:75, 46:18, 78:68, 78:84, 130:233; *f. nom. sg.* mycelu 132:320; mycel 14:90, 24:137, 26:11, 36:232, 42:119, 48:56, 62:136; micel 94:70; myccle 140:119,

150:92, 150:115; *nt. nom. sg.* mycel 32:146, 64:143, 102:107; *f. acc. sg.* mycle 94:72, 110:315; myccle 10:12, 26:23, 44:150, 56:237, 64:137; miccle 140:118, 146:21; *nt. acc. sg.* mycel 14:91, 16:144, 44:150, 58:32, 58:38, 60:77; *m. dat. sg.* myclum 158:4, 158:42; mycclum 12:67, 34:218, 138:87, 140:117, 142:165; *m. inst. sg.* mycle 98:12, 94, 164; myclen [→mycle] 7; *f. inst. sg.* mycelre 100:80, 106:199, 114:34; *nt. inst. sg.* mycle 86:117; myccle 26:42, 38:33, 42:128, 42:130, 66:200, 68:31, 112:327; miccle 142:161, 146:12, 154:195; *m. nom. pl.* myccle 64:156, 114:9, 126:148; *nt. nom. pl.* mycele 88:182; *m. acc. pl.* micle 132:311; *m. dat. pl.* myclum 76:36; *f. nom. pl.* myclum 92:16; mycclum 76:3, 126:165, 130:234; *nt. dat. pl.* mycclum 42:100; *def. m. nom. sg.* myccla 124:112; *f. nom. sg.* myccle 70:51, 88:145; *nt. nom. sg.* mycele 36:231; mycclle 106:197a, 106:197b; *m. acc. sg.* myclan 92:2; mycclan 34:207; *f. acc. sg.* myclan 22:98, 94:58; mycclan 10:35, 52:172, 54:184, 90:193, 104:179; *f. gen. sg.* mycclan 94:59; *nt. gen. sg.* mycclan 54:185; *f. dat. sg.* myclan 88:160, 88:181; mycclan 6:129, 30:113, 60:76; miclan 92:5; *m. nom. pl.* mycclan 70:53, 78:78; *f. nom. pl.* mycclan 34:204; myccllan 44:142; *nt. nom. pl.* mycclan 70:44

myċelnes *f.* greatness; *acc. sg.* mycelnesse 110:307, 118:100; *dat. sg.* mycelnesse 102:110, 126:149

mynetere *m.* money-changer; *gen. pl.* mynetera 48:78

myndgian (2) to remind, admonish; *ind. pres. 1 sg.* myngige 76:27; myngie 76:1; *3 sg.* myngaþ 136:1; mynegaþ 114:1

mynster *nt.* monastery; *acc. sg.* mynster 148:83, 152:138; *dat. sg.* mynstre 154:202

myntan (1) to purpose; *ind. pret. 3 sg.* mynte 152:170, 152:171, 152:172, 152:177, 154:202

myrecels [miercels] *m.* sign; *acc. sg.*
myrecels 60:65

myrgenliċ *adj.* of the morning; *def. m.*
inst. sg. myrgenlican 100:67

myrþra *m.* murderer; *nom. sg.* 34:220;
nom. pl. myrþran 42:96

N

nā *adv.* not 12:82, 14:106, 22:107, 22:115,
22:134, 28:55, 42:94, 46:41, 48:51, 52:155,
54:211, 58:33, 66:190, 70:88 >
nacod *adj.* naked; *m. nom. sg.* 146:42; *m.*
acc. sg. nacodne 24:161; *m. acc. pl.*
nacode 146:30
Nadzarenisca (see Nazarenisca)
nǣdder *f.* serpent; *acc. sg.* nǣddran 2:15;
acc. pl. nǣddran 120:42; *gen. pl.*
nǣddrena 118:121
nǣfre *adv.* never 4:87, 14:95, 16:163, 24:162,
26:17, 28:44, 30:107, 34:189, 42:116, 44:155,
46:32, 50:109, 88:155, 126:155 >
nægl *m.* nail; *gen. pl.* nægla [nægle →
nægla] 62:113; *dat. pl.* næglum 58:24
nǣnig *adj.* none; *m. nom. sg.* 8:153, 14:126,
20:62, 24:157, 34:189, 88:154; *f. nom. sg.*
nǣnigu 24:151, 102:105; **nǣnigo** 114:26;
nǣnig 16:168, 60:66, 72:112; *nt. nom. sg.*
nǣnig 20:78, 64:158; *m. acc. sg.* nǣnigne
4:62, 58:3, 154:189; *f. acc. sg.* nǣnige 20:80,
38:40, 54:187, 88:158, 110:289, 138:71; *nt. acc.*
sg. nǣnig 72:101; *m. gen. sg.* nǣniges
106:213, 114:6; nǣnges 66:198; *nt. gen. sg.*
nǣnges 122:59; *m. dat. sg.* nǣnigum
114:16, 154:186, 154:190; *f. dat. sg.*
nǣnigre 26:36, 88:158 [ǣnigre → nǣnigre],
124:118; *nt. dat. sg.* nǣnigum 152:147; *nt.*
inst. sg. nǣnige 28:89; *m. nom. pl.* nǣnige
110:288, 128:201; *nt. nom. pl.* nǣnige
66:199; *m. acc. pl.* nǣnige 126:155
nǣren (→ne wǣren) (anom.) be not; *ind. pret.*
2 sg. nǣre 156; *3 sg.* næs 12:82, 20:49, 20:52,
48:50, 60:66, 62:116, 88:176, 142:170; *pl.*

nǣron 10:30, 60:74, 64:170, 82:17, 110:288;
subj. pret. 3 sg. nǣre 16:163, 22:115, 26:20,
28:77, 82:26, 84:43, 114:18, 122:59, 146:27; *pl.*
nǣron 64:167
næs *adv.* not 2:18, 126:153; næs na 42:91,
66:190, 76:35/6, 128:219; næs no 6:136
næsþȳrl *nt.* nostrils; *nom. pl.* næsþȳrlo
40:65
nafað (→ ne habban) (see habban)
naht *adv.* naught 28:68, 34:229, 36:234,
148:47; to nahte 38:27/8
nāhte (→ ne habban); *ind. pret. 3 sg.* 152:173
(see habban)
nāhwǣr *adv.* nowhere 40:71, 126:152,
132:316
nam (see niman)
nama *m.* name; *nom. sg.* 4:85, 46:15, 46:25,
54:209, 62:103, 98:7; *acc. sg.* naman 42:122,
60:84, 98:8, 98:19, 102:113, 104:136, 136:22;
dat. sg. naman 26:32, 32:177, 34:217, 48:72,
54:219, 92:21; *inst. sg.* naman 52:170
nān *adj.* none; *m. nom. sg.* 44:152, 52:168,
70:64, 78:43, 78:60, 78:72, 148:46; *nt. nom. sg.*
nān 20:88, 22:90, 78:74; *m. acc. sg.* nānne
28:47, 50:90, 50:91; *f. acc. sg.* nāne 104:148,
118:125; *nt. acc. sg.* nān 10:9, 60:52, 62:119,
162:98; *m. gen. sg.* nānes 28:56; *f. gen. sg.*
nānre 126:163; *m. dat. sg.* nānum 28:78,
152:166; *f. dat. sg.* nānre 14:97, 44:154
nard [Lt. nardus] *m.* nard; *nom. sg.* 50:108
nāst [ne witan] (pret. pres.) to know not; *ind.*
pret. pl. nāstan [næstan → nāstan] 10:36
Nawmachia *prop. n.* Naumachia; *dat. sg.*
Nawmachian 132:309
nawþer ne … ne *conj.* neither … nor
28:88, 54:211, 124:117/8; nawðer ne … ne
152:165/6
Nazarenisca *adj.* Nazarene; *def. m. nom.*
sg. Nazarenisca 10:14, 122:67;
Nadzarenisca 48:75; *m. gen. sg.*
Nadzarenisca 122:66
Nazareþ *prop. n.* Nazareth; *nom. sg.*
122:68
ne *adv.* not (see Appendix, p. 151)

99

nēadian (2) to force, compel; *ind. pret. pl.* nȳddon 146:17

nēah *adj.* near; *m. nom. sg.* 76:12; *superl. m. nom. sg.* nēhsta 120:4; *f. acc. sg.* nēhstan 86:120; *m. dat. sg.* nēhstan 14:113

nēah *adv.* near (see Appendix, p. 151)

nēalēcan (1) to draw nigh; *ind. pres. 3 sg.* nēalǣceþ 26:2, 34:192, 62:128, 130:241; nēalǣcþ 76:27; *pret. 3 sg.* nēalǣhte 10:3, 52:162; *pl.* nēalǣhton 108:260; *subj. pres. sg.* nēalǣce 140:135

nēalīċe *adv.* nearly, almost 142:160 (EWS)

Neapolite *prop. n.* Neapolitan; *nom. pl.* Neapolite 138:68; *acc. pl.* Neapolite [þonc apulite → Neapulite]140:96

nēar, nēah *adv.* near (see Appendix, p. 151)

nearo *adj.* narrow; *def. m. dat. pl.* nearwan 72:94

nēawist [nēarwest] *f.* neighbourhood; *nom. sg.* 78:74; *dat. sg.* nēawiste 28:48; nēaweste 34:219, 40:66, 136:14

nēd [nīed] *m.* need; *dat. sg.* nede 32:156, 58:22

nēde *adv.* needs 32:139, 82:35, 146:9, 146:32

nēdþearf *f.* necessity; *nom. sg.* 18:23, 26:11, 68:2, 68:20, 68:31, 76:38; nēdþearf 78:61, 92:28; *acc. sg.* nēdþearfe 14:114, 14:130, 56:237, 78:49; *gen. sg.* nēdðearfe 106:208

nēdþearfliċ *adj.* needful; *m. nom. sg.* nedþearflic 154:215

nefne *conj.* except, but 154:193 (A) (M)

nēh (see nēah)

nēhgebur *m.* neighbour; *nom. pl.* nēhgeburas 138:68

nēhmǣg *m.* kinsman; *gen. pl.* nēhmǣga 78:86; *dat. pl.* nēhmǣgum 78:72

nēhsta *m.* neighbour; *acc. sg.*; nēhstan 24:167, 38:13; *dat. sg.* nēhstan 24:165, 38:14; *gen. pl.* nēhstena 90:219

nēhstan *adv.* 58:24, 64:178, 136:28, 136:35

nēhste *f.* kinswoman; *nom. sg.* 110:287

nelle [→ne bēon] (anom.) am not (see bēon)

nemne *conj.* except 12:73 (A) (M)

nemnan (1) to name; *ind. pres. 2 sg.* nemnest 4:60; *pret. 3 sg.* nemde 8:141, 52:170, 52:172; *3 pl.* nemdon 46:15; *imp. 2 sg.* nemn 126:144; *pp.* nemned 54:209, 92:32, 92:33, 94:51 [nemed → nemned], 98:9, 118:112, 134:326, 136:15

nemþe *conj.* except 114:7 (A)

nēolnes *f.* abyss; *nom. pl.* nēolnessa 64:153

neoman [niman] (IV) take away; *ind. pres. pl.* neomaþ 88:165

neorxna-wang [neorxna wang → neorxna-wang] *m.* paradise; *acc. sg.* neorxna-wang 108:261; *gen. sg.* neorxna-wanges 10:38, 60:48, 110:305; *dat. sg.* neorxna-wange 102:88, 108:262; neorxna-wonge 110:304

nēosian (1) to visit 86:135

nēowe *adj.* new; *def. f. dat. sg.*; nēowan 94:79

neoþan *adv.* beneath 14:129; neoðan 144:204

neoþer *adj.* lower; *comp. m. nom. sg.*; neoþeran 62:105; *superl. f. acc. pl.* neoþermestan 128:198

Nergend *m.* protector; *acc. sg.* Nergend 74:10

Nerōn *pers. n.* Nero; *nom. sg.* 122:56, 122:67, 122:69, 122:71, 122:77, 124:107, 124:128, 124:132, 126:136, 126:138, 126:156, 126:161, 126:163, 126:169, 126:172, 126:178, 128:187, 128:223, 130:233, 130:235, 130:243, 130:246, 130:250, 130:256, 130:269, 130:273, 130:275, 132:281; *acc. sg.* Nerōn 132:290; Nerōnem 132:312; *gen. sg.* Nerōnes 120:35, 132:282; *dat. sg.* Nerōne 120:21, 120:32, 122:53, 122:60, 126:153, 126:175, 128:184

nēten [nietan] *nt.* beast; *dat. pl.* nētenum 62:90

nēþer *adv.* down 70:56

ne witan (pret. pres.) to know; *ind. pret. 2 sg.* nystest 60:51, 60:52; *3 sg.* nyste 12:82, 148:46, 152:177; *3 pl.* nystan 70:48, 106:193; *subj. pres. 3 sg.* nyte 124:133

nigon *num.* nine 62:98, 74:9, 82:38; nigan 6:97, 32:166, 32:167; nigen 144:195

nicor *m.* monster; *nom. pl.* nicras 144:207; *gen. pl.* niccra 144:201; nicra 144:203

nigoþa *num. adj.* ninth; *f. acc. sg.* 100:59; nigoþan 10:59; *m. dat. pl.* nigeoþan 34:224

niht *f.* night; *acc. sg.* niht 30:121, 64:160, 90:185, 90:188, 90:191, 138:51, 154:228; *gen. sg.* nihtes 142:170; *dat. sg.* nihte 142:141, 108; niht 148:56; *acc. pl.* niht 30:101, 82:18; *gen. pl.* nihta 18:3, 22:128, 24:139, 92:34, 158:17; *dat. pl.* nihtum 50:92, 92:1

nihtes *adv.* by night 30:115, 88:180, 98:3

nihtlic̄ *adj.* nightly; *m. dat. sg.* nihtlicum 6:117, 6:120

niman (IV) to take 122:80; *ind. pres. 3 sg.* nimeþ 88:170; *pl.* nimaþ 42:103, 52:154; *pret. 3 sg.* nam 20:67, 20:68, 38:30, 84:77, 104:163; *pl.* naman 48:57, 48:69

nis [→ ne bēon] (anom.) is not 16:167, 16:168, 20:78, 22:90, 22:92, 36:236, 42:128, 44:152, 58:35, 60:45, 72:95, 72:99, 78:74, 82:24, 82:29, 82:34, 82:40, 96:92 > (see bēon)

nīwan *adv.* lately 122:83

nīwe *adj.* new; *f. acc. sg.* nīwe 104:154; *def. m. nom. sg.* nīwa 116:50; *f. gen. sg.* nīwan 116:46

niwe *adv.* newly 151

nīð *m.* malice; *nom. sg.* 124:101; *gen. pl.* nīþa 76:40; *dat. pl.* nīþum 120:22

niþer *adv.* down 12:49; niðer [niðerġewitað → niðer ġewitað] 144:198, 144:206; nyþer 18:8, 20:46

niþera *adj.* lower; *m. acc. pl.* niþeran 32

nō *adv.* not 2:28, 4:74, 6:135, 6:136, 8:137, 12:54, 26:9, 28:55, 40:73, 42:128, 58:35, 60:51, 82:29 [ne → no], 102:106 >

nōht *adv.* naught, not 70:57, 104:140, 114:32, 120:12, 148:70; nōhtes 34:197

noma *m.* name; *nom. sg.* 4:49, 114:21, 150:106; *acc. sg.* noman 6:136, 10:22, 28:75, 28:76, 72:106, 102:93, 116:64; *gen. sg.* noman 120:17; *dat. sg.* noman 26:8, 26:30, 26:34, 54:228, 100:48, 140:125

nōntīd *f.* hour of none; *acc. sg.* nōntīd 30:120

norð *adv.* north 144:199

norðanweard *adj.* northward; *m. acc. sg.* norðanweardne 144:198

norþdæl *m.* north part; *dat. sg.* norþdæle 64:139

norðduru *f.* north door; *dat. sg.* norðdura 140:110

norþende *m.* north end; *dat. sg.* norþende 64:152

norðhealf *m.* north side; *acc. sg.* norðhealfe 142:173

nōwiht *adv.* not at all 84:50

nū *adv.* now 14:118, 14:119, 16:137, 16:154 [nē → nū], 16:158, 16:159, 16:160, 16:161, 20:80, 22:129, 24:137, 24:140, 24:148, 24:173, 26:1, 26:2, 76:23, 86:96 >

nugēt *adv.* still 82:33, 88:176; nugīt 154:206, 154:214

nȳddon (see neadian)

nȳdþearf *m.* need; *acc. sg.* nȳdþearfe 70:80

nȳrwian [nierwian] (2) to be troubled; *ind. pret. 3 sg.* nȳrugde 32:144

nyt [nytt] *adj.* advantageous; *f. nom. sg.* 38:23; *f. acc. sg.* nytte 154:193; *nt. nom. sg.* nyt 26:32, 38:3, 38:28; *comp. nt. nom. sg.* nyttre 20:78, 52:138

nyte (see ne witan)

nyten *nt.* animal, beast; *nom. sg.* 18:28; *gen. sg.* nytenes 48:66; *acc. pl.* nytenu 14:95, 119

nytlic̄ *adj.* profitable; *nt. nom. sg.* 76:39

nyttnes *f.* advantage; *dat. sg.* nyttnesse 38:30

nytwyrð [nytweorð] *adj.* useful; nytwyrðe *nt. nom. sg.* 152:140

O

o *adv.* ever 12:86

of *prep.* (with *dat.*) of, off, from (see Appendix, p. 150)

ofbeon [of beon] (anom.) away; *ind. pres. 3 sg.* of biþ [ofbiþ → of biþ] 78:75

ofdūne *adv.* down 132:284, 132:289

ofer *prep.* (with *acc.* / *dat.*) over, above, upon, after (see Appendix, p. 150)

oferbrǽdan (1) to cover; *pp.* oferbrǽded 136:25, 142:155, 142:164

ofercuman (IV) to overcome 84:53, 94:62, 138:76; *ind. pres. pl.* ofercumon 140:96; *pp.* ofercumen 124:110; *pl.* ofercumene 130:257

ofercweþan (V) to repeat 10:24

oferfēolan (III) fell upon; *ind. pret. pl.* oferfēollan 140:97

oferfōn (VII) to seize; *ind. pret. pl.* oferfēngon 124:96

oferfyll *f.* excess; *nom. sg.* 24:155; *acc. sg.* oferfylle 112:323

oferġeotolnes *f.* forgetfulness; *dat. sg.* ofergeotolnesse 72:97

oferġetimbran (1) to build over; *ind. pret. pl.* ofergetimbredon 140:116

oferġīetan (V) to forget; *pres. p.* ofergȳ tende 160:70

oferherġian (2) to ravage; *ind. pret. pl.* oferhergodan 138:71

oferhogian (2) to despise; *ind. pres. 3 sg.* oferhogaþ 32:145; *pret. 3 sg.* oferhogode 136:27; *pl.* oferhogodan 32:145; oforhogodan 84:49, 84:53

oferhrȳfan [oferhrēfan] (1) to roof over; *pp.* oferhrȳfde 88:146

oferhydig *adj.* proud; *f. dat. pl.* oferhydigum 100:48

oferhygd *m.* pride; *acc. sg.* oferhygde 16:143; oforhygde 16:147; oferhygd 148:70; *dat. pl.* oferhygdum 110:319; oforhygdum 86:94

oferlǽdan (1) overtaken; *pp.* oferlǽded 138:87

ofermēd *m.* pride; *acc. sg.* ofermēdu 128:205

ofermōd *adj.* proud; *m. nom. pl.* ofermōde 110:316; *def. m. nom pl.* oformōdan 42:104

ofermōdlīċe *adv.* proudly 136:37, 138:72

oferscīnan (1) to shine over; *ind. pres. 3 sg.* oferscīneþ 90:187

oferstīgan (1) to surpass; *ind. pres 3 sg.* oferstīgeþ 118:105; *pret. 3 sg.* oforstāg 116:49

oferswīþan (1) to overcome 18:26, 94:63; oferswīðan 122:75; oforswīþan 20:80, 42:102, 122:77; *ind. pres. 2 sg.* oferswīþest 100:49; *3 sg.* oferswīþ 118:106; *pret. 2 sg.* oferswīþdest 110:280; *3 sg.* oferswīþde 20:69, 22:110, 46:16, 116:89; oforswīþde 4:55, 22:94, 22:100; oferswīþe 20:79; *pp.* oferswīþed 22:117; oforswīþed 20:66; *pl.* oferswīþede 126:157; oferswīþde 102:109

oferswōgan (1) to overhang; *pp.* oferswōgen 138:89

oferweaxan (VII) to increase; *subj. pret. sg.* oferweoxe 112:330; *pp.* oferwexen 142:164

oferwryċan [oferwrohtan] (I) to comprehend; *ind. pres. 3 sg.* oferwryhþ 12:77; oforwryhþ 64:144

oferwyrċean (1) to cover 88:155; *pp.* oferworhte 88:145

oflinnan (III) to cease; *ind. pret. 3 sg.* oflān 132

ofor (see ofer)

ofordruncennes *f.* drunkenness; *nom. pl.* ofordruncennessa 34:204/5

oforflōwnes *f.* abundance; *dat. pl* oforflōwnessum 34:202

oforgēotan (VII) to flood; *ind. pret. 3 sg.* oforgēat 58:30

oforġedrync *m.* excessive drinking; *acc. sg.* oforgedrync 68:40

oforhyd *f.* pride; *dat. sg.* oforhydo 20:65

oforsēon (V) to see; *ind. pret. pl.* oforsēgon 84:66

oforþēċċan (1) to cover; *ind. pret. 3 sg.* oforþēcþ 64:139, 64:144; *pp.* oforþēaht 64:147

ofscēotan (1) to shoot; *pp.* ofscēoten 138:55

ofslēan (VI) to slay, kill 52:158, 106:189; *ind. pres. pl.* ofslēað 10:8; ofslēaþ 64:180; *pret. 3 sg.* ofslōg 54:194; *pl.* ofslōgan 140:106; *pp.* ofslēgene 54:195, 108:231

oft *adv.* often 12:61, 18:24, 22:101, 22:127, 38:40, 44:150, 52:170, 74:1 >; *superl.* oftost 144:186, 144:190

oftēon (II) to deprive 24:166

ofweorpan (III) to strike (with missile); *ind. pret. 3 sg.* ofwearp 20:69

ofþynċan (1) to repent; *ind. pres. 3 sg.* ofþynceþ 122:67

oht [āwiht] *nt.* something; *nom. sg.* 22:101, 154:193

oleċċung *f.* flattery; *acc. sg.* olecunga 154:186

olfend *m.* camel; *gen. pl.* olfenda 118:116

Oliuete *prop. n.* Olivet; *nom. sg.* 98:9; *gen. sg.* Oliuetes 48:60, 88:141

ōlyhtword *nt.* false praise; *acc. pl.* ōlyhtword 70:45

on *prep.* (with *acc. / dat.*) on, upon, in into, among (see Appendix, p. 150)

onāþryccan (1) to impress; *pp.* onāþrycte 88:177

onbæcling *adv.* backwards 18:14, 20:64, 152:173

onbærnan (1) to burn; *pp.* onbærnde 16:148

onbecuman (IV) to become; *ind. pret. 3 sg.* onbecom 78:86

onbegan [onbugan] (II) to bend 84:53

onbīdan (I) 160:62, 160:65; *ind. pret. 3 sg.* onbād 52:183; *imp. 2 sg.* onbīd 158:16, 25

onblāwnes *f.* inspiration; *nom. sg.* 4:65

onbringan (1) to bring; *ind. pres. 3 pl.* onbringað 162:103

onbryrdan (1) to stir up; *ind. pret. 3 sg.* onbryrde 74:24; *pp.* onbryrded 30:132; *pl.* onbryrde 22:102, [onbryde → onbryrde] 84:52

onbryrdnes *f.* inspiration; *acc. sg.* onbryrdnesse 84:51

onbūgan (II) to submit 154:187

onbyrhtan (1) to illuminate; *ind. pret. 3 sg.* onbyrhte [onbyrhton → onbyrhte] 74:21

onbyriġan (1) to taste; *ind. pret. 3 pl.* onbyrigdon 142:179

onbyrignes *f.* taste; *acc. sg.* onbyrignesse 142:181; *dat. sg.* onbyrignesse 142:179

oncierran (1) to turn, reverse; *pp.* oncerred 86:101

oncnāwan (VII) to know 48:81, 64:182, 74:19, 74:22, 76:11, 80:113; *ind. pret. pl.* oncnēowan 124:94; *subj. pret. pl.* oncnēowon 132:303; *imp. 2 sg.* oncnāw 80:100

oncunnan (pret. pres.) to know; *ind. pret. pl.* oncuðon 148:54

oncyrran (1) to turn, reverse 156:238; *ind. pret. pl.* oncyrde 128:188, 128:223; *subj. pl.* oncyrran 88:171, *imp. 3 pl.* oncyrron 76:34; *pp.* oncyrred 2:2

ond [and] *conj.* and (see Appendix, p. 149)

ondetnes *f.* confession; *dat. sg.* ondetnesse 108:248

ōndettan (1) to confess; *ind. pres. pl.* ōndettaþ 12:79, 62:107; *imp. 1 pl.* ōndetton 110:307

ondfeng *adj.* acceptable; *m. nom. pl.* ondfenge 70:72

ondġit [onġiet] *nt.* understanding; *acc. sg.* ondgit 14:121; *dat. sg.* ondgite 44:138

ondrǣdan (VII) (with *acc. / dat.*) to fear 116:63; ondrǣdon 124:121, 132:297; *ind. pres. 1 sg.* ondrǣde 124:120; *2 sg.* ondrǣdest 124:123; *3 sg.* ondrǣdeþ 100:75; *pl.* ondrǣdað 4:50; ondrǣdaþ 26:34, 110:315; *pret. pl.* ondrēdon 160:75, 160:77, 88; ondrǣdon 138; *subj. pres. 3 sg.* ondrǣde 58:35; *imp. 2 sg.* ondrǣd 4:59, 158:14, 113; *3 pl.* ondrǣdaþ 160:78, 141; *pres. p. def. m. acc. pl.* ondrǣdendan 76:8

ondrysne *adj.* terrible; *m. nom. sg.* 146:26

ondrysnu *f.* fear; *nom. sg.* 140:119

ondswarian (2) (with *dat.*) to answer; *ind. pret. 3 sg.* ondswarode 4:89, 18:5, 18:10, 46:29, 48:75; ondswarede 14:124, 48:45, 82:23; ondswerede 10:19, 52:178, 100:83,

160:146; ondswarode 18:10, *pl.*
ondswaredon 100:51; ondsworedon 10:13;
imp. 2 sg. ondswara 4:70
ondweard *adj.* present; *m. nom. sg.* 12:77,
14:130, 48:88, 92:8; *m. acc. sg.* ondweardne
52:151; *m. gen. sg.* ondweardes 112:336; *f.
nom. sg.* ondweard 68:32; *nt. nom. sg.*
ondweard 150:98; *def. m. acc. sg.*
ondweardan 96:91; *m. gen. sg.*
ondweardran 96:90; *m. dat. sg.*
ondweardran 92:3; *f. acc. sg.* ondweardan
24:139, 58:3, 58:18, 62:127 *f. dat. sg.*
ondweardan 10:2
ondweardlīċe *adv.* in presence
[onweardlīċe → ondweardlīċe] 92:19
ondweardnes *f.* presence; *nom. sg.*
52:152
ondwleota *m.* face; *acc. sg.* ondwleotan
162:109
ōnettan (1) to hasten; *ind. pres. 3 sg.*
ōnetteþ 40:48
onfæþmnes *f.* embrace; *gen. sg.*
onfæþmnesse 4:66
onfindan (III) to discover; *ind. pret. 1 sg.*
onfand 122:83
onfēng *f.* receiving; *dat. sg.* onfēng [→
onfēnge] 144:197
onfēngnes *f.* reception; *acc. sg.*
onfēngnesse 94:83
onfeohtan (III) [→ on feohtan] to fight 138:86
onflǣscnes *f.* incarnation; *dat. sg.*
onflǣscnesse 56:231
onfōn (VII) (with *acc. / dat.*) to accept 18:30,
28:82, 32:140, 58:7, 70:79, 88:158, 108:248,
128:201, 146:18, 97; *ind. pres. 3 sg.* onfēhþ
2:27, 24:164, 38:36, 42:110, 112:325; onfēhþ
[onfēh → onfēhþ] 108:249; *pl.* onfoþ 30:103,
32:152, 84:45, 108:235, 134:330; onfō [→
onfōþ] 32:162; *pret. 2 sg.* onfēnge 108:234; *3
sg.* onfēng 2:42, 6:95, 12:47, 12:64, 14:109,
14:110, 14:131, 18:28, 28:75, 32:144, 50:99,
62:120, 114:41; *pl.* onfengon 92:38, 94:82,
102:124, 112:323, 120:6, 124:103, 124:105,
140:101, 142:178, 144:207, 31; *subj. pres. sg.*
onfō 26:29, 32:139, 42:111, 50:121, 70:83; *pl.*

onfōn 26:28, 26:34; *pret. sg.* onfēnge 18:29,
108:258, 116:86, 152:183; *pl.* onfengon
16:142; *imp. 2 sg.* onfōh 98:4, 98:22, 108:229,
160:47; *2 pl.* onfōþ 110:303; *pp.* onfangen
116:77
onġēan *prep.* (with *acc. / dat.*) against 48:61,
116:75, 116:80, 118:91, 122:45, 132:294, 138:81,
138:84, 138:89, 142:175, 152:143, 152:144,
152:145
onġēan *adv.* against 136:40, 138:89
onġebringan (1) to bring upon 162:106, 36
onġelīefan (1) to believe; *subj. pres. pl.*
ongelȳfan 54:223
onġin *m.* beginning; *nom. sg.* 4:87; *gen.
sg.* onginnes 146:14; *dat. sg.* onginne
130:239
onġinnan (III) to begin; *ind. pret. 2 sg.*
onginnest 130:241; *3 sg.* onginneþ 14:112,
14:113; *pl.* onginnað 158:8; *pret. 2 sg.*
ongunne 130:255; *3 sg.* ongan 20:49, 38:8,
74:2, 80:92, 80:105, 100:74, 106:185, 110:291,
116:74, 136:38, 152:138, 152:140, 152:143,
152:148, 42; ongon 104:181; *pl.* ongunnon
106:188, 138:70; ongunnan 106:191; *imp. 2
sg.* ongin 130:241; *pp.* ongunnen 22:118; *pl.*
ongunnen 142:152
ongrysla *m.* horror; *dat. sg.* ongryslan
138:87
onġieldan [onguldan] (III) to render; *ind.
pret. 3 pl.* onguldon 150:136
onġytan (V) to understand 10:37, 12:87,
14:120, 22:113, 34:206, 64:183, 74:22, 126:171,
154:192; ongeotan 10:9, 10:31, 68:13, 74:19,
76:11, 76:26, 92:12, 130:272; ongyton 114:4;
ind. pres. 2 sg. ongytest 126:168; *3 sg.*
ongyteþ 12:54, 44:149; *pl.* ongytaþ 40:87,
42:90, 44:155, 76:15; ongeotaþ 90:192; *pret.
1 sg.* ongeat 4:62, 60:89, 162:97; *3 sg.*
ongeat 6:132, 148:44, 148:71, 150:97, 150:107,
123, 130; *pl.* ongēaton 20:46, 46:8, 94:63,
94:71, 140:101, 140:113, 150:131; *subj.
pres. sg.* ongyte 76:3; *pl.* ongyton 14:114;
ongieton 62; *pret. sg.* ongeate 148:59; *pl.*
ongēaton 10:33; *imp. 2 sg.* ongyt 80:99; *2
pl.* ongytaþ 34:208; ongytað 160:87; *infl.*

inf. to ongytene 54:225; *pp.* ongyten 48:88, 116:48

onherian (2) to imitate 50:130

onhnīgan (I) to bow down 88:164; *ind. pres. pl.* onhnīgan 140:100

onhōfan (I) to lift up; *pret. 3 sg.* onhōf 104:174

onhrēran (1) to move; *pp.* onhrēred 62:135, 64:142

onhwyrfan (1) to turn 106:200

onhyrian (2) to imitate; *imp. 1 pl.* onhyrgean 14:92

onlēsnes *f.* redemption; *gen. sg.* onlēsnesse 54:226; *dat. sg.* onlēsnesse 46:6

onlīc *adj.* similar; *nt. nom. sg.* onlīc 144:184, 150:109, 152:149, 152:175; *nt. acc. sg.* onlīc 148:48

onlīcnes *f.* image; *nom. sg.* 117; *acc. sg.* onlīcnesse 52:140, 104:141, 43; *dat sg.* onlīcnesse 32:145, 92:36, 92:39, 94:45, 94:53, 136:13, 142:157, 144:203; onlīcnysse 51

onliehtan (1) to illuminate, shine; *ind. pret. 3 sg.* onlyhte 10:40, 12:71, 102:104, 158:11; *ind. pret. pl.* onlihton 94:85; *subj. pres. sg.* onlyhte 102:114; *infl. inf.* to onlyhtenne 4:71; *pres. p.* onlyhtende 124:90; *pp.* onlyhte 114:10

onlūtan (II) bowed down; *ind. pret. pl.* onlūton 48:58, 60:59

onlyhte (see onliehtan)

onlȳsan (1) to deliver; *ind. pret. 2 sg.* onlȳsdest 60:86; *3 sg.* onlȳsde 118:95; *pp.* onlȳsed 32:149; *pl.* onlȳsede 62:103; onlȳsde 58:41, 60:74, 60:82,

onmunan (pret. pres.) to think; *imp. 2 sg.* onmun 126:163

onrihtlīċe *adv.* rightly 28:60

onsæġdnes *f.* sacrifice; *gen. sg.* onsægdnesse 52:154

onsǣlan (1) to untie; *imp. 2 pl.* onsǣlaþ 48:62

onscunian (2) to shun; *ind. pret. pl.* onscunodan 122:50; *infl. inf.* onscunienne 44:156; *pres. p.* onscungend 78:73

onsecgan (3) to present; *ind. pret. pl.* onsǣgdon 138:63; *imp. 2 pl.* onsecggaþ 26:25

onseald [on seald → onseald] see syllan

onsendan (1) to send; *ind. pret. 3 sg.* onsende 58:26, 132:306, 140:131, 39; *subj. pres. sg.* onsende 158:31; *pp.* onsended 4:75, 92:4

onsetton (1) to set upon, attack 140:95

onsīen *f.* countenance; *dat. sg.* onsīene 85, 87

onslǣpan (VII) to fall asleep; *ind. pret. 3 sg.* onslēp 160:80

onspringan (III) to leap; *ind. pret. 3 sg.* onsprang 116:80

onstellan (1) to set, appoint 54:213; *ind. pres. 1 sg.* onstelle 156:235; *pret. 3 sg.* onstealde 4:52, 14:126, 18:30, 22:101, 52:145, 72:90; *subj. pres. pl.* onstellan 28:86

onstyrian (2) stirs, moves; *ind. pres. 3 sg.* onstyreþ 14:106; *pp.* onstyred 48:73, 136:37, 154:212; *pl.* onstyrede 12:63

onsundrum *adv.* especially 138:57

onsȳn *f.* appearance; *acc. sg.* onsȳne 10:7, 16:139, 24:177, 62:92, 72:108, 160:45; *dat. sg.* onsȳne 64:165, 72:111, 88:172, 118:110, 136:7, 154:217

ontēon (VII) to untie; *ind. pres. 3 sg.* ontȳ neþ 26:17, 32:173; *pret. 3 sg.* ontȳnde 74:24, 100:65, 112:329, 136; *pp.* ontēned 4:76; ontȳ ned 42:92; *pl.* ontȳnede 18

ontimbran (1) to instruct; *pp.* ontimbred 148:86

ontwa *adv.* in two 148:50

ontȳnnes *f.* opening; *acc. sg.* ontȳnnesse 64:163

onunwīsdōm *m.* folly; *gen. sg.* onunwīsdōmes 62:91

onwacan (II) to spring; *ind. pret. 2 sg.* onwoce 62:99

onwalg *adj.* whole; *m. nom. pl.* onwalge 88:172

onwalhnes *f.* wholeness; *acc. sg.* onwalhnesse 88:178

onweald *m.* power; *gen. sg.* onwaldes 96:94; *dat. sg.* onwalde 60:63, 68:3, 72:95; onwealde 32:179, 34:195

onweardliċe [see ondweardliċe]

onwedenheorte *adj.* insane; *m. nom. sg.* 136:33

onweġ *adv.* away 38:6, 82:6, 88:176, 126:152, 132:293

onwendan (1) to change, invert 58:39; *ind. pres. 3 sg.* onwendeþ 42:110; *pl.* onwendaþ 42:107; *pret. 3 sg.* onwende 80:104; *pl.* onwendan 122:71; *imp. 2 sg.* onwend 80:102; *pp.* onwended 34:215, 62:135, 64:154, 132:286, 8, 158:3; *pl.* onwende 76:34

onwendnesse *f.* change; *nom. sg.* 12:75

onwrigennes *f.* revelation; *nom. sg.* 130:242

onwrēon (1) to reveal; *ind. pres. 3 sg.* onwrȳhþ 130:237; *pret. 3 sg.* onwrēah 74:25; *pp.* onwrīgen 2:1, 128:197

open *adj.* open; *m. nom. sg.* 64:142; *f. nom. sg.* open 88:147; *f. acc. sg.* opene 46; *nt. nom. sg.* open 88:150, 128:196; *nt. acc. sg.* open 47; *def. m. acc. sg.* openan 64:143

openian (2) to open; *imp. 3 sg.* openige 4:64

openlīċe *adv.* openly 54:223, 126:162, 132:314, 150:105

openung *f.* opening; *nom. sg.* 62:128

orcēape *m.* free; *nom. sg.* 26:27

ord *m.* sword; *dat. pl.* ordum 132:277

ordfruma *m.* origin; *nom. sg.* 8:147; *dat. sg.* ordfruman 20:84

orleahtre *adj.* faultless; *m. nom. pl.* orleahtre 114:39

orsorh *adj.* secure; *nt. acc. sg.* orsorh 106:199

ortrȳwnes *f.* distrust; *nom. sg.* 62:114

orwēn *adj.* hopeless; *m. nom. pl.* orwēne 60:45; *def. m. dat. sg.* orwēnan 128:190

orþonc *adj.* skillful; *def. f. nom. sg.* orþonce 70:49

Ostensi *prop. n.* Ostensian; *dat. sg.* 132:283, 134:326

owiht [awiht] *nt.* aught; *nom. sg.* 124:117

owōp *m.* weep; *dat. sg.* owōpe 60:87

oþ *prep.* (with acc.) until (see Appendix, p. 150)

ōþer *adj.* another; *m. nom. sg.* 70:64; ōþor 78:87 [ōþer → ōþor] ; *f. nom. sg.* ōþru 54:188; *nt. nom. sg.* ōþer 18:28, 30:95, 150:109, 152:149, 152:175; *m. acc. sg.* ōþerne 14:118, 44:147, 44:149, 88:171, 120:14; *f. acc. sg.* ōþre 140:130, 156:238; ōðre 118:124; ōþer 128:214; *nt. acc. sg.* ōþer 150:122, 152:141; ōðer 140:125; ōþor 54:206, 72:101; *m. gen. sg.* ōþres 24:166, 52:136, 52:137, 78:88, 80:107; ōþræs 136:27; *nt. gen. sg.* ōþres 156:235; *m. dat. sg.* ōþrum 44:145, 52:181, 76:13, 104:181, 106:185, 128:204; ōðrum 98:36; *f. dat. sg.* ōþerre 12:74, 146:27; *nt. dat. sg.* ōðrum 152:147; *m. inst. sg.* ōþre 30:119, 122:65, 130:235, 132:295, 73; *m. nom. pl.* ōþre 100:76, 102:122, 104:145, 104:163, 128:201, 152:169; *m. acc. pl.* ōþre 150:91, 150:102; *m. acc. pl.* ōþre 32:142, 42:135, 50:132, 58:35, 66:198, 150:116; ōðre 150:95; *nt. acc. pl.* ōþre 124:93; ōþru 6:128; *f. gen. pl.* ōþerra 44:148; *m. inst. pl.* ōþrum 142:183

ōþer…ōþer *adj.* one … the other (no definite form) *m. nom. sg.* 120:4

oþon [on þon → oþon] *conj.* in that 14:97

oþspornan (III) to stumble; *subj. pres. sg.* oþsporne 18:10; *pret. 3 sg.* oþspurne 20:50

oþþæt *conj.* until 6:101, 14:108, 54:192, 102:102, 108:253, 108:259, 128:228, 132:297, 134:323, 140:95, 160:63, 67, 158 >; oðþæt [oð þæt] 33

oþþe *conj.* or 14:99, 14:100, 14:104, 14:106, 18:31, 18:32, 26:29, 28:87, 30:101, 30:106, 32:140, 34:228, 38:28, 44:148, 66:187, 66:188 >; oþþe … oþþe *conj.* either … or 32:157/8, 92:23

P

palmtwig *nt.* palm branch; *nom. sg.*
98:10; *acc. sg.* palmtwig 98:14, 104:166,
104:169, 106:201; *dat. sg.* palmtwige 98:5,
108:230, 108:234; *acc. pl.* palmtwigu 46:10,
48:57; *dat. pl.* palmtwigum 46:12
Pannania *prop. n.* Pannonia; *dat. sg.*
Pannania 146:4
pāpa *m.* pope; *nom. sg.* 140:131; *acc. sg.*
pāpan 140:129; *dat. sg.* pāpan 140:128
pāpseld *nt.* papal see; *acc. sg.* pāpseld
140:129
Paulus *pers. n.* Paul; *nom. sg.* 28:45, 28:63,
28:68 [Pauwlus → Paulus], 28:77, 28:80, 30:92,
32:146, 34:208, 50:134, 98:38 [Pawlus → Paulus],
116:75, 120:5, 122:62, 128:188, 128:189,
128:224, 130:237, 130:238, 130:240, 130:248,
130:253, 132:282, 144:197, 144:197 >; *acc. sg.*
Paulus 130:235, 130:243, 130:267; *gen. sg.*
Paules 100:42, 120:28, 134:326; *dat. sg.*
Paule 98:38, 126:158, 128:188, 130:252
peneg [penig] *m.* penny; *gen. pl.* penega
46:40, 52:139
Pentecosten *prop. n.* Pentecost; *nom. sg.*
92:33
Petrus *pers. n.* Peter; *nom. sg.* 98:38,
100:42, 100:43, 100:56, 102:98, 102:112,
102:116, 102:121, 104:142, 104:163, 104:166,
104:174, 106:208, 106:210, 106:212, 106:226,
108:229, 108:238, 108:244, 108:246, 110:277,
120:4, 120:26, 120:30, 120:40, 122:51, 122:57 >;
acc. sg. Petrus 130:235, 130:271; *gen sg.*
Petres 120:1, 134:325, 140:123; *dat. sg.*
Petre 14:123, 48:60, 102:111, 104:143, 104:152,
122:62, 122:71, 124:116, 124:131, 126:169,
128:223
pīcen *adj.* made of pitch; *def. f. dat. sg.*
pīcenan 28:70
Pictauie *prop. n.* Poitiers; *dat. sg.*
Pictauie 148:75
Pilatus *pers. n.* Pilate; *gen. sg.* Pilatus
122:80
plega *m.* sports, games; *nom. pl.* plegan
68:37; *acc. pl.* plegen [→ plegan] 68:40
plagian (2) to play; *ind. pret. 2 sg.*
plegodest 58:38

portic *m.* porch, portico; *gen. sg.*
portices 142:150; *inst. sg.* portice 142:153;
nom. pl. porticas 88:144
pund [Lt. pondo] *nt.* pound; *acc. sg.* pund
46:33, 50:105

R

racentēag *f.* chain; *dat. sg.* racentēage
142:175
racent *f.* chain; *dat. pl.* racentum 28:73
rǣd *m.* advice; *gen. sg.* rǣdes 112:336;
dat. sg. rǣde 80:102, 138:48, 138:73, 140:122,
140:130, 154:226; *inst. sg.* rǣd 72:97
rǣdan (1) to read 10:23, 78:62, 122:82; *pp.*
rǣden 118:109; rǣdd 114:6
rǣpling *m.* captive; *nom. sg.* 120:30
rǣran (1) to raise; *imp. 2 sg.* rǣre 130:252
rǣsan (1) to rush; *ind. pret. pl.* rǣsdon
126:149
ræst *f.* bed; *nom. sg.* 156:231; ræste 6:118,
44:162, 100:49; *acc. sg.* ræste 28:45, 56:238,
70:76, 100:47a, 100:47b, 102:122, 102:132; *gen.
pl.* ræsta 70:50
ræstġemanan *m.* bedfellowship; *acc. sg.*
ræstgemanan 120:37
rāp *m.* rope; *acc. sg.* rāp 66, 69
raþe *adv.* quickly 14:101, 40:59, 48:63,
48:80, 60:82, 62:102, 62:110, 106:184, 108:235,
110:282, 126:169, 128:191, 128:196, 130:258,
17; raðe 16; *superl.* raþost 28:66, 126:164;
raðost 140:128
rēadnes *f.* redness; *nom. sg.* 4:68
rēafian (2) to rob, plunder; *subj. pres. pl.*
rēafian 42:129
reċċean [reċċan] (1) to tell, relate, explain
38:20, 58:2, 78:62; *ind. pres. 3 sg.* recþ
62:123, 84:78; *pret. 3 sg.* rehte 120:29,
120:31 (A)
reċċend *m.* ruler; *nom sg.* 128:216
reġn *m.* rain; *nom. sg.* 64:144; *acc. sg.*
regn 64:140; *gen. sg.* regnes 88:152; *nom.
pl.* regnas 32:180
reliquias *m. pl.* [Lt. reliquiae] relics; *dat. pl.*
reliquium 88:166, 88:169, 92:29

rēnian (2) to arrange; *infl. inf.* to rēnigenne 76:42
restan (1) to rest; *ind. pres. pl.* restaþ 54:210, 112:332; *pret. 3 sg.* reste 102:130, 156:231; *subj. pres. sg.* ræste 30:121
reste *f.* bed; *nom. sg.* 6:115
rētan (1) to comfort; *ind. pres 3 sg.* rēteþ 26:41
rēþe *adj.* fierce, cruel, severe; *m. acc. sg.* rēþne 66:202; *comp. m. nom. sg.* rēþra 66:199; reðra 152:169
rēþnes *f.* cruelty; *dat. sg.* rēþnesse 28:71
rīce *nt.* kingdom, dominion; *nom. sg.* 16:167, 20:61, 20:75, 44:158, 44:163, 82:19, 122:63, 126:161; *acc. sg.* rīce 16:142, 78:58, 82:15, 82:16, 82:20, 86:123, 96:95, 128:194, 128:226; *gen. sg.* rīces 4:87, 6:104, 20:61, 28:46, 38:12, 40:50, 40:89, 42:92, 46:21, 74:27; *dat. sg.* rīce 4:52, 60:65, 70:85, 126:160; rīcu 6:93, 20:59a, 20:59b
rīce *adj.* rich, powerful; *m. nom. sg.* 136:20; *m. gen. sg.* rīces 28:56; *m dat. sg.* rīcum 86:131; *m. dat. pl.* rīcum 114:12; *def. m. gen. sg.* rīcan 34:218; *comp. m. nom. sg.* rīcra 150:126
riht *adj.* straight, upright; rihtne *m. acc. sg.* rihtne 52:153, 76:32a, 76:32b; *m. dat. sg.* rihtum 52:166; *f. acc. sg.* rihte 132:285; *f. dat. sg.* rihtre 108:248; *nt. nom. sg.* riht 22:121, 154:187; *nt. dat. sg.* rihtum 44:138; *m. nom. pl.* rihte 60:88, 142:157; *m. acc. pl.* rihte 42:107; *def. m. nom. sg.* rihta 14:98, 78:58; *m. acc. sg.* rihtan 42:111, 78:51
riht *nt.* right; *acc. sg.* riht 32:175, 42:93 [rihtdōndum → riht dōndum], 44:140, 78:81, 90:212, 154:188; rihtes *gen. sg.* 94:64, 122:58; *dat. sg.* rihte 28:50, 28:52, 28:54, 30:98, 30:100, 30:136, 34:223, 40:45, 42:124, 86:97, 122:87
riht [onriht → on riht] *adv.* alright; 28:83/4, 30:94, 30:134, 32:138, 36:237
rihtan (1) to correct, direct 132:304; *ind. pres. pl.* rihtaþ 42:129, 42:135
rihtcynecynnes *m.* true royal line; *gen. sg.* 14:136
rihte *adv.* rightly 28:56, 152:153, 154:197

rihtġelȳfed *adj.* having right faith; *nt. nom. sg.* 118:98; *m. dat. pl.* rihtġelȳfdum 120:8; *def. m. acc. pl.* rihtgelȳfedan 78:55
rihtġelȳfend *m.* rightly believing; *dat. pl.* rihtgelȳfendum 42:92, 128:221
rihtliċ *adj.* proper; *nt. nom. sg.* 12:50, 18:39
rihtlīċe *adv.* rightly 42:108, 50:131, 50:133, 54:230, 76:28
rihtwīs *adj.* righteous, just; *m. nom. pl.* rihtwīse 66:197; *nt. dat. pl.* rihtwīsum 50:104
rihtwīsnes *f.* righteousness; *dat. sg.* rihtwīsnesse 20:82/3
rīman (1) to count; *ind. pres. 3 sg.* rīmeþ 124:126
rīnan (1) to rain; *ind. pres. 3 sg.* rīneþ 64:140
rīxian (2) to rule, reign 126:160; *ind. pres. 3 sg.* rīxaþ 24:178, 66:208, 74:28, 80:131; rīxað 8:153, 56:239, 74:28, 90:221; rīxiaþ 120:23; *pres. p.* rīxiende 110:280
rōd *f.* cross, rood; *nom. sg.* 62:131, 132:288; *acc. sg.* rōde 132:285, 132:289; *gen. sg.* rōde 6:102, 30:115, 30:119, 68:3, 68:5, 100:46, 237 21; *dat. sg.* rōde 4:54, 16:141, 18:22, 22:92, 50:96, 52:182 [ond rōde → on rōde], 54:190, 58:24, 60:50, 68:6, 120:27, 124:98, 132:284, 132:288, 132:296
rōdetācn *f.* [rōdetānc → rōdetācn] sign of the cross *nom. sg.* 87, 114
Roman *prop. n.* Roman; *nom. pl.* Romane 132:293 ; *gen. pl.* Romana 54:189, 128:225, 130:235
Rome *prop. n.* Rome; *dat. sg.* Rome 132:295, 132:296, 132:322, 134:327, 140:128
rōse *f.* rose; *gen. sg.* rōsan 4:68
rumlīċe *adv.* largely, abundantly 32:161
rummōd *adj.* liberal; *m. nom. pl.* rummōde 76:29
rummōdlīċe *adv.* liberally, bountifully 32:172

S

sace *m.* strife; *acc. sg.* sace 42:114

sācerd *m.* priest; *gen. pl.* sācerda 52:157 [sācreda → sācerda], 106:219, 108:237, 108:244, 124:95, 48

Sacra Uia *prop. n.* Sacred Way; *nom. sg.* 130:264

sǣ *f. / m.* sea; *nom. sg.* 62:129, 62:134; *acc. sg.* sǣ 14:128, 130:231; *gen. sg.* sǣs 100:72, 124:92, 158:35; *dat. sg.* sǣ 136:15, 158:41, 160:77

sǣd *nt.* seed; *nom. sg.* 38:22, 112:330; *acc. sg.* sǣd 2:8

sǣgen *m.* sayings; *dat. pl.* sǣgenum 138:84

Sǣteresdæg *m.* Saturday; *dat. sg.* Sǣteresdæge 48:87

sǣw *f.* sea; *gen. sg.* sǣwe 160:61, 160:70, 160:73

Saleman *pers. n.* Solomon; *gen. sg.* Salemannes 48:77; Salemones 6:115, 6:118

sam *conj.* or 34:229

Samaria *prop. n.* Samaria; *dat. sg.* 84:56 [Lt. Sameria (84:55)]

samne (see tosamne)

samnian (2) to gather; *subj. pres. sg.* samnige 64:138

samninga *adv.* suddenly 102:107

samod *adv.* together 100:84

sancta *f.* saint; *nom. sg.* 2:39, 4:88, 98:8, 102:134, 110:321 >; sancte 110:312; *acc. sg.* sancta 6:110, 112:335 >; *gen. sg.* sancta 116:79; sanctæ 140:124; *dat. sg.* sancta 62:97, 74:12, 98:2 >

sanctus *m.* saint; *nom. sg.* 28:45, 28:63, 28:68, 28:77, 30:92, 32:146, 64:179, 66:185, 82:11, 118:114, 144:191, 148:83, 148:87, 152:151 >; sancta 114:42; *acc. sg.* sanctus 144:195, 144:209, 148:76 > ; *gen. sg.* sancte 114:3, 114:25, 114:38, 118:90, 118:97, 118:100, 118:110, 118:132, 120:1, 140:123, 140:125, 146:2, 152:146 >; *dat. sg.* sancta 104:139, 114:8, 124:115, 124:131; sancte 148:74 >

sang *m.* song; *dat. sg.* sange 30:105

sangere *m.* singer; *acc. pl.* sangeras 142:168

sār *nt.* sorrow, grief, pain; *nom. sg.* 16:167, 72:112, 150:115 >; *acc. sg.* Sār 42:114; *dat. sg.* sāre 2:37, 2:38, 40:60, 40:74, 40:82, 40:84, 62:94 >; *acc. pl.* sār 10:26, 40:81, 84:52 >

sār *adj.* sore, painful; *def. m. acc. pl.* sāran 68:7

sārliċ *adj.* sorrowful; *def. m. nom. sg.* sārlica 86:100

sārlīċe *adv.* sorrowfully 154:204

Satanas *m.* Satan; *nom. sg.* 106:184, 110:318 >

sāwan (1) to sow; *ind. pret. 3 sg.* seow 2:8; *pp.* sāwen 94:50

sāwl [sāwol] *f.* soul; *nom. sg.* 14:104, 14:105, 14:106, 26:42 [se sāwl → seo sāwl], 78:76 >; sāul 4:46, 6:134, 38:31, 38:32, 38:35, 40:53 >; *acc. sg.* sāwle 14:102, 108:262, 110:285 > ; sāuwle 28:66, 110:309; sāule 60:80, 62:105, 70:61, 72:101 >; *gen. sg.* sāwle 52:159 >; sāuwle 68:10, 68:20; sāule 40:49, 68:32, 72:104, 76:22 >; *dat. sg.* sāwle 98:22, 108:258, 108:260 >; sāule 34:197, 62:125, 78:81 >; *nom. pl.* sāwla 60:69; sāula 54:210, 144:202, 144:206, 144:207 > ; *acc. pl.* sāwla 6:124, 14:103 >; sāuwla 46:19; sāula 30:111, 42:121, 50:110, 64:177, 144:209 >; *gen. pl.* sāula 60:58, 60:67, 70:67, 70:81, 74:11 >; *dat. pl.* sāwlum 86:92; sāula 26:33, 40:45, 62:106, 66:193 >

Scariot *pers. n.* Scariot; *nom. sg.* 46:38

Scariothisca *pres. n.* Iscariot; *nom. sg.* 46:38

sceaft *m.* taper; *dat. sg.* sceafte 90:186

sceand *adj.* shameful; *m. nom. sg.* 122:58

sċēap *nt.* sheep; *nom. sg.* 60:78; *gen. sg.* sċēapes 128:183; sċēpes 126:180; *nom. pl.* sċēap 132:301; *acc. pl.* sċēap 23

sceat *m.* money, tithes; *acc. pl.* sceat 26:14; *nom. pl.* sceattas 26:37, 32:169; *acc. pl.* sceattas 28:49, 32:150; *dat. pl.* sceatum 94:50

sċēat *m.* bosom; *dat. sg.* sċēate 2:26

sċēawian (2) to behold, look upon 24:177, 72:108, 80:93; *ind. pres. 3 sg.* sċēawaþ 20:62; *pret. 3 sg.* sċēawode 4:47; *pl.* sċēawodan 138:63, 140:103; *subj. pres. sg.*

scēawige 40:52, 76:3; *imp. 2 sg.* scēawa 80:97, 110:311; *infl. inf.* to scēawigenne 80:95

scēawung *f.* spectacle; *dat. sg.* scēawunga 130:234

sceaþa *m.* thief; *nom. sg.* 46:42; *gen. pl.* sceaþena 42:123; *dat. pl.* sceaþum 48:79

sceldig *adj.* guilty; *m. nom. sg.* 34:220

scendan (1) to be illusory; *pres. p.* scendende 34:213

sceomol *m.* stool, benches; *acc. pl.* sceomolas 48:77

sceones *f.* suggestion, temptation; *dat. sg.* sceonesse 2:15; *acc. pl.* sceonessa 12:61; *dat. pl.* sceonessum 16:151

sceoran (1) to projected; *ind. pret. pl.* sceoredon 142:158

sceōrt *adj.* short; *nt. nom. sg.* 44:157; *def. f. nom. sg.* sceortan 56:238; *comp. nt. nom. sg.* scyrtre 82:41

scēotan (II) to shoot 136:39; *ind. pres. 3 sg.* scēoteð 78:47; *pret. 3 sg.* scēat 136:42

Sceppend *m.* Creator; *acc. sg.* Sceppend 4:44

sceþwrac *adj.* hurtful, noxious; *def. f. gen. sg.* sceþwracan 114:25

sceþþan (VI) (with *dat.*) to harm, injure 90:198, 152:147; *ind. pret. 3 sg.* sceþede 114:25, 118:119

sciccels *m.* cloak; *acc. sg.* sciccels 148:49

scieldan (1) to shield; *ind. pres. pl.* sealdað [scealað → sealdað] 6:123

scīnan (I) to shine 90:189, 90:191, 90:203; *ind. pres. 3 sg.* scīneþ 4:69, 40:50, 90:186, 136:6; *pl.* scīnaþ 90:184; *pres. p.* scīndende 98:10; *m. dat. sg.* scīndendum 32:144; *def. nt. dat. sg.* scīnendan 58:30

scinlac *m.* magic; *dat. pl.* scinlacum 42:106

scinlæc *m.* magician; *nom. pl.* scinlæcan 42:104

scip *nt.* ship; *acc. sg.* scip 158:36, 158:41, 160:47, 160:51, 160:58, 160:59; 160:72 >; *gen. sg.* scipes 160:60; *dat. sg.* scipe 160:44b, 160:88, 162:92 >; *inst. sg.* scipe 160:44a

scipbroc *m.* shipwrecks; *acc. pl.* scipbrocu 120:29

scræf *nt.* den, cave; *acc. sg.* scræf 138:65; *gen. sg.* scræfes 136:13, 136:31, 136:36, 142:157; *dat. pl.* scrāfum 48:79

scrift *m.* confessor; *dat. sg.* scrifte 28:64; *dat. pl.* scriftum 134:329

scriftbōc *m.* confessional books; *acc. pl.* scriftbēc 28:54

scrȳdan (1) to clothe 146:30

scua [scuwa] *m.* shadow; *dat. sg.* scuan 60:81 (A)

scucc *m.* devil; *gen. pl.* scucna 130:259

sculdor *m.* shoulder; *nom. pl.* sculdro 88:163

sculan (pret. pres.) must, ought to; *ind. pres. 1 sg.* sceal 118:132 >; *2 sg.* scealt 14:125, 34:209, 46:31, 86:102, 128:196 >; *3 sg.* sceal 24:159, 26:40, 28:43, 28:82, 30:99, 30:123, 30:126, 32:139 >; *pl.* sceolon 24:148, 82:9 >; sceolan 6:131, 10:24, 10:34, 12:66, 12:67, 14:96, 14:98, 30:100 >; sculon 22:127, 12, 28 >; *ind. pres. 1 sg.* sceolde 100:85, 108:267 >; *3 sg.* sceolde 2:33, 2:37, 26:21, 46:39, 52:175, 58:37, 82:19, 86:92 >; scolde 2, 44; *pl.* sceoldon 92:22; sceoldan 12:87, 28:89, 30:96, 42:125, 48:80, 60:51, 70:49, 76:21, 76:22, 76:25 >; *subj. sg.* sceole 68:11, 68:16, 82:41, 122:75, 124:116, 128:189, 128:197, 140:132 >

scȳld *m.* shield; *nom. sg.* 8:139, 20:51, 62:90

scyld *f.* sin, guilt; *nom. sg.* 114:25, 118:118; *acc. sg.* scylde 130:271; *dat. sg.* scylde 42:124

scyldan (1) to shield 30:124; *ind. pres. 2 sg.* scyldest 154:208

scyldend *m.* protector; *nom. sg.* 100:49

scyldiġ *adj.* guilty; *m. nom. sg.* 122:58, 132:280; *m. acc. sg.* scyldigne 122:50; *m. nom. pl.* scyldige 60:123, 44:154, 44:155; *m. acc. pl.* scyldige 60:54; *def. m. acc. pl.* scyldigan 42:131

scylf *m.* shelf; *acc. sg.* scylf 18:8

scylfring *f.* fretwork; *nom. sg.* 70:52

Scyppend *m.* creator; *nom. sg.* 24:164, 58:4, 62:101, 94:67, 128:215, 130:230, 138:59; *acc. sg.* Scyppend 28:76, 74:9, 76:9, 84:88, 130:260; *gen. sg.* Scyppendes 6:92, 24:177, 88:178; *dat. sg.* Scyppende 8:142, 70:88, 86:98

scyttel *m.* bolt, bar; *nom. pl.* scyttelas 60:57; *acc. pl.* scyttelas 58:28

se, sēo, þæt *def. art. & dem. pron.* the, he, she, it, that (see Appendix, p. 146)

se, sēo, þæt *pronom.* who, which, that (see Appendix, p.148)

sealmsang *m.* psalmsinging; *dat. sg.* sealmsange 138:50

sealmsceop *m.* psalmist; *nom. sg.* 38:8, 38:24; *nom. pl.* sealmsceopas 74:3

sealt *m.* salt; *nom. sg.* 118

searo *nt.* deceit; *acc. sg.* searo 76:42, 138:76; *acc. pl.* searwa 58:23, 120:31

seax *nt.* knife; *nom. sg.* 152:177; *acc. sg.* seax 148:49; *inst. sg.* seaxe 152:176

sēcan (1) to seek 14:96, 14:99, 14:118; sēcean 120:37; *ind. pres. 2 sg.* sēcest [sēcestu → sēcest þu] 98:8; *3 sg.* sēcþ 50:103; *pl.* sēcaþ 64; sēceaþ 134:328; *pret. 3 sg.* sohte 120:30, 142:161, 54:218; *pl.* sohton 36:234, 88:148, 61; sohtan 138:54, 138:61; *subj. pres. pl.* sēcan 30:128, 68:20; *imp. 2 sg.* sēc 60:78; *2 pl.* sēcað 52; sēceað 142:145; *infl. inf.* to sēcenne 116:59, 140:135

secgan (3) to say 82:1, 82:7, 84:63, 84:68, 86:108 >; secgean 86:98, 118:132 >; secggan 38:20, 72:98, 74:1, 76:16 >; secggean 58:2, 78:63, 84:58, 146:1 >; sæcgan 146:37; *ind. pres. 1 sg.* secge 12:60, 116:46, 116:59, 118:130 >; secgge 34:216, 48:48, 52:179 [seccge → secgge], 138:57 >; *2 sg.* sagast 124:122; *3 sg.* sagaþ 18:1; sagað 82:10, 122:78; segeþ 136:20; segþ 38:1, 98:1, 3 >; segð 1, 3, 6 >; sægþ 26:20, 26:37, 28:79, 30:131, 46:1, 62:124, 128:225 >; sæg 124:108; *pl.* secgaþ 86:136; *pret. 1 sg.* sægde 146:28, 148:74 >; sæde 124:127; *3 sg.* sægde 4:86, 6:91, 10:1, 26:1, 28:68, 28:77 >; sæde 10:25;

pl. sægdon 56:233, 74:2, 74:4, 122:50a, 122:50b, 124:97 >; sædon 48:86, 124:104 >; *subj. pres. 1 sg.* secge 124:128; *pl.* secgan 100:84; secggan 30:127; *imp. 2 sg.* sege 124:129, 126:143; sæge 160:56; saga 124:107; *3 sg.* secge 124:126, 124:131, 126:138 >; secgge 126:139 >; *1 pl.* secggan 72:104; *2 pl.* secgað 124:102; secggaþ 48:63, 48:65 >; *infl. inf.* to secggenne 42:128 >; *pres. p.* secgende 114:15; *pp.* sægd 38:23, 42:98, 42:111, 44:147, 48:48 >

sefa *m.* mind, heart; *dat. sg.* sefan 94:88

segnbora *m.* standardbearer; *nom. sg.* 116:44

seldon *adv.* seldom 44:148

selest *superl. adv.* best 70:70; selost 54:197

self *adj.* self, himself; *def. m. nom. sg.* selfa 116:52, 116:53, 116:58, 118:103, 126:142; *nt. nom. sg.* selfe 133

sēlra *adj.* better; *comp. m. nom. sg.* 114:42; *m. acc. sg.* sēlran 116:60; *m. dat. sg.* sēlran 76:5; *m. nom. pl.* sēlran 78:64; *superl. nt. nom. sg.* sēlest 140:134; sēlost 46:31; *def. m. nom. sg.* sēlosta 8:139; *m. acc. sg.* sēlestan 34:198; *nt. dat. sg.* sēlestan 98:17

semninga *adv.* suddenly 100:60, 102:123, 102:128, 104:156, 108:256, 152:156 >; sæmninga 100:61 (A) (M)

sendan (1) to send 64:177, 86:126, 122:86, 122:88 >; sendon 66; *ind. pres. 1 sg.* sende 92:10, 94:80, 118:110, 158:17, 26 >; *3 sg.* sēndeþ 32:173 [sendaþ → sendeþ], 66:193, 140:93a, 140:93b >; sendeð 92:20; *pret. 3 sg.* sende 48:85, 52:165, 54:188, 108:242, 122:80, 128:220 >; sende [sendde → sende] 118; *pl.* sendon 2, 158:1, 24, 69, 72; *subj. pres. sg.* sende 98:21, 90; *pret. pl.* sendon 140:128; *imp. 2 sg.* send 18:8, 20:46, 120, 132, 144; sænd 115; *infl. inf.* to sendenne 126:154; *pp.* send 140; sended 6:94, 92:26, 92:36, 108:267, 136:41, 144:192, 160:63 >; *pl.* sende 14:118, 98:6, 104:146 >

senn [synn] *m.* sin; *acc. pl.* senna 28:59

sēo (see se, sēo, þæt)

sēoc *adj.* sick; *def. m. gen. sg.* sēocan 40:77

sēod *m.* wallet; *acc. pl.* sēodas 46:42

seofon *num.* seven 158:16, 15, 46, 79, 158, 164, 166; seofan 30:118, 104:141, 132:322

seofoþa *num. adj.* seventh; *m. dat. sg.* seofoþan 66:184; *m. inst. sg.* seofoþan 30:121

seolf *adj.* himself; *m. dat. sg* seolfum114:9; *def. m. nom. sg.* seolfa 94:64

seolfer *m.* silver; *gen. sg.* seolfres 12:89, 34:197, 70:47; *dat. sg.* seolfre 88:156, 88:162

seolfren *adj.* made of silver; *f. dat. sg.* seolfrenre 142:175

seoþþan *adv.* afterwards; 24:176, 32:140, 52:182, 54:220, 74:16, 74:23, 84:49, 84:69, 88:154b, 132:316, 140:117, 150:106, 150:125 >

seoþþan *conj.* after, since; 42:98, 74:6, 88:154a, 88:159, 128:225, 150:124 >; seoððan 10:38, 78:75

Sepontanus *prop. n.* Sepontanus; *nom. sg.* 138:70

Sepontus *prop. n.* Sepontus; *nom. sg.* 136:16, 138:46

sete (see settan)

setl *nt.* settle, seat, couch; *dat. sg.* setle 82:5, 86:90, 90:195, 110:317; *nom. pl.* setl 86:93; *acc. pl.* setl 48:78; *gen. pl.* setla 70:51

setlgang *m.* setting of the sun; *dat. sg.* setlgange 64:157

settan (1) to set, place 86:130; *ind. pret. 3 sg.* sette 31; *pl.* setton 16:140, 108:255; settan 124:99; *imp. 2 sg.* sete 60:66

setung *f.* treachery; *nom. sg.*; *acc. pl.* setunga 58:23

si (see eom)

sib [sibb] *f.* peace; *nom. sg.* 108:257, 108:265, 158:19, 158:37; sibb 36:240; *acc. sg.* sibbe 76:30, 110:300, 110:301, 128:202, 154:194; *gen. sg.* sibbe 54:208, 54:209,

80:123; *dat. sg.* sibbe 72:108, 72:115, 154:200; *gen. pl.* sibba 80:117

sibliċ *adj.* peaceful; *def. f. acc. pl.* siblecan 78:50

sīde *f.* side; *acc. sg.* sīdan 156:238; *dat. sg.* sīdan 28:69

sien (see bēon)

sige (see bēon)

sige *m.* victory; *nom. sg.* 140:133; *acc. sg.* sige 20:82, 46:11, 46:15, 138:78; *gen. sg.* siges 46:13, 46:15, 124:111, 130:266, 140:109, 140:115; *dat. sg.* sige 138:85

sigebeorht *adj.* victorious; *m. nom. pl.* sigebeorhte 140:107

sigefæst *adj.* more victorious; *comp. m. nom. sg.* sigefæstra 118:107

sigetācen *nt.* token of victory; *acc. sg.* sigetācen 68:5

simle *adv.* always 32:160, 86:107, 86:134, 88:180, 88:183, 92:8, 118:135, 128:202, 138:56, 158:3, 55 >

Simon *pers. n.* Simon; *nom. sg.* 120:31, 120:39, 122:48, 122:51, 122:60, 122:68, 122:70, 122:78, 124:115, 124:131, 126:139, 126:140, 126:141, 126:146, 126:156, 126:162a, 126:162b, 126:165, 126:169, 126:171, 126:173, 126:174, 130:245, 130:247; *acc. sg.* Simon 122:50, 130:241, 130:254; *gen. sg.* Simones 50:93, 120:41, 130:258, 130:270; *dat. sg.* Simone 120:25, 120:32, 122:51, 124:114, 126:156, 126:162

sin *pron.* his; *m. nom. sg.* 88:142

singallīċe *adv.* perpetually 70:76

signan (III) to sing; *ind. pres. 3 sg.* singeþ 106:182; *pl.* singaþ 54:230; *pret. 3 sg.* sang 2:21, 4:46, 110:309; *pl.* sungon 74:3; *imp. 2 pl.* singaþ 110:303; *pres. sg.* singende 102:131, 104:176, 106:196, 158:20, 19; *pp.* sungen 52:163

Sion *prop. n.* Zion; *gen. sg.* Siones 48:65

sittan (V) to sit 54:205; sitton 19; *ind. pres. 2 sg.* sitest 100:45; *3 sg.* siteþ 12:53, 50:126; *pret. 3 sg.* sæt 10:11, 50:95, 50:115, 50:127, 102:121, 146:42a, 146:42b; *subj. pret. sg.* sæte 12:51; *imp. 2 pl.* sittað 33; *pres. p.*

sittende 14:120, 46:33, 48:66, 108:270, 158:42 (A)

sīð m. journey; acc. sg. sīð 132:298; dat. sg. sīþe 120:30; inst. sg. sīþe 18:11, 30:119, 30:120a, 30:120b, 30:120c, 30:121, 132:296, 152:175; sīðe 146:39, 148:85, 150:109, 152:138, 152:167; inst. pl. sīþum 30:118, 54:196, 104:141

sīþfæt m. journey; nom. sg. 158:33; acc. sg. sīþfæt 158:34

siþþon conj. after 14:116; siþþan 142:171

siþþon adv. afterwards 40:60

slæp m. sleep; inst. sg. slæpe 140:115

slæpan (VII) to sleep; ind. pret. 3 sg. slēp 148:57, 160:81; 3 pl. slēpan 102:124, 104:165; pres. p. slēpende 160:72, 160:86

slēan (VI) to stroke, slay 106:191, 152:143, 152:170, 152:171, 152:172; ind. pret. 3 sg. slōg 100:64, 152:140, 152:144; pl. slōgan 16:139, 106:192; subj. pres. sg. sleā 30:117, 132:277; pp. slēgene 108:241

slef m. sleeves; acc. pl. slefan 126:146

slege m. slaughter; nom. sg. 80:124

slitan (I) to bite; pres. p. slitende 42:123

smēagan (1) to inquire 38:8; ind. pres. 3 sg. smēaþ 124:126; pret. 3 sg. smēade 4:57; subj. pres. 3 sg. smēage 76:28; imp. 1 pl. smēagean 12:58; infl. inf. to smēagenne 22:98

smearcian (2) to smile; ind. pret. 3 sg. smercode 130:256

smerenes f. ointment; nom. sg. 50:107; acc. sg. smerenesse 50:94; gen. sg. smerenesse 46:34, 46:36; dat. sg. smerenesse 52:138 (A)

smerian (2) to anoint 50:110, 50:135; ind. pret 3 sg. smerede 46:34, 50:130; smyrede 50:106

smyltnes f. serenity, calmness; nom. sg. 80:116, 160:76

smyrenes f. ointment; nom. sg. 46:39; gen. sg. smyrenesse 50:105 (A)

snāw m. snow; nom. sg. 104:141, 104:151

snotorlīce adv. wisely, prudently 66:205

snottor adj. wise; m. acc. pl. snottre 76:2

snyttro f. wisdom; nom. sg. 70:49, 84:78; snytro 114:37 (EWS)

Sodom prop. n. Sodom; gen. sg. Sodoma 108:240

Sodomwar prop. n. people of Sodom; dat. pl. Sodomwarum 54:189

somne [ætsomne] adv. together 68:6, 70:63

somnunga adv. suddenly 50

sona adv. soon, at once, immediately 10:20, 10:21, 12:48, 12:70, 12:79, 14:107, 18:19, 22:105, 22:108, 22:110, 22:19 >

sorg f. sorrow; nom. sg. 72:113; sorh 94:70; dat. sg. sorge 94:72; nom. pl. sorga 94:68; acc. pl. sorga 94:77; dat. pl. sorghum 2:37

sorgian (2) to be sorrowful 68:15; ind. pres. pl. sorgiað 68:29 [he gelomlīce → ge gelomlīce (68:28)]

sōþ adj. true; m. nom. sg. 20:47, 22:111, 22:112, 22:115, 106:216, 130:231 >; sōð 152:164; nt. nom. sg. sōþ 34:216, 48:48, 52:179 >; f. acc. sg. sōþe 24:143, 70:60, 76:30 >; sōðe 68:23; nt. acc. sg. sōð 118:130; f. dat. sg. sōþre 16:157, 90:204, 120:7; m. nom. pl. sōþe 130:249; nt. nom. pl. sōþe 128:224; f. dat. pl. sōþum 124:124; def. f. nom. sg. sōþe 16:157, 70:59; m. acc. sg. sōþan 30:95, 74:9, 84:88; f. acc. sg. sōþan 66:207, 78:53; f. gen. sg. sōþan 18:33, 116:51; m. dat. sg. sōþan 76:5; f. dat. sg. sōþan 56:231; sōðan 16:160; nt. dat. sg. sōþan 76:7

sōð nt. truth; nom. sg. 130:236; acc. sg. sōð 154:187; sōþ 90:212; dat. sg. sōðe 10:29

sōþfæst adj. true; m. nom. sg. 60:87, 130:247; m. nom. pl. sōþfæste 52:143; f. acc. pl. sōþfæste 66:206; m. gen. pl. sōþfæstra 42:107, 92:12; f. dat. pl. sōþfæstum 66:193, 70:75

sōþfæstnes f. truth; acc. sg. sōðfæstnesse 38:10, 128:228; gen. sg. sōðfæstnesse 12:51; sōþfæstnesse 26:26, 52:141, 116:57

113

sōþlīċe *adv.* truly 20:55, 40:80, 76:37, 92:23, 98:5, 98:10, 100:49, 104:161, 104:174, 104:176, 106:183 >; sōðlice 98:33 [we sōðlice → is sōðlice], 154:189, 140, 169 >

sōþsecgende *adj.* truth-telling; *m. nom. sg.* 130:247

spætlan (1) to spit; *ind. pres. pl.* spætliað 10:7; *pret pl.* spætledon 16:139; spætlædon 162:108

spēd *m.* power; *nom. pl.* spēda 124:114

spel *m.* story; *nom. sg.* 120:T

spellboda *m.* messenger; *nom. sg.* 116:44; spelboda 116:84

spellian (2) to proclaim; *ind. pret. pl.* spellodan 114:15

spīca *m.* drug; *nom. sg.* 50:108

spīwan (VI) to spew; *pres. p.* spīwende 38:29

sprǣc *f.* speech; *acc. sg.* sprǣce 154:193, 156:240; *nom. pl.* sprǣca 34:204

sprecan (V) to speak 38:14, 128:189; *ind. pres. 2 sg.* sprecst 128:188; *3 sg.* spreceþ 120:14, 122:63; sprecþ 38:10; *pl.* sprecaþ 64:152, 120:13; *pret. 3 sg.* sprǣc 12:81, 20:58, 82:16, 92:19, 100:66, 116:61, 154:211, 156:242, 60 >; *pl.* spǣcon 28:69; sprǣcan 52:177; sprecan 70:45; *subj. pres. sg.* sprece 78; *pl.* sprecan 120:12; *imp. 2 sg.* sprec 108:231, 160:69; *pres. p.* sprecende 2:16, 26:13, 38:1, 42:108, 108:245, 112:329, 154:188 [specende → sprecende], 158:37, 162:92, 162:96

stǣnen *adj.* made of stone; *f. acc. sg.* stǣnenne 113; *f. gen. sg.* stǣnenre 74:18; *m. acc. pl.* stǣnene 122:43; *def. f. dat. sg.* stǣnenan 130:263, 131

stæðhlyplīċe *adv.* steeply 142:158

stal *f.* theft; *gen. sg.* stale 52:146

stān *m.* stone, rock; *nom. sg.* 14:106, 50:127, 52:81 [sān → stān]; *acc. sg.* stān 52:81, 110:284, 144:199; *dat. sg.* stāne 20:50, 140:112, 142:172, 144:199, 144:201; *nom. pl.* stānas 18:4, 142:158; *acc. pl.* stānas 20:68, 130:265; *gen. pl.* stāna 142:162

standan (VI) to stand 156:243, 16, 43; *ind. pres. 1 sg.* stande 154:221; *2 sg.* standest 156:244; *3 sg.* standeþ 34:216, 76:35, 136:18; *pl.* standaþ 98:39; *pres. p.* standende 70:78

staðelian (2) to establish 78:51; staþelian 80:110

staþol *m.* support; *nom. sg.* 8:139

staðolfæst *adj.* steadfast; *m. nom. sg.* 148:79

staþolfæstlīċe *adv.* steadfastly 12:72

stefn *f.* voice; *nom. sg.* 60:55, 64:141, 102:110, 104:180, 128:227, 158:11, 103; *acc. sg.* stefne 12:78, 62:93, 64:137, 102:112, 104:174, 116:52, 118:94, 57; *dat. sg.* stefne 34:190, 106:200, 116:58, 148:61, 150:101, 150:111, 154:213; *inst. sg.* stefne 4:89, 10:14, 54:218, 60:75, 62:107, 100:80, 106:205, 126:147

stemn *f.* voice; *nom. sg.* 12:63, 20:47

stenc *m.* odour, smell; *nom. sg.* 102:123; *acc. sg.* stenc 40:64, 50:115, 50:134; *gen. sg.* stences 50:109; *dat. sg.* stence 46:35, 50:107; *nom. pl.* stencas 40:56

stēopcild *nt.* orphan; *dat. pl.* stēopcildum 28:77

steorra *m.* star; *nom. sg.* 98:11; *nom. pl.* steorran 64:159

stēorreþra *m.* steerman; *nom. sg.* 160:44; stēorreðra 160:89; *dat. pl.* stēorreþran 160:60

stēran [stīeran] (1) to rule 42:125

stīgan (I) to ascend; *ind. pres. 3 sg.* stīgeþ 20:61

stihtan (1) to command, order; *ind. pres. 3 sg.* stihtaþ 84:78

stihtung *f.* arrangement; *nom. sg.* 56:231

stille *adv.* still 142:174

stilnes *f.* stillness; *acc. sg.* stilnesse 124:92

stocc *m.* stock; *acc. sg.* stocc 130:263; stoc 130:265

stōndan (VI) to stand 122:63, 135:39, 138:45; *ind. pres. 1 sg.* stōnde 138:56; *3 sg.* stōndeþ 12:72, 88:147, 136:7; stōndeð 52:169 [stōndað → stōndeð]; *pl.* stōndaþ 86:112; *pret. 3 sg.* stōd 88:137, 90:201, 100:66, 122:54,

126:150, 136:36, 152:139, 146; *pl.* stōdan 70:44, 84:83, 88:159, 120:20; *pres. p.* stōndende 6:120

stōpl *m.* footstep, footprints; *nom. pl* stōplas 88:177; *dat. pl.* stōplum 88:171

storm *m.* storm; *nom. sg.* 138:88

stōw *f.* place; *nom. sg.* 24:151, 88:137, 88:140, 88:154; *acc. sg.* stōwe 12:77, 72:114, 88:142, 88:148, 88:182, 90:206, 100:60; *gen. sg.* stōwe 138:59; *dat. sg.* stōwe 10:3, 12:74, 46:6, 64:142, 90:188, 90:189, 90:201, 90:203, 90:211, 92:35, 94:43, 100:87; *acc. pl.* stōwa 14:129; *dat. pl.* stōwum 52:170, 76:18, 90:211

strǣl *m.* arrow, dart; *nom. sg.* 136:39, 136:40, 55; *dat. sg.* strǣle 136:38, 138:55; *nom. pl.* strǣlas 138:89; *dat. pl.* strǣlum 140:105

strǣt *m.* street; *dat. sg.* strǣte 130:264

strang *adj.* strong; *m. nom. sg.* 58:31, 76:40; *nt. nom. sg.* strang 2:36, 54:203; *m. nom. pl.* strange 94:84; *superl. m. dat. pl.* strengestum 6:116

strangan (1) to strengthen; *pres. p.* strangende 165

stream *m.* stream; *nom. sg.* 40:71

strēnan [stēonan] (1) to gain, acquire; *ind. pres. pl.* strēnaþ 36:237

strengu *f.* strength; *gen. sg.* strenge 94:76; *dat. sg.* strenge 94:82

strengo *f.* strength; *nom. sg.* 4:85

strengþ *m.* forces; *dat. pl.* strengþum [strengum → strenþgum] 106:188

streownes *f.* litter; *acc. sg.* streownesse 156:232/3

streowian (2) to scatter; *ind. pret. pl.* streowodan 48:69, 48:70 (EWS)

stregdan (III) to scatter, spread; *pp.* strogden 94:50

stronglīċe *adv.* strongly 118:120

strudan (VII) to ravage, destroy 52:140

strynde *f.* lineage, race; *dat. sg.* strynde 14:135 (A)

styccemælum *adv.* piecemeal, in places 142:163

stȳran (1) to move, steer 42:128, 42:133, 132:304; *ind. pret. 3 sg.* stȳrde 12:59, 132:292; *pl.* stȳrdon 10:16; stȳredan 122:43a, 122:43b

subdiacon *m.* subdeacon; *dat. pl.* subdiaconum 76:38

sum *adj.* some; *m. nom. sg.* 10:11, 46:37, 78:86, 106:182, 136:20, 140:111, 146:42 [→ sum þearfa], 150:113 >; *f. nom. sg.* sum 136:14; *nt. nom. sg.* sum 136:27, 152:140; *m. acc. sg.* sumne 144:199, 154:197, 52; *f. acc. sg.* sume 112:327, 152:153, 156:232; *nt. acc. sg.* sum 148:83, 152:138, 152:167, 152:175; *m. gen. sg.* sumes 136:12, 150:110; *nt. gen. sg.* sumes 136:31, 136:36; *m. dat. sg.* sumum 64:143, 152:149; *f. dat. sg.* sumre 82:39, 142:159, 142:160, 148:88, 43 >; sumere 82:40; *m. inst. sg.* sume 150:109; *f. inst. sg.* sumre 160:71; *m. nom. pl.* sume 14:99, 42:128, 48:69, 132:317, 148:53, 126 >; *f. nom. pl.* sume 28:61; *m. acc. pl.* sume 146:37

sumor *m.* summer; *gen. sg.* sumores 40:57

sundor *adv.* apart 10:4 (A)

sundorgenga *adv.* going alone, solidary 136:28

sundorweorþung *f.* special honour; *dat. sg.* sundorweorþunge 136:6

sundran *adv.* especially 138:59:

Sunnandæġ *m.* Sunday; *dat. sg.* Sunnandæge 48:88; *inst. sg.* Sunnandæge 84:48; *acc. pl.* Sunnandagas 22:133; *inst. pl.* Sunnandagum 30:128

sunne *f.* sun; *nom. sg.* 62:130; *acc. sg.* sunnan 6:98; *gen. sg.* sunnan 32:181, 64:157, 116:51

sunu *m.* son; *nom. sg.* 6:132, 18:4, 18:8, 18:21, 20:73, 48:71, 50:92, 54:218, 106:214, 106:215 >; *acc. sg.* sunu 4:43, 4:60, 20:46, 116:64, 122:87 >; *gen. sg.* suna 20:72, 108:249, 116:44, 118:135 >; *dat. sg.* suna 4:81, 10:6, 100:50, 118:91, 134:332 >; *acc. pl.* suna 128:209

sutole *adv.* plainly 64:160

suðduru *f.* south door; *nom. sg.* 138:64
suðwag *m.* south wall; *acc. sg.* suðwag 142:154
swā *adv., conj.* so (See Appendix, p. 149)
swæþ *nt.* footstep, track; *dat. sg.* swæþe 50:132
swæðhlype *adv.* precipitously 138:65
swat *m.* sweat; *dat. sg.* swate 40:84
swað *m.* footstep; *nom. pl.* swaðo 142:151; *acc. pl.* swaðu 140:111; *gen. pl.* swaþa 88:181
swē [swē → swā] (See Appendix, p. 149)
sweart *adj.* swart, black; *nt. nom. sg.* 144:204; *nt. nom. pl.* swearte 144:202
swēġ *m.* sound; *nom. sg.* 44:161, 92:35, 92:36, 92:40, 94:47, 94:51
sweltan (III) to die; *ind. pres. 3 sg.* swelt 108; *pl.* sweltaþ 34:219; *subj. pres. sg.* swelte 67; *pl.* swelton 34:191; *pres. p. m. acc. sg.* sweltendne 10:28
swencean (1) to trouble, afflict 54:213; *ind. pres. 3 sg.* swenceþ 37 (A)
swēora *m.* neck; *acc. sg.* swēoran 69; *dat. sg.* swēoran 152:171
sweord *m.* sword; *acc. sg.* sweord 6:117; *dat. sg.* sweorde 30:117; *inst. sg.* sweorde 152:169; *dat. pl.* sweordum 106:188
sweostor *f.* sister; *nom. sg.* 46:24, 46:25, 46:28, 100:66
sweotol *adj.* manifest; *f. acc. sg.* sweotole 58:2, 68:34
sweotollīċe *adv.* manifestly, plainly 18:21, 68:13, 150:134
swēr [swēor] *m.* pillar, column; *nom. sg.* 98:39, 146; *acc. sg.* swēr 43, 112; *dat. sg.* swēre 44
swēte *adj.* sweet, pleasant; *m. nom. sg.* 102:123; *m. acc. sg.* swētne 50:115, 50:133; *m. nom. pl.* swēte 40:62; *def. m. dat. sg.* swētan 46:35, 50:107; *m. nom. pl.* swētan 40:56 *superl.* swētast 34:209
swētnes *f.* sweetness; *nom. sg.* 40:67; *acc. sg.* swētnesse 38:16, 38:17; *dat. sg.* swētnesse 24:150

swīgian (2) to be silent; *subj. pret. sg.* swīgode 12:65; swīgade 10:15; *pres. p.* swīgende 4:58, 40:52
swīgung *f.* silence; *gen. sg.* swīgunge 118:95; swīgunga 118:119
swilċe *adv.* so, also 152:149, 70
swingan (III) scourge; *ind. pres. pl.* swingaþ 10:7; *pret. pl.* swungon 16:138, 162:108; *imp. 2 pl.* swingað 77; *pp.* swungen 132:315
swingel *f.* scourging; *dat. sg.* swinglan 10:8
swīðe *adj.* strong, great; *def. m. inst. sg.* swīðan 140:115
swīþe *adv.* greatly, very 12:63, 14:98, 14:101, 18:12, 20:87, 24:164, 28:61, 32:183, 34:192; swīðe 68:21, 68:37, 70:71, 78:84 >; *comp.* swīþor 22:110, 34:203, 40:81, 42:129, 42:130, 42:132, 100:77, 112:323, 146:24, 152:144, 152:145, 154:187 >; swīðor 38:34, 142:157, 142:161, 146:12 >; *superl.* swīþost 154:185
swīþra *adj.* right; *f. acc. sg.* swīþran 62:116, 66:192, 104:153; *f. dat. sg.* swīþran 106:204
sworettan (1) to sigh; *ind. pret. pl.* sworettan 60:43
swūra *m.* neck; *acc. sg.* swūran 124
swutol *adj.* plain, manifest; *m. nom. pl.* swutole 140:112
swutollīċe [swutolīċe → swutollīċe] *adv.* plainly 126:155
swylc *adj.* such; *m. nom. sg.* 58:33a, 58:33b; *nt. nom. sg.* swylc 40:79; *f. acc. sg.* swylce 130:271; *nt. acc. sg.* swylc 138:44; *nt. dat. sg.* swylcum 66:189
swylce *conj.* so, like, also, as it were, as if (See Appendix, p. 149)
swyltan (1) to die 40:78; *ind. pres. pl.* swyltaþ 30:107; *pret. pl.* swultan 34:214, 54:192, 54:195; *subj. pres. sg.* swylte 132:315; *pres. p.* swyltende 52:148
swȳra *m.* neck; *acc. sg.* swȳran 67
swȳþe *adv.* much, very 24:163, 28:80, 30:104, 30:123, 40:80, 46:37, 52:138, 58:28,

70:83 >; *comp.* swȳþor 10:16, 22:102, 78:87 >
sylf *adj.* self, himself, herself; *m. nom. sg.* 26:21, 28:57, 32:152, 32:169, 46:17, 54:212, 70:65 >; *f. nom. sg.* sylf 8:141, 88:157; *nt. nom. sg.* sylf 88:150; *m. acc. sg.* sylfne 6:129, 20:64, 22:91, 24:168, 70:70, 76:3, 80:99, 124:95 >; *f. acc. sg.* sylfe 6:92; *nt. acc. sg.* sylf 130:236; *m. gen. sg.* sylfes 40:55, 58:22, 68:2, 70:79, 84:62, 86:122, 90:197, 114:7, 128:194 >; *m. dat. sg.* syflum 8:144, 44:146, 50:101, 66:202, 76:36, 80:115, 86:104 >; *f. dat. sg.* sylfre 2:35; *m. nom. pl.* sylfe 34:194, 54:202, 152:180 >; *m. acc. pl.* sylfe 30:127, 66:190, 68:25, 88:155, 122:47 >; *f. acc. pl.* sylfe 120:35; *m. gen. pl.* sylfra 72:97, 124:98 >; *f. gen. pl.* sylfra 14:103, 42:121 >; *nt. gen. pl.* sylfra 84:66, 90:192 >; *m. dat. pl.* sylfum 28:86, 28:86, 28:88, 42:123, 92:12, 118:132, 152:165 >; *def. m. nom. sg.* sylfa 8:151, 12:51, 26:4, 26:13, 30:92, 38:26, 64:178, 66:198, 72:108, 76:24 >; *f. acc. sg.* sylfan 120:12; *m. dat. sg.* sylfan 118:134; *f. nom. pl.* sylfan 160:74
syllan (1) to give 20:59, 22:130, 26:24, 34:219, 44:152, 70:70, 90:209, 124:130; *ind. pres. 1 sg.* sylle 18:13, 20:54, 110:301; *2 sg.* sylest 100:47; *3 sg.* sylþ 34:228; syleþ 24:172, 26:17, 32:160, 44:163; *pl.* syllaþ 26:28, 26:32, 26:34, 26:35; *pret. 2 sg.* sealdest 60:62, 132:303, 75; *3 sg.* sealde 6:102, 26:4, 26:6, 32:162, 32:177, 34:185, 50:95, 104:139, 106:198, 106:199; *pl.* sealdon 54:199, 124:101, 6, 10; *subj. pres. sg.* sylle 34:227; *pl.* syllon 32:150, 36:238; *pret. pl.* sealdon 26:22; *imp. 2 sg.* syle 158:9; *3 sg.* sylle 34:225, 116:52; *2 pl.* syllaþ 28:49, 160:51; *infl. inf.* to syllenne 14:133/4; *pp.* seald 32:154, 96:91, 96:92, 96:93, 128:219, 140:133 [onseald → on seald]
syllic *adj.* marvellous; *nt. nom. pl.* syllice 62:135; *m. acc. pl.* syllice 130:265
sylra *adj.* better, more excellent; *comp. m. nom. sg.* 114:18

symbeldæġ *m.* feast day; *acc. sg.* symbeldæg 92:2; *dat. sg.* symbeldæge 48:56
symbelnes *f.* festivity, festival; *nom. sg.* 44:162; *nom. pl.* symbelnessa 40:68
symle *adv.* always 16:152, 24:175, 26:5, 26:8, 28:56, 32:144, 32:158, 32:171, 34:223, 38:14, 38:16, 42:125 >
synbyrþen *m.* sin-burdens; *acc. pl.* synbyrþenna 78:44
synderliċ *adj.* various; *nt. acc. sg.* synderlic 48:86; *f. dat. sg.* synderlicre 100:86
synderlīċe *adv.* in several ways, variously 146:26
synfull *adj.* sinful; *f. gen. pl.* synfulra 50:92; *m. acc. pl.* synfulle 52:143; *m. dat. pl.* synnfullum 28:59; *def. m. nom. sg.* synnfulla 40:85; *m. gen. sg.* synfullon [symfullon → synfullon] 68:22; *m. nom. pl.* synfullan 20:83; *m. acc. pl.* synfullan 50:91; *m. dat. pl.* synnfullum 42:93
syngallīċe *adv.* constantly 144:194
syngian (2) to sin; *pres. p. m. acc. pl.* syngiende 42:135
synliċ *adj.* sinful; *nt. acc. pl.* synlicu 76:20
synlīċe *adv.* sinfully 138:77
synlust *m.* sinful lust; *dat. pl.* synlustum 40:43
synn *f.* sin; *nom. sg.* 2:19, 36:233, 44:146, 118:119; syn 2:2; synne 44:144; *acc. sg.* synne 26:23, 44:150; *dat. sg.* synne 32:167, 40:82; *nom. pl.* synna 28:64; *acc. pl.* synna 12:79, 16:155, 16:158, 24:138, 28:60, 40:46, 42:99, 44:142; *gen. pl.* synna 12:54, 24:144, 28:82, 32:152, 32:155, 44:148, 50:126, 78:56; *dat. pl.* synnum 4:79, 22:96, 22:97, 24:148, 24:152, 24:155, 30:107, 34:191, 52:180, 94:56
syx *num.* six 22:133a, 22:133b, 22:134, 46:23, 48:82, 48:86, 62:135 >
syxta *num. adj.* sixth; *f. dat. sg.* syxtan 48:83, 102:122; *m. inst. sg.* syxtan 30:121, 50:96, 64:174, 116:76
syxtig *num.* sixty 6:120, 22:132; syxtigum 6:115

117

sȳþ *m.* time; *inst. pl.* sȳþum 54:198, 54:200

syþþan [siþþan] *conj.* since, after, afterwards (See Appendix, p. 149)

T

tācen *nt.* token, sign; *acc. sg.* tācen 114:15, 17; tācn 60:66, 118:101, 142:138; *dat. sg.* tācne 4:56, 30:115, 30:119, 142:147, 142:180; *inst. sg.* tācne 84:79; *nom. pl.* tācno 76:23, 82:29; *dat. pl.* tācnum 138:58

tācnian (2) to signify, denote; *ind. pres. 3 sg.* tācnaþ 10:37, 12:47, 12:78, 46:15, 50:100, 54:205, 54:211, 54:214, 54:220; tācnað 12:45; *pl.* tācniaþ 12:43, 24:140, 52:165; tācnaþ 24:139; *pret. 3 sg.* tācnode 12:59, 12:60, 90:200

tæcan (1) to teach 28:54, 28:60, 74:18; *imp. 3 pl.* tæcean 76:32

tælan (1) to blame, reproach; *ind. pret. pl.* tældon 148:52; *subj. pres. sg.* tæle 44:146, 44:147; *pres. p. def. m. nom. pl.* tælendan 44:153

tælend *m.* slanderer, backbiter; *nom. sg.* 44:149

talian (2) to reckon; *ind. pres. pl.* talge 114:29

tān *m.* lot; *dat. pl.* tānum 84:72 (A)

tānc [tānc → tācn] (see tācen)

tēah (see tēon)

teala *adv.* well, good 48:47, 50:132, 50:135

teallan [tellan] (1) to reckon; *ind. pret. pl.* tēaldon 82:18

tēar *m.* tear; *acc. pl.* tēaras 2:5; *gen. pl.* tēara 42:102; *dat. pl.* tēarum 106:205, 130:254

templ [Lt. templum] *nt.* temple; *nom. sg.* 2:30, 50:103, 104:161, 106:223, 110:288; *acc. sg.* templ 48:77, 150:135; *gen. sg.* temples 18:8, 52:176; *dat. sg.* temple 108:274

ten *num.* ten 22:123, 82:18, 92:1

teolian (2) to endeavour 78:64, 90:215; *ind. pret. 3 sg.* teolode 116:82, 150:119; *subj. pres. pl.* teolian 86:134; *imp. 1 pl.* teolian 90:219

tēon (II) to draw, pull 67; *ind. pret. 3 sg.* tēah 80:119; *pl.* tugon 102:88, 70, 93; *pp.* togen 70

tēona *m.* wrong, anger, grief; *nom. sg.* 30:111; *acc. sg.* tēonan 22:104; *dat. sg.* tēonan 32:171, 34:218, 124:116, 152:152, 152:156

tēontig (see hund tēontig)

tēoþa *num. adj.* tenth; *m. acc. sg.* tēoþan 22:130, 22:131, 22:135, 24:137, 26:5, 26:8, 26:38, 32:153, 32:158, 32:167, 34:224; tēoðan 26:14; *m. gen. sg.* tēoþan 32:168; *m. inst. sg.* tēoþan 84:47; *m. nom. pl.* tēoþan 26:37, 32:169; *m. acc. pl.* tēoþan 28:49, 32:150

tēoþian (2) to tithe; *subj. pres. pl.* tēoþian 26:24

tēoþungceap *m.* tithe; *dat. sg.* tēoþungceape 26:2

tēoþungsceat *m.* of tithing; *gen. pl.* tēoþungsceatta 34:219

Ticinan *prop. n.* Ticinan; *dat. sg.* Ticino 146:5

tīd *f.* time, hour; *nom. sg.* 58:11, 82:25, 86:96, 86:131, 90:219, 140:135 >; *acc. sg.* tīde 82:7, 82:25, 84:48, 120:13, 130:262 >; tīd 12:88, 18:20, 18:21, 24:146, 24:148, 24:153, 24:173, 58:3, 58:11, 58:18, 62:127 >; *gen. sg.* tīde 46:1, 82:2, 114:2; *dat. sg.* tīde 10:2, 10:3, 20:56, 52:162, 56:238, 58:16, 62:124, 98:37 >; *nom. pl.* tīda 22:126, 90:215; *gen. pl.* tīda 58:11; *dat. pl.* tīdum 20:74, 72:104; *inst. pl.* tīdum 158:16

tīdsang *m.* hour-services; *acc. pl.* tīdsangas 30:135

tintreġ *nt.* torment; *nom. pl.* tintrega 95; *acc. pl.* tintregu 35; tintrego 11, 90; tintrega 84:52, 158:8, 162:103; *dat. pl.* tintregum 80:108, 120:9, 102

tintrian (2) to afflict; *ind. pres. 3 sg.* tintregaþ 40:79

Tītus *pres. n.* Titus; *nom. sg.* 54:189, 54:191, 54:200

tō *prep.* (with *dat.*) to, at, for (see Appendix, p. 150)

tō *adv.* too 28:57, 28:58, 28:68, 76:40a, 76:40b, 76:41a, 76:41b, 78:66, 78:67, 80:110 >
tōberan (IV) to carry off; *subj. pret. pl.*
tōbǣron 66:188
tōbelimpan (III) to belong; *subj. pres. sg.*
tōbelimpe 30:136
tōbrecan (IV) to break in pieces; *ind. pret. 3 sg.* tōbrǣc 58:29, 126:146; *pp.* tōbrocen 58:41; *pl.* tōbrocene 60:57
tōberstan [tōbyrstan] (III) to break apart; *ind. pret. 3 sg.* tōbyrst 64:162; *pret. 3 sg.* tōbǣrst 130:264
tōclēofan (II) to cleave; *ind. pres. 3 sg.* tōclēofeð 78:47
tōclipian (2) to call to; *ind. pret. pl.* tōcleopodan 80:94
tōcuman (IV) to come; *ind. pres. 3 sg.* tōcymeþ 40:63; *pret. 3 sg.* tōcom 132:316; *subj. pres. 3 sg.* tōcyme 34
tōcweþan (V) to say to; *ind. pret. 3 sg.* tōcwæþ 10:18, 10:20, 18:8, 18:13, 20:52, 46:28, 102:119, 130:236, 27 >; tō-cwæð 20, 25, 32, 36, 51, 57, 62, 86, 90/1 >
tōcyme *m.* coming, advent; *acc. sg.* tōcyme 10:40, 20:78, 54:216, 74:15, 92:3, 118:98; *gen. sg.* tōcymes 72:93; *dat. sg.* tōcyme 22:121, 54:229, 60:56, 62:109, 74:1
tōdæġe *adv.* today 98:33, 98:37, 132:300; todæg 92:3, 100:57, 100:58, 100:84, 114:2
tōdǣldan (1) to scatter; *ind. pret. 3 sg.* tōdǣlde 110:316
tōdōn (anom.) to put to, applies; *ind. pres. 3 sg.* tōdēþ 88:167
tōdrīfan (I) to scatter; *ind. pres. pl.* tōdrīfað 154:207
tōēacan *prep.* besides 148:78 (EWS)
tōgan (anom.) to go to; *ind. pret. pl.* tōēodan 18:16
tōgædere *adv.* together 68:42
tōgēanes *post prep.* (with *dat.*) towards, before 34:226, 46:10, 46:12, 48:58, 48:69 >
tōgecweðan (V) to speak; *pp. m. nom sg.* tōgecweden 2:3

tōhlīdan (1) to open; *ind. pret. pl.* tōhlīdon 74:6
tōhlēotan (VII) to divide by lot; *ind. pret. 3 pl.* tōhlūton 84:72
tōhwirfan (1) to returned to; *ind. pret. 3 sg.* tōhwirfde 32
tohwon *adv.* wherefore, why 60:43, 60:52 > (A)
tōlǣtan (VII) to leave to, grant; *ind. pres. 3 sg.* tōlǣteþ 32:183
tōlīesan (1) to loosen, undo; *pp.* tōlēsed 8
tōlesnes *f.* breach; *nom. sg.* 80:123
tōlōcian (2) to look on; *ind. pret. pl.* tōlōcodan 152:161; *pres. p. m. inst. pl.* tōlōciendum 126:167
tōlȳsan [tōlīesan] (1) to dissolve, destroy; *pp.* tōlȳsedu 158:3
tōmorgenne *adv.* tomorrow 126:172; tōmorgne [tō morgne → tōmorgne] 142:146
tor *m.* tower; *acc. sg.* tor 126:165, 130:233; torr 130:245
tōsamne [tō samne] *adv.* together 120:29, 128:183, 132:290
tōsēcan (1) to seek, require; *ind. pres. 3 sg.* tōsēcþ 66:202
tōsendan (1) to sent to; *ind. pret. 3 sg.* tōsende 108:245
tōsendan (1) to send apart, dispersed; *ind. pret. pl.* tōsendon 54:199
tōslītan (1) to tear in pieces; *subj. pret. pl.* tōslītan 66:188
tōsnīðan (VI) to cut up; *ind. pret. 3 sg.* tōsnað 148:50
tōsprēcan (V) to speak to; *ind. pret. 3 sg.* tōsprǣc 138:52
tōstregdan (III) to scatter; *ind. pres. pl.* tōstenceað 162:104
tōweard *adj.* future *m. nom. sg.* 56:236, 82:30, 140:113; *m. acc. sg.* toweardne 48:85, 54:191, 56:233, 82:17, 138:79; *nt. nom. sg.* toweard 52:174, 114:10; *m. acc. pl.* tōwearde 4:86; *def. m. acc. sg.* tōwerdon 34:206; *f. dat. sg.* tōweardan 10:2, 36:231; *m. acc. pl.* tōweardan 86:129

tōweardnes *f.* future coming; *acc. sg.*
tōweardnesse 84:59

tōwitan (pret. pres.) to show; *subj. pret. pl.*
tōwiston 128:212

tōweorpan (III) to throw down; *pp.*
tōworpene 52:180

tōþæs *adv.* so 2:36 [tō þæs → tōþæs], 82:26a,
82:26b; tōðæs 78:68

tōþon *adv.* so 28:61, 80:118a, 80:118b, 94:76,
94:84 >; tō þon 84:51, 90:184 >; tōðon 78:69,
78:71, 94:83, 94:87a, 94:87b, 94:88 >; tōþon
þæt 48:80; tōþon þa 60:66

trahtian (2) to expound 20:49

trēow *nt.* tree, beam, log; *nom. sg.*
14:106; *acc. sg.* trēow 106; *dat. pl.*
trēowum 48:69, 130:233

trēowleas *adj.* faithless *m. nom. pl.*
trēowlease 122:72; *def. m. dat. sg.*
trēowleasan 128:190

trum *adj.* firm, strong, sound *m. nom. sg.*
trume 120:22; *superl. m. nom. sg.*
trumesta 8:139

trūwian (2) to trust in; *subj. pret. pl.*
trūwodon 128:205

trymian (1) to prepare; *subj. pres. sg.*
trymme 64:138; *subj. pret. pl.* trymedan
138:81

trymman (1) to strengthen, comfort; *ind.*
pret. 3 sg. trymede 68:21, 102:116; *subj.*
pret. sg. tremede 28:53

tūddor *nt.* offspring, issue; *gen. sg.*
tūddres 4:61, 80:117

tūgon (see tēon)

tūn *m.* town; *nom. sg.* 52:163; *dat. sg.*
tūne 46:38, 48:59, 146:5, 150:110, 150:111,
152:149, 152:160

tunce [tunece] *f.* tunic; *acc. pl.* tuncean
118:124

tunge *f.* tongue; *nom. sg.* 116:60; *acc. sg.*
tungan 118:95; *dat. sg.* tungan 38:11,
106:220; tungon 2:14

tungol *nt.* star; *gen. pl.* tungla 62:130,
62:132

Turan *prop. n.* Tours; *dat. sg.* Turan
150:124

turtur [Lt. turtur] *m.* turtle-dove; *nom. pl.*
turturan 14:135

twēġen *num.* two 14:134a, 14:134b, 52:165,
84:83, 132:307, 152:156, 160:45; twā 48:85;
118:124, 124:114, 126:146, 138:63, 138:70,
140:124, 152:145, 38; twǣm 148:72

twelf *num.* twelve 10:4, 26:5, 26:8, 84:72,
90:220, 108:271, 108:272, 136:16, 144:205

twentig *num.* twenty 148:72, 158:17

twēo *m.* doubt; *nom. sg.* 44:152, 140:120;
acc. sg. twēon 62:112

twēogan (1) to doubt 100:74; twēogean
28:47, 58:3; *ind. pres. pl.* twēogaþ 26:33;
imp. 3 sg. twēoge 100:78

tweonum (see betweonum)

twig *nt.* branch, twig; *nom. pl.* twigo
144:206; *acc. pl.* twigu 48:69; *dat. pl.*
twigum 144:206

twyfeald *adj.* twofold, double *f. gen. sg.*
twyfealdre 32:164; *f. dat. sg.* twyfealdre
70:73; *nt. nom. sg.* twyfeald 122:62; *nt.*
acc. sg. twyfeald 160:55

tȳdder *adj.* weak; *def. f. gen. sg.* tyddran
18:28; *f. acc. sg.* tȳdran 22:113; *f. dat. sg.*
tȳdran 12:47

tȳddernes *f.* weakness, frailty; *acc. sg.*
tȳddernysse 97; *gen. sg.* tȳddernesse
136:9; *dat. sg.* tȳdernesse 20:78, 70:87; *dat.*
pl. tȳddernessum 40:61

tyhtan (1) to incite, urge; *ind. pret. pl.*
tyhton 146:13

tȳn *num.* ten 146:12

tynan (1) to annoy; *subj. pres. pl.* tynan
30:115

þ

þā *pron.* (see se, sēo, þæt)

þā *adv.* then (see Appendix, p. 147)

þǣm (see se, sēo, þæt))

þǣne (see se, sēo, þæt)

þǣr *adv.* there (see Appendix. p. 147)

þǣr æfter *adv.* thereafter (see Appendix. p. 151)

þǣre (see se, sēo, þæt)

þǣrin *adv.* wherein 50:93

þǣron [→ þær on] *adv.* therein, thereon 48:68, 88:156, 136:20

ðǣrscwold *m.* threshold; *dat. sg.* ðǣrscwolde 142:151

þǣr ūte *adv.* outside 138:66, 150:102

þæs (see se, sēo, þæt)

þæs þe *adv.* after 18:18, 22:119, 24:154, 46:9, 50:124, 154:226 >

þæt (see se, sēo, þæt)

þæt *conj.* that 2:26, 2:29, 2:33, 2:36, 4:45, 4:57, 4:72, 6:91, 6:104, 6:112, 6:113, 6:129 >; ðæt 138:81 >

þætte [þæt þe] (see se, sēo, þæt)

þætte *conj.* that 18:1, 18:18, 28:45, 36:236, 42:91, 52:165, 60:56, 102:124, 160:70, 162:104 >

þagen [þe agen] who again 118:91

þagȳt *adv.* as yet, still 10:10, 10:30, 60:74, 60:87, 82:17; ðagīt 158:37; þagȳt 146:23, 146:27

þām (see se, sēo, þæt)

þan [þon] (see se, sēo, þæt)

þanc *m.* thank; *acc. sg.* þanc 72:104, 86:108, 132:301, 150:102; *acc. pl.* þancas 26:3, 111

þancfull *adj.* thankful; *m. nom. pl.* þancfulle 118:126

þancian (2) to thank 28:58; *ind. pret. pl.* þancudon 140:109; *subj. pret. pl.* þancodon 128:208

þancung *f.* thanking; *gen. pl.* þancunga 50:122

ðane (see se, sēo, þæt)

þānon *adv.* thence 24, 39, 79, 154

þāra (see se, sēo, þæt)

þǣre (see se, sēo, þæt)

þās (see se, sēo, þæt)

þǣs (see se, sēo, þæt)

þē (see þū)

þe *indcl. rel. pron.* (used for any number, gender or case) who, which, that 4:49, 4:50, 4:75, 6:113, 6:116, 6:120, 10:3, 10:5, 10:20, 10:24, 12:44, 12:52, 12:83, 14:92, 14:94, 14:95, 14:98, 14:100, 14:107, 14:112, 14:113 >; ðe 118:128, 118:129, 140:133, 152:166 >

þē *conj.* than 148:72

þē *conj.* or 68:12a, 68:12b, 82:21 >

þē [→ þā] then 150:91

þēah *conj.* though, although (see Appendix, p. 150)

þearf *f.* necessity; *nom. sg.* 24:137, 42:119, 68:10, 88:180, 122:59, 142:142, 160:50; ðearf 86:134; *acc. sg.* þearfe 32:176, 48:63, 68:11, 68:32, 70:81, 84:75; *gen. sg.* þearfe 16:164, 70:67, 72:104; *gen. pl.* þearfa 154:210

þearf (see þurfan)

þearfa *m.* beggar; *nom. sg.* 10:12, 146:42; *acc. sg.* þearfan 148:45; *gen. sg.* þearfan 26:16; *dat. sg.* þearfan 28:78, 148:50, 148:55, 148:58, 148:59; *acc. pl.* þearfan 48:46, 52:148, 76:2, 128:207; *dat. pl.* þearfum 34:222; þearfan 52:149

þearft (see þurfan)

þearlwis *adj.* severe; *comp. m. nom. sg.* þearlwisra 66:199

þearlwislīċe *adv.* severely 42:132

þēaw *m.* custom; *nom. sg.* 46:10; *dat. sg.* ðēawe 142:146; *dat. pl.* þēawum 138:69; ðēawum 148:79

þeġenrǣden *f.* thaneship, service; *dat. sg.* þegenrǣdene 120:38

þeġn *m.* servant, disciple; *nom. sg.* 46:22, 146:7; *gen. sg.* ðegnes 140:124; *nom. pl.* þegnas 10:9, 10:30, 48:67, 54:210, 102:122, 112:328, 122:66; *acc. pl.* þegnas 10:4, 52:165, 122:76, 142:169; *gen. pl.* þegna 46:37, 50:94, 146:8; ðegna 146:9, 146:18; *dat. pl.* þegnum 8:145, 10:25, 46:33, 48:60, 50:92, 54:204, 94:68; ðegnum 146:40

þeġnian (2) (with *dat.*) to serve, minister 30:101, 46:28; *ind. pres. pl.* þegniaþ 22:117; *pret. pl.* þegnedon 22:113; þegnedan 18:17; *subj. pret. sg.* þegnode 46:27, 50:99; *pl.* þegnodon 22:116

þeġnung f. service; acc. sg. þegnunga
118:93, 122:56; þegnunge 160:63, 33; gen.
sg. ðegnunge 144:191
þēh conj. though, although, however (see
Appendix, p. 150)
þēh hweþre conj. yet, nevertheless
90:211, 150:127
þenċan (1) to think 38:8, 38:34 >; þencean
146:34; ind. pret. 1 sg. þence 126:138,
126:139, 126:143 >; 3 sg. þencþ 38:15;
þenceþ 126:140; pret. 3 sg. ðōhte 4:58;
þōhte 126:153; pl. þōhton 106:188, 65;
þōhtan 48:54, 52:157; subj. pres sg. þence
26:29, 122:64, 124:127, 124:128, 124:129 >; pl.
þencan 14:99; imp. 1 pl. þencan 12:58; infl.
inf. to þencenne 68:10
þēo (see se, sēo, þæt)
þēod f. nation; nom. sg. 76:15; acc. sg.
þēode 84:73; dat. sg. þēode 76:15; acc. pl.
þēoda 48:76, 128:203; gen. pl. þēoda
116:45; dat. pl. þēodum 20:77, 108:271
þēodland nt. country; acc. sg. þēodland
76:14
þēodscipe m. society; acc. sg. þēodscipe
76:32, 128:209; dat. sg. þēodscipe 92:23
þēof m. thief; acc. sg. þēof 52:142; nom.
pl. þēofas 42:102; acc. pl. þēofas 52:143;
dat. pl. þēofum 42:125
þēos (see þes, þēos, þis)
þēostro nt. darkness; nom. pl. þēostra
64:158; acc. pl. þēostra 12:54; þeostro
10:39, 58:29, 58:40, 72:109, 104:149; gen. pl.
þēostra 58:14, 58:27; dat. pl. þēostrum
44:159, 64:147, 72:94, 126:178
þēote f. fountain; acc. pl. þēotan 26:17,
32:173
þēow m. servant; nom. sg. þēow 32:138,
42:136; acc. sg. þēow 60:78; gen. sg.
þēowes 32:140; dat. sg. þēowe 75; ðēowe
158:7; nom. pl. þēowas 130:249, 156:237;
acc. pl. þēowas 30:135; gen. pl. þēowa
70:52, 148:84; dat. pl. þēowum 26:39,
162:91
þēowa m. servant; nom. sg. 140

þēowdōm m. bondage; acc. sg.
þēowdōm 30:95, 146:16, 148:77; ðēowdōm
146:11; gen. sg. þēowdōmes 14:127, 32:139,
96:94; dat. sg. þēowdōme 46:4, 46:20, 50:97,
120:38
þēowe f. handmaiden; dat. sg. þēowan
110:280
þēowen f. handmaiden; nom. sg. 6:90,
8:140, 8:141; gen. sg. þēowene 4:48; dat.
sg. ðēowene 6:92; þēowene 62:93, 62:96
þēowian (2) (with dat.) to serve 18:25, 20:64,
30:100, 32:138, 72:107; ind. pres. pl.
þēowiaþ 20:82; subj. pres. pl. þēowdon
128:217; imp. 2 sg. þēowa 18:16
þes, þēos, þis dem. adj. & dem. pron.
this; m., f. & nt. (see Appendix, p. 146)
þes, þēos, þis pronom. this; m., f. & nt.
(see Appendix, p. 148)
þicce adv. thickly, closely 140:90
þider adv. thither whither 88:149, 158:32,
36 >
þīn pers. pron. yours (see Appendix, p. 145)
þīn (see þu)
þinċan [þynċan] (1) to seem; ind. pres. 3 sg.
þincþ 20:86, 124:116; þincð 78:74
þing nt. thing; acc. sg. þing 62:121; gen.
sg. þinges 82:22, 122:59; ðinges 156:235;
dat. sg. þinge 150:129; nom. pl. þing
62:129, 76:24; acc. pl. þing 22:125, 58:18,
62:125, 64:161, 66:205, 92:21, 92:22, 130:231;
gen. pl. þinga 46:30, 140:90, 152:151; dat.
pl. þingum 6:133, 6:136, 8:137, 18:40, 24:141,
26:19, 26:25, 32:157, 32:170, 38:34, 38:35,
38:36, 66:184; ðingum 146:21, 146:24
þingere m. advocate, intercessor; nom.
sg. 94:81, 112:335
þingian (2) (with dat.) to intercede 74:2; ind.
pres. pl. þingiaþ 30:105
þingung f. intercession; nom. pl.
þingunga 66:199
þis (see þes, þēos, þis)
þisliċ adj. of this kind, such nt. acc. sg.
þislic 140:130
þisle f. pole; dat. pl. þislum [þilum →
þislum] 132:277

þissum (see þes, þēos, þis)

þō [→þā]

þoncung *f.* thanksgiving; *dat. sg.*
þoncunga 20:71

þon (see se, sēo, þæt)

þonan *adv.* thence (see Appendix, p 147)

þonne *adv.* then, therefore (see Appendix, p. 147)

þonne *conj.* then, therefore (see Appendix, p. 150)

þonon *adv.* thence (see Appendix, p. 147)

þorn *m.* thorn; *dat. pl.* þornum 16:140

þrafian (2) to urge, compel 28:83

þrāg *f.* season; *acc. sg.* þrāge 82:25, 92:9 (EWS)

þrē *num.* three 102:125; þrēo 22:132, 50:108, 82:39, 104:163, 148:73; þrēora 44:145, 138:73; þrim 18:40, 20:43, 20:66, 46:40, 52:139, 98:5, 108:271, 130:231, 158:30; ðrim 162:99; þry 88:144, 122:65, 130:270, 138:48, 148:88, 152:154, 158:23, 158:28, 158:42, 21

þrēa *m.* vanity; *acc. pl.* þrēas 146:12

þrēan [þrēagan] (1) to rebuke; *ind. pret. 3 sg.* þrēade 12:65, 80:91, 118:120; *pp.* þrēad 32:155

þrēat *m.* troop, host; *dat. sg.* þrēate 64:179; *nom. pl.* þrēatas 6:112, 70:53; *acc. pl.* þrēatas 6:122, 82:5, 84:49, 86:105

þrēatigean [þrēatian] (2) to urge 30:134 (A)

þrēatung *f.* threatening; *acc. sg.* þrēatunge 138:72

þremmes (see þrym)

þridda *num. adj.* third; *m. nom. sg.* 102:98; *m. acc. sg.* þriddan 130:261; *m. dat. sg.* þriddan 82:8, 128:186; ðridan 124:134; *f. dat. sg.* þriddan 108:263, 138:81; *m. inst. sg.* þriddan 10:8, 18:11, 30:120, 50:91, 64:152, 90:200, 126:174, 126:176, 128:184, 130:268, 130:270; ðriddan 124:100

þrim (see þrēo)

ðrim (see þrēo)

þrītig *num.* thirty; þrīttigum [þrīttigun → þrīttigum] 54:200

þrōwian (2) to suffer 10:3, 46:3, 52:162, 64:172, 70:59; ðrōwian 46:6; *ind. pres. 1 sg.* þrōwige 60:88; *2 sg.* þrōwast 110:289; *pret.*

2 sg. þrōwodest 95; *3 sg.* þrōwode 16:141, 18:22, 52:183, 68:8; þrōwade 68:6; *pl.* þrōwodan 10:40; *subj. pres. pl.* þrōwian 22:101; *pres. p.* ðrōwiende 162:108

þrōwung *f.* suffering, passion; *acc. sg.* þrōwunga 4:54, 10:25, 54:217, 122:81; þrōwunge 108:268, 110:289; *gen. sg.* þrōwunge 58:7; *dat. sg.* þrōwunga 18:20, 22:120, 48:86, 56:233, 58:13, 58:19, 68:3, 72:95, 82:7, 82:19, 84:64, 88:175, 120:4; þrōwunge 120:6; *acc. pl.* þrōwunga 108:246, 120:25

þrōwungtīd *f.* passiontide *acc. sg.* þrōwungtīde 120:2

þrūh *m.* tomb; *acc. sg.* þrūh 132:309

þry (see þrēo)

þryċċan (1) to oppress; *subj. pres. sg.* þrycce 50:127

þrym *m.* majesty, glory; *acc. sg.* þrym 52:176; *gen. sg.* þrymmes 44:137, 46:3; þremmes 50:118; *dat. sg.* þrymme 84:81; *acc. pl.* þrymmas 46:21; *dat. pl.* þrymmum 2:25, 14:97

þrymliċ *adj.* glorious, magnificent; *f. nom. sg.* þrymlic 88:141; *nt. nom. sg.* þrymlic 52:177

þrymrīċ *nt.* realm of glory; *dat. sg.* þrymrīce 74:4

þrymsetl *nt.* throne; *dat. sg.* þrymsetle 70:78; *acc. pl.* þrymsetl 20:61

Þrȳnes *f.* Trinity; *acc. sg.* Þrȳnesse 54:229, 142:137; *gen. sg.* Þrȳnesse 18:35; *dat. sg.* Þrȳnnysse 169

þū, ġit, ġe *pron.* you; *m. f. & nt.* (see Appendix, p. 145)

þūhte (see þynċan)

þunor *m.* thunder; *nom. sg.* 64:140; *nom. pl.* þuneras 64:156

þunorrād *f.* thunder; *nom. sg.* 102:123

þurfan (pret. pres.) to need; *ind. pres. 2 sg.* þearft 132:297

þurh *prep.* (with acc. / dat.) through, by means of (see Appendix, p. 151)

þurhtēon (II) to accomplish; *pp. m. nom. sg.* þurhtōgen 124:111

þurhwunian (2) to preserve, continue 52:166; *ind. pres. 3 sg.* þurhwunaþ 14:113, 44:158, 44:163; *pl.* þurhwuniað 130:250; *pret. 3 sg.* þurhwunode 2:10, 60:87; *pl.* þurhwunodan 120:8, 120:19 þurhwunedon 54:187; *pres. p.* þurhwunigende 158:19; *m. dat. pl.* þurhwuniggendum 120:9
þurst *m.* thirst; *nom. sg.* 44:160, 72:113; *acc. sg.* þurst 42:115; *dat. sg.* þurste 40:83; *inst. sg.* þurste 38:33
þus *adv.* thus 2:16, 2:21, 4:46, 4:59, 4:61a, 4:61b, 4:89, 6:98, 6:114, 6:134, 10:14, 10:16, 20:70, 38:9 >; ðus 154:213, 103 >
þūsend *num.* thousand 82:39 82:41; þūsenda 54:196, 54:198, 54:199, 54:201
þūsendliċ *num. adj.* thousand; *def. m. nom. pl.* þūsendlican 12:68
þwēal *m.* washing; *dat. sg.* þwēale 104:145
þwēan (II) to wash; *ind. pret. 3 sg.* þwōh 50:94, 98:16; *pl.* þwōgan 104:164
þȳ (see se, sēo, þæt)
þyder *adv.* thither 18:37, 18:38, 46:18, 46:20, 48:50, 48:56, 86:136, 88:148, 106:188, 120:30, 142:144, 142:150, 142:171, 156:237, 156:241, 158:33, 160:48, 160:50 >; ðyder 154:199 >
þȳwan (1) to press, urge; *subj. pres. pl.* þ ȳdon 80:128
þȳlǣs [þȳ lǣs] *conj.* lest 146:34
þyllic *adj.* such; *m. nom. sg.* 40:71
þynċan (1) to seem; *ind. pres. 3 sg.* þynceþ 122:75, 132:279; *pl.* þencaþ 40:63; *pret. 3 sg.* þuhte 76:17, 140:130, 154:226; ðuhte 152:141; *subj. pret. sg.* þuhte 127
þyrstan (1) (with *gen.*) to thirst 110:322
þyslīċ *adj.* such; *nt. nom. pl.* þyslīco 76:23
þysne [þisne] (see þes, þēos, þis)
þysse [þisne] (see þes, þēos, þis)
þȳstrogenip *nt.* mists of darkness; *nom. pl.* þȳstrogenipo 144:200; *dat. pl.* þȳ strogenipum 138:88

U
Uaticanus [Lt. Vaticanus] *prop. n.* Vatican; *nom. sg.* 132:310, 134:326
ufan *adv.* above, from above 4:73, 12:77, 32:173, 88:145, 88:147, 88:150, 88:151, 88:155 >; ufon 4:63 >
ufancund *adj.* supreme; *def. m. gen. sg.* ufancudan [→ ufancundan] 116:45
ufer *adj.* upper, further; *m. inst. sg.* uferan 84:48
ufeweard *adj.* upward; *f. dat. sg.* ufeweardre 88:141
ūhta *m.* dawn; *dat. sg.* ūhtan 30:121
unāblinnendlīċe *adv.* unceasingly 86:107
unāgǣledlīċe [unāgǣledlīċe → unāgǣledlīċe] *adv.* unremittingly 84:69
ūnālyfd *adj.* unlawful; *def. nt. dat. pl.* ūnālyfdum 36:233
unānrǣdnes *f.* inconstancy; *acc. sg.* unānrǣdnesse 20:81
unārǣfnedliċ *adj.* intolerable; *def. f. nom. sg.* unārǣfnedlice 50:128; *m. gen. sg.* unārǣfnedlican 96:94
unārīmed *adj.* unnumbered; *f. nom. sg.* 136:24; *m. nom. pl.* unārīmede 142:183; *def. f. nom. sg.* unārīmede 60:67; *nt. inst. sg.* ūnārīmedan 16:171
unārīmedliċ *adj.* innumerable; unārīmedlico *f. nom. sg.* 132:290; *def. f. sg.* unārīmedlice 60:58
unāsecggendliċ *adj.* unspeakable; *m. dat. sg.* unāsecggendlicum 60:69; *def. nt. nom. sg.* ūnāsecggenlice 16:162; ūnāsecggendlice 44:163
unbegrīpendliċ *adj.* incomprehensible; *m. acc. sg.* unbegrīpendlic[n]e 128:218; *def. m. nom. sg.* unbegrīpendlica 124:113
unberend *adj.* barren; *m. nom. pl.* unberende 64:169
ūnbesmiten *adj.* undefiled; *def. m. acc. sg.* ūnbesmitenan 2:8; *nt. dat. sg.* ūnbesmitenan 108:273/4

124

unblīþe *adj.* sad; *comp. nt. nom. pl.* unblīþran 92:14

unc (see wit)

uncer *dual pron.* our, us two; *m. nom. sg.* 130:244; *f. nom. sg.* uncer 130:242; *m. dat. pl.* uncrum 140:136

unclǣn *adj.* unclean; *def. m. dat. sg.* unclǣnan 16:148

uncūþ *adj.* unknown, uncertain; *nt. nom. sg.* 34:192, 82:42, 86:130

uncȳm *adj.* mean; *f. acc. sg.* uncȳme 156:232

uncȳst *f.* vice; *nom. sg.* 24:152, 44:156; *acc. pl.* uncȳsta 12:61; *dat. pl.* uncȳstum 16:150, 16:152

undēaþliċ *adj.* immortal; *m. nom. sg.* 14:109

under *prep.*(with *acc. / dat.*) under, among 22:129, 26:27, 68:25, 144:200, 144:204, 33 >

undern *m.* the third hour; *acc. sg.* undern 64:156; *dat. sg.* underne 64:162, 64:174

underṅereord *m.* morning-feasts; *acc. pl.* underngereordu 68:42

underntīd *f.* third hour; *acc sg.* underntīd 30:119, 94:45 (EWS)

underwreþian (2) to support, uphold; *ind. pres. 3 sg.* underwreþeþ 14:129

underþēodan (1) to subject, subdue; *pp.* underþēoded 18:38, 58:32, 58:37; *nom. pl.* underþēodde 54:206, 76:36

unēaþe *adj.* uneasy, difficult; *m. nom. sg.* 40:66; *nt. gen. sg.* unēaþes 22:101

unēþnes *f.* uneasiness, trouble; *nom. sg.* 72:113

unfæġer *adj.* foul; *f. nom. sg.* 78:74

unfeor *adv.* near 156:242

unforht *adj.* fearless, undaunted; *nt. inst. sg.* unforhte 46:5

unforwealwod *adj.* unwithered; *m. acc. sg.* unforwealwodne 50:111

unfyrn *adv.* not long ago 92:1

unġēara *adv.* suddenly unawares 70:77

ūnġecoren *adj.* reprobate; *m. nom. pl.* ūngecorene 52:174

unġecyndeliċ *adj.* unnatural, monstrous; *nt. acc. pl.* ungecyndelico 76:13/4

unġecyneliċ *adj.* strange; *m. acc. pl.* ungecynelice 76:14

ūnġeendod *adj.* infinite; *nt. nom. sg.* 136:23; *def. nt. nom. sg.* ūngeendode 16:162, 16:167

unġefulwad *adj.* unbaptized; *m. nom. sg.* 150:92; ungefullad 150:90

unġehāten *adj.* unpromising; *nt. nom. sg.* 130:275

unġelǣred *adj.* illiterate; *m. acc. sg.* ungelǣredne 124:117

unġelēaf *m.* unbelief; *dat. sg.* ungelēafan 52:173

unġelēaf *adj.* unbelieving; *m. nom. pl.* ungelēafsume 90:205

unġelēafful *adj.* unbelieving; *m. gen. pl.* ungelēaffulra 130:260; *def. m. dat. pl.* ungeleaffullum 62:113

unġelēaffulnes *f.* unbelief; *dat. sg.* ungelēaffulnesse 162:107, 76

ūnġelīċ *adj.* different; *m. nom. sg.* 68:17

unġelimpliċ *adj.* unfortunate; *nt. nom. pl.* ungelimplico 76:15

unġelyfed *adj.* unbelieving; *def. m. dat. pl.* ungelyfedum 42:133; ungelyfdum 38:24

unġemetliċ *adj.* immoderate; *def. m. nom. pl.* ungemetlican 40:69

unġeorne *adv.* negligently 128:182

unġerēclic *adj.* unbelieving; *def. f. acc. pl.* ungerēclican 12:60

unġerisne *adj.* unseemly; *f. inst. sg.* ungerisnre 132:278

unġesælignes *f.* misery; *gen. sg.* ungesælignesse 2:2

unġesælig *adj.* unhappy; *superl. f. nom. sg.* ungesæligost 62:101

unġesibb *adj.* hostile; *m. nom. pl.* ungesibbe 154:198

unġesȳnelič [unġesīeneliċ] *adj.* invisible; *m. acc. sg.* ungesȳnelicne 128:219; *def. f. nom. sg.* ungesȳnelice 14:104, 14:106
unġewider *m.* bad weather; *gen. sg.* ungewidres 88:152 *acc. pl.* ungewidro 88:152
unġeþwǣr *adj.* at variance, disagreeing; *m. nom. pl.* ungeþwǣre 154:198
unġeþyld *m.* impatience; *nom. sg.* 22:105
unġeþyldig *adj.* impatient; *m. nom. sg.* 116:84
unġyrwan [ungierwan] (1) to divest; *ind. pret. 3 sg.* ungyrede 70:86
unhierliċ *adj.* fierce, wild; *m. nom. sg.* 138:87
unhȳrsumnes *f.* disobedience; *dat. sg.* unhȳrsumnesse 60:48, 64:181
ūnlǣd *adj.* wicked; *def. nt. dat. sg.* ūnlǣdan 68:7; *m. nom. pl.* ūnlǣdan 52:158; *m. dat. pl.* ūnlǣdum 16:138, 58:23; ūnlǣdon 16:163
unlǣred *adj.* unlearned; *m. nom. pl.* unlǣrede 126:168
unmǣt *adj.* immense; *def. nt. nom. sg.* unmǣte 70:47
unnan (pret. pres.) to grant, wish; *ind. pret. 3 sg.* uþe 34:196
unnyt *adj.* useless; *m. nom. sg.* 152:165
unoferhrēfed *adj.* unroofed *f. nom. sg.* unoferhrēfed 88:147; *nt. nom. sg.* unoferhrēfed 88:151
unrǣdliċ *adj.* thoughtless; *f. acc. pl.* unrǣdlice 68:41
unriht *nt.* wrong, wickedness; *nom. sg.* 122:59; *acc. sg.* unriht 122:73; *gen. sg.* unrihtes 78:48, 134:329; *dat. sg.* ūnrihte 144:208; *dat. pl.* unrihtum 76:34, 134:330
unriht *adj.* wrong, wickedness; *m. nom. pl.* unrihte 44; *def. m. nom. pl.* unrihtan 158:21; *nt. dat. pl.* unrihtum 16:146
unrihtdōnde *m.* evil-doer; *dat. pl.* unriht dōndum [→ unrihtdōndum] 42:125

unrihtġestrēon *m.* unrighteous gain; *acc. sg.* unrihtgestrēon 42:122
unrihtġītsung *f.* wrongful greed; *nom. sg.* 36:332
unrihthǣmed *f.* adultery; *acc. sg.* unrihthǣmed 128:214
unrihthǣmend *m.* adulterers; *dat. pl.* unriht-hǣmendum 42:126
unrihtlīče *adv.* wrongfully 40:70, 154:190
unrihtnes *f.* wickness; *dat. sg.* unrihtnesse 55
unrihtwīs *adj.* unrighteousness; *nt. nom. pl.* unrihtwīse 22:90; *f. gen. pl.* unrihtwīsra 20:89; *m. dat. pl.* unrihtwīsum 30:97
unrihtwīsnes *f.* unrighteousness *acc. sg.* unrihtwīsnesse 62:96; *acc. pl.* unrihtwīsnessa 60:77; *dat. pl.* unrihtwīsnessum 60:85
unrihtwrigels *nt.* evil-covering; *acc. sg.* unriht wrigels [→ unrihtwrigels] 74:20
unrihtwyrcend *m.* wrongdoing; *dat. pl.* unrihtwyrcendum 42:94
unrōt *adj.* sad, sorrowful; *m. nom. pl.* unrōte 94:65, 94:73, 132:299, 150:91, 154:204
unrōtmōd *adj.* sadhearted; *m. nom. sg.* 78:89
unrōtnes *f.* sadness; *nom. sg.* 25 31; *dat. sg.* unrōtnesse 2:3, 40:84, 44:160, 60:50, 72:112
unsceþþend *adj.* harmless, innocent; *def. m. acc. sg.* unsceþþendan 2:5
unscyldig *adj.* innocent *m. acc. sg.* unscyldigne 60:53; *m. acc. pl.* unscyldige 42:129; *def. m. acc. pl.* unscyldigan 42:131
unscyldigliċ *adj.* excusable; *comp. nt. nom. sg.* unscyldiglicre 132:279
unsnottor *adj.* unwise; *m. nom. sg.* 34:212; *def. m. nom. sg.* unsnottra 32:163
unsōfte *adv.* severely 140:95
unsorh *adj.* free from care; *m. nom. sg.* 150:98
unsȳferliċ *adj.* impure; *f. nom. pl.* unsȳferlice 28:61

126

untrum *adj.* sick, ill; *m. nom. sg.* 148:87, 148:89, 152:183, 154:203; *m. dat. sg.* untruman 154:184; *m. gen. pl.* untrumra 144:189

untrumnes *f.* sickness; *acc. sg.* untrumnesse 152:181; *dat. sg.* untrumnesse 100:78, 154:229, 156:233; *nom. pl.* untrumnessa 142:183; untrumnesse 88:166; *dat. pl.* untrumnessum 142:181

untwēogend *adj.* undoubting; *nt. inst. sg.* untwēogende 120:7

untwēogendlīċe *adv.* undoubtedly 120:10

unwǣr *adj.* unwary; *m. acc. pl.* unwǣre 42:105

unwǣrlīċe *adv.* unwarily 38:30, 42:133

unwǣstmfǣst *adj.* barren; *f. nom. sg.* 114:31

unwǣstmfǣstnes *f.* barrenness; *nom. sg.* 114:40

unwar *adj.* unwary; *m. acc. pl.* unware 128:195; *def. m. acc. sg.* unwaran 38:17

unwemm *adj.* undefiled; *m. dat. sg.* unwemmum 62:111; *f. dat. sg.* unwemre 118:103; *m. acc. pl.* unwemme 72:101; *def. f. dat. sg.* unwemman 74:12

unwins *adj.* unpleasant; *nt. dat. sg.* unwinsumum 152:154

unwīs *adj.* foolish; *m. nom. pl.* unwīse 40:72; *m. acc. pl.* unwīse 76:2; *nt. dat. pl.* unwīsum 62:90

unwitweorc *nt.* work of folly; *dat. pl.* unwitweorcum 78:50

ūp *adv.* up 60:71, 86:109, 86:112, 86:113, 88:149, 88:157, 88:161, 102:88, 110:296, 110:297, 110:304 >

ūpāhebban (VI) to raise up; *ind. pres. 3 sg.* ūpāhefþ 110:320; *pret. 3 sg.* ūpāhof 150:99; *pp.* ūpāhafen 132:285; *m. nom. pl.* ūpāhafene 12:50, 16:147

ūpāstandan (VI) to stand up; *ind. pres. 3 pl.* ūpāstandaþ 78:48

ūpāstīġan (I) to ascend; *pres. p. m. acc. sg.* ūpāstīgendne 84:83

ūpāstīġnes *f.* ascension; *acc. sg.* ūpāstīgnesse 54:217; ūpāstīgenesse 84:65; *dat. sg.* ūpāstīgenesse 82:10 ūpāstīgnesse 84:76, 120:5

ūpgang *m.* ascent; *acc. sg.* ūpgang 138:66

ūpheah *adv.* aloft 150:119

ūpliċ *adj.* on high; *m. gen. pl.* ūplicra 136:11; *def. m. nom. sg.* ūplica 66:202; *f. nom. sg.* ūpplice 70:83; *nt. dat. sg.* ūplican 60:65; *nt. acc. pl.* ūplican 6:93

ūpon [ūppan] *prep.* (with acc. or dat.) upon 18:11, 90:202 >

ūprǣcan (1) to reach up; *ind. pret. 3 sg.* ūprǣhte 152:172

ūpstīġ *m* ascension; *gen. sg.* ūpstīges 92:2; *dat. sg.* ūpstīge 6:102, 60:73, 92:22, 98:3

ūpweardes *adv.* upwards 156:236 >

ūre *poss. adj.* our; *pron.* ours (see Appendix, p. 145)

ūs *pron.* our; *nt. dat. pl.* ūssum 106:198

ūs *pron.* (see wē)

ūt *adv.* out 34:199, 40:70, 48:77, 60:80, 102:118, 150:95 >

ūtālǣdan (1) to lead out; *ind. pres. 3 sg.* ūtālǣdeþ 158:17; ūtālǣt 26; *pret. 3 sg.* ūtālǣdde 53

ūtan (see ūton)

ūtan *adv.* outside 136:7

ūtāstungan [ūtāstungan] (III) to put out; *ind. pres. pl.* ūtāstungon 6; ūtāstungan 10

ūte *adv.* out 4:56

ūtēodan [ūtgān] (anom.) to go out; *ind. pret. 3 sg.* ūtēode 6:98, [ūt ēode → ūtēode] 62:110, 42, 133

ūteweard *adv.* on the outside 142:163

ūtfēran (1) to go out; *subj. pret. 3 pl.* ūtfērdon 122:47

ūtflōwan (VII) to flow out; *pres. p. m. nom. sg.* ūtflōwende 142:174

ūtgangan [ūtgongan] (VII) to go out 163

ūtġelǣdan [ūtġelǣddan] (1) to bring out; *subj. pret. pl.* ūtgelǣddon 45

ūtlǣdan (1) to bring out 158:21

ūton *adv.* (with *inf.*) let us 58:20 [uuton → ūton], 62:118, 62:122, 62:126, 66:196, 66:204, 76:25, 80:113, 80:127, 66:128, 86:128, 86:129, 86:130, 86:131 >; **ūtan** 24:175, 112:334, 127 >

ūtwearde *adv.* outwards 142:151

uþe (see unnan)

uþgān (anom.) to flow, fleet *pres. p. m. gen. pl.* uþgendra 128:205

W

wā *m.* woe; *nom. sg.* 16:161, 40:87, 108:239, 125, 138

wacian (2) to keep awake 12:73; *ind. pret. 3 sg.* wacode 154:228; *pl.* wacodon 104:164; *subj. pres. pl.* wacian 98:28; *pret. pl.* wacedon 102:125

wæċċa *m.* vigil; *nom. pl.* wæccan 50:113; *dat. pl.* wæccum 24:149

wæċċan (1) to watch; *pres. p.* wæccende 98:2; *m. acc. pl.* wæccende 102:103

wædl *f.* poverty, need; *gen. sg.* wædle 128:208

wædla *m.* beggar; *acc. sg.* wædlan 24:161

wædlian (2) to be poor; *pres.p. sg.* wædliende 12:51, 12:53

wæfersēon [wæferſēon → wæfersēon] *m.* spectacle; *dat. pl.* wæfersēonum 130:236

wælgrim *adj.* bloody; *m. nom. sg.* 156:244

wælhhreow *adj.* cruel, fierce; *def. m. acc. sg.* wælhreowan 20:79

wǣpen *nt.* weapon; *acc. sg.* wǣpn 116:87; *dat. pl.* wǣpnum 140:95, 140:105, 146:20, 154:220

wǣpnedmann *m.* man; *dat. pl.* wǣpnedmannum 54:196

wǣr *m.* covenant, agreement; *acc. pl.* wæra 78:50

wærnes *f.* wariness, caution; *acc. sg.* wærnesse 146:21, 146:24

wæstm *m.* fruit, increase; *nom. sg.* 2:32; *acc. sg.* wæstm 38:3, 38:6, 38:21, 50:90, 50:91, 50:111, 132:300; *dat. sg.* wæstme 156; *acc. pl.* wæstmas 26:3a, 26:3b, 26:7,

32:181; *gen. pl.* wæstma 26:18, 26:22, 32:153; *dat. pl.* wæstmum 26:9, 26:26, 32:159, 80:93, 33

wæstmberende *adj.* bearing fruit; *nt. nom. sg.* 106

wæstmian (2) to bear fruit 76:19

wǣta *m.* moisture; *nom. sg.* 142:174; *gen. sg.* wǣtan 142:176, 142:181

wǣta *f.* water; *gen. sg.* wǣtan 142:178

wæter *nt.* water; *nom. sg.* 144:204, 162:105, 71, 124, 132, 133; *acc. sg.* wæter 115, 118, 131, 137; *gen. sg.* wæteres 40:70, 44:161[wætres → wæteres]; *dat. sg.* wætere 22:125, 28:66, 66:187, 144:199, 144:205 [wætre → wætere], 145; *inst. sg.* wætere 141, 144; *nom. pl.* wætero 144:198

wæterscipe *m.* portion of water; *dat. sg.* wæterscipe 142:175

wāfian (2) to gaze at; *ind. pret. pl.* wāfodon 120:42

wāg *m.* wall; *gen. sg.* wāges 142:155; *nom. pl.* wāgas 142:157; *acc. pl.* wāgas 106:193

waldend [wealend] *m.* ruler; *nom. sg.* 94:47

wamb *f.* stomach; *acc. sg.* wambe 26:16

wana *adj.* wanting, lacking; *m. nom. sg.* 12:55

wandian (2) to fear; *ind. pres. 3 sg.* wandaþ 28:62; *imp. 3 sg.* wandige 28:55 (EWS)

wang *m.* field, land, world; *acc. sg.* wang 74:6

wanian (2) to diminish 54:211; *ind. pres. 3 sg.* wanað 12:45

wanung *f.* waning; *acc. sg.* wanunge 12:46

waroð *nt.* shore; *dat. sg.* waroðe 158:35, 158:36; warþe 158:42

wē (see iċ, wit, wē)

wēa *m.* misery; *acc. sg.* wēan 64:178; *dat. sg.* wēan 34:221; *acc. pl.* wēan 84:49; *gen. pl.* wēana 42:115 (A)

wealdend *m.* ruler; *nom. sg.* 35, 89

wealdan (VII) to rule; *ind. pres. 2 sg.* waldest 102:90; *3 sg.* wealdeþ 20:76 (A)

weallan (VII) to be fervent, to be zealous; *pres. p.* weallende 116:84; *m. acc. sg.* weallendene 42:114

weall *m.* wall, rampart; *dat. pl.* weallum 136:16

weard *m.* guard; *dat. pl.* weardum 6:115, 124:102

wearg *m.* wolf; *gen. pl.* wearga 144:201

weaxan (VII) to grow; *ind. pres. 3 sg.* weaxeþ 126:160; *pret. 3 sg.* weox 124; *subj. pret. sg.* weoxe 22:109

webbian (2) to weave; *infl. inf.* webgenne 76:41

weccan (1) to wake; *ind. pres. pl.* weccaþ 32:181

wedd *m.* pledge; *dat. sg.* wedde 92:5

weġ *m.* road; *nom. sg.* 12:51, 14:98, 88:149, 156:241; *acc. sg.* weg 48:70, 54:214, 76:32, 84:87, 118:111, 132:299, 158:33, 160:56; [on]weg 128:183, 130:265, 85, 92; *dat. sg.* wege 10:12, 10:41, 12:51, 12:53, 14:120, 132:283, 134:236, 155; *inst. sg.* wege 132:321; *nom. pl.* wegas 194:85; *acc. pl.* wegas 90:200

wegan (V) to carry; *ind. pret. 3 sg.* wæg 146:19

wel *adv.* well, very 4:85, 8:143, 8:145, 20:48, 20:67, 46:13, 52:161, 54:227, 76:39, 78:59, 128:205, 140:103, 148:86, 154:201, 154:227 >

wela *m.* wealth, riches; *nom. sg.* 34:188, 70:47; *acc. sg.* welan 16:137, 78:69, 78:84, 136:23; *gen. sg.* welan 14:93; *nom. pl.* welan 36:231, 70:43, 78:76, 80:100; *acc. pl.* welan 32:161, 60:47, 122:323; *gen. pl.* welena 128:205; *dat. pl.* welum 36:233

weleġ *m.* wealthy, rich; *acc. pl.* welegan 2:22, 76:2

weliġ *adj.* wealthy, rich; *m. nom. pl.* welige 68:34; *m. acc. pl.* welige 14:132; *m. gen. pl.* weligra 68:34; *def. m. nom. sg.* welega 32:165, 136:22; *m. acc. sg.* welegan 136:41; *m. gen. sg.* welegan 34:219, 136:23; *comp. m. nom. sg.* weligra 66:201

welm *m.* fervour; *dat. sg.* welme 18:33

welwyrcend *m.* well-doer; *dat. pl.* welwyrcendum 96:95

wēn *m.* expectation, supposition; *nom. sg.* 26:28, 124:125, 158:30, 162:97, 35, 49, 89, 127

wēnan (1) (with *gen.*) to think 26:27, 34:215, 42:116, 70:64, 78:43 >; *ind. pres. 1 sg.* wēne 123:156; *2 sg.* wēnstu 128:189; *3 sg.* wēnþ 38:14; wēneþ 124:110, 124:111, 128:197; *pl.* wēnaþ 28:58, 34:187, 44:144; wēne 58:36; *pret. 3 sg.* wēnde 122:57, 130:267, 130:270 >; *3 pl.* wēndon 58:36; *subj. pres. sg.* wēne 124:106

wendan (1) to go; *ind. pret. pl.* wendan 34:214; *imp. 2 pl.* wendaþ 132:284

wēninga [wēnung] *f.* expectation; *acc. sg.* wēninge 146:35

wēofod *nt.* altar; *nom. sg.* 142:154; *acc. sg.* wēofod 140:116; *gen. sg.* wēofodes 142:173; *dat. sg.* wēofode 52:154; *acc. pl.* wēofodu [wēofedu → wēofodu]140:124

weorc *nt.* work; *nom. sg.* 12:62, 30:111; *acc. sg.* weorc 48:46, 48:86, 50:131, 52:146, 78:60, 148:48; *gen. sg.* weorces 48:45, 142:142, 142:156, 154:228; *dat. sg.* weorce 10:33, 154:216; *nom. pl.* weorc 38:9, 122:79; *acc. pl.* weorc 66:206, 76:21; *gen. pl.* weorca 50:91, 50:112, 50:115, 76:26; *dat. pl.* weorcum 24:159, 50:104, 52:167, 86:122

weorce *f.* trouble, distress; *nom. sg.* 140:119, 150:92, 150:115

weorld *f.* world; *acc. sg.* weorld 24:139; *gen. sg.* weorlde 40:48

weorod *nt.* throng, company, troop; *nom. sg.* 54:220; *acc. sg.* weorod [weorad → weorod] 120:32; weorod 136:34, 152:159; *dat. sg.* weorode 10:4, 100:66, 112:327; *inst. sg.* weorode 16:171; *nom. pl.* weorod 70:44; *dat. pl.* weorodum 92:8

weoroldlīċe *adv.* worldly 138:53

weorpan (III) to throw; *ind. pret. 3 sg.* wearp 88:157

weorð *adj.* worthy, respected; *m. nom. sg.* 146:26, 150:107, 152:139

weorþ *nt.* worth, price; *acc. sg.* weorþ 70:62, 70:63; *dat. sg.* weorþe 62:98

weorþan (III) to become 52:175, 82:20, 86:92, 90:212, 90:215, 128:198; weorðan 86:103; *ind. pres. 3 sg.* wyrþ 14:107, 32:171; weorðeþ 4:87; weorþeð 52:179; weorþeþ 34:211, 120:12; *pl.* weorþaþ 34:204, 34:205; *pret 1 sg.* wearþ 108:272; *3 sg.* wearþ 20:84, 58:34, 86:97, 106:203, 118:101, 120:39, 122:54; wearð 78:85, 86:100, 122:64, 126:146, 136:41, 148:87, 150:118, 152:146, 154:185, 154:203; *pl.* wurdon 32:141, 40:73, 74:13, 110:319, 122:44, 138:43; wurdan 56:233, 60:57, 108:251, 142:181; *subj. pres. sg.* weorþe 34:215, 70:81; *pl.* weorþon 34:194; *pret sg.* wurde 122:60

weorþe *m.* worth; *nom. sg.* 116:48

weorþe *adj.* worthy, fit; *f. nom. sg.* 114:37

weorþian (2) to worship 20:63, 72:106, 114:3; weorðian 68:4; *ind. pres. 2 sg.* weorþast 18:14, 20:55; *3 sg.* weorþaþ 34:195, 48:53, 90:206; weorþeþ 20:55; *pl.* weorþiað 26:40, 82:3, 82:10; weorðiað 146:3; *pret. 3 sg.* weorþode10:21; weorðode 142:170; *pl.* weorþodan 48:58, 92:1, 140:117; weorðodan 146:26, 152:150; *subj. pret. sg.* weorþode 20:60; *imp. 2 sg.* weorþa 18:15; *1 pl.* weorþian 6:109, 6:110, 22:114, 92:3; weorðian 120:1; *2 pl.* weorþiaþ 26:25; *3 pl.* weorðian 2:41; *pp.* weorþod 46:7; weorðod 144:190; weorþad 48:89; *infl. inf.* to weorþienne 114:5, 136:3

weorþlīċe *adv.* worthily, honourably 88:143; *superl.* weorþlicost 88:143

weorþmynd *f.* or *nt.* honour; *nom. sg.* 44:166; weorðmynd 86:106; *dat. sg.* weorþmende 60:89; *gen. pl.* weorþmenda 86:98; *dat. pl.* weorþmyndum 62:100

weorþung *f.* honour, worship; *nom. sg.* 116:78, 118:97, 118:100; weorðung 118:136, 144:186; *acc. sg.* weorðunga 96:90; weorþunga 116:57; *dat. sg.* weorþunge

6:127; weorþunga 30:112, 88:181, 92:32, 114:2, 118:106

wēpan (VII) to weep; *ind. pres. 3 pl.* wēpað 16:159, 16:161; *pret. 2 sg.* wēop 150:91, 154:211; *imp. 2 sg.* wēp 100:71; *1 pl.* wēpan 16:158; *pres. p.* wēpende 100:68, 106:205; *f. dat. sg.* wēpendre 60:59, 154:213; *f. inst. sg.* wēpendre 60:75; *nt. acc. sg.* wēpende 100:74; *pl.* wēpende 157; *m. acc. pl.* wēpende 108:239, 154:211; *nt. dat. pl.* wēpendum 108:244

wer *m.* man; *nom. sg.* 128:214, 146:37, 148:44, 148:57, 148:69, 148:83, 150:105, 150:110, 154:189, 154:195 >; *acc. sg.* wer 4:62, 148:76, 150:122, 152:174 >; *gen. sg.* weres 34:196, 146:2 >; *dat. sg.* were 128:214, 148:68, 154:222 >; *nom. pl.* weras 84:84, 86:111, 132:307, 138 >; *acc. pl.* weras 76:1, 128:212, 158:42 >; *gen. pl.* wera 2:33, 2:40, 6:120, 120:37, 30, 38 >; *dat. pl.* werum 6:116,

wercan (1) to work 46:31

werian (2) to defend 54:193

wēriġ *adj.* accursed, wicked; *m. gen. pl.* wērigra 58:5; *def. m. dat. sg.* wērgan 94:62

werrest *adj.* worst; *superl. m. acc. pl.* werrestan 158:8

wesan (anom.) to be (see beon)

west *adv.* westward 90:188

westan *m.* west; *nom. sg.* 88:162

westdǣl *m.* west quarter; *acc. sg.* westdǣl 64:163

wēsten *nt.* wilderness; *acc. sg.* wēsten 18:2, 18:37, 18:40, 18:41, 22:119, 136:28, 136:30, 136:32; *dat. sg.* wēstenne 116:59, 118:117

wex *m.* wax; *nom. sg.* 90:186; *dat. sg.* wexe 140:112

weaxan [wascan] (VII) to wax; *ind. pres. 3 sg.* wexeþ 12:44; *pres. p.* wexende 76:19

wīc *nt.* village; *acc. sg.* wīc 52:169; *nom. pl.* wīc 52:170

wīcsceawere *m.* harbinger; *gen. sg.* wīcsceaweres 114:35

wide *adj.* wide, vast; *nt. dat. sg.* widan 44:165, 72:107; *comp. nt. nom. sg.* widdre 88:161

wīde *adv.* widely, far 54:199, 88:168

wīdgill [wīdgal] *adj.* spacious; *def. m. acc. sg.* wīdgillan 136:33

wīf *f.* woman, wife; *nom. sg.* 50:94, 116:63, 120:35a, 120:35b, 128:215 >; *acc. sg.* wīf 128:214 >; *gen. sg.* wīfes 2:18, 34:196, 114:21 >; *acc. pl.* wīf 68:39, 76:2, 128:211> ; *gen. pl.* wīfa 2:33, 2:40, 8:143, 62:101, 114:18, 118:101, 39 >; *dat. pl.* wīfum 42:97

wīfcynn *f.* womankind; *acc. pl.* wīfcyn 100:82

wīfmon *f.* woman; *acc. sg.* wīfmon 2:15 *dat. pl.* wīfmannum 54:195

wig *m.* war; *acc. sg.* wig 138:72

wiht *m.* creature; *nom. sg.* 60:52, 62:119, 36

wild *adj.* wild; *nt. nom. sg.* wilde 66:200

wildēor *nt.* wild beast; *nom. pl.* wildēor 66:187

wīlewise *m.* basketwise; *dat. sg.* wīlewisan 88:142 (EWS)

willa *m.* desire; *nom. sg.* 30:103, 140:121, 140:135, 154:208, 154:216, 154:220, 154:222; *acc. sg.* willan 16:155, 22:126, 32:177, 42:102, 42:113, 46:5, 46:31, 154:218, 91; *gen sg.* willan 64:150; *dat. sg.* willan 24:137, 24:166, 50:123, 54:207, 58:22, 68:16, 68:18, 70:71, 70:83, 84:78, 130:244; wyllan 18:38; *nom. pl.* willan 78:79; *acc. pl.* willan 12:60

willan (anom.) to wish, desire; *ind. pres. 1 sg.* wille 68:22, 106:200, 132:295 >; *2 sg.* wilt 10:18, 12:82, 58:39, 82:14, 124:132, 126:171, 128:193; *3 sg.* wile 12:83, 16:153, 28:82, 30:112, 32:176, 34:188, 38:7, 38:14, 38:16, 38:17 >; *pl.* willaþ 14:119, 22:106, 26:24, 28:51, 30:100, 32:172, 42:133; willað 158:24 >; wille 16:143, 110:276, 160:43 160:48 >; *pret. 1 sg.* wolde 128:186; *2 sg.* woldest 60:52; *3 sg.* wolde 10:3, 10:26, 10:27, 12:49, 12:122, 16:142, 18:30, 18:39, 18:41, 20:54, 20:58, 20:60, 20:68, 20:72 >; *pl.* woldon 54:202, 152:158, 160:62, 119;

woldan 30:99, 48:43, 48:51, 48:54, 52:157, 54:184, 94:85, 106:188, 120:21>; *subj. pres. sg.* wille 26:30, 28:57, 78:45, 82:41, 86:132, 86:135, 122:79, 160:55 >; *pl.* willon 30:127, 30:130, 34:193, 42:100, 42:109, 64:175, 66:195; willan 128:213 >

wilnian (2) (with *gen.*) to desire; *ind. pret. pl.* wilnodan 72:94, 150:133, 152:166; *subj. pret. pl.* wilnodan 138:49, 138:76

wīn *nt.* wine; *acc. sg.* wīn 38:28, 116:66; *dat sg.* wīne 50:96

wind *m.* wind; *nom. sg.* 44:161, 152:140, 152:144b; *acc. sg.* wind 94:46, 152:144a; *gen. sg.* windes 92:36, 94:45, 94:47, 136:40; *dat. sg.* winde 94:48, 152:145, 160:73, 160:76; *nom. pl.* windas 32:180; *dat. pl.* windum 124:92

wīngeard *m.* vineyard; *nom. pl.* wīngeardas 32:174; *dat. pl.* wīngeardum 68:36

winnan (III) to strive 68:15; *ind. pres. pl.* winnað 68:28; *pret. 3 sg.* wan 42:18; *pl.* wunnon 100:48; *subj. pres. pl.* winnon 68:32; *pres. p. m. dat. pl.* winnendum 146:29 (A)

winter *m.* winter, year; *nom. sg.* 146:41; *gen. pl.* wintra 48:85, 52:182, 54:184, 80:90, 82:38, 82:39, 90:198, 148:72; wintre 146:12, 146:17; *dat. sg.* [middum]wintra 146:41

wīsdōm *m.* wisdom; *acc. sg.* wīsdōm 128:195; *dat. sg.* wīsdōme 32:158

wīse *f.* wise; *nom. sg.* 20:87, 38:13, 38:16; *acc. sg.* wīsan 66:188, 114:28, 124:105, 126:135, 132:281, 140:130; *dat. sg.* wīsan 20:67, 94:70; *dat. pl.* wīsum 124:124

wīsfæst *adj.* constant in wisdom; *f. dat. pl.* wīsfæstum 84:81 (A)

wīslīċe *adv.* wisely 66:205, 138:53

wisnian (2) to dry up; *ind. pret. 3 sg.* wisnode 80:121

wist *f.* food, meal, feast; *acc. sg.* wiste 68:40; *nom. pl.* wista 78:77

wit *dual pron.* we two; *nom.* 126:156, 130:237, 130:249, 130:258, 140:135; *acc.* unc 130:244; *dat.* unc 130:255

wita *m.* wise man, elder; *nom. pl.* witan 48:54

witan (pret. pres.) to know 82:22, 122:79; witon 30:123, 114:4; *ind. pres. 1 sg.* wāt 124:122, 126:140, 162:91, 57, 106; *2 sg.* wāst 62:95, 62:98, 122:74, 126:173, 130:249, 158:32, 97; *3 sg.* wāt 12:83, 12:86, 124:126, 126:141; *pl.* witon 8:148, 14:90, 22:132, 40:47, 40:55, 88:149, 88; witan 106:215; *pl.* witon; *pret. 1 sg.* wiste 126:153; *3 sg.* wiste 48:50, 52:174, 70:89, 92:15, 94:65, 154:195, 154:197, 160:80; *pl.* wiston 6:113, 6:122, 54:191, 54:216, 86:91, 138:84, 148:154; *subj. pres. sg.* wite 82:40, 126:142; *pl.* witan 82:24; *pret. 2 sg.* wistest 60:50; *3 sg.* wiste 128:204, 154:199; *pl.* wiston 8:147, 84:44; *imp. 2 sg.* wit 126:175; wite 126:141, 126:159, 126:177, 138:54; *3 sg.* wite 12:55; *2 pl.* wite 132:311; *infl. inf.* to witenne 42:119, 44:144, 90:207, 144:188

wīte *nt.* punishment, torment; *nom. sg.* 16:162, 34:189, 54:203; *acc. sg.* wīte 2:36, 14:118, 38:42, 52:156, 52:174, 58:14; *dat. sg.* wīte 56:234, 68:12; *acc. pl.* wītu 58:35, 64:177, 76:14, 128:199; *dat. pl.* wītum 24:147, 32:155, 42:100, 42:113, 42:120, 58:10, 60:64, 60:71, 68:8, 70:65, 80:107, 120:22, 130:269, 132:278, 132:279

wītedōm *m.* prophecy; *nom. sg.* 48:64 (A)

wītestōw *m.* place of torment; *dat. sg.* wītestōwe [wīte stōwe → wītestōwe] 60:46

wītga *m.* prophet; *nom. sg.* 6:97, 20:76, 24:160, 24:169, 48:75, 58:15, 118:109, 140:91; *acc. sg.* wītgan 26:13, 46:17, 94:48, 116:59, 116:60; *gen. sg.* wītgan 98:34, 116:69; *nom. pl.* wītgan 60:61, 72:111, 114:8; wītigan 105 9; *acc. pl.* wītgan 48:85, 122:85; *gen. pl.* wītgena 54:216; wītgana 114:7; *dat. pl.* wītgum 30:91, 58:18; wītgan 118:104

wītegian (2) to prophesy; *ind. pret. 3 sg.* wītgode [wītgade → wītgode] 58:16, 94:46; *pl.* wītgodan 114:11, 122:86; wītigodan 74:30; *pp.* wītgod 94:48

wītnian (2) to torment, afflict 42:100, 132:278; *subj. pres. sg.* wītnige 126:164

wītnung *f.* torture; *gen. sg.* wītnunge 132:314

witodlīce *adv.* certainly 44:153, 108:235, 108:250, 108:252, 122:85, 126:136, 126:153, 128:197 >

wiþ (wið) *prep.* against, towards, from with (see Appendix, p. 151)

wiþcweþan (V) to forbid; *subj. pres. 1 sg.* wiþcweþe 48:63

wiþerbreca *m.* adversary; *nom. sg.* 122:58 (A)

wiþermēd *adj.* perverse; *f. nom. sg.* wiþermēde 62:90

wiþersynes *adv.* adverse, hostile 64:159

wiþerweard *adj.* adverse, hostile; *m. nom. pl.* wiþerwearde 94:63, 152:179; *nt. dat. pl.* wiðerweardum 8:137

wiþerwearda *m.* adversary; *nom. sg.* 18:15, 42:99; *dat. sg.* wiþerweardan 28:64, 28:67

wiþerweardnes *f.* opposition, adversary; *nom. sg.* 16:168

wiþone [wiþ þone] *prep.* from the 14:105

wiðsacan (VI) (with dat.) to refuse; *ind. pres. 1 sg.* wiðsace 154:215, 154:219; *pret. 3 pl.* wiþsocan 32:141; *imp. 2 pl.* wiþsacaþ 36:233

wiþstandan (VI) (with dat.) to withstand, resist 20:81, 94:62, 114:12, 152:163; wiþstondan 16:153; *ind. pret 3 sg.* wiþstod 46:16; *pl.* wiðstodan 152:152

wlanc *adj.* rich; *m. acc. pl.* wlance 128:204

wlēnco *f.* pride, riches; *acc. sg.* wlēncu 136:31; *nom. pl.* wlēnca 68:35; wlēncea 78:77; *dat. pl.* wlēncum 34:221, 68:37, 70:59

wlite *m.* beauty; *nom. sg.* 40:47, 40:49, 40:59; *acc. sg.* wlite 80:119; *dat. sg.* wlite 80:93, 136:5

wlitelīce *adv.* handsomely 140:116

wlitiġ *adj.* beautiful; *nt. nom. sg.* 76:17

wlitiġnes *f.* beauty, splendour; *nom. sg.* 70:50; *dat. sg.* wlitignesse 6:126

wōh [on wōh] *m.* wrongfully; 28:85, 30:92, 42:103, 42:107, 52:154

wōhdǽd *m.* unrighteous deeds; *nom. pl.* wōhdǽda 76:12; *acc. pl.* wōhdǽda 30:99; *gen. pl.* wōhdǽda 30:98

wōhhǽmed *m.* adultry; *acc. sg.* wōhhǽmed 42:96

wolcen *nt.* cloud; *nom. sg.* 64:138, 100:60; wolcn 40:70, 84:75 84:76a; wolc 122; *acc. sg.* wolcn 84:76b; *gen. sg.* wolcnes 84:75; *dat sg.* wolcne 64:139, 84:79, 84:80, 86:115, 245 29; *dat. pl.* wolcnum 102:128, 104:177, 106:190, 108:258, 108:261, 110:297, 110:298, 110:305

woldan (see willan)

wolīċe *adv.* wrongly 76:33

wōliċ *adj.* wrongful; *f. dat. pl.* wōlicum 76:15

wom *m.* spot, blemish; *dat. pl.* wommum 78:82

won *adj.* lacking, absent; *m. nom. sg.* 92:7

wones *f.* wrong; *nom. pl.* wonessa 76:13; *dat. pl.* wonessum 76:34

wōp *m.* weeping; *nom. sg.* 4:56, 60:45, 72:113, 80:123, 128:199, 157; *acc. sg.* wōp 42:115, 150:111; *dat. sg.* wōpe 40:84, 158:4; *inst. sg.* wōpe 94

word *nt.* word; *nom. sg.* 122:53; *acc. sg.* word 10:33, 22:126, 100:61; *gen. sg.* wordes 94:82; *dat. sg.* worde 18:6, 22:100, 38:33, 122:46, 124:118, 162:100; *nom. pl.* word 40:69, 128:224, 98; *acc. pl.* word 10:31, 20:58, 38:2, 38:4, 38:11, 38:14, 38:18, 46:26, 124:105, 132:306, 140:131, 154:211; *gen. pl.* worda 10:9, 38:16, 126:172; *dat. pl.* wordum 2:32, 6:90, 6:134, 6:135, 8:140, 20:63, 24:175, 48:53, 52:147; *inst. pl.* wordum 2:41

world *f.* world; *nom. sg.* 80:111, 80:112, 80:126; *acc. sg.* world 2:37, 12:43, 24:172, 56:236, 64:159, 74:2, 74:5, 74:11, 74:29, 80:131, 96:97, 98:20, 100:51, 102:93, 110:295, 118:136, 134:332; *gen. sg.* worlde 10:39, 16:137, 16:152, 38:35, 40:43a, 40:43b, 40:87, 42:110, 62:106; *dat. sg.* worlde 24:141, 24:143, 28:79,

32:151, 36:231, 40:45, 40:54, 44:138, 44:141, 80:110; *gen. pl.* worlda 36:240, 74:29, 80:131, 96:97, 98:20, 100:51, 102:93, 110:295, 118:136, 134:332; *dat. pl.* worldum 20:72

worldcund *adj.* worldly; *f. acc. sg.* worldcunde 58:12

worldfrǽtwung *f.* worldly ornament; *dat. sg.* worldfrǽtwunga 88:156

worldfrēond *m.* worldly friend; *gen. pl.* worldfrēonda 78:87; *dat. pl.* worldfrēondum 78:72

worldġeþoht *m.* worldy thoughts; *dat. pl.* worldgeþohtum 10:10

worldgleng *m.* worldly splendour; *gen. pl.* worldglenga 12:89

worldliċ *adj.* worldly; *f. dat. sg.* worldlicre 88:158; *m. acc. pl.* worldlice 84:52; *nt. acc. pl.* worldlicu 76:20

worldrīċe *m.* the whole world; *dat. sg.* 76:40

worldriċe *adj.* having worldly power; *m. dat. sg.* worldricum 78:84; *m. gen. pl.* worldricra 76:16

worldspēd *m.* worldly wealth; *acc. pl.* worldspēda 14:133, 24:172; *gen. pl.* worldspēda 22:130

woroldliċ *adj.* worldly; *nt. dat. pl.* woroldlicum 146:18

woroldwǽpen *nt.* world weapons; *acc. pl.* woroldwǽpno 146:19

woruld *f.* world; *acc. sg.* woruld 112:330, 146:4; *dat sg.* worolde 68:25; *gen. pl.* worulda 169

woruldfolgað *m.* worldly occupation; *acc. sg.* woroldfolgað 148:74; *dat. sg.* woruldfolgaðe 146:11, 146:13

woruldmon *m.* worldly men; *acc. pl.* woruldmen 146:20

woruldrīċe *adj.* powerful; *m. dat. sg.* woruldrīcum 154:186

wrǣc *nt.* vengeance, banishment; *nom. sg.* 16:162; *acc. sg.* wrǣc 58:14; *dat. sg.* wrǣce 18:42

wræc *f.* vengeance; *acc. sg.* wræce
54:188; *dat. sg.* wræce 54:201
wræcsīþ *m.* banishment, exile; *acc. sg.*
wræcsīþ 14:118
wræcwīte *nt.* vengeance, punishment;
acc. sg. wræcwīte 2:34, 2:35
wrecan (v) to avenge, punish; *ind. pres 3
sg.* wreceþ 128:215; *pret. 3 sg.* wræc
54:190
wrēgan (1) to accuse; *ind. pret. 3 sg.*
wrēgde 114:26, 120:32
wrigels *nt.* covering, veil; *acc. sg.*
wrigels 74:20; *dat. sg.* wrigelse 42:98
wrītan (1) to write; *ind. pret. 3 sg.* wrāt
114:20, 114:22, 116:47; *pl.* wrīton 92:23
wrītere *m.* writer; *nom. sg.* 50:105
wrōht *m.* accusation; *acc. pl.* wrōhtas
76:41
wucu *f.* week; *gen. sg.* wucan 92:26; *dat.
pl.* wucan 22:133
wudu *m.* wood, forest; *nom. sg.* 40:54;
acc. sg. wudu 136:34; *inst. sg.* wuda
142:164; *dat. pl.* wudum 132:318
wuduhunig *m.* wild honey; *dat. sg.*
wuduhunige [wudu hunige → wuduhunige]
118:114
wuduwyrt *f.* wood plant; *gen. pl.*
wuduwyrta 40:57
wuht *nt.* person; *nom. sg.* 20:60; *acc. sg.*
wuht 162:98
wuldor *nt.* glory; *nom. sg.* 36:240, 44:157,
44:158, 44:166, 64:150, 96:97, 102:107,
118:136; *acc. sg.* wuldor 14:118, 18:12,
40:89, 50:121, 86:98, 102:126, 106:199,
106:220; *gen. sg.* wuldres 16:166, 26:12,
46:14, 60:65, 60:66, 62:100, 110:287; *dat. sg.*
wuldre 62:97, 68:13, 72:115, 110:281, 120:23,
193 25; *dat. pl.* wuldrum 88:139
wuldorcyning *m.* king of glory; *nom. sg.*
6:99
wuldorfæst *adj.* glorious; *def. m. acc. sg.*
wuldorfæstan 58:26; *f. acc. sg.*
wuldorfæstan 72:108; *nt. nom. sg.*
wuldorfæste 72:110

wuldorhelm *m.* crown of glory; *dat. sg.*
wuldorhelme 32:144
wuldorlīce *adv.* gloriously 114:14, 146:16
wuldorlič *adj.* glorious; *def. f. acc. sg.*
wuldorlican 84:64/5; *f. dat. sg.*
wuldorlican 82:8
wuldorþrymm *m.* glory; *acc. pl.*
wuldorþrymmas 78:63
wuldrian (2) to glorify 110:292; *infl. inf.*
to wuldrienne 136:3
wulf *m.* wulf; *nom. sg.* 144:204; *nom. pl.*
wulfas 42:123, 132:317, 154:207; *dat. pl.*
wulfum 24
wund *m.* wound; *acc. pl.* wunda 62:113
wundian (2) to wound; *ind. pret. pl.*
wundan 16:140
wundor *nt.* wonder, miracle; *nom. sg.*
20:89, 22:90, 78:75, 122:75, 124:116, 144:190,
150:109, 152:175, 49; wunder 152:149; *acc.
sg.* wundor 10:22, 12:70, 48:81, 88:178,
138:44, 135:47; *gen. sg.* wundres 48:51; *acc.
pl.* wundro 54:217, 124:93; wundor 10:34,
150:121, 150:125; *gen. pl.* wundra 58:20,
74:17, 150:105; *dat. pl.* wundrum 72:90
wundordǣd *m.* wonderful deed; *acc. pl.*
wundordǣda 120:41
wundorġeweorc *nt.* miracle; *acc. sg.*
wundorgeweorc 4:52, 46:8
wundorlič *adj.* wonderful; *m. nom. sg.*
98:8; *f. acc. sg.* wundorlice 150:103; *f. dat.
sg.* wundorlicre 126:149; *nt. acc. sg.*
wundorlic 142:138; *def. f. nom. pl.*
wundorlican 106:225; *superl. m. nom. pl.*
wundorlicost 88:167
wundorlīce *adv.* wondrously 120:22
wundorweorc *m.* wondrous work,
miracle; *dat. pl.* wundorweorcum 114:14
wundrian (2) to wonder; *ind. pres. pl.*
wundriað 86:112; *pret 3 sg.* wundrode
108:246; *infl. inf.* to wundrigenne 22:93;
pres. p. m. nom. sg. wundrigende 106:224
wunian (2) to dwell 12:62, 16:171, 40:85,
42:113 [wunan → wunian], 58:10, 60:64, 72:114,
78:51, 94:71; *ind. pres. 2 sg.* wunast 100:50;

3 sg. wunaþ 40:45, 40:50, 74:28, 102:93, 108:250, 108:275, 120:24; wunað 70:57, 120:17; *pl.* wuniaþ 72:103, 72:111; *pret. 3 sg.* wunode 6:101, 74:7, 74:16, 80:90, 41, 164; *pl.* wunedon 94:44; wunodan 142:174; *subj. pret. sg.* wunode 92:9; *imp. 2 sg.* wuna 150; *pres. p.*wunigende 50:124, 116:72; *pl.* wunigende 92:35; *m. dat. pl.* wunigendium 120:9

wunung *f.* abode, dwelling; *nom. sg.* 8:149; *acc. pl.* wununga 50:101

wuton (see uton)

wydew [widuwe] *f.* widow; *dat. pl.* wydewum 28:77

wylder *adj.* fierce; *comp. m. nom. pl.* wyldran 106:191

wylǣdan (1) to roll; *subj. pret. sg.* wylēde 110:284

wynsum *adj.* joyful, merry, pleasant, delightful; *m. nom. sg.* 80:120, 142:173; *f. nom. sg.* wynsumu 142:179; *nt. nom. sg.* wynsum 98:35; *def. m. gen. sg.* wynsuman 142:176

wynsumian (2) to rejoice 62:118; *ind. pres. 3 sg.* wynsumaþ 4:47; *subj. pres. sg.* wynsumige 110:310; *imp. 2 pl.* wynsumiaþ 132:311; *pres. p.* wynsumiende 98:11; wynsumigende 102:89

wynsumliċ *adj.* pleasant; *m. nom. sg.* 80:118; *nt. nom. sg.* wynsumlic 76:17, 78:71

wynsumliċor *comp. adv.* more pleasing 94:58

wynsumnes *f.* pleasantness, delight; *acc. sg.* wynsumnesse 80:119; *dat. sg.* wynsumnesse 78:85, 80:115; *acc. pl.* wynsumnessa 20:57

wyorþmynd *m.* honour; *dat. pl.* wyorþmyndum 46:13

wyrċean (1) to work 32:177, 78:60, 118:123, 124:93, 126:161; wyricean 75 13; *ind. pres. 3 sg.* wyrceþ 14:104; *pl.* wyrceað 118:130; wyrce 26:23; *pret. 3 sg.* worhte 10:35,

12:70, 20:88, 42:113, 54:217, 72:91, 74:17, 118:133; *pres. p.* wyrcende 48:46, 52:147 (A)

wyrd *f.* fate; *nom. sg.* 58:3, 152:143; *acc. sg.* wyrd 150:103; *gen. sg.* wyrde 78:45; *dat. sg.* wyrde 62:130, 94:79

wyrgan (1) to curse; *ind. pret. pl.* wyrgdon 132:290

wyrhta *m.* worker 78:60; *gen. sg.* wyrhtan 140:121; *nom. pl.* wyrhtan 78:58

wyrm *m.* worm; *gen. sg.* wyrmes 80:96; *gen. pl.* wyrma 78:76; *dat. pl.* wyrmum 68:31; *inst. pl.* wyrmum 70:56

wyrnan (1) (with gen.) to refuse; *ind. pres. 3 sg.* wyrneþ 32:172

wyrrest *adv.* worst 34:196

wyrse *adj.* worse; *comp. nt. nom. sg.* 26:23; *nt. acc. pl.* wyrsan 90; *superl. m. nom. sg.* wyresta 46:42, 48:43; wyrresta 128:195; *m. acc. sg.* wyrrestan 132:312; *nt. acc. sg.* wyrste 26:24; *nt. acc. pl.* wyrstan 35; *nt. dat. pl.* wyrstan 101

wyrt *f.* wort, herb; *nom. pl.* wyrta 40:54; *dat. pl.* wyrtum 50:108, 118:114

wyrtruma *m.* root; *nom. sg.* 38:5, 44:147

wyrþe *adj.* worthy; *m. nom. sg.* 50:121, 132:288; *m. acc. sg.* wyrþne 126:163; *f. nom. sg.* wyrþe 26:20; *m. nom. pl.* wyrþe 30:124, 54:207

wȳscan (1) to wish; *ind. pres. pl.* wȳscaþ 64:167; *pret. 2 sg.* wȳsctest 60:50; *pl.* wȳscton 72:93

Y

yfel *nt.* evil, ill, wickedness; *nom. sg.* 20:65, 72:113, 80:124, 122: 62, 126:161; *acc. sg.* yfel 28:75, 52:144, 60:77, 70:79, 76:19; *gen. sg.* yfeles 34:185, 54:185; yfles 60:52; *dat. sg.* yfele 38:18, 154:190; *gen. pl.* yfela 26:19; yfla 120:40; *dat. pl.* yfelum 54:187

yfel *adj.* evil, bad, wicked; *f. nom. sg.* yeflu 24:151; yefl 114:26; *nt. gen. sg.* yfeles 136:7; *f. dat. sg.* yfelre 130:274; *m. nom. pl.* yfele 30:94; *m. gen. pl.* yfelra 12:67; *m. dat. pl.* yflum 22:92, 24:154;

135

yfflum 22:102; *nt. dat. pl.* yfelum 24:75, 114:12; *def. m. nom. sg.* yfela 42:110; *f. dat. sg.* yfelan 2:15

yfeldǣd *f.* evil deed; *gen. pl.* yfeldǣda 68:24

yfele *adv.* miserably 127

yfelian (2) to work evil 52:140

yfelsacian (2) to blaspheme; *subj. pret. 3 sg.* yfelsacode [yfel sacode → yfelsacode] 130:273

yfelsacung *f.* reproach; *acc. pl.* yfelsacunga [yfel sacunga → yfelsacunga] 120:31

ylda *f.* old age; *nom. sg.* 114:40; *dat. sg.* ylda 114:34

yldan (1) to delay; *ind. pres. 2 sg.* yldest 126:164; yldestu 4:71

ylding *f.* delay; *nom. sg.* 40:77, 40:80; *dat. sg.* yldinge 60:56, 130:248

yldo *f.* age, old age; *nom. sg.*114:30; *dat. sg.* yldo 72:112

yldor [see ealdor] *m.* leader, parent; *nom. pl.* yldran 34:214, 146:6, 146:13, 146:17; *acc. pl.* yldran 14:133; *dat. pl.* yldrum 120:15, 128:210

yldu *f.* old age; *dat. sg.* ylde 40:59, 44:159, 48:83

ymb(e) *prep.* (with *acc.*) about, concerning; *adv.* around (see Appendix, p. 151)

ymbfaran (VI) to embrace, comprehend; *ind. pres. 3 sg.* ymbfehþ 14:129; *pret. 3 sg.* ymbfeng 110:291

ymbhwyrft *m.* world; *acc. sg.* ymbhwyrft 6:125; *dat. sg.* ymbhwyrfte 136:3

ymbhygdig *adj.* anxious, heedful; *nt. inst. pl.* ymbhygdigum 38:20

ymbhygd *m.* anxiety; *dat. pl.* ymbhygdum 92:16

ymbscīnan (I) to shine round; *ind. pres. 3 sg.* ymbscīneþ [ymbscīncþ → ymbscīneþ] 4:73

ymbsellan (1) to surround; *ind. pret 3 sg.* ymbsealde 123; *pp.* ymbseald 6:121 (A)

ymbsettan (I) to surround; *pp.* ymbseted 6:115

ymbstandan (VI) to stand around; *ind. pres. 3 sg.* ymbstandeþ 100:74

ymbþonc *m.* consideration; *nom. sg.* 126:172

ymen [Lt. hymnus] *m.* hymn; *acc. pl.* ymen 102:130, 106:196

yppe *adj.* manifest, plain; *nt. nom. sg.* yppe 122:59

yppe *nt.* upper room; *dat. sg.* yppan 94:44

yrf *nt.* cattle; *dat. sg.* yrfe 136:29

yrfeweard *m.* heir; *nom. pl.* yrfeweardas 34:193

yrmþu *f.* misery; *acc. sg.* yrmþo 140:97; *acc. pl.* yrmþa 40:87

yrnan (III) to run; *ind. pres. pl.* yrnaþ 64:159; *pret. 3 sg.* ārn 100:53, 152:142, 64; *pl.* ūrnon 122:43, 60

yrre *nt.* anger, wrath; *nom. sg.* 106:197; *dat. sg.* yrre 136:36

yrre *adj.* angry; *m. acc. sg.* yrne 154:190; *m. nom. pl.* yrre 132:291

ȳtmesta [ūterra] *adj.* last; *superl. m. nom. sg.* 70:82; *m. dat. sg.* ȳtmestan 32:171, 34:184, 38:37; ȳtmæstan 42:109; *nt. acc. pl.* ȳtmestan 94:51; *f. dat. pl.* ȳtmestsan 84:56

ȳþ *f.* wave; *nom. pl.* ȳþa 160:74; *acc. pl.* ȳþa 124:93

Z

Zacharias *pers. n.* Zacharias; *nom. sg.* 114:21, 116:63; *acc. sg.* Zachariam 116:62

S. ANDREAS

[Camb. CCC MS 198, fols 386r–94v]

Her segð þæt æfter þam þe Drihten Hælend Crist to heofonum astah, þæt þa apostoli
wæron ætsomne, ond hie sendon hlot him betweonum, hwider hyra gehwylc faran scolde
to læranne. Segþ þæt se eadiga Matheus gehleat to Marmadonia þære ceastre. Segð þonne
þæt þa men þe on þære ceastre wæron þæt hi hláf ne æton, ne wæter ne druncon, ác æton
5 manna lichaman, ond heora blód druncon. Ond æghwylc man þe on þære ceastre com
ælþeodisc, segð þæt hie hine sona genámon ond his eagan útastungon; ond hie him sealdon
attor drincan þæt mid myclen lybcræfte wæs geblanden; ond mid þy þe hie þone drenc
druncon, hraþe heora heorta wæs tolesed ond heora mod onwended.
  Se eadiga Matheus þa ineode on þa ceastre, ond hraðe hie hine genamon ond his eagan
10 útastungan, ond hie him sealdon attor drinccan [→ drincan], ond hine …

[The part is extant in the Blickling Manuscript, fols. 136r- 139v]

… Gemūne ge hu manega earfoðness …Gehiere me Andreas, and aræfna þas tintrego,
forþon manige synt on þisse ceastre þa sculon geleofan on minne naman.' Mid þi he þis
cwæð, Drihten Hælend Crist, he astah on heofonas.
  Se haliga Andreas þa ineode on þa ceastre mid his discipulum, ond nænig man hine ne
15 mihte geseon. Mid þi þe hie comon to þæs carcernes dyru, hie þær gemetton seofon hyrdas
standan. Se haliga Andreas þa gebæd on his heortan, ond raðe hio wæron deade. Se halga
Andreas þe eode to þæs carcernes duru, ond he worhte Cristes rode tacen, ond raþe þa dura
wæron ontynede, ond he ineode on þæt carcern mid his discipulum, ond he geseah þone
eadigan Matheus ænne sitton singende. Se eadiga Matheus þa ond se haliga Andreas hie
20 wæron cyssende him betwéonon. Se halga Andreas him to-cwæð, 'Hwæt is þæt, broþor?
Hú eart þu her gemet? Nu þry dagas to lafe syndon þæt hie þe willaþ acwellan, ond him to
mete gedón.' Se halga Matheus him andswarode, and he cwæð, 'Broþor Andreas, ac ne
gehyrdest þu Drihten cweþende, forþon þe ic eow sende swá swá sceap on middum
wulfum? Þanon wæs geworden, mid þy þe hie me sendon on þis carcern, ic bæd urne
25 Drihten þæt he hine æteowde, ond hraþe he me hine æteowde, ond he me to-cwæð, 'Onbid
hér xxvii daga, ond æfter þon ic sende to þe Andreas þinne broþor, ond he þe útalæt of
þissum carcerne ond ealle þa mid þe syndon.' Swa me Drihten to-cwæþ, 'Ic gesie, broðor,
hwæt sculon we nu dón?'
  Se halga Andreas þa ond se halga Matheus gebædon to Drihtne, ond æfter þon gebede
30 se haliga Andreas sette his hand ofer þara wera eagan þe þær on lande wæron, ond gesihþe
hie onfengon. Ond eft he sette his hand ofer hiora heortan, ond heora andgeat him eft
tohwirfde. Se haliga Andreas him to-cwæð, 'Gangað on þas niþeran dælas þisse ceastre,
ond ge þær gemétað mycel fíctreow; sittað under him ond etað ð his wæstmum oð þæt ic
eow tócyme.' Hi cwædon to þam halgan Andrea, 'Cum nu mid us, forþon þe þu éart úre
35 wealdend, þy læs wén is þæt hi us eft genimon ond on þa wyrstan tintregu hie us
ongebringan.' Se haliga Andreas him to-cwæð, 'Farað þider, forþon þe eow nænig wiht ne
dera ð ne ne swenceþ.' Ond hraðe hie þa ealle ferdon, swa him se halga Andreas bebead.
Ond þær wæron on þæm carcerne twá hund ond eahta ond feowertig wera, ond nigon ond
feowertig wifa, ða se haliga Andreas þánon onsende. Ond þone eadigan Matheum he
40 gedyde gangan to þam east-dæle mid his discipulum ond se haliga Andreas asetton on þa
dune þær se eadiga Petrus se apostol wæs. Ond he þær wunode mid him. Se haliga Andreas

þa úteode of þæm carcerne, ond he ongan gangan út þurh midde þa ceastre, ond he com to sumre stowe, ond he þær geseah swer standan, ond ofer þone swer ǽrne onlicnesse. On he gesæt be þam swere ánbidende hwæt him gelimpan scolde. Ða únrihte men þa eodon þæt
45 hie þa men útgelæddon, ond hie to mete gedón. Ond hie gemetton þæs carcernes duru opene, ond þa seofon hyrdas deade licgan. Mid þy þe hie þæt gesawon hie eft hwirfdon to hiora ealdormannum, ond hie cwædon, 'Þín carcern open we gemetton, ond ingangende nænig [MS mænige] we þær gemetton.' Mid þi þe hie gehyrdon þara sacerda ealdormen, ond hie cwædon him betweonan, 'Hwæt wile þis wesan? Wén is þæt hwilc wundor ineode on
50 þæt carcern ond þa hyrdas acwælde, ond somnunga [alysde] þy þær betynede wǽron.'
Ǽfter þiossum him æteowde deofol on cnihtes onlicnysse, ond him tó-cwæð, 'Gehyrað me, ond secað her sumne ælþeodigne man þæs nama is Andreas, ond acwellað hine. He þæt is se þa gebundenan of þissum carcerne útalædde, ond he is nú on þisse ceastre. Ge hine nú witon, efstað mine bearn ond acwellað hine.' Se haliga Andreas þa cwæð to þam
55 deofle, 'Ana þu heardeste stræl to æghwilcre únrihtnesse; þu þe simle fihtest wið manna cyn. Mín Drihten Hælend Crist þe gehnæde in helle.' Þæt deofol þe his þis gehyrde, he him to-cwæð, 'Þine stefne ic gehiere, ác ic ne wát hwær þu eart.' Se haliga Andreas him tó-cwæð, 'Forþon þe þu eart blínd þe ne gesihst ænigne óf Godes þam halgum.'
Þæt deofol þa cwæð to þam folce, 'Behealdað eow ond geseoð hine, forþon þe he þæt is
60 se þe wið me spræc.' Ða burhleode þa úrnon, ond hi betyndon þære ceastre gátu, ond hie sohton þæne halgan Andreas þæt hie hine genamon. Drihten Hælend hine þa æteowde þam haligan Andrea, ond him tó-cwæð, 'Andrea arís, ond gecýð him þæt hie ongieton mín mægen on þe wesan.' Se haliga Andreas þa arás on þæs folces gesihþe, ond he cwæð, 'Ic eom sé Andreas þe ge secaþ.' Þæt folc þa árn, ond hie hine genámon ond cwædon, 'Forþon
65 þu us þus dydest we hit þe forgyldað.' Ond hie þohton hu hie hine acwellan meahton. Þa wæs se deofol ingangende, ond cwæð to þam folce, 'Gif eow swá licige uton sendon ráp on his swyran, ond hine teon þurh þisse ceastre lanan, ond þis uton we don oþþæt he swelte. Ond mid þi þe he dead sie, uton we dælan his lichaman urum burhleodum.' Ond þa eall þæt folc þæt gehierde, hit him licode, ond hraðe hie sendon ráp on his sweoran, ond hie
70 hine tugon geond þære ceastre lanan. Mid þi þe se eadiga Andreas wæs togen his lichama wæs gemengeð mid þære eorðan, swa þæt blod fleow ofer eorðan swá wæter. Ða æfen geworden wæs, hi hine sendon on þæt carcern, ond hie gebunden his handa behindan, ond hie hine forleton; ond eall his lichama [wæs] gelysed. Swilce oþre dæge þæt ilce hie dydon. Se haliga Andreas þa weóp, ond hé cwæð, 'Min Drihten Hælend Crist, cum ond geseoh
75 þæt hie me doð þinum þeowe; ond eall íc hit aræfnie for þínum gebode, þe þu me sealdest, ond þu cwæde, 'Ne dó æfter hiora úngeleafulnesse.' Beheald, Drihten, ond geseoh hu hie me doð.' Mid þi he þus cwæð, þæt deofol cwæð tó þam folce, 'Swingað hine on his muð, þæt he þus ne sprece.' Ða geworden wæs þæt hie hine eft betyndon on þam carcerne.
Ðæt deofol þa genam mid him oþre seofon deoflo, þa þe [se] haliga Andreas þanon
80 afliemde, ond ingangende on þæt carcern hie gestodon on gesihþe þæs eadigan Andreas, ond hine bismriende mid myclere bismre, ond hie cwædon, 'Hwæt is þu her gemetest? Hwilc gefreolseð þe nú of úrum gewealde? Hwær is þin gilp ond þin hiht?' Þæt deofol þa cwæð to þam oðrum deoflum, 'Mine bearn, acwellað hine, forþon he us gescende ond ure weorc.' Þa deofla þe blæstan hie ofer þone halgan Andreas, ond hie gesawon Cristes
85 ródetácen on his onsiene, hi ne dorston hine genealæcan, ac hraðe hie on weg flugon. Þæt deofol him tocwæð, 'Mine bearn, for hwon ne acwealdon ge hine?' Hie him andswarodon ond hie cwædon, 'We ne mihton, forþon þe Cristes ródetácn [MS ródetánc] on his onsiene we gesawon, ond we us ondredon. We witon forþon þe ǽr he on þæs earfoðnesse com he úre wæs wealdend. Gif þu mæge, acwel hine; we þe on þissum ne hersumiað, þy læs wén sie
90 þæt hine God gefreolsige ond us sende on wyrsan tintrego.' Se haliga Andreas him to-

cwæð, 'Þeah þe ge me acwellan, ne dó ic eowerne willan, ac ic dó willan mínes Drihtnes
Hælendes Cristes.' Ond þus hi geherdon ond on weg flugon.

On mergen þa geworden wæs eft hie tugon þone halgan Andreas, ond he cigde mid
mycle wópe to Drihtne, ond cwæð, 'Mín Drihten Hælend Crist, me genihtsumiað þas
95   tintrega, forþon ic eom geteorod. Min Drihten Hælend Crist, áne tid on róde þu þrowodest
ond þu cwæde, 'Fæder, for hwon forléte þu mé?' Nú III dagas syndon syððan ic wæs
getogen þurh þisse ceastre lanum. Þu wast, Drihten, þa menniscan tyddernysse, hát onfón
minne gast. Hwær syndon þine wórd, Drihten, on þam þu us gestrangodest, ond þu cwæde,
'Gif ge me gehyrað ond ge me beoð flygende, ne án loc of eowrum heafde forwyrð?'
100 Beheald, Drihten, ond geseoh for[þi] þinum lichaman ond loccas mines heafdes mid þisse
eorðan synd gemengde. Áne III dagas syndon syððan ic wæs getogan to þæm wyrstan
tintregum, ond þu me ne æteowdest. Mín Drihten Hælend Crist, gestranga mine heortan.'

Ðus gebiddende þam halgan Andrea Drihtnes stefn wæs geworden on Ebreisc,
cweþende, 'Mín Andreas, heofon ond eorðe mæg gewítan; min word næfre ne gewítaþ.
105 Beheald æfter þe ond geseoh þinne lichaman ond loccas þines heafdes, hwæt hie syndon
gewordene.' Se haliga Andreas þa lociende he geseah geblowen treow wæstmberende; ond
he cwæð, 'Nú ic wat, Drihten, forþon þæt þu ne forlet mé.' On æfenne þa geworden hie
hine betyndon on þam carcerne, ond hio cwædon him betwynum, 'Forþon þe þisse nihte he
swelt.' Him æteowde Drihten Hælend Crist on þæm carcerne, ond he aþenede his hand ond
110 genam, ond he cwæð, 'Andreas, arís.' Mid þi þe he þæt gehyrde hraþe he þa arás gesúnd,
ond he hine gebæd, ond he cwæð, 'Þancas ic þe dó, mín Drihten Hælend Crist.' Se haliga
Andreas þa lociende he geseah on middum þæm carcerne swer standan, ond ofer þone swer
stænenne anlicnesse. Ond he aþenede his handa ond hiere to-cwæð, 'Ondræd þe Drihten
ond his ródetácn [MS ródetánc], beforan þæm forhtigað heofon ond eorþe. Nú þonne,
115 anlicnes, dó þæt ic bidde on naman mines Drihtnes Hælendes Cristes; sænd mycel wæter
þurh þinne muþ, swá þæt sien gewemmede ealle þa on þisse ceastre syndon.'

Mid þi [þe] he þus cwæð, se eadiga Andreas, hraþe sio stænene [MS stefne] onlicnes
sendde [→ sende] mycel wæter þurh hiora muþ swa sealt, ond hie æt manna lichaman, ond
hit acwealde heora bearn ond hyra nytenu. Ond hie ealle woldon fleon of þære ceastre. Se
120 haliga Andreas þa cwæð, 'Mín Drihten Hælend Crist, ne forlæt me, ac send me þinne engel
of heofonum on fyrenum wolcne, þæt þa embgange ealle þas ceastre þæt ne magen
geneosian for þæm fyre.' Ond þus cweþende, fyren wolc astah of heofonum, ond hit
ymbsealde ealle þa ceastre. Mid þy þæt ongeat se eadiga Andreas, he bletsode Drihten. Þæt
wæter weox oþ mannes swuran, ond swiþe hit æt hyra líchaman. Ond hie ealle cigdon ond
125 cwædon, 'Wá ús, forþon þe þas ealle úp cóman for þissum ælþeodigum, þe we on þissum
carcerne betýned hæbbað. Hwæt beo we dónde?' Sume hie cwædon, 'Gif eow swa líce
þuhte, utan gangan on þissum carcerne ond hine út forlætan, þy læs wén sie þæt we yfele
forweorþon; ond uton we ealle cigean ond cweþen, forþon þe we geleofað on Drihten
þyses ælþeodigan mannes; þonne afyrseþ he þas earfoðnesse fram ús.'
130 Mid þi se eadiga Andreas ongeat þæt hie to Drihtene wæron gehwerfede, he cwæð to
þære stænenan ánlicnesse, 'Ara nú þurh mægen úres Drihtenes, ond ma wæter of þinum
muþe þu ne sénd.' Ond þa gecweden þæt wæter oflán, ond ma of heora muþe hit ne eode.
Se haliga Andreas þa úteode of þam carcerne, ond þæt selfe wæter þegnunge gearwode
beforan his fotum. Ond þa þær to lafe wæron, ond he comon tó þæs carcernes duru, ond hie
135 cwædon, 'Gemiltsa us God, ond ne dó us swá swá we dydon on þisne ælþeodigan.' Se
haliga Andreas þa gebæd on þæs folces gesihþe, ond seo eorþe hie ontynde ond hio
forswealh þæt wæter mid þam mannum.

Þa weras þa þæt gesawon hie him swiþe ondrædon, ond hie cwædon, 'Wá us, forþon þe
þes deað fram Gode is, ond he us wile acwellan for þissum earfoðnessum þe we þissum

140   mannan dydon. Soðlice fram Gode he is send, ond he is Godes þeowa.' Se halga Andreas
him to-cwæð, 'Mine bearn, ne ondrædaþ ge eow forþon þe þas þe on þis wætere syndon eft
hie libbað. Ac þis is forþon þus geworden þæt ge geleofon minum Drihtne Hælendum
Criste.' Se haliga Andreas þa gebæd to Drihtne ond cwæð, 'Mín Drihten Hælend Crist,
send þinne þone Halgan Gast, þæt áwecce ealle þa þe on þisse wǽtere syndon, þæt hie
145   geliefon on þinne naman.' Drihten þa het ealle arisan þe on þam wǽtere wǽron. Ond æfter
þissum se haliga Andreas het cyrican getimbrian on þære stowe þær se swer stod. Ond he
him sealde bebodu Drihtnes Hælendes [MS Hælendest] Cristes, 'Ond lufiað hine forþon
mycel is his mægen.' Ond ænne of heora aldormannum to bisceope he him gesette, ond he
hi gefullode ond cwæð, 'Nu þonne ic eom gearo þæt ic gange to minum discipulum.' Hie
150   ealle hine bædon ond hie cwædon, 'Médmycel fæc nu gyt wuna mid ús, þæt þu us gedefra
gedó, forþon þe we niwe syndon to þissum geleafan gedón.' Se halga Andreas hie þa nolde
gehieran, ác he hie grette ond hie swá forlet.
    Him fylgede mycel manigo þæs wepende ond hrymende. Ond þa ascán leoht ofer
hieora heafod, mid þi se halga Andreas þanon wæs farende [ond] him ætiwde Drihten
155   Hælend Crist on þam wege on ánsine fægeres cildes, ond him to-cwæð, 'Andreas, for hwan
gæst þu swá buton wæstme þines gewinnes, ond þu forlete þa þe þe bǽdon, ond þu nære
miltsiend ofer heora cild þa þe wǽron fyliende ond wepende? Þara círm ond wóp to me
astah on heofonas. Nu þonne hwyrf eft on þa ceastre ond beo þær seofon dagas, oþþæt þu
gestrangie heora mod on minne geleáfan. Gang þonne to þǽre ceastre mid þinum
160   discipulum, ond þa þe [MS ge] on minne geleafan geleofan.' Mid þi he þis cwæð, Drihten
Hælend Crist, he astah on heofonas. Se eadiga Andreas þa wæs eft hwyrfende on
Marmadonia ceastre, ond he cwæð, 'Ic þe bletsige mín Drihten Hælend Crist, þu þe
gehwyrfest ealle saula, forþón þu me ne forlete útgangan mid minre hatheortan of þisse
ceastre.' Hio wæron gefeonde mycle gefean, ond he þær wunode mid him seofon dagas,
165   lǽrende ond strangende hira heortan on geleafan ures Drihtnes Hælendes Cristes.
    Mid þí þe þa wǽron gefyllede seofon dagas swá swa him Drihten bebead, he ferde of
[Mar]madonia ceastre efstende to his discipulum. Ond ealle þæt folc hine lædde mid
gefean ond hie cwædon, 'An is Drihten God, se is Hælend Crist, ond se Halga Gast, þam is
wuldor ond geweald on þære Halgan Þrynnysse þurh ealra worulda woruld soðlice a butan
170   ende.'

APPENDIX

NOUNS

Strong ('Masculine')

	Singular	Plural
Nom.	se cyning	þā cyningas
Acc.	ðone cyning	þā cyningas
Gen.	ðæs cyninges	þāra cyninga
Dat.	ðǣm cyninge	þǣm cyningum

Weak ('Masculine')

	Singular	Plural
Nom.	se guma	þā guman
Acc.	ðone guman	þā guman
Gen.	ðæs guman	þāra gumena
Dat.	ðǣm guman	þǣm gumum

Strong ('Feminine')

	Singular	Plural
Nom.	sēo lufu	þā lofa, –e
Acc.	þā lufe	þā lofa, –e
Gen.	þǣre lufe	þāra lufa, –ena
Dat.	þǣre lufe	þǣm lufum

Weak ('Feminine')

	Singular	*Plural*
Nom.	sēo heorte	þā heortan
Acc.	þā heortan	þā heortan
Gen.	þǣre heortan	þāra heortena
Dat.	þǣre heortan	þǣm heortum

Strong ('Neuter')

	Singular	*Plural*
Nom.	þæt weorc / hof	þā weorc / hofu
Acc.	þæt weorc / hof	þā weorc / hofu
Gen.	þæs weorces / hofes	þāra weorca / hofa
Dat.	þǣm weorce / hofe	þǣm weorcum / hofum

Weak ('Neuter')

	Singular	*Plural*
Nom.	þæt ēage	þā ēagan
Acc.	þæt ēage	þā ēagan
Gen.	þæs ēagan	þāra ēagena
Dat.	þǣm ēagan	þǣm ēagum

INDEFINITE ADJECTIVES ('STRONG')

Singular

	Masculine	*Feminine*	*Neuter*
Nom.	gōd /dol	gōd / dolu	gōd / dol
Acc.	gōdne / dolne	gōde / dole	gōd / dol
Gen.	gōdes / doles	gōdre / dolre	gōdes / doles
Dat.	gōdum / dolum	gōdre / dolre	gōdum / dolum

Plural

	Masculine	Feminine	Neuter
Nom.	gōde /dole	gōde,-a / dole,-a	gōd(e) / dolu
Acc.	gōde / dole	gōde,-a / dole, -a	gōd(e) / dolu
Gen.	gōdra / dolra	gōdra / dolra	gōdra / dolra
Dat.	gōdum / dolum	gōdum / dolum	gōdum / dolum

DEFINITE ADJECTIVES ('WEAK')

Singular

	Masculine	Feminine	Neuter
Nom.	gōda /dola	gōde / dole	gōde / dole
Acc.	gōdan / dolan	gōdan / dolan	gōde / dole
Gen.	gōdan / dolan	gōdan / dolan	gōdan / dolan
Dat.	gōdan / dolan	gōdan / dolan	gōdan / dolan

Plural

	Masculine	Feminine	Neuter
Nom.	gōdan /dolan	gōdan / dolan	gōdan / dolan
Acc.	gōdan / dolan	gōdan / dolan	gōdan / dolan
Gen.	gōdra / dolra -ena -ena	gōdra / dolra -ena -ena	gōdra / dolra -ena -ena
Dat.	gōdum / dolum	gōdum / dolum	gōdum / dolum

POSSESSIVE ADJECTIVES

Genitive-case pronouns function as designators; they can be used anywhere that can also be replaced by a determinatior (*se*, *sēo*, *þæt*) or specifier (*þes*, *þēos*, *þis*). In this function, genitive-case pronoun forms for 'Speaker' and 'Addressee' (1st and 2nd person) *mīn*, *ūre*, *incer*, etc. are declined as indefinite ('strong') adjectives only. The remaining 'Other' possessive pronoun forms (*his* & *hiere*) do not take adjective inflections.

COMPARISON OF ADJECTIVES

As well as occurring with permanent inflections to single case, number and gender, adjective stems may also occur with fixed forms for comparison. These comparative morphemes should be classed as postbase forms; they precede the syntax-signalling inflections that occur directly after the adjective root to create the following sequence:

Adjective Root   +   Postbase of Degree   +   Inflection

The comparative degree is signified usually by /-r-/ and the superlative degree by /-ost-/ or /-est-/. The positive degree is not designated by any explicit form; it can be signified as -ø- after the stem (see *OEG*, p. 657, *OES*, pp. 181-8).

Noncompared	Comparative	Superlative
root -ø- I	root -r- I	root -Vst- I
ǣðel(e)-ø-e, etc.	ǣðel-r-a, etc.	ǣðel-est-an, etc.

NUMERALS

The cardinal numerals are used as adjectives agreeing with a noun in gender, number and case, e.g. *On ānum dæġe bēoð fēower and twentiġ tīda.* 'In one day there are twenty-four hours.' They are also used as nouns, followed by the partitive genitive, e.g. *to anre þara burga* 'to one of the cities' and *twentig cyninga* 'twenty kings'. The numeral *an* 'one', for example, is declined like a strong adjective, can be only singular, but has masculine, neuter and feminine genders. It is the source of the indefinite article 'a' and 'an' in ME: 'a house' literally means 'one house'.

Ordinal numbers (*first, second, third,* etc.) are always adjectives, and all of them are declined weak, e.g. *Þone forman dæġ hīe hēton Sunnandæġ.* 'They called the first day Sunday.' An exception is *ōðer* 'second', which is always declined strong, e.g. *Þone ōðerne dæġ hīe hēton Mōnandæġ.* 'They called the second day Monday.' Ordinal numerals use the suffix *-ta* or *–ða* (e.g. *siexta* 'sixth' / *niogða* 'ninth')

The two variants for the word 'first' actually mean different attributes: *forma* is translated as 'forward' and *fyresta* is 'the farthest' or 'the first'. Again double variants for the second nominal mean respectively 'the other' and 'the following'. In OE ordinal numerals were used with the demonstrative pronoun *þā* before them. This is where the definite article as in 'the first', 'the second' originates.

PRONOUNS

First and Second Personal

	Singular	*Dual*	*Plural*
Nom.	iċ	wit	wē
Acc.	mē, meċ	unc	ūs
Gen.	mīn	uncer	ūre
Dat.	mē	unc	ūs

	Singular	*Dual*	*Plural*
Nom.	þū	ġit	ġe
Acc.	þē, þeċ	inc	ēow / ēowiċ
Gen.	þīn	incer	ēower
Dat.	þē	inc	ēow

Third Personal

Singular				*Plural*
	m.	*f.*	*nt.*	*All genders*
Nom.	hē	hēo, hīo	hit	hīe, hī
Acc.	hine	hīe, hī	hit	hīe, hī
Gen.	his	hire	his	hira, hiera
				heora, hiora
Dat.	him	hire	him	him, heom

se 'the, that'

	Singular			Plural
	m.	*f.*	*nt.*	*All genders*
Nom.	se	sēo, sīo	þæt	þā
Acc.	þone	þā	þæt	þā
Gen.	þæs	þǣre	þæs	þāra, þǣra
Dat.	þǣm, þām	þǣre	þǣm, þām	þǣm, þām
Inst.	þȳ, þon	—	þȳ, þon	—

þes   'this'

	Singular			Plural
	m.	*f.*	*nt.*	*All genders*
Nom.	þes	þēos	þis	þās
Acc.	þisne	þās	þis	þās
Gen.	þisses	þisse, þisre	þisses	þissa, þisra
Dat.	þissum	þisse, þisra	þissum	þissum
Inst.	þȳs	—	þȳs	—

	m. and f.	*nt.*
Nom.	hwā	hwæt
Acc.	hwone	hwæt
Gen.	hwæs	hwæs
Dat.	hwǣm, hwām	hwǣm, hwām
Inst.	hwȳ	hwȳ, hwon

Indefinite Pronominals

Pronominals relate to or function similar to pronouns. Resembling a pronoun, as by specifying a person, place or thing, while functioning primarily as another part of speech (e.g. *his* in '*his* choice') is a pronominal adjective). These forms are not inflected for case or number or gender but do have syntactic qualities like indefinite pronominals. The long-standing tradition of classifying these forms as adverbs had its genesis in the grammar of the classics (especially Latin). Their characteristics within English, however, associate them with the prenominals. While none of these forms are inflected, the forms do make up prenominals of another kind, as is apparent in the following sentences: *On ðǣre byriġ þǣr se cyning ofslæġen læġ.* 'In that fortress where the king lay slain.' and *Iċ næbbe hwyder iċ mīne wæstmas gadriġe.* 'I do not have anywhere where I may store my crops.' Unlike MnE cognate forms, the 'þ–' forms are used correlatively in OE, e.g. *Þǣr ēower goldhord is, þǣr byð ēower heorte.* 'Where your treasure is, there is your heart.' (see *OES*, pp. 348–54, 363-77).

HW—	Personal	Non-personal
Nom.	hwā 'who'	hwæt 'what
Acc.	hwone	hwæt
Gen.	hwæs	hwæs
Dat.	hwǣm, hwām	hwǣm, hwām
Inst.	hwȳ	hwȳ, hwon

Some Related Forms

hēr	'here
hider	'hither'
heonan	'hence'
[nū	'now']

þā	'then'
þǣr	'there'
þider	'thither'
þonan	'thence'
þonon	'thence'
þonne	'then'
hū	'how'
hwȳ	'why'

hwǣr	'where'
hwider	'whither'
hwonan	'whence'
hwanne	'when'

Designators

Two sets of pronominals have functions comparable to those of MnE forms 'that / those' and 'this / these'. One set have the citation forms 'se, sēo & þæt' and the other 'þes, þēos & þis'. Like third person pronouns, they are inflected for grammatical gender, number and case.

Singular

	m.		*f.*		*nt.*	
Nom.	se	þes	sēo	þēos	þæt	þis
Acc.	þone	þisne	þā	þās	þæt	þis
Gen.	þæs	þisse	þǣre	þisse, þisre	þæs	þisses
Dat.	þǣm	þissum	þǣre	þisse	þǣm	þissum
Inst.	þ̄y	þ̄ys			þ̄y	þ̄ys

Plural (*All genders*)

Nom.	þā	þās
Acc.	þā	þās
Gen.	þāra , þǣra	þissa, þisra
Dat.	þǣm, þām	þissum

Other Indefinite Pronominals: hwylċ 'which', hwæðer 'which of two', hūlīċ 'of what sort'. They have grammatical forms similar to those of 'strong' adjectives and are inflected for number, gender and case. Their inflectional endings are similar to the determinators and specifiers.

Singular

Nom.	hwilċ	hwilċ	hwilċ
Acc.	hwilċne	hwilċe	hwilċ
Gen.	hwilċes	hwilċere	hwilċes
Dat.	hwilcum	hwilċere	hwilcum

Plural

Nom.	hwilċe	hwilċe, -a	hwilċ
Acc.	hwilċe	hwilċe, -a	hwilċ
Gen.	hwilcra	hwilcra	hwilcra
Dat.	hwilcum	hwilcum	hwilcum

Conjunctions

ac	'but'
ǣr	'before'
ah	'but'
and	'and'
būtan, būton	'except that, but' + *ind.*
būtan, būton	'unless, if not, but' + *subj.*
for	'because'
for þǣm	'because'
for þǣm þe	'because'
forþon, forðon	'because'
ġe	'and'
ġe... ġe	'both... and'
ġif	'if, whether' (introducing a dependant clause)
ġif	'if' (introducing conditional clauses)
hwonne	'when, until' (temporal)
nefne, nemne,	(Anglian of *būtan, būton*)
nū	'now that'
nymþe	(Anglian of *būtan, būton*)
ond	'and'
oð	'until' (denoting temporal and/or local limit)
sam ... sam	'whether ... or' (in concessive clauses)
siþþan, syþþan	(i) *ex quo* 'since'
	(ii) *postquam* 'after'
	(iii) 'when, as soon as'
swā	'so'
swā þæt	'so that' (introducing result clauses)
swelīċe, swilċe, swylċe	(i) 'such as'
	(ii) 'because'
	(iii) 'as if' (with subjunctive or without verb)
þā	(i) 'when' (used only with the past indicative of a single completed act in the past)
þā ... furþum	'as soon as'
þā ... ǣrest	'as soon as'
þā hwīle þe	'as long as'
þanon	'whence'
þǣr	(i) 'where' (alone, doubled *þǣr þǣr*, or correlative *þǣr ... þǣr*)
	(ii) 'whither, to the place where'
	(iii) 'wherever'
	(iv) 'if' (with past subjunctive)
	(v) 'if only' (with past subjunctive)
þæs	(i) of time 'from that, after'
	(ii) of extent or comparison 'to the extent, so'
þæs (þe)	'when, after, since' (time)
	'as' (comparison)
þæs ... þæt	'so that'

149

þe, þȳ	'who, which' (rel. pron.)
	'when' (time)
	'as' (comparative)
þeah ... þe	'whether ... or'
þeah, þēh (þe)	'however, yet'
	'although'
þenden	'meanwhile'
	'as long as, while' (time)
þider	'thither, whither' (place)
þon ma þe	'more than'
þonne	'then, when' (time)
	'whenever' (time)
	'than, than that' (comparison)
þȳ	'because'
þȳ þe	'because'
þȳ lǣs (þe)	'lest' (with subj.)

Prepositions

æfter	with *acc. / dat.*	'after, along, according to'
ǣr	with *acc. / dat.*	'before'
æt	with *acc.*	'as far as, onto, until'
æt	with *dat.*	'at, from, by, on'
be	with *acc. / dat.*	'by, along, alongside, about'
beforan	with *acc. / dat.*	'before, in front of'
betweox	with *acc. / dat.*	'among, between'
binnan	with *acc. / dat.*	'within, into'
bufan	with *acc. / dat.*	'above, upon'
būtan, būton	with *acc. / dat.*	'except, outside, without'
ēac	with *dat.*	'besides, in addition to'
for, fore	with *acc. / dat.*	'for'
fram, from	with *dat.*	'from, by (of agent)'
ġeond	with *acc. / dat.*	'throughout'
in	with *acc. / dat.*	'in, into'
inne	with *acc. / dat.*	'in, within' (occasionally with *gen.*)
into	with *acc.*	'into'
mid	with *acc. / dat.*	'among, with, by means of'
of	with *dat.*	'from, of'
ofer	with *acc. / dat.*	'above, over, on'
on, an	with *acc. / dat.*	'in, into, on, at'
ongēan	with *acc. / dat.*	'against, towards'
oþ, oð	with *acc. / dat.*	'up to, until'
tō	with *acc.*	'towards'
tō	with *gen.*	'at, for, to such an extent, so'
tō	with *dat.*	'as'*
tōġēanes	with *dat.*	'against, towards'

þurh	with *acc. / dat.*	'through, throughout, by means of'
under	with *acc. / dat.*	'under, beneath'
wiþ	with *acc. / dat.*	'towards, opposite, against, in exchange for'
ymb(e)	with *acc. / dat.*	'after, about, concerning'

to frofre ('as a consolation')

Interjections

ēalā	'alas!, O!'
efne	'behold, indeed, truly!'
huru	'indeed, surely, at least'
hwæt	'ah! lo!'
men þa leofstan	'dearly beloved!'
wā	'woe!'

Common Adverbs

ā	'always'	lǣs	'less'
ābuton	'about, around'	nē	'not'
ǣfre	'ever'	neah, near	'near'
ēac	'also'	þǣr	'there'
fōran	'before'	þǣr æfter	'thereafter'
ġīt	'yet, still'	ymb	'around'
hu	'how'		

Verbs ('Weak')

'Weak' verbs (also called 'consonantal' verbs) are typified by past tense forms with a suffix morpheme containing a dental consonant, either [d] or [t]; they follow the stem and precede person-number inflection. There are three classes of weak verbs. Class I is a relative large group with several subclasses and Class 2 is also a relatively large with a distinctive –od- form for the past-tense morpheme. Class 3 has only four verbs with at least three of them being very common in occurrence.

Weak verbs have three principal past forms:

Class	Infinitive	Past (1 sg.)	Past Participle
1	deman 'to judge'	demde	demed
2	lufian 'to love'	lufode	lufod
3	habban 'to have'	hæfde	hæfd

Verbs ('Strong')

'Strong' verbs (also called 'vocalic' verbs) are typified by past and non-past forms that are marked by changing the stem-vowel (and not by suffixed past-tense inflections). There are seven classes of strong verbs distinguished by differences in the base form (the infinitive stem) and the ablaut series of the principal parts; in verbs, ablaut or vowel-gradation, is essentially a systematic variation of the vocalic elements in forms of the same root in relation to tense. Because past-tense forms of most classes have two different stem-vowels, four principal parts are conventionally cited for strong verbs.

Class Participle	Infinitive	Past (1 sg.)	Past Plural	Past
I	stīgan 'to ascend'	stāg, stāh	stigon	stigen
II	flēogan 'to fly'	flēag, flēah	flugon	flogen
	brucan 'to bend'	brēac	brucon	brocen
III	bindan 'to bind'	band	bundon	bunden
	beorgan 'to protect'	bearh	burgon	borgen
	sweltan 'to die'	swealt	swulton	swolten
IV	beran 'to bear'	bær	bǣron	boren
V	wrecan 'to avenge'	wræc	wrǣcon	wrecen
VI	faran 'to go'	fōr	fōron	faren
VII	hātan 'to command'	hēt	hēton	hāten

Verbs ('Anomalous')

OE has a small number of verbs whose inflectional forms do not conform to the pattern of inflections for any other verbs. They are frequently used in OE and are the ancestral forms of 'be', 'do', 'go' and 'will'. The verb bēon / wesan 'to be' has a number of functions. It is a copula (e.g. *Iċ hit eom* 'It is I'); it forms phrases using the present participle (e.g. *Hī ðus sprecende wǣron* 'They were speaking thus'); and it forms phrases using the passive participle (e.g. *Hyt is gecwǣden...* 'It is said...').

The verb dōn 'to do' in OE had developed none of the auxiliary senses that it now has in contemporary English usage. It had no negative marker 'He did not' nor formed yes/no questions 'Did he understand?' nor signified emphatic stress 'He did understand'.

The verb willan 'to will / wish' has a range of meanings. Along with the preterite-present verbs it also was evolving as an auxiliary, having the infinitive of another verb as its complement. It was not yet a 'future auxiliary', although that function was developing during the OE period.

Bēon / Wesan 'to be, exist, become'

Indicative			Subjunctive	
		Non-past		
eom	syndon		sīe	sīen
eart	synd		sī	sīn
is	sint		sȳ	sy̅n
bēo	bēoþ		bēo	bēon
bist	bēoþ		bēo	bēon
bið	bēoþ		bēo	bēon
		Past		
wæs				
wǣre	wǣron		wǣre	wǣren
wæs				

bēon; wesan	(Infinitive)
	(Inflected infinitive)
bēonde; wesende (Present participle)	
	(Passive participle)
wes	(Imperative singular)
bēoþ; wesaþ	(Imperative plural)

Dōn 'to do, make, cause'

Indicative			Subjunctive	
		Non-past		
dō				
dēst	dōþ		dō	dōn
dēþ				
		Past		
dyde				
dydest	dydon		dyde	dyden
dyde				

dōn	(Infinitive)
tō dōnne	(Inflected infinitive)
dōnde	(Present participle)
dōn	(Passive participle)
dō	(Imperative singular)
dōþ	(Imperative plural)

Gān 'to go, come, walk, move, happen'

Indicative		Subjunctive	
	Non-past		
gā			
gǣst	gāþ	gā	gān
gǣþ			

	Past		
ēode			
ēodest	ēodon	ēode	ēoden
ēode			

gān	(Infinitive)
tō gānne	(Inflected infinitive)
	(Present participle)
gān	(Passive participle)
gā	(Imperative singular)
gāþ	(Imperative plural)

Willan 'to will, wish, desire, be willing'

Indicative		Subjunctive	
	Non-past		
wil(l)e			
wilt	willaþ	wille	willen
wil(l)			

	Past		
wolde			
woldest	woldon	wolde	wolden
wolde			

willan	(Infinitive)
	(Inflected infinitive)
willende	(Present participle)
	(Passive participle)
	(Imperative singular)
nyllað*	(Imperative plural)

[*negative]

Verbs ('Preterite-Present)

Like anomalous verbs and Class 3 weak verbs, several of these preterite-present verbs occur frequently. Their present tense forms resemble the preterite forms of string verbs classes from which, in fact, they originated; hence the name 'preterite-present'. The past tense forms resemble those of weak verbs. The selection of forms for the principal parts of these verbs, consequently, differs from that for either string or weak verbs. These verbs also customarily are labelled with the strong verb class from which they originally derived. (The asterisk signifies that the infinitive is not recorded.)

(Non-Past) Infinitive	Non-past 1st Pers. Sg.	Non-past Plural	Past 1st Per. Sg
I. witan ('to know')	wāt	witon	wisse, wiste
I. āgan ('to possess')	āh	āgon	āhte
II. dugan ('to avail')	dēag	dugon	dohte
III. annan ('to grant')	ann	unnon	ūðe
III. cunnan ('to know')	cann	cunnon	cūðe
III. durran* ('to dare')	dearr	durron	dorste
III. þurfan ('to need')	þearf	þurfon	þorfte
IV. sculan* ('to be obligated')	sceal	sculon	scolde
IV. ġemunan ('to remember')	ġeman	ġemummon	ġemunde
VI. mōtan* ('to be permitted')	mōt	mōtan	mōste
? magan ('to be able')	mæġ	magon	meahte

These verbs belong together because of their morphological similarities. In their grammatical and syntactical functions, though, they are not alike. Some of them co-occur with an infinitive, resembling the modal auxiliary verbs of MnE, such as 'can', 'may', 'ought', 'must', 'dare' (e.g. *Ne mihte hē þǣr nænne ġeseon þe hē gecnawān cūþe.* 'He might not see anyone there whom he could recognize.'). Even so, some of the preterite-present verbs are not ancestral forms of modern modal auxiliaries: *ġemunan, unnan, witan* & *dugan*. Some of these actually function as independent verbs, which is clearest when the verb has no direct object (e.g. *Ġif hē þæt eal ġemunon* 'If he remembers all that').

With the verb *sculan* – as well as the weak verb *willan* – the resemblance to their MnE descendent forms is only partial, in that the use of these with a following infinitive form did not constitute a future tense expression, even though futurity of the action expressed by the infinitive was implicit in the meaning of the phrase. This is the construction in which the phrasal future tense in English has its beginning, but only its very beginning in OE.

Variations of Spelling

a = æ, ea	f = w	ps = sp
æ = a, æg, e, ea	fn = mn	pt = ft
æi, æig = æg	g = h, w, x	qu = cw
æo = ea	ge = g	sc = s
b = f	gg = cg	sce = sc
c = g, h	gi = g	sci = sc
ce = c	gu = geo	sþ = st
ch = c, h	h = c, g	t = þ
ci = c	hs = sc, x	th = þ

cs = sc, x
ct = ht
d = þ
dd = þd
ds = ts
ð = þ
e = æ, ea, eg, eo, ie, y
ea = æ, ea, eg, eo, gea, i
ei = e, eg
eo = e, ea, geo, i, ie, oe (= e)
eu = eo, eow
ew = eow

i = eo, g, ie, ig, ige, y
ia = eo
ig = i
io = eo
iu = eo, geo
iw – eow
k = c
m = mn, n
nc = c(e)n, ng
ng = g(e)n
o = a, og
oe = e, æ

u = f, ug, v, w
uu = ū, w
v = f
weo = wo, wu
wi = wu
wo = weo
wu = w, weo, wo, wy
wy = weo, wi
x = cs, hs, sc
y = e, i, ie, yg

Pronunciation and Phonetic Notation

The phonetic symbols for vowels and consonants used in the Concordance are based on those of the International Phonetic Alphabet. The table that follows brings all these symbols together and lists them in sequence. Phonetic notation is enclosed in square brackets; phonemic notation is denoted by the numbers 1, 2, 3, 4 & 5 which are referenced at the end of the tables.

Vowels

Phonetic Symbol	Phonetic Notation	OE Spelling	Editorial System
i:	[bi:]	i	ī
i	[bɪt]	i	i
ü:	(1)	y	ȳ
ü	(2)	y	y
e:	[be:]	e	ē
ɛ	[bɛt]	e	e
æ:	(3)	æ	ǣ
æ	[bæt]	æ	æ
α	[bɑt]	a	a
ɔ	[bɔt]	a	a
α:	[bɑ:]	a	ā
ɒ	[hɒt]	o	o
o:	[no:]	o	ō
u	[luk]	u	u
u:	[nu: nju:]	u	ū

(1) German **kühn**, **grün**
(2) German **müssenn**, French **reçu**
(3) The [æ] sound lengthened

156

Consonants

Phonetic Symbol	Phonetic Notation	OE Spelling	Editorial System
p	[pɪp]	p	p
b	[bɪb]	b	b
t	[tot]	t	t
d	[dɪd]	d	d
k	[kɪk]	c, k	c, k
g	[gɪg]	g	g
m	[mem]	m	m
n	[nun]	n	n
ŋ	[sɪŋ]	n	n
l	[lɑl]	l	l
r	[ror]	r	r
w	[wik]	p, u, uu	w
h	[hit]	h	h
s	[sis]	s	s
z	[zonz]	s	s
f	[fɪt]	f	f
v	[vælv]	f, u	f
θ	[θm̩l]	þ, ð	þ, ð
ð	[brið]	þ, ð	þ, ð
x	(4)	h	h
ɣ	(5)	g	g
j	[jɛt]	g	ġ
tʃ or č	[č]	c	ċ
dʒ or ĵ	[ʒĵ]	cg, g	cg, ĝ
ʃ or š	[šu:]	sc	sc

(4) German **machen**
(5) North German **sagen**

BIBLIOGRAPHY

Alexander, J. J. G. *Insular manuscripts, 6th to the 9th Century* (London, 1978).

Barney, S. A. *Word-Hoard: An Introduction to Old English Vocabulary* (New Haven, CT, and London, 1977).

Bassett, S., ed. *The Origins of Anglo-Saxon Kingdoms* (London, 1989).

Baudrillart, A., ed. *Dictionaire d'histore et de géographie ecclésiastiques* (Paris, 1912).

Blair, J. and **Sharpe**, R., eds. *Pastoral Care before the Parish* (Leicester, 1992).

Blaise, A. H., ed. *Dictionnaire Latin - Français des Auteurs Chrétiens: Addenda et corrigenda* (Turnhout, 1967).

Blatt, F. ed. *Dei lateinischen Bearbeitungen der Acta Andreae et Matthiae apud anthropophagos* (Zeitschrift für die neutestamentliche Wissenschaft, Beihft 12, 1930).

Bolton, W. F. *A History of Anglo-Latin Literature* i. *597–740* (Princeton, NJ, 1967).

Bosworth, J. and **Toller**, T. N. *An Anglo-Saxon Dictionary* (Oxford, 1898). *Supplement* by T.N. Toller (Oxford, 1921). *Enlarged Addenda and Corrigenda* by A. Campbell (Oxford, 1972).

Browne, R. E., **Fitzmyer**, J. A. and **Murphy**, R. E., eds. *The New Jerome Biblical Commentary* (London and New York, 1968; repr. 1996).

Bülbring, K. D. *Altenglisches Elementarbuch* (Heidelberg, 1902)

Butler, L. A. S. and **Morris**, R. K., eds. *The Anglo-Saxon Church: Papers on History, Architecture and Archaeology in Honour of Dr. H. M. Taylor* (London, 1986).

Carbol, F. and **LeClercq**, H. M. *Dictionaire d'archéologie chrétienne et de liturgie*, 15 vols. (Paris, 1907–53).

Campbell, A. *Old English Grammar* (Oxford, 1959; rept.1962 and 1977).

Campbell, J. *Essays in Anglo-Saxon History* (London, 1986).

Carpentier, D. P., ed. *Glossarium ad Scriptores Mediae et Infimae Latinitatis*, 4 vols (Paris, 1766).

Clark Hall, J. R. *A Concise Anglo-Saxon Dictionary*, 4th edn with a supplement by H. Meritt (Cambridge, 1960; repr. Toronto, 1984).

Douglas, D. C. *English Historical Documents* ii. *1042–1189*, 2nd edn (London, 1981).

Dumville, D. N. *Wessex and England from Alfred to Edgar* (Aldershot, 1992).

Dumville, D. N. *Britons and Anglo –Saxons in the Early Middle Ages* (Aldershot, 1993).

Ekwall, E. *The Concise Oxford Dictionary of English Place Names*, 4th edn (Oxford, 1960).

Ettmüller, L., ed. *Lexicon Anglo-saxonicum* (Leipzig, 1851)

Ferguson, E., ed. *Encyclopedia of Early Christianity*, 2 vols, 2nd edn (New York and London, 1998).

Frank, R. and **Cameron**, A. *A Plan for the Dictionary of Old English* (Toronto, 1973).

Godden, M. and **Lapidge**, M. *The Cambridge Companion to Old English Literature* (Cambridge, 1991).

Grein, C. W. M., ed. *Sprachschatz der Angelsächsischen Dichter* , (Kassel, 1912–1914).

Haddan, A. W. and **Stubbs**, W., eds. *Councils and Ecclesiastical Documents relating to Great Britain and Ireland*, 3 vols, (Oxford, 1869-78).

Hardy, A. K. *Die Sprache der Blickling Homilien* (Leipzig, 1899).

Haslam, J. *Anglo-Saxon Towns in Southern England (*(Oxford, 1981).

Healey, A. diP. et al. *Dictionary of Old English* (Toronto, 1986–).

Healey, A. diP., and **Venesky**, R. L. *A Microfiche Concordance to Old English: The High Frequency Words* (Toronto, 1980).

Hecht, H. *Bishof Wæferths von Worcester Übersetzung der Dialoge Gregors des Grossen* (Hamburg, 1907).

Jespersen, O. *Growth and Structure of the English Language*, 10th edn. (Oxford, 1983).

Jordan, R. *Eigentümlichkeiten des Anglischen Wortschatzes* (Heidelberg, 1906).

Kelly, R. J., ed. & trans. *The Blickling Homilies: Edition and Translation* (London and New York, 2003).

Ker, N. R., *Catalogue of Manuscripts containing Anglo-Saxon* (Oxford, 1957).

Keynes, S. and **Lapidge**, M., eds. & trans. *Alfred the Great. Asser's Life of King Alfred and other Contemporary Sources* (Harmondsworth, 1983).

Kirby, T. and **Woolf**, H. B., eds. *Philologica: The Malone Anniversary Studies* (Baltimore: 1949).

McClure, J. and **Collins**, R., trans. *The Ecclesiastical History of the English People; The Greater Chronicle; Bede's Letter to Egbert* (Oxford, 1994).

Lapidge, M. *Anglo-Latin Literature 600-899* (London, 1996).

Lapidge, M. *Anglo-Latin Literature 900-1066* (London, 1993).

Lapidge, M. and **Gneuss**, H., eds. *Learning and Literature in Anglo-Saxon England. Studies presented to Peter Clemoes* (Cambridge, 1985).

Latham, R. E., ed. *Revised Medieval Latin Word-List from British and Irish Sources* (London, 1965).

Law, V. *The Insular Latin Grammarians* (Woodbridge, 1982).

Law, V. *History of Linguistic Thought in the Early Middle Ages* (Amsterdam, 1993).

Law, V. *Grammar and Grammarians in the early Middle Ages* (London, 1977).

Lewis, C. T. and **Short**, C., eds. *A Latin Dictionary* (Oxford, 1966).

Liebermann, F. *Die Gesetze der Angelsachsesn*, 3 vols. (Halle, 1903–16).

Lowe, E.A., ed. *Codices Latini Antiquiores*, 11 vols. with supp. (Oxford, 1934-17; 2ⁿᵈ ed. of vol. ii, 1972).

Menner, R. J. 'The Anglian Vocabulary of *The Blickling Homilies*' in **Kirby** and **Woolf** (1949), pp. 56–64.

Migne, J. –P., ed. *Patrologia Latina*, 221 vols. (Paris, 1844–64).

Miller, T. , ed. *The Old English Version of Bede's Ecclesiastical History*, EETS os 95 (Oxford, 1890).

Mitchell, B. *Old English Syntax*, 2 vols. (Oxford, 1985).

Moore, S. and **Knott**, T. *The Elements of Old English* (Ann Arbor, 1925).

Morris, R., ed. & trans. *The Blickling Homilies*, EETS os 58, 63, 73 (Oxford, 1874, 1876, 1880); repr. as 1 vol. (Oxford, 1967).

Niermeyer, J. F., ed. *Mediae Latinitatis Lexicon Minus*, 2ⁿᵈ rev. edn by J. W. J. Burges (Leiden, 2002).

Ohlgren, T. H. *Insular and Anglo-Saxon Illuminated Manuscripts: an Iconographic Catalogue c. AD 625 to 1100* (Binghamton, NY, 1986).

Plummer, C., ed. *Venerabilis Baedae Opera Historica*, 2 vols. (Oxford, 1896; repr. 1969).

Roberts, J, ed. *Alfred the Wise. Studies in Honour of Janet Bately on the Occasion of her sixty-fifth Birthday* (Cambridge, 1997).

Rauh, H., *Der Wortschatz der altenglischen Uebersetzungen des Matthaeus-Evangeliums* (Berlin, 1936).

Scherer, G. *Zur Geographie und Chronologie des angelsächsischen Wortschatzes im Anschluss an Bischof Wæferth's Übersetzung des 'Dialoge' Gregors* (Leipzig, 1928).

Sharpe, R. *A Handlist of the Latin Writers of Great Britain and Ireland before 1540* (Turnhout, 1977).

Smith, A.H. ed. *English Place-Name Elements*, EPNS, vols 25, 26, 2ⁿᵈ rev. edn (Cambridge, 1970).

Stratford, P. *Unification and Conquest. A Political and Social History of England in the Tenth and Eleventh Centuries* (London, 1989).

Stenton, F. *Anglo-Saxon England*, 3ʳᵈ ed. (Oxford, 1971).

Temple, E. *Anglo-Saxon Manuscripts, 900-1066* (London, 1976).

Visser, F. Th. *An Historical Syntax of the English Language*, 4 vols. (Leiden, 1963–1973).

Whitelock, D., ed. *English Historical Documents* i. c. 500–1042, 2ⁿᵈ ed. (London 1979).

Whitelock, D. *From Bede to Alfred: Studies in Early Anglo-Saxon Literature and History* (London, 1980).

Whitelock, D. *History, Law and Literature in 10ᵗʰ and 11ᵗʰ Century English* (London, 1981).

Whitelock, D., **Brett**, M. and **Brooke**, C.N.L., eds. *Councils & Synods with other Documents relating to the English Church* I. *AD 871–1204*, 2 vols. (Oxford, 1981).

Wood, I. and **Lund**, N. *People and Places in Northern Europe 500–1600. Essays in Honour of Peter Hayes Sawyer* (Woodbridge, 1991).

Wrenn, C. L. and **Quirke**, R. *An Old English Grammar*, 2nd edn (London, 1977).

Wright, J. and **Wright**, E. M. Old English Grammar, 3rd edn (Oxford, 1925; rpt. 1972).

Wyld, H. C. *Short History of English*, 2nd edn (London, 1921).

Yerkes, D. *The Two Versions of Wæferth's Translation of Gregory's Dialogues* (Toronto, 1979).

Yorke, B. *Kings and Kingdoms of Early Anglo-Saxon England* (London, 1990).

Yorke, B. *Wessex in the Early Middle Ages.* London, 1995.